Theorising Performance

THEORISING PERFORMANCE

Greek Drama, Cultural History and Critical Practice

Edited by
Edith Hall & Stephe Harrop

Duckworth

First published in 2010 by
Gerald Duckworth & Co. Ltd.
90-93 Cowcross Street, London EC1M 6BF
Tel: 020 7490 7300
Fax: 020 7490 0080
info@duckworth-publishers.co.uk
www.ducknet.co.uk

A catalogue record for this book is available
from the British Library

ISBN 978 0 7156 3826 2

Typeset by Ray Davies
Printed and bound in Great Britain by
CPI Antony Rowe, Chippenham and Eastbourne

Contents

Contents

List of Illustrations

Contributors

Felix Budelmann teaches Classics at the University of Oxford. He is the author of *The Language of Sophocles* (2000) and editor of the *The Cambridge Companion to Greek Lyric* (2009). He is currently working on a commentary on selections from Greek lyric poetry and is in the early stages of a project exploiting cognitive science for the study of Greek tragedy.

Freddy Decreus is a classical philologist, specialising in the reception of classical antiquity during the nineteenth and twentieth centuries. He works at the University of Gent, where he is responsible for courses in Latin Literature, Literary Theory, Comparative Literature and Theatre History. Recently he published (together with Mieke Kolk) two volumes on rereading classics in 'East' and 'West': *Post-colonial Perspectives on the Tragic* (2004) and *The Performance of the Comic in Arabic Theatre*: *Cultural Heritage, Western Models, Post-colonial Hybridity* (2005). Currently he is working on a project *Lacan and Classical Mythology* (2007-2010).

Zachary Dunbar is a freelance writer, director, composer and producer. He has created and staged several musicals and commissioned plays at the Edinburgh Fringe, in Hertfordshire, and in London. As artistic director of Zeb Fontaine (a multimedia performance group) he has focused on re-conceptualisations of Greek tragedy in works such as 'Delphi, Texas', a radio podcast 'The Ballad of Eddy Tyrone', and a dance theatre piece 'The Cows Come Home'. He is a lecturer at Central School of Speech and Drama.

Erika Fischer-Lichte is Professor of Theatre Studies at the Freie Universität Berlin. From 1995 to 1999 she was President of the International Federation for Theatre Research. She is a member of the Academia Europaea, the Academy of Sciences at Göttingen, and the Berlin-Brandenburg Academy of Sciences. She also heads the Institute for Advanced Studies on 'Interweaving Performance Cultures'. She has published widely in the fields of aesthetics, theory of literature, art and theatre, in particular on semiotics and performativity, theatre history and contemporary theatre. Among her numerous publications are *The Transformative Power of Performance: A New Aesthetics* (2008, German 2004), *Theatre, Sacrifice, Ritual: Exploring Forms of Political Theatre* (2005), *History of European Drama and Theatre* (2002, German 1990), *The Show and the*

Gaze of Theatre: A European Perspective (1997), *The Semiotics of Theatre* (1992, German 1983), and *The Dramatic Touch of Difference: Theatre, Own and Foreign* (1990).

Helene Foley is Professor of Classics at Barnard College, Columbia University. She is the author of *Ritual Irony: Poetry and Sacrifice in Euripides* (1985), *The Homeric Hymn to Demeter* (1994), *Women in the Classical World: Image and Text* (co-authored with Elaine Fantham, Natalie Kampen, Sarah Pomeroy and Alan Shapiro, 1994) and *Female Acts in Greek Tragedy* (1995). She is editor of *Reflections of Women in Antiquity* (1981) and co-editor of *Visualizing the Tragic* (2007). She has been the recipient of Guggenheim, NEH, National Humanities Center, and ACLS fellowships, has served as president of the American Philological Association, and was Sather Professor of Classics at Berkeley in Spring 2008.

Mary-Kay Gamel is Professor of Classics, Comparative Literature and Theatre Arts at Cowell College, University of California-Santa Cruz. Her work has been appeared in multiple scholarly journals including *American Journal of Philology, Helios* and *Amphora*, and her publications include *Women on the Edge: Four Plays by Euripides* (co-editor, 1998). She also has professional experience as a producer, director and actor in numerous theatrical performances.

Simon Goldhill is Professor of Greek at the University of Cambridge. He has published widely on Greek literature, including *Reading Greek Tragedy* (1986), *The Poet's Voice* (1991), *Foucault's Virginity* (1995), *Who Needs Greek?* (2002) and most recently *How to Stage Greek Tragedy Today* (2007) and *Sophocles and the Greek Tragic Tradition* (2009, co-edited with Edith Hall). He is Director of the Cambridge Victorian Studies Group, and a fellow of King's College, Cambridge.

Edith Hall is Professor of Classics and Drama at Royal Holloway, University of London, where she also directs the Centre for the Reception of Greece and Rome. While a lecturer at the University of Oxford in 1996 she co-founded the Archive of Performances of Greek and Roman Drama with Oliver Taplin. Her books include *Inventing the Barbarian* (1989), an edition of Aeschylus' *Persians* (1996), *Greek and Roman Actors* (2002, co-edited with Pat Easterling), *Greek Tragedy and British Theatre* (2005, co-authored with Fiona Macintosh), *The Theatrical Cast of Athens* (2006), and *The Return of Ulysses: A Cultural History of Homer's Odyssey* (2008). She is currently working on a book entitled *Classics and Class*.

Lorna Hardwick teaches at the Open University where she is Professor of Classical Studies and Director of the Reception of Classical Texts research project. She is especially interested in the theory and practice of translation and in classics in postcolonial contexts. She is the editor of the *Classical Receptions Journal* and (with Jim Porter) of the Oxford University Press series Classical Presences.

Stephe Harrop is an academic and theatre-maker, whose research centres upon the relationship between text and physical performance. She completed her practice-based PhD in 2007, and has since worked at Royal Holloway, Goldsmiths and Rose Bruford Colleges, and the Archive of Performances of Greek and Roman Drama. Her recent publications include 'Poetic Language and Corporeality in Translations of Greek Tragedy', *New Theatre Quarterly* (with David Wiles, 2008).

Eleftheria Ioannidou holds a degree from the Department of Theatre Studies of the University of Athens and a Masters in Theatre Research from Royal Holloway, University of London. She received her DPhil in Classics from Oxford University. Her thesis maps out the dialogue between the reception of Greek tragedy and major theoretical investigations of the last three decades. She currently works for the European Network of Research and Documentation of Performances of Ancient Greek Drama.

Charles Martindale is Professor of Latin at the University of Bristol, and has written extensively on the reception of classical poetry. His recent publications include *Redeeming the Text: Latin Poetry and the Hermeneutics of Reception (1993), Shakespeare and the Classics* (2004), *Latin Poetry and the Judgement of Taste* (2005) and *Classics and the Uses of Reception* (with Richard F. Thomas, 2006).

Pantelis Michelakis is Senior Lecturer in Classics at Bristol University and Honorary Research Fellow at the Archive and Performances of Greek and Roman Drama. He is the author of *Achilles in Greek Tragedy* (2002) and *A Companion to Euripides' Iphigenia at Aulis* (2006), co-editor of *Homer, Tragedy and Beyond: Essays in Honour of P.E. Easterling* (2001) and *Agamemnon in Performance, 458 BC to AD 2004* (2005). He is currently working on the reception of Greek tragedy on the modern stage and on screen.

Paul Monaghan has lectured in Theatre Studies at the University of Melbourne, with a specialist interest in the reception of Greek Tragedy in the modern world, for the past ten years. In 2009 he begins teaching at the Victorian College of the Arts (Performing Arts), a professional arts training school, now a Faculty of the University of Melbourne. He previously worked in the professional theatre industry for sixteen years in a variety of roles, and continues to direct as part of his teaching. Paul is co-convenor/co-editor of *Double Dialogues* conference and journal, and co-convenor of the *Dramaturgies Project*, which examines dramaturgical practices in contemporary Australian theatre.

Jane Montgomery Griffiths is a specialist in Greek drama in contemporary performance and has combined academic teaching and research in the UK and Australia with professional performance practice as an award-winning actor and director. She has held university positions in both Drama and Classics departments, and currently convenes the Classical Studies Program at Monash University. She is editor-in-chief of *Didaskalia*, and her publications include *The Spaces of Greek and Roman Theatre* (2009).

Blake Morrison was born in Skipton, Yorkshire, and educated at Nottingham University, McMaster University and University College London. After working for the *Times Literary Supplement*, he went on to become literary editor of both the *Observer* and the *Independent on Sunday* before becoming a full-time writer in 1995. His published works include several collections of poems (including *Selected Poems*, 1999) and a bestselling memoir, *And When Did You Last See Your Father?* which was made into a film in 2007. He has produced many adaptations for the stage including *Oedipus* (2001), *Antigone* (2003) and *Lisa's Sex Strike* (2007), all produced by Northern Broadsides.

Simon Perris took his DPhil in Classical Languages and Literature at Magdalen College, Oxford with a thesis on the literary reception of Euripides' *Bacchae*. He teaches Classics at Victoria University of Wellington, and is currently researching domestic relationships in Greek tragedy.

David Wiles is Professor of Theatre at Royal Holloway, University of London. His publications include *Tragedy in Athens: Performance Space and Theatrical Meaning* (1997), *Greek Theatre Performance: An Introduction* (2000), *A Short History of Western Performance Space* (2003) and *Mask and Performance in Greek Tragedy* (2007). His current research is centred upon the relationship between theatre and citizenship.

Rosie Wyles is post-doctoral research fellow at the University of Nottingham. She completed her doctoral thesis 'The Stage Life of Costume in Euripides' *Telephus*, *Heracles* and *Andromeda*: An Aspect of Performance Reception within Graeco-Roman Antiquity' at Royal Holloway, University of London in 2007. Since then she has held posts at Oxford and National University of Ireland, Maynooth. Her research interests include theatre costume, and the reception of classical drama especially in Ireland. Her most recent project has been *New Directions in Ancient Pantomime* (2008), which she co-edited with Edith Hall.

Acknowledgements

The research underlying this book was made possible by a major research grant to the Archive of Performances of Greek and Roman Drama (APGRD) from the Arts and Humanities Research Council, for which we are extremely grateful. The conference at which early drafts of most of the papers contained in this volume were delivered was held at Oxford on 14 and 15 September 2007, with generous support from the British Academy, the Classical Association, the Classics Faculty at the University of Oxford, the Jowett Trustees, Magdalen College, and the Society for the Promotion of Hellenic Studies.

Too many people have been involved in the intellectual work centring on the APGRD since its foundation in 1996 (with the assistance of a research grant from the Leverhulme Trust) for us to be able to record or thank each of them individually. We do however owe particular gratitude to our colleagues at the APGRD, especially Peter Brown, Pantelis Michelakis, Fiona Macintosh, Oliver Taplin and Rosie Wyles; Scott Scullion, Helen Damon and Amanda Wrigley laboured nobly to ensure the successful organisation of the Theorising Performance conference.

For their help and support with different aspects of the conference and the book we wish to thank Erica Clarke, Robert Day, Neil Leeder, Geraint Lewis, Ronald Melzack, Luca del Pia and Paul Sawyer. We are also indebted to those contributors who have stimulated our thoughts in ways far beyond the provision of chapters, notably Felix Budelmann, Helene Foley and Lorna Hardwick. We are grateful to Deborah Blake at Duckworth for her constructive and enthusiastic support of this project from its inception. Finally, this book is dedicated to our mothers, Brenda Hall and Marilyn Harrop.

Introduction

Edith Hall and Stephe Harrop

The aim of this volume is to explore one simple and fundamental question – is there anything distinctive about the intellectual framework that underlies scholarship on ancient Greek and Roman drama in post-Renaissance performance? The intention is not to provide a definitive answer, but to offer readers a variety of studies, by international specialists in the field, that will allow them to arrive at their own opinion rather better informed than hitherto. The study of the reception of ancient drama in performance, although still a new field, is now a fast-expanding and increasingly respected and influential one. A handful of courageous and enlightened individuals pioneered the field with what are now recognised as pathbreaking contributions before and in the early 1980s.[1] By the early 1990s, the scale and global scope of the revival of Greek theatre in performance became acknowledged and analysed in a series of important books that set a new, international agenda.[2] Since the millennium the number of productions of ancient drama – and studies of its history and practice of performance – has mushroomed across the planet.[3]

Performance reception of Greek theatre is now studied internationally by thousands of scholars and students in departments not only of Classics and of Drama, Theatre and Performance Studies, and on interdisciplinary programmes, but also in Media Studies, Film Studies, Comparative Literature, Modern Languages, and Social and Intellectual History. It is drawn upon by numerous directors and other practitioners in both the professional and amateur theatre worldwide, and thus informs new productions in an unceasing process of cross-fertilisation between academy and performance space.

The volume's particular stimulus was an international conference, 'Theorising Performance', organised by the Archive of Performances of Greek and Roman Drama (APGRD) at Magdalen College, Oxford, in September 2007. The conference convenors were Edith Hall and Scott Scullion. The idea for the conference, and for the book, was one of the elements in the second research project (2004-2009) generously funded by the Arts and Humanities Research Council at the APGRD. The idea arose in direct response to our experience as scholars at the APGRD, along with other researchers across the world who are working in the same field and with whom we are in regular contact. Several of us have been documenting and analysing the performance history of ancient drama for a decade or two, and publishing books upon the subject independently and collectively, without necessarily feeling any pain at the absence of a defined body of theory. Yet paradigms emerge from an accumulated body of data and hermeneutic work upon it, and the field has begin to acquire its own 'canon' of pathbreaking productions – for example, 'Mendelssohn's' *Antigone*, Koun's *Birds*, Ninagawa's *Medea* or Mnouchkine's *Les Atrides* – to which discussion constantly returns. The work of particular translators – for example, Hölderlin, W.B. Yeats or Tony Harrison – has become identified as crucially influential. Certain directors – Suzuki, Stein, Mnouchkine, Sellars – stimulate endless reassessments because they seem to have selected Greek plays when attempting to make critical avant-garde statements about the social role of the practice of theatre.

Methods of archiving, documentation and analysis have emerged from engagement with the source material and actual performances; interpretative agendas have been established in accordance with individual scholars' backgrounds, temperaments and politics; questions have been formulated because they seemed intuitively important and pressing rather than because they were rendered obligatory by a master paradigm or theoretical agenda. But things have now moved on. Sometimes the avalanche of publications and conferences can begin to feel overwhelming: the terrain is vast (and grows every day, as new performances are mounted), but the analytical routes through have sometimes begun to feel to many of us as if they are too often discovered by accident or invented *ad hoc* without sufficient intellectual preparation.

Studying the performance of ancient Greek and Roman drama, however widespread it may now be in the Humanities, is an activity that was born at the meeting-place of two established academic disciplines, Classics and Theatre Studies. Subsequently, it has been enriched by contact with several other fields, including Philosophy, Musicology, Cognitive Psychology, Postcolonial Studies and Film Studies. Distinctive contributions have also been made by practitioners – actors and translators as well as directors – whose responses to their own experience of Greek plays expand the hermeneutic toolkit available to the analytical and theoretical researcher. The field discussed in this book has become a leading example within the Humanities of not only of *interdisciplinarity* but of exemplary *multidisciplinarity* (see Dunbar in this volume). It is a feature of this book (as it was of the conference) that it self-consciously aims to bring together contributors from different intellectual worlds in the hope of arriving at a richer picture of our activities and the intellectual paradigms that underlie them through dialogue and cross-fertilisation.

To ask our over-riding question – is there anything unique and distinctive about the theories that underpin the study of the performance of ancient plays? – is to address two complementary distinctions that are often made, but the legitimacy of which is seldom examined. The first distinction is one that primarily affects theatre historians, since it as-sumes a difference between scholarship on the performance history of ancient drama and scholarship on the performance history of other theat-rical traditions (for example, Shakespeare or Ibsen). Do we need a different kind of theory to approach the performance history of a pagan 'classic' playscript that is two millennia old from the theory we need to shape our enquiries into a Renaissance Christian one?

The second distinction that needs to be examined is one that has more bearing on the subject-area understood by the term 'Classics': how does investigating the reception of an ancient Greek or Roman play in perform-ance differ from investigating the reception of an ancient text in a non-performed medium such as the novel or statuary?

The probing of these distinctions in this book has made inevitable the fulfilling of our second aim, which is to identify the key intellectual models and theories of art and culture which have informed the practice of research into the post-Renaissance performance of ancient drama. The essays encompass discussion of a broad range of philosophical and critical-theoretical approaches, from Vico's New Science to Kantian Idealism and onwards to Marxist cultural materialism, Saussurean Semiotics, La-canian psychanalysis, Derridean deconstruction and Jauss' Konstanz School of *Rezeptionsästhetik*. The narrative discusses and indeed applies the theories and methods of theatre critics and practitioners from Aristotle to Artaud and Hans-Thies Lehmann's provocative *Postdramatisches Theater*. It covers texts from Humanist Latin 'cribs' of the Greek drama-tists to Yorkshire dialect versions of Aristophanic obscenity in 2007. It adduces examples from performance media ranging from classical music to video installations. Its evidence ranges from performances of Greek plays in high Victorian 'authentic' revivals to playwrights whose works use Greek texts in heavily disguised manner and to the avant-garde practitio-ner Romeo Castellucci, in whose *Tragedia Endogonidia* the psychological repression reflected in the whole idea of theatre as a paradigm of human consciousness is referred back to the Greek tradition.

Most of the essays began life as papers delivered at the conference, although others have been specially commissioned or included in response to interventions during the discussions that took place at the conference itself. They fall into four sections, although there is considerable dialogue between individual contributions across the section boundaries. Section 1, 'Paradigms', marks out the terrain covered by the book and examines a series of paradigms, essential conceptual models and terminology, the meaning of which is constantly under negotiation within the field – 'performance', 'live performance', 'reception', 'classic', 'text', 'artwork', 'event', 'aesthetic experience'. Chapter 2, Hall's 'Towards a Theory of Performance Reception', is a revised version of an article originally pub-lished in *Arion* (2004), at the time the conference was at planning stage, in order to define some of the central issues, identify theoretical contributions that were already available, and stimulate debate. It is an attempt to pinpoint an intellectual ancestry for scholarship on performance reception, thereby to identify what it is about performance arts that makes the study of them, including their use of Greek and Roman antiquity, different from the study of non-performed arts. It surveys a range of schools of thought within philosophical and cultural theory that might offer concepts that could help us hone our analytical tools in studying ancient plays in performance. It advocates a fundamentally cultural materialist approach that is however radically qualified by an engagement with a consistent (and, paradoxically, idealist) philosophical line which can be traced from Vico's rediscovery of the sensually conveyed wisdom of pagan art, via Kant to Kierkegaard, Husserlian Phenomenology, Symbolism and French Existentialism. It concludes that no single paradigm or model can ever be sufficient to the complicated task of analysing performance, especially of 'classic' texts, and that different problems are susceptible to unravelling by different conceptual means. We should not be afraid to order our theory eclectically '*à la carte*'.

Erika Fischer-Lichte in Chapter 3 attacks the disputed concept of 'Reception' head-on in order to fuse the senses in which Classicists and Theatre specialists use it; this process produces her argument that participation in the performance of Greek drama *does* have a distinct and unique history in that it has often been related to an attempt to make spectators *aware* of their own aesthetic experience as a particular kind of liminal experience. Wiles' essay comes from another angle, to think about the conceptual paradigms inherent within post-war Shakespeare scholarship, especially the relationship between different understandings of the term 'reception', to ask if these can illuminate the current state of play in Classics, and the recent evolution in the documentation and historiography of the performance of ancient drama.

Fischer-Lichte's analysis of the concept of aesthetic experience, and Wiles' anatomy of the different meanings of 'reception' relative to the 'classic' plays of antiquity and Shakespeare respectively, lead directly into the next two chapters, 5 and 6, which articulate a major tension in Classics today. This concerns aesthetic evaluation and hierarchy and therefore the very meaning and appropriate field of Classical Reception. Simon Goldhill and Charles Martindale collide head-to-head on the degree to which the historical contextualisation of any text in reception, performed or otherwise, should or can take priority over the study of its literary 'stemma' – its relation to its ancient archetype(s). The argument returns inevitably to the validity of the concept of 'disinterestedness' in the contemplation of an art object, as defined in Kant's *Critique of Judgement* (1790), and to the bifurcated tradition of cultural analysis that has followed or rejected the paradigm of the Kantian idea of beauty and the non-self-interested contemplation which is, to Kantians such as Stolnitz, the correct moral response to it.

1. Introduction

The debate between Goldhill and Martindale ranges over a wide variety of genres and media, from painting to poetry and opera. In debating the very nature of what constitutes 'Classics', the question of boundaries between disciplines is inevitably raised, along with the established academic model of 'interdisciplinarity'. In Chapter 7, Zachary Dunbar explores the status of the study of ancient plays in performance in the evolution of critical practice from reliance on the paradigm of interdisciplinarity to a more flexible and inclusive model of multidisciplinarity. Dunbar is himself an instantiation of multidisciplinarity in practice, as a classical pianist with a degree in drama history and performance who now both writes and directs. But multidisciplinarity still needs its research resources, and the question of the recording and documentation of performance forms the central question explored in Chapter 8, 'Archiving Events, Performing Documents: On the Seductions and Challenges of Performance Archives', by Pantelis Michelakis, a Classicist with a long-standing interest in the murky theoretical interstices between Greek and Roman texts, theatre performance, and cinema. Here he thinks about the implications of the 'archive' model of research that has been the scholarly response to the ephemeral and highly dispersed social activity of ancient drama performance, by comparing the Derridean and Foucauldian accounts of the ideological work done by agglomerative and centralised archival institutions.

The second section tackles the complex relationship between the performed representation of the human mind in action, the biological and socially constructed human body, and tragedy. On a basic biological and neurological level, neither the body nor the brain has changed much over the last two and a half millennia, the period during which tragedy has intermittently flourished as a prestige art form. But the understanding of the relationship between mind, body, and the human suffering that is represented in tragedy has of course been transformed almost beyond recognition. This section therefore investigates that relationship from three different perspectives, and in doing so encompasses some of the major theoretical models and disciplines offering concepts and methods that may be able to illuminate the remarkable cultural longevity of Greek drama. In Chapter 9, Budelmann looks at Cognitive Science and the intercultural recognition of neurological markers for pain. Decreus on the other hand draws on the tradition of French post-structuralism, especially Deleuze, to infer a theoretical model with which to approach Romeo Castellucci's *Tragedia Endogonidia*, a major work of art on the relationship between history, representation and the body that was created over a period of three years (2002-4, still in performance in 2007). Foley's essay (Chapter 11) draws on the history of genre theory that stretches back beyond Bakhtin to the great Renaissance drama theorists such as Ludovico Castelvetro in order to argue that studies of the reception of Greek tragedy on the stage must account more fully for the generic expectations that audiences, directors and playwrights bring to the theatre in different eras. The theorisation of tragedy, the tragic, the comic and the tragicomic is culturally conditioned and returns repeatedly to questions of tone, bodily representation, and intellectual stance on the subject-matter, core components of the increasingly burlesque and flippant idiom of some recent productions of tragedy, which have imported laughter and deconstructed traditional generic boundaries.

The third, central section discusses the challenges of transcultural and transhistorical 'translation' – not only of texts but of the entire multimedial performances that constituted ancient drama. Mary-Kay Gamel (Chapter 12) discovers a rich seam of theoretical ideas in scholarship on the 'authentic' performance of classical music, ideas with which to approach the question of authenticity in transferring ancient scripts to modern performance contexts. In Chapter 13, Rosie Wyles addresses the 'translation' of the socialised theatrical body through costume. Utilising theories developed in Linguistics and Semiotics, she proposes a set of distinctions between the different functions of costume in relation to some recent performances of ancient theatre-scripts that have appropriated or rigorously resisted longstanding costuming strategies. It is the thorny issue of the status of the transmitted texts of ancient drama in the form taken by their publication in modern-language translations, relative to the status of their performances, however, that Simon Perris tackles in Chapter 14. He argues that the important point is less whether one is more *important* than the other than that they are simply distinct. Spectating and reading are different modes of aesthetic experience, and therefore performance reception and literary reception through published translations and adaptations require different modes of analysis. He presses the (in Theatre Studies currently unfashionable) case that Classicists and cultural historians simply cannot take the history of literary translation and reading out of the history of performance, any more than classical scholarship was ever justified in marginalising the experience of contemporary performance.

Lorna Hardwick's attention is focused on the actual procedures involved in translation for performance, and through a series of case-studies in Chapter 15 she argues that the traditional polarities between source and target languages, and between concepts of 'translation' and 'rewriting', need to be reviewed. Translation and adaptation for the stage involves a considerable number of contributory agents (designers, musicians, actors and choreographers), but it also reflects back on the work of future scholars and translators in a continuous and dialectically evolving process. Eleftheria Ioannidou concludes this section in an essay (Chapter 16) that tackles the troublesome distinction between adaptation and translation of ancient plays – which are after all in languages spoken by nobody alive and portray a religion practised nowhere today – with the help of Nietzsche, Benjamin and Barthes (and, in an unexpected but

6

productive dialectic, Dryden). Her particular focus is the untranslatability of religious ideas and the language that goes with them, especially in live performance.

Indeed, there can be no practice to theorise without practitioners, and in section IV five individuals who have worked on the front line of significant productions of ancient drama reflect on the intellectual assumptions and concepts that have underlain their own work, and that of others, in the practice of acting, scenography and translation respectively. Jane Montgomery Griffiths has both directed and acted in numerous productions; in Chapter 17 she argues through an analysis of accounts by performers of the leading role in Sophocles' *Electra* that the response of an actor to an ancient theatrical role can be seen as a synecdoche for the whole process of classical reception, since the actor's emotional and somatic connection in part comprises the field of signification for the source text. Stephe Harrop (Chapter 18) examines the work of voice practitioners and theorists, to analyse the elusive relationship between vocality and physical performance, and the ways in which the translation of ancient theatre-texts impacts upon their corporeal enactment. In Chapter 19 Paul Monaghan, writing from the perspective of the scenographer, outlines some key terms and categories for the study of lighting and stage design, and their role in shaping the performance history and reception of ancient tragedy.

Finally, Blake Morrison, who knows no Greek, has translated Sophocles and adapted Aristophanes for Northern Broadsides; here, in the final essay (Chapter 20) he assesses the principles and methods that he and others have used in creating working modern-language performance scripts out of the texts of ancient Greek drama – both tragedy and comedy. He explores the metaphors used by other theorists of translation for stage performance in order to clarify the relationship between original text and what is eventually communicated to a contemporary audience; his own encounter with Greek archetypes has suggested the notions of service, of rendering the alien intelligible and retaining its integrity without imposing undue contraints on the emergence of the new artwork. In doing so he produces a new definition of the 'classic' drama that is, as it happens, a corollary of Vidal-Naquet's Marxist-inflected and relativist historical model, developed when discussing what is commonly held to be the first full staging of an ancient Greek tragedy in the Renaissance. Vidal-Naquet argued that the longevity of Greek drama in performance – what has made so many plays 'classics' of the repertoire – is a product of its exceptional susceptibility to reinterpretation.[4] Morrison takes takes this argument one step further: 'The classics always adapt; *that's why they're classics.*'

To return to our over-riding question – is there anything unique about what we are doing when we study ancient Greek and Roman drama in performance? – we are well aware that there are numerous other types of theatrical practice, as well as theory, which could have been included in this collaborative attempt to find answers. Among other absences, we regret the lack of any contribution to this volume dealing diectly with feminist, gender or post-colonial theory, and their place in the ongoing discussion of performance reception.[5] We would also have liked to include a more extensive survey of practitioners, including chapters written from the perspective of the theatre director or dramaturg.

We are also aware, and in this case indeed gratified, that our contributors do not agree on the answer to our fundamental question. Some say that the models used for studying classic theatre are largely the same regardless of whether it is Greek, Renaissance or the more recent theatrical canon under scrutiny. Others argue that there must be something unique about studying plays produced in a society whose languages are now unspoken and whose metaphysics were so radically different from any religious beliefs current today; still others maintain that ancient drama is indeed unique *because it has a unique history* – two long periods of living existence in performance that are however separated by a period of hibernation from performance that lasted more than a thousand years. Some have argued that idealist aesthetics and traditional methods of literary criticism that draw upon them are of no use to the scholar of performance history, while others have asserted that good art is good art regardless of where and by whom it is produced and consumed. But in the course of explaining their different viewpoints and supporting them with arguments and examples, the contributors to this volume have identified and assembled (and contested) an unprecedented series of key topics, landmark productions, and productive theories that will, it is hoped, prove of considerable benefit to future study in the field. For the story of the performance of ancient drama, its practice, its documentation *and* its theorisation, is not only complex and dialectical, but it is renewable inifinitely.

Notes

1. E.g. Marianne McDonald, *Euripides in Cinema* (1983); Michael Walton, *The Greek Sense of Theatre* (1984); Kenneth MacKinnon, *Greek Tragedy into Film* (1986). Alexis Solomos' remarkably prescient *The Living Aristophanes* was first published in English translation, with help from Marvin Felheim, by the University of Michigan Press in 1974, but had actually been published in Greek as early as 1961.

2. Oliver Taplin, *Greek Tragedy in Action* (1978); Bruce R. Smith, *Ancient Scripts and Modern Experience on the English Stage, 1500-1700* (1988); Helmut Flashar, *Inszenierung der Antike* (1991); Marianne McDonald, *Ancient Sun, Modern Light* (1992).

3. Full bibliography until 2003 is available in Edith Hall, Fiona Macintosh and Amanda Wrigley (eds) *Dionysus Since 69* (2004); although it is invidious to single out any of the numerous subsequent contributions, a list would include the excellent study by Barbara Goff and Michael Simpson, *Crossroads in the Black Aegean: Oedipus, Antigone, and Dramas of the African Diaspora* (2007); Edith Hall and Fiona Macintosh, *Greek Tragedy and the British Theatre 1660-1914* (2005);

1. Introduction

David Wiles, *Mask and Performance in Greek Tragedy* (2007); Edith Hall, Fiona Macintosh, Pantelis Michelakis and Oliver Taplin (eds), *Agamemnon in Performance* (2005); Edith Hall and Amanda Wrigley (eds), *Aristophanes in Performance* (2007); Michael Walton, *Found in Translation: Greek Drama in English* (2006); John Dillon and Stephen Wilmer (eds), *Rebel Women: Staging Ancient Greek Drama Today* (2005); and numerous articles in collections edited by Lorna Hardwick and colleagues, including Lorna Hardwick and Christopher Stray (eds), *A Companion to Classical Receptions* (2008).

4. P. Vidal-Naquet, 'Oedipus in Vicenza and Paris', in J.P. Vernant and P. Vidal-Naquet, *Myth and Tragedy in Ancient Greece* (1998).

5. Key studies elsewhere include Froma Zeitlin, *Playing the Other: Gender and Society in Classical Greek Literature* (1996); Helene Foley, *Female Acts in Greek Tragedy* (2001); Kevin J. Wetmore, *The Athenian Sun in an African Sky: Modern African American Adaptations of Classical Greek Tragedy* (2002); Barbara Goff (ed.), *Classics and Colonialism* (2005); Lorna Hardwick and Carol Gillespie (eds), *Classics in Post-Colonial Worlds* (2007).

Towards a Theory of Performance Reception

Edith Hall

The most important nights in the theatre were seen by only a tiny fraction of the population and yet they have passed into the history of the world.

Peter Sellars

1. Introduction

This essay outlines some theoretical issues involved in studying the reception of ancient Greece and Rome in performed media. It attempts to identify an intellectual ancestry for such scholarship, and thereby to identify what it is about performance arts that makes the study of them, including their use of Greek and Roman antiquity, different from the study of non-performed arts. Since this enquiry addresses itself to cultural phenomena extending from the Renaissance to the twenty-first century, it does not engage with the controversy surrounding the legitimacy of the concept of 'performance' in relation to the ancient world, which knew neither the term nor the category it denotes.[1] While acknowledging that 'performance' is a concept with its own (relatively recent) historical specificity, the discussion nevertheless assumes a 'commonsense' definition of the word 'performance' as it is used now: to say that something from ancient Greece or Rome has been 'performed' implies an aesthetic phenomenon in which humans have realised an archetypal text, narrative or idea by acting, puppet manipulation, dance, recital or song; the category 'Performance Reception' therefore excludes individuals reading a text to themselves, or the visual arts (except, hypothetically, when they are of a type requiring the label 'performance art').

The history of the consumption of all 'classic' drama and episodes from ancient history, Shakespeare or Racine or historical movies as much as the Greek plays, is inherently interesting since it reveals the contingent historical perspectives which have been brought to bear on these texts in public arenas of consumption. But there is a danger that Performance Reception in practice (of which there have been some outstanding examples) has run in advance of the theory. Performance Reception is a subcategory of what has conventionally been called 'The Classical Tradition', 'The *Nachleben*', or 'The Reception' of ancient Greece and Rome. Performances may have taken the form of dramas, operas, ballets, films, radio, television or audio-recordings, but they have all involved audiences responding to performers using their bodies, voices and/or musical instruments in a visual or aural representation of material derived from a 'classical' source. In an oft-cited definition of theatre, Bentley said that its essential quality was that *A* impersonates *B* before *C*.[2] Performance Reception of Greek and Roman antiquity, at its most reductively defined, analyses the process by which *A* impersonates a *B* derived from a classical prototype before *C*. Although other contributing subjectivities (of translators, adaptors, authors, directors) are usually involved, it is the dynamic *triangular* relationship between ancient text, *performer* and audience that distinguishes 'Performance Reception' from the study of the ways in which ancient texts have been 'received' in scholarship, curricula, private reading, adaptations into other literary genres designed to be read privately (for example, the novel), or in the visual arts.

A little of what follows applies to Performance Reception outside the theatre, including Classics in cinema, television and radio. Some of it applies to the theatrical Reception of ancient material other than drama: to plays drawing on Homer's *Odyssey*,[3] Ovid's *Metamorphoses* and Plutarch's *Lives*, or to gladiatorial spectacles in Victorian amphitheatres. Much of it applies to the performance genres most closely allied to theatre – live ballet and opera. Almost all of it applies to the investigation of ways in which ancient theatrical genres, conventions, acting styles and performance spaces have inspired people of the theatre – especially those consciously involved in the aesthetic *avant-garde* of any generation – even when they have not been performing ancient texts or subject-matter at all: examples would be the founding fathers of opera and subsequently ballet, who claimed their media originated in ancient tragedy and pantomime respectively.[4] Even more of the arguments here will apply to Performance Reception within antiquity – the thousand-year-long process of revival and adaptation undergone by the 'classics' of the repertoire across the Greek and Roman worlds (the evidence for which has usually been ignored by scholars tracing particular themes diachronically across antiquity, with problematic results).[5] But the areas of overlap with, and distinctions between, all these phenomena and my own material will not be investigated in detail here: for the sake of precision the focus of the argument will be the post-Renaissance history of *theatrical* performances of Greek and Roman *drama*.

2. Performance Reception within Classical Reception

The last three decades have seen the development of methods and theoretical infrastructures for the more generalised study of 'Classical Reception', which inevitably provide a frame of reference for the aspiring theorist of Performance Reception. Martindale's *Redeeming the Classics* expounds two helpful theses in the practice of Reception-theory. The first contends that 'numerous unexplored insights into ancient literature are locked up in imitations, translations and so forth'; the second that 'our current interpretations of ancient texts ... are ... constructed by the chain of receptions through which their continued readability has been effected'.[6] These two sensible propositions will inform any intelligent exercise in Performance Reception. I want to stress the first thesis, that our appreciation of the original texts can be refined by excavating their afterlife, what they have 'meant' in cultures and epochs other than those which originally produced them. A new understanding of the epistemological vacuum central to *Iphigenia in Aulis* can be gained, for example, by comparing this play's experiences at the hands of Protestants and Catholics respectively.[7]

The value of Martindale's theses is nevertheless limited for our purposes because it explicitly puts the *reader* at the centre of Reception. Ancient plays are, of course, frequently read without (or prior to) being performed, and there is a dialectical relationship between the processes whereby they are realised as texts that are read and as texts that are performed in the consciousness of different individuals and generations. Browning's transformation of Euripides' *Alcestis* into a poetic monologue in *Balaustion's Adventure* (1871) is a reaction *against* the vulgarities he perceived in the spectacular mid-Victorian theatre. James Thomson, the author of an important eighteenth-century *Agamemnon*, knew no English version, used Thomas Stanley's Latin crib, but had studied advanced Greek at Edinburgh University.[8] There used to be a convention by which respectable scholars erased all mention of performances of ancient drama in which they had been involved from their scholarly publications.[9] There has certainly been a disreputable tendency amongst literary scholars to censure theatre people, and *vice versa*, but it is unnecessary if we accept that neither 'script-alone' nor 'script-as-performed' is superior to the other: it is merely *different*.[10]

Moreover, Performance Reception requires reading other texts, especially those by directors. Certain ancient plays have achieved prominence amongst theatre professionals because one of their own canonical works of theory has reminded them of it. An example is Artaud's description of Seneca as 'the greatest tragic author in history, an initiate in the secrets who knew better than Aeschylus how to put them into words. I cry as I read his inspired theatre, and underneath the sound of his syllables, I sense the transparent seething of the forces of chaos frothing at his mouth'.[11] This encomium, because of the cult status of its author, lies behind Peter Brook's interest in Senecan drama and will always stimulate attempts at staging it.

Drama originated in enactment rather than literary culture, but this does not mean that we privilege performance reception over literary reception. By the time that ancient drama became consolidated into a canon, Aristotle could already decree that a good tragic plot could induce emotion in readers as well as spectators (*Poetics* 14.1453b). Performance

2. Towards a Theory of Performance Reception

Reception must embrace the history of reading scripts-alone, although if it fails to address performances altogether it will cease to be Performance Reception. Performance issues sometimes need thinking about in the negative: why was a play's performance banned at a particular time (as Shirley's Whig *Electra* was censored in 1762), or why were there no attempts to stage *Trojan Women* in the nineteenth century?[12] But performance will never be absent altogether from the Performance Reception scholar's perspective, as it has too often been omitted from the discussions of scholars in departments of English Studies, Comparative Literature, or Modern Languages (e.g. in the case of Goethe's *Iphigenie auf Tauris*) as well as Classics and Ancient History.

No two scholars will practise Performance Reception in the same way, any more than they will interpret an ancient artwork identically in the context of its original creation. This is not just a matter of personal taste, but of theoretical models operating alongside the Reception-related conception of a text. Some scholars in Performance Reception, for example, may be more informed by Formalism or Narratology if they study the different translations of certain speech-acts in an ancient text (command, wish, question, insult). They may draw on psychoanalytical theory if they trace shifts in sexual identity and representations of the body within the history of antiquity-related performances. The Performance Reception of ancient comedy is likely to adduce the Bakhtinian notion of Carnival. In the application of inter-cultural models of ritual theatre, anthropological theory may be dominant. Feminist theorists engaged in Performance Reception may, alternatively, draw on the idea of the 'resisting reader' in witnessing how versions of, say, *Medea*, have reacted to ancient male authors' patriarchal control of the female characters' voices within their texts. Some Classicists engaged in Performance Reception concentrate on the poststructuralist assault on the notions of literary canon and aesthetic value, and excavate the legacy of the *scurra* or the afterlife in performance of 'low' ancient genres, such as mime, novel or fable.

Although certain ideas descended from German Idealism have clarified my own thinking about Performance Reception (see below), by a dialectical irony my usual model of cultural analysis has derived from the historical Materialism pioneered in reaction *against* Idealism by Marx and Engels.[13] The relationship between cultural phenomena and sociopolitical issues informed the study Fiona Macintosh and I conducted in *Greek Tragedy and the British Theatre* (2005). When dealing with the portrayal of women, we sensed the relevance of Bakhtin's notion (itself produced by the interplay of Formalism and Marxism) that a measure of the greatness of literature is the degree to which it holds 'prefigurative' meanings that can only be released by readings far away in the future.[14] We drew help from Vidal-Naquet's Marxist-inflected historical relativism, which locates Greek tragedy's power to transcend history in its susceptibility to different interpretations; this explains, for example, why *Iphigenia in Tauris* could

isn't this true of all great literature?

13

be adapted into English with equal conviction, within fifty years, by an ardent Royalist, an obsessive Whig, and a self-consciously apolitical playwright.[15] Sometimes a more dialectical method emerged in arguing, with Vernant, that all significant artworks actively condition the shapes taken by future artworks, whether the conditioning takes the form of emulation, modification or rejection:[16] no dramatic author writing about mother-son incest can conceivably avoid forging a relationship with Sophocles' *Oedipus*. It became tempting to see Greek tragedy as conditioning the actual shapes taken by future society and its moral discourses, a position argued persuasively in relation to Shakespeare by Weimann.[17]

3. The special nature of Performance Reception

3.1. Translation

Performance Reception has always been bound up with the history of translation. Many early versions of plays were made with performance in mind, for example the imitation of Plautus' *Amphitryo* published in London anonymously in 1562-3 as *A New Enterlude for Chyldren to playe, named Jack Jugeler*.[18] Most Euripidean dramas remained unavailable in translation until after they had been Englished for performance, for example Richard West's *Hecuba*, designed for enactment at Drury Lane in 1725, decades before Euripides' complete works were translated into the English language.[19] Translations designed for performance also have distinctive features: the diction, register and phrasing of Tony Harrison's version of the *Oresteia* for the London National Theatre in 1980 were created specifically for *masked* delivery.

The poststructuralist assault on the stability of language is relevant here. Derrida took his position on the impossibility of translation even further than in 'Des tours de Babel',[20] when he said at a conference in California in June 2002: 'The paradox of translation is that the translator must strive to be as faithful as possible to the original author's style and intent, while at the same time recognizing that it's impossible to reconstitute the unique meaning of the original words. The alchemy of translation occurs precisely at that point where an essentially new work is created.'[21] Translation, in Derrida's view, entails what he calls 'contamination', a strong form of interpretation and the violent imposition of bias and meaning on a text. This can be an act of treachery (as the Italians say, *traduttore, traditore*), or of homage, when the concept of a benevolent counterfeit must become, as Barnstone insists, 'an epistemological paradox'; it may be an unconscious or a conscious process, but translation 'is not a mirror. Nor is it a mimetic copy. It is another creation', which owes form and content to its source.[22] A powerful instance in the Reception of drama (although it was not performed) of *conscious* imposition of new meaning is provided by the earliest English translation of Sophocles' *Electra*, an allegorical version by the Royalist Christopher Wase, circulated in 1649 after Charles I was executed. This explicitly equates Aegisthus with Oliver Cromwell. Visual images combined with the Italian translation used in a recent Roman production of *Frogs*, directed by Luca Ronconi, imposed too much contemporary meaning for Berlusconi's government, which intervened.[23]

Most performances of ancient Greek and Roman theatrical works are in translation or more extensive adaptation. They involve, in the form of new playscripts, a baseline ideological 'fixing' of meaning. This is because, according to Derrida, verbal translation necessitates such a strong form of interpretation. Some productions of ancient drama address this process directly: Peter Stein explored the impossibility of finding a single 'correct' translation of ancient Greek terms in the first production of his monumental *Oresteia* in Berlin (1980), often by providing several alternative substitutes for a Greek word or phrase.[24] When the degree of adaptation is more extensive, the 'anachronistic' new ideological trajectory it takes will become even more divorced from what the text originally 'meant' in the context of its ancient premiere. But when this strongly inflected ideological and cultural product is also then subjected to realisation in *performance*, a second act of translating (or traducing) occurs. This partly results from the plurality of individual agents (director, designer, composer, lighting designer, actors) whose subjectivities leave their traces on the 'carrying across', the 'trans-lation' of the text into the media of physical enactment and vocal delivery. The text is exposed to artillery from a whole battalion of human interpreters, rather than to single combat. In the theatre even more than in other media, classical material is subject less to 'Reception' than to wholesale Appropriation.

3.2. Body

In *The Life of the Drama* (1965), written just as the theatre approached its most climactic revolution in taste, subject-matter and subjectivity for decades, Eric Bentley presciently declared that the body and an inherent 'indecency' underpin the theatrical experience. Bentley argues (in a manner that feminists will read uneasily, especially his remarks about female strip artists at the Folies-Bergère) that while fine art deals with the nude, the theatre deals with the naked. Theatre has often involved costuming, make-up and masks, but what is concealed by such artifice is always the living, breathing, human body. If it is replaced by celluloid records or mechanical puppets, it ceases to be theatre and becomes a different form of mimesis.[25] Theatre, argues Bentley cogently, 'is shamelessly "low"; it cannot look down on the body, because it *is* the body.' To understand theatre art, we must accept that 'we *do* wish to see, and we do wish to be stimulated by seeing bodies ... We are prying into filthy secrets.'[26] Theatre is fundamentally indecent. Actors exhibit themselves; spectators are voyeurs. Just because most dramatists play out the indecency at a remove, and the nakedness becomes the laying bare of the mind rather than of the material body, 'the immediate reality of theatre is aggressively physical, corporeal'. This makes it different even from painting and sculpture in that 'only theatre thrusts at its audience the supreme object of sensual thoughts: the human body'.[27]

Common to both Greek comedy and satyr play is the display of a male body that is generically and often riotously hyper-male, which calls attention to theatre's uniquely corporeal status and medium of presentation. At its most ribald, Old Comedy even presented its audience either with naked women or with men pretending to be naked women. It is difficult to decide which would have been the more bodily emphatic. Greek tragedy is fascinated by its own imitation of beautiful, alluring bodies; at moments of quintessentially tragic emotion involving pity and fear, eros and thanatos, tragic figures (especially females) are often compared with paintings or statues, in an implicit acknowledgement of the visual objectification of the characters represented.[28] Moreover, at the core of tragedy lies the representation of a phenomenon whose claim to transhistorical invariability is great: physical agony. Philoctetes' screams drown out trendy cultural relativisation.[29] What happens to the nervous system and the neurological synapses during onslaughts of physical pain has not changed much over time, unlike the cultural codes for representing or coping with pain. For Performance Reception, therefore, the *somatic* quality of theatre means that it offers special evidence of a society's approach to such basic aspects of human experience as the body, gender, sexual desire, injury, and suffering, in addition to the physical rites of passage (mating, birth and death).

3.3. Mimesis

The body in the theatre belongs to the actor. Joseph Chaikin, himself a charismatic and influential actor/director, has described the inherently non-verbal dynamism (what Benjamin called the *aura*[30]) generated by a powerful actor's presence. 'It's a quality that makes you feel as though you're standing right next to the actor, no matter where you're sitting in the theatre … There may be nothing of this quality offstage or in any other circumstance in the life of such an actor. It's a kind of libidinal surrender which the performer reserves for his anonymous audience.'[31] This is, by any account, not the same type of encounter as that experienced by a reader with a Penguin Classic in her study.

What an actor brings to life is a *role*. A playwright must write not just a 'character' but a 'role'. Creating several roles for individual actors to sustain is more integral to playwriting than producing the separate parts for each musical instrument participating in an orchestral symphony. Every role, even a minor part, will be scrutinised as an individual entity by spectators in a manner impossible for a musical auditor, except where one of the instruments becomes so virtuoso that the symphony turns into a concerto. A role's full possibilities can only be revealed by great acting: a fine role well acted can, moreover, actually leave the stage and enter

general discourse, invent a new individual to add permanently to a culture's functional imaginative 'cast'. Clytemnestra, like her descendant
Lady Macbeth, ultimately lies behind the public vilification of countless
wives of powerful men.

Goldman argues that one thing everyone *always* 'recognises' in a play
is *the presence of acting*. Recognition 'has a unique inflection in the theater
because it is connected with a psychological mechanism that also achieves
a unique theatrical prominence, the mechanism we call *identification*'.[32]
Identification, indeed, is the linchpin of drama, a process by which an actor
sustains and projects an identity; it is therefore inevitable that the establishing and relinquishing of selfhood has been a theme of all types of drama
from all periods.[33] Performance Reception deals with nothing less than the
way in which successive generations have projected and explored their
own identities.

Dramatic plots often reflect the way that drama functions psychologi-
cally. It is true, of course, that one school of theatrical theory, usually
associated with Brecht, argues that the purpose of theatre is to 'alienate'
its spectators by making them semi-permanently aware of the formal
processes which maintain the cognitive fallacy that they are experiencing.
Moreover, some thinkers have seen the epistemological chasm yawning
between later audiences and the original consumers of ancient drama as
the source of its theatrical power: long before Brecht crystallised his theory
of Epic Theatre, Oscar Wilde argued that Hecuba's sorrows are still so
suited to tragedy because Realism is doomed to failure: the moment Art
surrenders its detachment from reality it is lost. Every artist needs to
avoid 'modernity of form and modernity of subject-matter ... any century
is a suitable object for art except our own'.[34] On this account, it is the
cultural chasm separating Hecuba from post-Euripidean audiences which
underlines her sorrow. Yet this hyper-intellectual approach has never
been shared by most regular theatre-goers, for whom it remains perenni-
ally true that at the core of live drama lie the twin processes of substitution
of one 'person' by another (i.e. by an actor) and identification of one person
(i.e. the spectator) *with* another (represented by the actor). Moreover,
these two processes, substitution and identification, have always affected
dramatic plots, which revel in regents, surrogates, and step-relatives. It
was not only in antiquity that drama was peopled by sons stepping into
their fathers' shoes, sisters who become spokespersons for dead brothers,
and mothers who murder their husbands in the name of slaughtered
daughters. Dramas have also always invited spectators to identify with
the suffering of individuals, whether the tyrant Alexander, embarrassed
because he wept for Hecuba and Andromache in *Trojan Women* (Plutarch,
Life of Pelopidas 29.4-6), or another fourth-century audience who identified with Electra's grief over Orestes' urn as enacted by the actor Polus
(Aulus Gellius, *Attic Nights* 6.35). Just as all humans substitute every
individual with whom they 'really' engage in a reliving of their primal

affective drama, so the family, the site of the primary drama, gravitated to the core of dramatic fiction shortly after the birth of tragedy. Performance Reception of ancient theatre thus offers the potential for discovering the most intimate sites of affective identification utilised by successive generations.[35]

Great acting also leaves traces on the text. All subsequent actors attempting the same role need to position their performance relative to the great forerunners. An experienced audience will comes to appreciate a new performance of a famous role only in comparison with a previous realisation: subsequent adapters have always had to contend as much with a great actor's earlier performance as with the transmitted playscript. It is the traces left by the actors in the historically specific moment of performance, as much as the serial adaptors and authors, that make Performance Reception require an unusual combination of *diachronic* and *synchronic* thinking.

Intellectual insights into Performance Reception take place at the intersection of the diachronic history of a text (especially but not exclusively its previous performance history) and the synchronic reconstruction of what the text will have meant at the time of the production being investigated. Productions *are* far more ephemeral than novels, lyric poems, or paintings. This quality makes the synchronic plane peculiarly important to understanding them. The power of theatre is inseparable from its ephemerality (see below). But theatrical productions have a dense accrued genealogical status, resulting from the contribution of previous *performers* and directors as well as previous writers, translators, adaptors. The influence of all these performances accumulates like compound interest on a capital sum. When Fiona Shaw performed Medea, her approach to the role was informed both by other recent realisations (notably Diana Rigg's), and by a long tradition of *divas* attempting to outdo the legendary performances of their predecessors. This can be traced back to Sarah Bernhardt, who herself was positioned in a Medean stemma that leads to the early nineteenth-century operatic star Giuditta Pasta.[36] The diachronic grasp of the stemmatic position of the individual production, the specific act of *mimesis*, is more complicated but more revealing than in other types of Classical Reception.

Some Phenomenologists argue that theatre has an unusual *truth value*. On this view, theatre is privileged precisely because it is so patently artificial, resulting in a potential to reveal the truth without the mendacious tendency of discursive practices which 'hypocritically' (the word originally meant 'like an actor', a *hupokritês*) stake false *claims* to veracity. Untrue or distorted news reportage, political oratory, travel guides or biographies can all 'masquerade' as truth. Theatre can never 'masquerade' as the truth because it *is* masquerade. Its insights into the society or subjectivity of the time of the production may therefore, paradoxically, be penetratingly veracious. The approach stems from Husserl, the founder of

18

Phenomenology, whose method entailed revealing the meaning of things and events through inspecting the structures underlying *their modes of appearing*. To one influential Phenomenological theorist of drama, 'theatre is a disciplined use of the fictionalizing imagination which can discover … aspects of actuality'.[37] An eloquent expression of this view can be found in the fiction of the dramatist Genet, whose 1941 novel *Notre-Dame des Fleurs* depicts, through the fantasies of its narrator, a gay *demi-monde* where the worlds and identities created by cabaret art and transvestism are more authentic than the duplicitous hypocrisy of the French legal system: at the cabaret on the Rue Lepic, 'It is customary to come in drag, *dressed as ourselves*.'[38] Theatre's truth results from its self-conscious fakery, in contrast with the falseness of people's conduct in 'real life'.

The future Athanasius of Alexandria, who grew up to dislike theatre's false images, nevertheless told the other children at playtime that he 'was' their bishop.[39] Further support of the 'truth' value of theatre could be elicited from the child psychologists who study play and its functions in the young.[40] Erik Erikson insisted that 'even where nobody sees it or does anything about it children proceed to express their vital problems in the metaphoric language of play – more consistently and less self-consciously than they are able or willing to in words'.[41] Human society, likewise, can express its problems in the metaphoric language of *the* play more consistently and less self-consciously than in words.

3.4. Memory

Performance history constitutes time travel into a personal, individual arena of human history. Watched in physical company with other spectators, it offers access to mass ideology, taste and prejudice. It is as a source for such phenomena that it is used by social historians. But it simultaneously permits access to the private imaginative worlds of the individual members of previous generations. Theatre happens, and leaves its psychological records, at the intersection of the collective and the individual, the 'ideological' and the 'subjective'. Theatre critics are also aware that there is something distinctive about the immanent presence of live performance in the memory. It may be an ephemeral art, but a compelling theatrical experience can leave a deeper impression on the memory than the printed word or painted image. Although Freud had access to Sophocles' *Oedipus Tyrannus* as a 'script-alone' in his youth, he never recovered from the experience of watching the great Jean Mounet-Sully perform the role of Oedipus at the Comédie-Française in Paris in 1885-6.[42]

Matthew Arnold was so overwhelmed by the lovely Helen Faucit's realisation of the role of Sophocles' Antigone in 1845 that he later designed his tragedy *Merope* along lines which he hoped would stimulate this tragedienne into performing it. The Irish writer Percy Fitzgerald confessed that his fantasy life was haunted by the same performance: the 'classical vision haunted my boyish dreams for weeks, and does still … It seemed some supernatural figure lent temporarily to this base earth.'[43] Faucit's Antigone affected both Arnold and Fitzgerald with an acute, libidinally charged version of what the scholar of myth Joseph Campbell was a few decades later to term 'Aesthetic Arrest'.[44]

In writing about film, the Marxist-formalist critic Jameson illuminates the impact made by any performance with a visual dimension:

> movies are a physical experience, and are remembered as such, stored up in bodily synapses that evade the thinking mind. Baudelaire and Proust showed us how memories are part of the body anyway ... or perhaps it would be better to say that memories are first and foremost memories of the senses, and that it is the senses that remember ...[45]

Memory is *primarily* sensual; the senses can 'jog' memory of a long-forgotten film (or theatrical performance) years after the event. Jameson continues by describing beautifully, in relation to film, how visual images saturate the psyche immediately after they are watched:

> in the seam between the day to day; the filmic images of the night before stain the morning and saturate it with half-conscious reminiscence, in a way calculated to raise moralizing alarm ... film is an addiction that leaves its traces in the body itself.[46]

This meditation on the specialness of the filmic experience is also suggestive for anyone trying to understand what happens in a theatre. In film, he says, the visual 'glues' things back together, it 'seals up the crevices in the form; it introduces a third thing alongside the classical Aristotelian question of Plot and the modern Benjaminian question of Experience';[47] in a modified form, the theatrical 'visual' has been sealing up crevices in form for millennia. Many plays seem episodic to the critic who only reads them: A.W. Schlegel's indictment on the ground of disunity of a play that he (like all his early nineteenth-century contemporaries) had only read (*Trojan Women*), ensured that it was despised for decades subsequently.[48] Yet it suddenly made sense when theatrically performed. It became glaringly obvious in performance that one character (Hecuba) visually supplied the axis around which every emotion and encounter revolves.[49]

3.5. Psyche

The importance of the sensuous dimension of theatre was brilliantly advocated by Susan Sontag in 'Against Interpretation'.[50] But the genealogy of the theoretical rehabilitation of the theatrical experience can be traced back to the early eighteenth century, which saw the first theoretical revolution in the understanding of theatre seriously to challenge the anti-performance prejudices inherited from Plato.[51] Plato's attack on the theatre was a function, of course, of his appreciation of its power. He understood theatre's fusion of identities and its annihilation of the boundaries demarcating *I* from the actor and from the acted role so well that the verb *mimeisthai* and its cognates are stretched to breaking-point in books 2-3 of the *Republic*. They are made to cover not only what the poet does, what *oratio recta* (direct speech) does, and what the narrator's persona does, but what the poem does, the rhapsode does, the actor does, and arguably even what the theatrical audience contributes to the experience.[52] The thinker who first produced a theoretical model with the potential to cast the visual and bodily dimensions of theatrical *mimesis* in a more positive light (however elliptically) was Vico, in his *Scienza nuova* of 1725. Vico's proto-anthropological approach probed behind the rational, proto-scientific and cerebrally sophisticated analytical thinking of the classical Greeks in order to recover their pre-verbal, emotional and sensual experiences of the natural and the supernatural, above all in the 'poetic metaphysics' and 'poetic wisdom' of Homer. In an appendix, however, Vico extended his thesis to the scripts of the Greek theatre, beneath which lay the bodies of the chorus members and actors like Thespis, who engaged his spectators from a wagon in a mimetic enactment of primordial myths.[53]

It was via a route through Kantian Idealism that Vico's characterisation of the sensual wisdom of the Greek poets led to Søren Kierkegaard. In 1843 he published *Either/Or*, in which theatre provides a paradigm of the aesthetic consciousness which enters the sphere of the existential. Kierkegaard philosophically legitimises the notions of the selectivity of memory, the aesthetic categories by which it prioritises types of experience, and in particular the cognitive and emotional power of performed language and music (in his case, Mozartian opera). He believed that there is a difference in the experience of theatre between physical and mental time. For Kierkegaard, the immediacy of 'the Moment' of apprehension of a performance transcends time, for the images it leaves on the mind are indelible. The moment of performance ideally gains its emotive force from the 'immanent acceleration' in the representation as well as its sensual wholeness, grounded in the material instantiation of the characters and events. This moment is in one sense lost forever, but even its details can also be held in the consciousness until death.[54] Ibsen is influenced by this argument when he makes the eponymous hero of his *Brand* (1885) observe at the end of Act IV that 'Only what is lost can be possessed for ever.'[55]

The susceptibility of theatrical imagery to the human *sub*conscious also contributes to the special nature of Performance Reception. Even in antiquity people experienced theatrical dreams. Demosthenes was said to have dreamed that he was an actor, competing in a tragic competition against Archias ([Plutarch], *Life of Demosthenes* 28-9). Before the battle of Arginusae, one of the Athenian admirals dreamt that he and his six colleagues were playing the roles of the Seven against Thebes in Euripides' *Phoenician Women*, while the Spartan leaders were competing against them as the sons of the Seven in his *Suppliant Women* (Diodorus 13.97-8). Artemidorus' *On the Interpretation of Dreams* includes discussions of dreams in which the subject performs in the theatre.[56] Freud would not have been surprised by these ancient accounts, since he was convinced of the affinity between the world of the theatre and dreamscapes.

The Interpretation of Dreams (1900) proposes, in chapters 4 and 5, that mental images follow dramatic models and embody mimetic representations of living reality. Freud said that abstract thoughts become conveyed by dreams in a 'pictorial language' of dynamic images derived from dramaturgic principles; dreamers incorporate their ideas, transformed into pictures, into a *stage* setting. This process effectively 'dramatises' the idea.[57] In the essays comprising *Totem and Taboo* (1912-1913), he analysed ancient rituals as dramatic enactments of myth, emotion and history; from them emerged the earliest true drama, whose mimetic function aimed to restore absent objects in the ceremonial arena.[58] The later twentieth-century feminist reaction against Freud supplemented his picture with the 'sexual scenography' Irigaray identifies in Plato's metaphysics, above all in the myth of the womblike cave of *Republic* book 5, and the 'return' of Kristeva's 'maternal "repressed" … asking for new spaces, and therefore, new representations'.[59] These psychoanalytical concepts are important to Performance Reception because they imply that the theatre, more than any other art form (except cinema, a largely post-Freudian development), has supplied the furniture equipping the place where each society's inmost fantasies reside.

3.6. Contingency

Jameson's notion of *contingency*, explored in his discussion of film, can aid this quest for a theory to underpin the theatre-centred practice of Performance Reception.[60] Jameson has been affected by a theoretical insight of Jean-Paul Sartre, himself a movie-goer from the age of three.[61] Sartre records that the theory of contingency, the fundamental experience of his novel *Nausea* and the linchpin of his brand of Existentialism, emerged from pondering on the mysterious difference between the images in the film and the 'real' world outside the film. The film will always be identical, and its images always happen in the sequence ordered by the director. Life outside, on the other hand, is always contingent, often unpredictable, the images it presents subject to no directorial control. If movies are entirely *uncontingent*, and life is entirely *contingent*, then a live theatrical performance must lie somewhere between these two poles. Performed plays have a script similar to a film's. Except, of course, in avant-garde experiments such as Schechner's 'interactive' *Dionysus in 69*, a notorious reworking of *Bacchae* which actually opened in 1968, they are largely expected to be performed in a linear movement, more or less from begin to end, at every performance. Most plays are rehearsed by actors so that the way in which phrases and speeches are delivered, the use of the physical body and of props, the underlying tempo are all intended to be identical each night. That is, conventional, polished performances try to eradicate the effects of contingency. On the other hand, the performance must always interact with the responses (or lack of them) evinced by the audience, which will be different at each performance, and no one gesture or phrase can *ever* be performed in an absolutely identical manner. Moreover, the performances even of hallowed examples of the classical repertoire are always subject to actors' changes in timing, memory lapses, interpolations, and spontaneous elaborations of gesture or expression. They are vulnerable to disastrous eventualities – electricity failure, actors who pass out, 'corpse', or trip on their hemlines.

Fundamentally, the contingency attending upon a theatrical performance, except one that is being experienced via a video recording, is both the greatest threat to the success of the performance and the source of its greatest power.[62] One of the most popular plays in antiquity, said by its Alexandrian hypothesis-writer to work wonderfully on the stage, is *Orestes*, at whose premiere the house was brought down when its leading actor, Hegelochus, fluffed a line.[63] The sheer performability of that text was thus in antiquity associated with the contingent excitement of experiencing it in performance by demonstrably fallible actors. The 'electrical' current that passes between a live actor communicating effectively with an audience (Benjamin's 'aura') may not be the same as the psychic saturation offered by the indelible manufactured images of cinema, but it is as powerful. Unlike the aura of physical presence in the theatre, the specious intimacy and proximity which film offers is actually 'based on a mutual absence mediated by the camera'.[64] Practitioners of Performance Reception need to bear this in mind, especially when dealing with now legendary performances – Laurence Olivier as Oedipus, Barrie Rutter as Silenus.

Hornby addresses the difference between productions which are so ineptly acted that they fail to create any sustained identification in their audiences, and those in which the audience is so involved that a deliberate shattering of the dramatic illusion strips away the imaginary framework of role and play temporarily, only to affirm it. He cites as an example of such 'metadramatic' technique the moment in Schechner's *Dionysus in 69* when the true name and identity of the actor playing Pentheus – Bill Shephard – was suddenly acknowledged.[65] Stripping away the fiction of performance is to draw 'upon the very essence of live theatre', which combines a presence with the ever-present threat of *absence*. The actuality of sweating actors is present alongside the imminent absence of the identities they have assumed if the electric current charging the performance fails. 'The special, magical feeling that we experience in the theatre is the result of our awareness that there is so much than can go wrong, that a performance always teeters on the brink of the disaster', despite the physicality and tangible presence of the performers.[66] This excitement was

23

for me exemplified by watching Greg Hicks as Dionysus carry off Peter Hall's unremarkable *Bacchai* in 2001 by the sustained force of his presence and actorly expertise.

Orthodox Structuralists see the live nature of theatre as a frame; it is part of the *langue* in which the theatrical *parole* (specific utterance and gesture) takes place. Live-ness, therefore, is not the *defining* feature of theatre, since listening to an after-dinner speaker perform in his or her 'real' persona does not offer the same degree or type of engagement as a theatrical performance. It is the *live-ness* of the representation of the *fictive identities*, the manner in which they are sustained through time and across action and encounter, and the contingent threat to their successful continuance – the imminence and immanence of *absence* – which is nearer to the essential nature of theatre. Moreover, mediocre theatre does not take its audience as close to the edge of breakdown of the conjured identities as good theatre; part of the effectiveness of a performance is the extent to which it can teeter on the edge of dissolution and anarchy (as the premiere of Euripides' *Orestes* did), but without actually collapsing.

3.7. Temporal orientation

The relative contingency of theatre is connected with its temporal orientation. The Symbolist Ernst Cassirer argued that art gives *form* to human feeling. Its effect is in consequence not fully analysable discursively in language: art forms *communicate the non-verbal*. Langer took this notion further, to argue that all art forms have discrete immanent laws, and offer us a 'virtual reality', a conceptual place with its own inner rhythms. Mimesis is not a hallucination or a delusion, but an 'affecting presence'. What distinguishes different art forms is the nature of the specific virtual space they create. Narrative literature provides a 'virtual past' or 'memory', lyric a 'virtual experience', but drama suggests a 'virtual *future*', on account of its orientation towards *what will happen next.*[67]

Even the remote time depicted in ancient tragedy (which is set in its original audience's past), or in ancient comedy (set in its original audience's present), is transformed by live enactment into a dynamic representation of the margin between 'now' and 'after now'. When we watch *Antigone*, we are always present in Thebes, wondering how this man who stands so visibly enraged before us will react to the teenage girl who is being so rude to him *right now*. Immediacy makes the Performance Reception of drama different from the Reception of, for example, an ancient historiographical work extending over innumerable printed pages. Szondi's famous study of time in Wilder's *The Long Christmas Dinner* identifies such nuances in the temporal dimension of drama as its spatialisation of time, its 'abstract evocation' of the passage of time, and the crucial distinction between between 'narrative time' (corresponding to the time of the performance) and the 'narrated time' covered by the enacted

24

events. Yet it nevertheless implies a reaffirmation of the inevitable 'presence' of the visible moment, 'a moment turned toward the future … one that destroys itself for the sake of the future movement'.[68]

This 'future' orientation of drama, an aspect of its semi-contingency, is also connected with its political potential. Theatre makes the future seem potentially *controllable*, or at least susceptible to intervention. This distinguishes it from film, whose non-contingency places it in a different relation to the twin poles of narrative (past) and theatre (future). Theatre's 'what will happen next?' question suggests the immanent power of the collective to alter that future – a sense conveyed by ancient choruses who want to intervene in domestic violence but are unable to actualise their desire. The sense of empowerment gives the theatre what, ever since the unorthodox Marxist Bloch's *Geist der Utopie* (first published at the poignant date of 1918, when German radicals were facing acute disappointment), has been called its 'utopian' tendency or signature. This designates its potential for transcending in fictive unreality the social limitations of the moment of its own production. All art can narrate or represent revolution, but only drama has the potential to *enact*, through both form and content, optimistic changes in power relations impossible in the society producing the drama. Even alongside its potential for inspecting the worst atrocities and trepidations humankind can imagine, theatre offers a sense that the future is *partly* in the hands of those creating it, and that it could be changed. There could be a world where no child was murdered, and tyrants always fell, if we collectively willed and then enacted such a world into being. The creation of an imaginative arena susceptible to the radical act of utopian thinking belongs to live theatre as to no other artistic medium.[69]

In revivals of the live theatre of previous eras, the radical potential of theatre is enhanced by the conception of the *relativity* of all historical phenomena. The thinker to whom this needs to be traced is another product of German Idealism, Dilthey, who was influenced by Husserl. Dilthey became convinced that understanding the changes which the world has continuously undergone prevents humans from allowing themselves to be bound irrevocably to any one conviction. Historical awareness makes humans free: 'The *historical consciousness* of the *finitude* of every historical phenomenon, of every human or social condition, of the relativity of every kind of faith, is the final step in the liberation of man.'[70] Historical understanding reveals new possibilities. When Dilthey says that man is a historical being, he means that man's historical attitude faces the future instead of gazing into the past.[71] The development of historical understanding can be nurtured by watching the drama of previous stages of historical development and responding actively to its social and political conundrums (as Iser argued cogently in respect of the lasting impact of Shakespeare's history plays).[72]

3.8. Political potency

Theatre's communal consumption lends it a collective aspect, but its enacted nature and face-to-face confrontations contribute to what Sontag called its unique 'adversarial power'.[73] 'Why stage declamatory Greeks ... unless to disguise what one was thinking under a fascist regime?' Sartre asked bluntly in 1944, referring to the moral conflict he had recently staged in *Les Mouches*.[74] This is one reason why Peter Sellars thinks that an important theatrical event can make waves far beyond its performance context, as cited in this chapter's epigraph.[75] Artaud savoured Augustine's censorious comparison of the potency of theatre, which induces extraordinary changes in the minds of nations, with the plague which can kill without even destroying individual organs.[76] Examples of nation-changing productions of ancient drama more recently include Fugard's *The Island* and Andrej Wajda's *Antygona*. Theatre's form can be peculiarly egalitarian, as Aristophanes noted in Euripides' boast that he made tragedy 'democratic' by allowing his women and slaves, individuals silenced in the public discourse of the Athenian city-state, to deliver public speeches (*Frogs* 949-52). There is a tension between the 'democratic' form of ancient drama and its often conservative content. This tension gives the plays an ideological complexity, a dialogism, that partly explains their perennial appeal.[77] The actor's art, as early Christian anti-theatrical polemicists already fumed, also abolishes social boundaries by allowing common, even servile players to pretend to be kings, or to enact the humiliation of kings.

Theatre has also, historically at least, been available to more people than knowledge of Latin and Greek. Low-income spectators for centuries spent their hard-earned pennies on acquiring familiarity with ancient mythology and history from the proletarian pits of Europe's theatre and opera houses.[78] The groundlings who leered at Antony and Cleopatra were 'doing Classics' as vigorously as the learned clerics of Oxenford, immersed in their ancient Rhetoric. But so were the French citizens who flocked to watch Talma, the thespian darling of the French Revolution, perform a star turn as Philoctete or Égiste in a new version of Sophocles at the Theatre of the Republic. To do Performance History is to excavate a more demotic and more widespread influence of the Classics.

4. Conclusion

No doubt this chapter reads as eccentrically eclectic. It defines a fundamentally cultural materialist approach to its subject-matter, but this is qualified by an engagement with a consistent philosophical line which can be traced from Vico's rediscovery of the sensually conveyed wisdom of pagan art, via German idealism to Kierkegaard, Husserlian Phenomenology, Symbolism, and French Existentialism. The discussion has also adduced the psychoanalyst Freud, theatre scholars such as Bentley, Goldman, Hornby and Weimann, literary theorists including Bakhtin (a 'Formalist') and Derrida (a 'Deconstructionist'), as well as a few Classicists (above all Fiona Macintosh, Lorna Hardwick and Helene Foley, who also provided indispensable help with this essay). This is theory ordered *à la carte*. But its aim is simply to open up dialogue within Classics by offering an account of the special features of the medium studied in Performance Reception.

Notes

1. See Goldhill 1999b: especially 1-20.

2. Bentley 1975: 150.

3. On which see Hall 2008b.

4. See Hall 2002a: 430-1; Hall and Wyles 2008. A different example would be the Plautine ancestry which Dario Fo claims for the Saturnalian spirit which has conditioned his own farces: see Scuderi 2000: 39-42.

5. See Hall 2005a on the longlasting effects of the ancient reception of Clytemnestra.

6. Martindale 1993: 7.

7. Hall 2005b.

8. Hall 2002: 432; Hall & Macintosh 2005: chs 4 and 15.

9. Wilamowitz's involvement in theatricals including the *Oresteia*, *Medea* and *Oedipus* (briefly described in his *Recollections* 1930: 306-8), is not apparent in his scholarship on the dramatists involved.

10. Bentley 1975: 149.

11. Letter of 16 December 1932, in Schumacher 1989: 722-3.

12. See Hall and Macintosh 2005: chs 6 and 17.

13. See Hall 2006: 4-6.

14. Bakhtin 1986; see also Hall 2008b: 6.

15. Vidal-Naquet 1988: 361-80; Hall and Macintosh 2005: ch. 2.

16. Vernant 1988: 237-47.

17. Weimann 1976: especially 46-56.

18. See also Warner 1595.

19. Hall and Macintosh 2005: ch. 3.

20. English translation published in Graham 1985.

21. See Johnson 2002.

22. Barnstone 1993: 261; see also Bassnett 2002: 1-10.

23. See Schironi 2007.

24. Fischer-Lichte 2004: 344-52.

25. Helene Foley points out to me that there have been effective combinations of live actors and puppets, in, for example, the musical *Avenue Q* at the Golden Theatre, Broadway, in 2003.

26. Bentley 1975: 117.

27. Bentley 1975: 117.

28. Hall 2006: 118-33.

29. Eagleton 2002: xiv, 29, 31.

30. Benjamin 1992: 231 eloquently described the absence of the *aura* from film: 'for the first time – and this is the effect of film – man has to operate with his whole living person, yet forgoing its aura. For aura is tied to presence; there is no replica of it.'

31. Chaikin 1972: 20.

32. Goldman 2000: 10.

33. Goldman 2000: 18; see also Goldman 1975: 123.

34. Wilde 1989: 222.

35. See Hall 2004b: 34 n. 63.

36. Macintosh 2000.

37. Wilshire 1982: 11.

38. My italics. Translation by Bernard Frechtman, from Genet 1963: 228.

39. Rufinus, *Historia Ecclesiastica* 10.15.

40. See Walton 1994, in reaction to Ernst Gombrich's famous essay 'Meditations on a Hobby Horse' (in Gombrich 1965).

41. Erikson 1975: 668.

42. See Frankland 2000: 30-2, 68, 142-3, 206.

43. Hall & Macintosh 2005: ch. 12.

44. For an account of which see Campbell 1968: 66.

45. Jameson 1990: 1-3.

46. Jameson 1990: 2.

47. Jameson 1990: 5.

48. English translation in Schlegel 1846: 136.

49. Bates 1927: 200-1.

50. This essay, dating from the early 1960s in *Evergreen Review*, is accessibly republished in Sontag 1994.

51.On which see the superb study by Barish 1981.

52. Hall 2006: 37-9.

53. Vico 1948: 295.

54. See Kierkegaard 1987: 42, 68, 117-18, 239, 486-7; and Pattison 1992: 95-124.

55. Translation taken from Ibsen 1972: 194.

56. See Hall 2006: 16-18.

57. See Rose 2001: 79; Lyotard 1977; and Frankland 2000: 131.

58. See the discussion of Rose 2001: 76-7.

59. Irigaray 1985, Kristeva 1977; both are reproduced in Murray 1997.

60. Jameson 1990: 4-5.

61. Sartre 1964: 96-102 and 1970: 53-4.

62. Performance reception of live theatre is compromised in different ways both by the necessity to study many performances via video recordings, and by many theatre professionals' refusal to allow their productions to be recorded at all.

63. See Aristophanes, *Frogs* 303 with scholion; Sannyrion fr. 8 and Strattis fr. 1.2-3 *Poetae Comici Graeci*.

64. Gilloch 2002: 188.

65. On which see Zeitlin 2004.

66. Hornby 1986: 98-9.

67. Langer 1953: 215, 307, 258-79, 307.

68. 77 Szondi 1965: 87.

69. 78 Jameson 1981: 290-1; Rose 1992: 36-42; Ryan 1989.

70. Dilthey 1913-58: vol. 7, 290, translated by Plantinga 1980: 133.

71. Plantinga 1980: 133.

72. Iser 1988, translated into English in Wilson 1993.

73. Quoted in Marranca and Dasgupta 1999. See also Gellrich 1988.

74. *Carrefour*, 9 September 1944, quoted in Contat and Rybalka 1976: 188.

75. Quoted in O'Mahony 2000: 7.

76. *City of God* 1.32; see Schumacher 1989: 114-15.

77. Hall 2010: ch. 3.

78. Hall 2008a.

Performance as Event – Reception as Transformation

Erika Fischer-Lichte

The last twenty years have seen the appearance of several histories of modern performances of ancient plays.[1] These all implicitly and explicitly reflect on the particular conditions, modes, theoretical assumptions, discourses and other prerequisites that have to be considered when writing a history of Performance Reception in the context of ancient drama on the modern stage. Yet despite the substantial progress achieved in this field, theorising Performance Reception still remains a challenge. To a large extent, the trouble arises from the usage of the two key terms – performance and reception. We usually assume that we all have more or less the same things in mind when using those terms. But is this really so? Even if we do agree on their definitions, are we always aware of the consequences they have on our work? In this essay I elaborate on these two concepts in order to attempt to theorise 'Performance Reception' and draw certain conclusions for its history. This procedure also has consequences for the analysis of present-day performances of ancient plays. To begin with defining the contested concept of *performance*, I shall consider four aspects of particular importance to our work.[2]

1. Co-presence

A performance takes place in and through the bodily co-presence of actors and spectators. Every performance requires two groups of people, the 'doers' (a group which may include technicians, stage crew, musicians etc., as well as performers) and the 'onlookers', who have to assemble at a certain time and place in order to share this situation, a span of lifetime. A performance arises out of their encounter and interaction. That is to say, the medial conditions in a performance are completely different from those underlying the production and reception of texts, artefacts and objects. While the actors *do* something – such as move through the space, perform gestures, manipulate objects, speak and sing – the spectators perceive them and react. It may well be the case that some of these reactions are internal – imaginative and cognitive – that is, limited to purely mental processes. However, most of the reactions and responses can be perceived by the other spectators and the actors, such as laughing, shouting, yawning, snoring, sobbing, crying, commenting on what is happening, getting up, running out, slamming the doors, and so on and so forth. The perception of these responses in turn leads to further perceptible reactions. Whatever the actors do, it has an effect on the spectators; and whatever the spectators do, it has an effect on the other spectators and the actors. A performance generates itself through the interactions between actors and spectators. From this it follows that its course can neither be fully planned nor predicted. Performance relies on an *autopoietic* process, which is characterised by a high degree of contingency. Nobody can foresee the exact course of a performance at its beginning. Many elements emerge in the course of a performance as a result of certain interactions.

Of course, the actors set the decisive preconditions for the progression of the performance – preconditions that have been fixed by the process of *mise-en-scène* (the design and arrangement of a production or performance) since the early twentieth century. However, the actors are not in a position fully to control the course of the performance. Ultimately, all participants generate the performance together. This condition not only minimises but precludes the possibility for an individual or a group fully to plan, steer and control its course. In other words, performance opens up the possibility for all participants to experience themselves as subjects able to co-determine the actions and behaviour of others, and whose own actions and behaviour are determined by others. Depending on the cultural and historical context, however, both groups, actors and spectators, are limited in the range of possible behavioural modes by the social rules governing public events like theatrical performances. The rules applied to a performance at the court of Louis XIV, *le Roi Soleil*, are different from those at a modern performance at Berlin's Volksbühne. This demonstrates that performances are not to be regarded solely as an artistic but always also as a social process. Different groups encounter, negotiate, and regulate their relationships differently in performances.

The social process turns political at that moment during a performance when a power struggle erupts between actors and spectators or between different groups of spectators. This might be because one group attempts to impose on the others certain definitions of the situation or their relationship, or certain convictions and modes of behaviour. Since all participants (to varying degrees) co-determine the course of a performance and are determined by it, there can be no 'passive' participants in a performance. In this sense, all participants bear the joint responsibility for what occurs. Furthermore, some kind of unity may arise among the spectators. A community may even emerge among the spectators or between actors and spectators, for the whole duration of the performance or at least for certain periods. Thus a performance might turn into a profoundly political process, without necessarily addressing an explicitly political subject-matter.

3. Performance as Event – Reception as Transformation

If we understand performance as that which occurs *between* actors and spectators, then a history of Performance Reception must take this into account. Consequently, sources telling us what occurred during a performance between actors and spectators, or even between different groups of spectators, are of utmost importance here. In order to make sense of such sources, we have to probe the performance's particular social and political context. We have to research those who initiated the performance for whatever purpose as well as the audience: its social composition, expectations, and responses. It is inadequate simply to examine the text version used and relate it to the performance's social and political context. Unfortunately, in some cases, we do not have access to many other sources.

At this point, a truism needs reasserting: a performance always takes place here and now; it belongs only to the present. Unlike pictures, statues, and other objects, we cannot behold past performances in a museum. Producers can never hope that another audience may arise in fifty or even a hundred years that will be able better to appreciate and understand their work. Performance takes place between present-day actors and spectators. It is embedded and engrained in the actual cultural, social, and political situation much more deeply than texts and objects. Performance cannot be detached from its context under any circumstances, whether of a contemporary play or ancient drama.

2. Ephemerality and intensity

The materiality of the performance cannot exist beyond its duration. Rather, its spatiality, corporeality and tonality are brought forth in the course of the performance. This leads us to an inherent paradox of performance: it is ephemeral and transitory; however, whatever happens and takes shape in its course comes into being *hic et nunc* (here and now) and is experienced by the participants as being present in a particularly intense way.

Even if, in this sense, performances exhaust themselves in this 'present-ness', that is in their permanent emerging and passing, this does not mean that material objects cannot be used in them. Such objects remain as traces of the performance and can be preserved. While the focus shifts to the object itself once it is exhibited in a theatre museum, during a performance the attention is primarily directed at the use made of the object – what actions were performed when an object was manipulated, how did a costume give shape to the body and the way it looked and moved, and what effect this had. These are questions theatre historians must answer when referring to such evidence.

Whatever appears in a performance results, on the one hand, from the intentions, plans, ideas, and imaginations of several subjects. The *mise-en-scène* defines what elements are to appear where and when on stage, how they are to move through the space, and whence and when they are to disappear from it. But, on the other hand, as we have seen above, the performance as a whole is generated from interactions. By a certain point in history, such phenomena as the spectators' perceivable responses have indeed been considered constitutive of the performance; this was the case in Max Reinhardt's *Oedipus the King* (1911) or in Richard Schechner's *Dionysus in 69* (1968). But this was not always so. Such elements have at other times been deemed disruptive, and the performance's materiality has been defined only as what was intentionally produced by the artists involved, as by Goethe in the performances of his *Ion* production (1802).[3] In either case, it needs reiterating that whatever appears during a performance co-constitutes the particular materiality of this performance. This is why we must clearly distinguish between the concept of *mise-en-scène*, of production, and that of performance. While '*mise-en-scène*' describes the materiality of the performance determined by the plans and intentions of the artists, 'performance' includes any kind of materiality elicited in its course. As such, the production is reproducible, whereas every performance is unique. When studying the *mise-en-scène*, one useful source of evidence might be the testimony of the participating artists, but in the case of the *performance*, such testimony forms only one small component of the sources that need to be taken into consideration.

One element from which the materiality of the performance of an ancient play comes into being is space. Performances of Greek tragedies since their Renaissance rediscovery have taken place in a variety of locations: in the dining halls, ballrooms, or fencing arenas of castles; in the first theatre of modern times, the Teatro Olimpico in Vicenza; in court or bourgeois theatre buildings; in circus tents and empty factories; and in the remains of the ancient theatres of Delphi, Epidaurus and Syracuse. Irrespective of the functions these spaces fulfil, the spatiality of the performances taking place in them is always ephemeral and transitory. We must distinguish between the architectural-geometric space, in which the performance takes place, and the performative space through which the performance comes into being. It is the performative space that enables particular possibilities for the relationship between actors and spectators, for movement and perception, which it also organises and structures. The ways in which such possibilities are used, realised, avoided, or resisted affect the performative space. Every movement of people, animals, objects, or light, and every sound, will change the performative space and produce its spatiality anew. In contrast to the architectural-geometric space, the performative space is unstable, permanently fluctuating and changing. In performance, spatiality does not exist but 'happen'. We have to keep this difference in mind when visiting a site where a particular performance of an ancient play took place.

The actors' bodies constitute the other basic material of performance. As the philosopher Hellmuth Plessner noted, the relationship of human beings to their bodies is characterised by a certain duality.[4] Human beings *are* their bodies; they are body-subjects. Yet, at the same time, they *have* a body which they can use as an object and tool serving different purposes, or as a sign conveying various meanings. However, because of this duality, the human body can never be used in the same way as any other object. For the human body is a living organism engaged in a permanent state of becoming; it is involved in an ongoing process of transformation. There is no state simply of 'being'; the body understands being only as becoming; it is always dynamic and never static, even when motionless. With each lowering of the eyelid, each breath, each movement, the body recreates itself, becomes another and embodies itself anew. The bodily being-in-the-world, the phenomenal body, which lives in the state of *becoming*, fiercely defies any definition of itself as an artwork in the sense of an object. The human body can turn into an artwork, an object, only as a dead body, a corpse. From that point onwards it can be used as material and shaped accordingly, not only for death rituals but also in artistic processes, as Gunter von Hagen demonstrated in his exhibition *Body-Worlds*.[5] As a living body, however, it stubbornly defies any attempt to turn it into a work of art.

Actors do not create works of art out of their bodies. Rather, they perform a process of embodiment which produces their particular individual corporeality, their phenomenal body. This process also allows them to bring forth their semiotic bodies, i.e. a dramatic figure. It is in this way that the body transforms itself, and creates itself anew. This is why it can never be completely controlled. On the other hand, in bringing forth their phenomenal bodies, actors also generate bodies of energy. The conjuring up of energy by actors is neither a purely physical process nor a purely mental one; it is both at the same time. When the spectators physically sense the energy emanating from an actor and circulating in the space among those present, they sense it as a mental as well as a physical force. They sense it as a transformative, and as such *vital* force emanating from the actor, and simultaneously as their own vital force. This is what we usually call experiencing the actor's PRESENCE. Through the actor's PRESENCE, the spectators experience the actors as well as themselves as embodied minds, as people engaged in the permanent process of becoming, and as living organisms gifted with consciousness.

This can happen only because of the bodily co-presence of actors and spectators. Judging by different sources from the sixteenth and seventeenth centuries, spectators then frequently sensed an actor's PRESENCE emanating from his/her phenomenal body. In that case, the consequences for research in Performance Reception will differ significantly from a situation in which the spectators tend to attribute the experience of PRESENCE to the actor's semiotic body, i.e. to the character he is embodying. We can assume that this was the case during the eighteenth and nineteenth centuries. In both cases, emotions were contagious. Besides contemporary theories of acting and manuals, we must also consider

33

discourses on the body, on emotion, and perception. Such an approach will allow us to understand why and how a particular performance of a Greek tragedy affected the senses and the minds of spectators, as was apparently the case in Tieck/Mendelssohn's 1841 *Antigone* in Potsdam with Auguste Crelinger in the title role, or in the 1845 *Antigone* at Covent Garden, starring Charlotte Vandenhoff, or in the *Antigone* of the same year in Dublin, starring Helen Faucit.[6]

The third source material, the play's text in whatever version, poses a serious problem. As a written text, it does not form a part of the performance's materiality. Rather, the particular materiality of the performance makes the text disappear. Instead of names and portions of text accorded to them as their lines, we have actors with a particular corporeality, including a specific voice, way of moving through the space, gesturing, manipulating objects, speaking, and/or singing. Not even the act of reciting the text, thus bringing forth tonality as vocality, is identical with the written text. As in the case of the body, we must distinguish between the material qualities of the voice and the sounds brought forth by the voice as signs, as words. Vocality always brings forth corporeality.

A voice creates all three types of materiality: corporeality, spatiality, and tonality. The intimate relationship between body and voice becomes particularly evident when a person screams, sighs, moans, sobs or laughs. Such sounds clearly involve the entire body as it bends over, contorts or stiffens. Yet, in performances, vocal expressions have largely become indivisibly linked to language, since they mostly use speaking or singing voices. Spoken language in a performance can therefore by no means be equated with the written text. Since the voice refers to a particular corporeality and rings out in a particular space, language cannot be analysed in the same manner as a written text. Rather, its relationship to all the other components at play must also be considered. This poses a serious problem when it comes to past performances and can be appropriately dealt with only in analysing present-day performances.

3. The production of meaning in performance

Scholars used to proceed from the assumption that performances transmit the specific, given meaning inherent in the dramatic text or a particular interpretation enabled by it. Such an assumption can no longer be maintained for various reasons. One is that every text of an ancient play is ambiguous. It does not contain a single fixed meaning or sense that we have to take as authoritative, but it can be interpreted in different ways. The problem is exacerbated by the use of translations of the ancient texts on the modern stage. Furthermore, the perspectives of co-presence and ephemerality, which I have already discussed, bluntly contradict such a notion. First, there are the unforeseen and unplanned elements that emerge from the interaction between actors and spectators during the performance and generate their own meanings. Secondly, focussing the attention on the particular presence of phenomenal bodies (and also objects and spaces) distracts it from the semiotic bodies, objects and spaces and thus runs counter to the idea that the text has a fixed and immanent meaning. Meanings come into being during the performance and are to be regarded as emergent. It is to miss the point to interpret the text, even the version used in the performance, and use this interpretation as a yardstick for judging the meanings generated by the performance. Theatre is neither a derivative art nor a philological institution.

But what happens to the text in performance? In another context, I have developed three different models for how the text might relate to the performance – sacrificial ritual, play and resonance.[7] Klaus Michael Grüber's production of *The Bacchae* (1974) inspired the idea for the first model.[8] To stage a text means to perform a *sparagmos* (tearing apart) and an *omophageia* (raw-flesh-eating). The artists involved in the production take the text apart and incorporate it into a performance piece by piece. They proceed in a manner similar to a Greek sacrificial meal as described by Walter Burkert,[9] for they incorporate only what they or some ruling 'Zeitgeist' consider palatable. What appears to them as 'bones', 'inedible innards', or even 'fatty vapour' is left to the 'gods'; in other words, it will be excluded from this particular production. In this sense, each and every production that uses a text performs its dismemberment, a ritual sacrifice. This also applies to productions that use unabridged texts. Even such a text has to be dismembered and incorporated by different actors, who transform them according to their particular corporeality. The outcome is consequently different in each case. In every instance the text had to be sacrificed in order to allow the appearance of something new – the performance.

In certain contexts, however, one of the two other models might be better suited to describing accurately how the text is used as one of the materials constituting the production. On the one hand, to play with the text means to exploit fully its potential for generating associations. On the other, the ludic process of creating a collision of the text with other materials which superficially bear no relationship to it, allows us to find out what kinds of new meanings can be generated. The productions of Frank Castorf and Peter Sellars frequently employ this method.[10] But the third model, the model of resonance, applies to all those cases in which a production uses only fragments of the text, while the rest of the text resonates in certain scenes, actions, movements, or behaviour without actually being spoken, or when a whole other production that used the text resonates in these dimensions of the production. In all three cases, the text as such does not appear on the stage. It is always dismembered and transformed. The transformation is achieved both by the process of incorporation and the ever-changing spatial constellation. By way of summary: in a performance, spectators are not confronted with a text – as they are

35

as readers. Instead, they encounter particular human bodies in a particular space uttering words and sentences in a specific voice and manner. While their words may also be found in the written text, they generate very different meanings in this specific constellation.

Even the careful examination of the underlying textual version that was used is therefore entirely inadequate as a strategy for discovering what meanings a past performance of a Greek play may have generated, for example Tieck's *Antigone* in 1841, which used the proclaimed literal translation by Jakob Christian Donner.[11] First, one must consider the particular constellation that emerged on the stage and its general cultural, political, social and philosophical context. In order to study the theatrical constellation of Tieck's *Antigone*, for example, we have to examine the particular space created for this performance in the Hoftheater im Neuen Palais in Potsdam. Remodelled according to Hans Christian Genelli's vision of a Greek theatre, it provided a space in which the ancient orchestra resonated in the area in front of the stage and was linked to the stage by steps in addition to incorporating the semicircle of the auditorium.[12] We must examine sources concerning the particular corporeality and acting style of the actors, including Auguste Crelinger as Antigone and Eduard Devrient as Haemon. Another significant dimension is the music composed by Felix Mendelssohn Bartholdy. Relating all these elements to each other may give us an idea of the possible meanings generated by the performance.

Furthermore, the general context in which the performance was embedded has to be studied with care. First, we have the political context. This particular production was staged more or less by order of the Prussian King Friedrich Wilhelm IV who had ascended the throne the previous year. One purpose of this performance was undeniably to articulate a new self-understanding of the Prussian state. Why *Antigone*? Here we have to trace the philosophical discussion surrounding the play, begun and dominated by Hegel and his successors, and identify possible connections to Goethe's somewhat unsuccessful Weimar *Antigone* of 1809. Moreover, we have to probe the composition of the audience, both during the premiere in Potsdam and during later performances at the Theatre Royal in Berlin. We have to investigate the academic discourse of the time on ancient Greek theatre (August Böckh from the Department of Classics at Berlin University had been involved in the production as advisor), as well as the widespread discourse, dating back to the mid-eighteenth century, on the relationship between ancient Greek and contemporary German culture. Lastly, we must see the great importance of the emergence of historicism, which shaped a completely new consciousness of and attitude towards the past, particularly ancient Greece. Meanings generated by individual spectators will ultimately remain a mystery, unidentifiable even if we scrutinise the reviews by critics and academics, or the reports by the artists involved, or even the spectators themselves. Yet considering all these contexts in their entirety will allow us to get an idea of the possible meanings generated in the performance.

We are, of course, in a wholly different but not necessarily better position when dealing with a performance nowadays. While we might be able to discuss the meanings we attributed to a performance while it was going on, or reflect on them later, during an actual performance we are never distanced observers, but always involved participants. In other words, we are analysing a process of which we form a part. But this situation helps us to relate the meanings we and others generate during or after the performance to the actual context, and, accordingly, to assess its topicality. Such performances offer the only opportunity for us to experience a performance aesthetically while participating in it, and therefore to think about the interplay between the generation of meaning and the aesthetic experience.

4. Performance as event

Performances are characterised by their nature as events. They enable a specific mode of experience that corresponds to a particular form of liminal experience. Since a performance comes into being by way of the interaction between actors and spectators and produces itself as an *autopoietic* process, it is impossible to label it an artwork in the sense of an object. Once the *autopoietic* process comes to an end, the performance does not stay behind as its result; the performance, too, has come to an end. It is over and therefore irretrievably lost. A performance exists only in the process of performing; it exists only as event.

Unlike the *mise-en-scène*, the performance as event is unique and cannot be repeated. It is impossible for exactly the same constellation between actors and spectators to occur another time. The spectators' responses and their effect on the actors and other spectators will be different in each and every performance. A performance must be regarded as an event that no participant can fully control. It constitutes an event that simply happens to its participants – particularly to the spectators. This holds true not only with respect to the consequences of the bodily co-presence of actors and spectators, but also in relation to the particular 'presentness' of the actors' bodies and the emergence of meaning.

Moreover, the particular nature of performance as event is characterised by a strange collapsing of binaries. The participants in a performance experience themselves as subjects co-determining its course and, at the same time, being determined by it. They live through the performance as an aesthetic and social, even political process, in the course of which relationships are negotiated, power struggles are fought out, communities are established and dissolved. The participants' perception shifts between focussing on the actors' phenomenal bodies and sensing their PRESENCE, and focussing on their semiotic bodies, repre-

37

senting a dramatic character. Thus, traditional oppositions and conceptual dichotomies in Western culture (e.g. autonomous subject / subject determined by others; art / social reality or politics; presence / representation) are not experienced as exclusive of one another by the participants in a performance but as complementary. The binaries collapse, the dichotomy dissolves.

The moment this happens, the moment one category may also be the other, our attention is attracted to the passage from one state to the other, by instability, which, in its turn, is experienced as an event. An interval opens up in the space between these opposites. The 'betwixt and between', defined by Victor Turner as constitutive for ritual experience,[13] thus also becomes a privileged category in a theatre performance. It points to the threshold between the spaces, a liminal state to which the performance's participants are all transferred. This insight is not news. We find it in almost all theories of theatre adhering to a *Wirkungsästhetik*, or an aesthetic of effect. When Aristotle described the effect of tragic theatre in chapter 6 of his *Poetics* as the excitement of *eleos* and *phobos*, pity and terror, he had in mind an exceptional affective state brought about by performance, articulated physically, and bearing the potential to alter the person concerned. *Katharsis*, the term introduced in the same passage to define the function of tragic theatre, cannot negate its ritual origins, and its idea of purging evokes healing rituals. While triggering affects will transfer the spectator into a liminal state, *katharsis* brings about the actual transformation. The concept of catharsis strongly influenced the discussion of aesthetic experience in performance until the late eighteenth century. While later concepts of catharsis still maintained the idea of liminality and transformation, it was defined quite differently.

At the turn of the eighteenth to the nineteenth century, the idea of the autonomy of art was established, leading to the end of the aesthetic of effect and the development of the concepts of aesthetics and aesthetic experience. In consequence, the notion of theatre's transformative power gradually became marginalised. Yet, it is not too far-fetched to identify signs of a new version of the idea of theatre's transformative potential in Goethe's or Schiller's *Bildungstheater*, particularly in Goethe's productions of ancient plays. Schiller's *Letters on the Aesthetic Education of Man* (1795) develops this idea.[14] Its central term can indeed be interpreted in terms of a 'betwixt and between', a liminal experience. In playing, the ordinary human being, in whom the sensuous, material instinct (*Stofftrieb*) and the formal instinct (*Formtrieb*) diverge and are at constant war with each other, undergoes a metamorphosis. The transformation is temporary; ideally, the aesthetic experience lasts for the duration of the performance and reconciles material and formal instincts. With Nietzsche's *Birth of Tragedy out of the Spirit of Music* (1872), a new aesthetic of effect was formulated that focussed on the transformative potential of performance and has proved influential until today.

3. Performance as Event – Reception as Transformation

It may actually be only in present-day performances that we can have aesthetic experiences, but the concept is by no means irrelevant to the study of past performances of ancient plays. There have always been theoretical discussions of the impact theatre performances may have had on spectators, regardless of whether this impact was deemed negative or positive. The transformative potential of performances was never seriously questioned. These discussions often drew heavily on discourses and examples from antiquity. It therefore seems particularly interesting to apply them to performances of ancient plays to find out in which of these particular elements the contemporaries saw the affective potential. Reports on the impact of performances on individual spectators will also be useful in order to be able to determine the function and significance of a particular performance.

Contemporary performances of ancient plays trigger a state of liminality using different artistic devices and seemingly serving different purposes. In Gotscheff's production of *The Persians* (Deutsches Theater Berlin 2006), it was primarily the manner of speech which transferred the spectators/listeners into such a state. Margit Bendokat acted as the chorus. She spoke slowly, with great involvement, wresting each individual word from her body. Her manner of speech created something of a maelstrom, hypnotic and at the same time somewhat distanced, slowly but inevitably dragging the spectator/listener into the stream of single words that followed each other without always making sense. This effect resulted especially from the version of the play used, a text created by Heiner Müller.[15] With the words spoken so slowly and with such a particular emphasis placed on each one, Müller's intentionally complicated syntax often prevented listeners from understanding. This manner of speech could indeed be understood as a particular form of choric speech. The actress was not speaking as an individual; rather, she acted as a medium for something else to speak through her. This manner of speech not only grabbed the listeners' attention but also transferred them into a liminal state.

Terzopoulos' production of *Ajax* (premiered 2005) created a similar effect through rhythm and repetition. In his production, Sophocles' text only *resonated*. The performance was conducted by three actors who, one after the other, enacted Ajax's madness. All three of them laugh and absently tell the story of the slaughter committed by Ajax, accompanied by the soft sounds of a waltz. Their bodies are evidently very tense, making jerky movements. Over the course of their narration, they begin to experience the ecstasy they are talking about. Their rhythmic and loud breathing as well as their repeated, synchronised movements transfer each of them into a Dionysian state at the end of their stories, although each time this occurs differently. This particular kind of repetition also allows the spectator to be gradually transferred into a state of liminality, though probably not into an ecstatic state.

Through the interplay of the particular space, the actors' bodies, and the

Erika Fischer-Lichte

chorus, Michael Thalheimer's production of the *Oresteia* (premiered 2006) created a comparable effect. The stage was closed off by a white wall smeared with blood and the auditorium was lit by cold neon light. The actors, whose bodies were or became smeared with blood, performed on the narrow passage between the wall and the auditorium.[16] The chorus was placed above and behind the spectators in the gallery; it shouted down at them and sometimes even shouted them down, creating a sense of claustrophobia.[17] Cooped up between the actors in front of the wall and the chorus behind their backs, exposed to the gaze of the actors and other spectators in the bright, cold, alienating light, the spectators were made to experience a particular kind of liminality.

Needless to say, all the devices discusses here could be employed in different kinds of productions. Yet it seems remarkable that they should have been displayed in these performances of Greek tragedies, thus somehow linking the experience of such a performance to the possibility of consciously entering a state of liminality. It seems that in these cases the participation in a performance of a Greek tragedy in particular was supposed to allow the spectators to become aware of their own aesthetic experience as a particular kind of liminal experience.

5. Conclusions: Performance Reception

My deliberations on the concept of performance and the conclusions drawn from them for the field of Performance Reception so far have also laid the ground for defining the concept of reception. Although the term seems to imply a passive process, when referring to the term 'performance', it can only signify an active one. Such a conception is partially based on the theory of reception as elaborated by Hans Robert Jauß and Wolfgang Iser as early as the 1970s.[18] Gunter Grimm later emphasised the active aspect of the process of reception when he coined the term 'productive reception'.[19] Our discussion of the concept of performance has led us to see that the reception of an ancient play through performance is always an active, creative and transformative process. From this inference I would like to draw some general conclusions.

First and most obviously, neither the original play text, nor any particular version of it, can serve as a yardstick for judging a performance of an ancient play. Other criteria derived from the four aspects of performance I have discussed need to be taken into consideration.

The second conclusion follows from the fact that the reception of an ancient play through performance is always a creative and transformative process. Does it really make sense, therefore, fundamentally to distinguish between performances that use and adapt translations of ancient plays and those that employ a text written by a modern author who draws heavily on an ancient drama, such as Racine's *Phèdre* or Dryden and Lee's *Oedipus*? There are some good reasons for and against such a distinction.

40

3. Performance as Event – Reception as Transformation

Flashar's decision to only consider performances claiming to be productions of Greek tragedies, if strongly adapted, is therefore just as legitimate as Hall's and Macintosh's decision to include performances of plays by modern authors for whom an ancient play served as model, pretext, or material. The specific approach and particular problem at hand always determines the selection.

The third conclusion concerns the question whether the spectators come to learn anything about ancient theatre and culture by participating in performances of ancient plays in any version whatsoever. Even as late as the age of historicism it was claimed that such performances were able to draw a more or less faithful picture of ancient Greek or Roman culture. This claim was undeniably upheld in reference to the Prussian *Antigone* of 1841 as well as by the production at the Meininger of the first two parts of *The Oresteia*, entitled *Orest*, in 1868.[20] In both cases, this claim was supported by invoking academic research on ancient Greece as formulated by scholars in Classics departments. These and other performances would certainly have conveyed a particular image of ancient Greek culture – an image, which, in its turn, also served particular political and ideological purposes linked to processes of nation-building, cultural identity, claims of cultural superiority and the like. But these connections with contemporary political and ideological contexts mean that the performance of ancient plays cannot be viewed as functioning simply within a framework of educating audiences about Classics-as-ancient-history.

Some interesting general questions therefore still remain. The questions of the purpose of staging an ancient play and the way that the performance worked can ultimately only be answered on an individual basis. In each case, the definition of the concept of performance that I have outlined above may serve as a useful parameter for this endeavour.

Notes

1. Notably Smith 1988, Flashar 1991, Hall and Macintosh 2005.
2. Regarding the following four aspects see Fischer-Lichte 2008, where the concept of performance is fully elaborated.
3. Euripides' *Ion* in August Wilhelm Schlegel's version was put on stage in Weimar on 2 January 1802 (repeated on 4 January, 27 July and 9 August 1802). Goethe's preparations for it had been lengthy and thoughtful. The actors playing the two old men wore masks; the postures and attitudes of Apollo and Ion were modelled after the Apollo Belvedere. It seems that in this case the audience did not appreciate Goethe's efforts. Spectators laughed at moments in the performance that seemed absolutely inappropriate to Goethe. He jumped to his feet and thundered at the audience: 'Stop laughing!' ('Man lache nicht'). See Genast 1862/66: 77.
4. Plessner 1970.
5. The exhibition 'Körperwelten' (Body Worlds) has been touring the world since 1997. Its exhibits are human corpses that are preserved and treated in a special manner through plastination. See da Fonseca and Kliche 2006 and weblink http://www.koerperwelten.com/de (accessed 16 December 2008).

41

6. Fischer-Lichte 2009a, Hall and Macintosh 2005: 316-49.

7. See Fischer-Lichte 2004, 2006, 2009b.

8. See Fischer-Lichte 2004.

9. Burkert 1983.

10. Regarding Castorf see Fischer-Lichte 2006. Sellars used this method, for example in his production of Sophocles' *Ajax* (1987 in Stuttgart) or in Euripides' *Heraclidae* (Bottrop, Ruhr-Triennale, Rome, Paris, Boston, Vienna 2002).

11. Johann Jakob Christian Donner's so-called literal translation, adhering to the metre of the original, was published by Winter in Heidelberg in 1839. By the nineteenth century, it was the most widely used translation for productions of *Antigone*. Surprisingly enough, the translation for the Covent Garden production of 1845 was based on Donner's German text. See Hall and Macintosh 2005: 321.

12. Christian Genelli, *Das Theater zu Athen*, 1818. Although the Greek Archeological Society had begun their excavations of the Theatre of Dionysus as early as 1839, nothing had been discovered that might have challenged Genelli's concept at the time of the preparations for the Potsdam production. However, the archaeologist E.H. Toelken from Berlin University subsequently raised some doubts about Genelli's concept, since he believed he had discovered some incongruities with Vitruvius' deliberations (Boeckh, Toelken and Foerster 1842: 49-71).

13. See Turner 1969 and 1977.

14. Schiller 1993.

15. See Rüter 1991.

16. Closing off the stage with a wall clearly alluded to Peter Stein's famous 1980 production of the tragedy at the Berlin Schaubühne. Here, the stage was closed off by a black wall during the first and the second part of the trilogy. See Fischer-Lichte 2004.

17. This way of dealing with the chorus was reminiscent of Einar Schleef's use of the chorus in his new tragic theatre which began in 1986 with the production of *The Mothers*, a compilation of Euripides' *Suppliant Women* and Aeschylus' *Seven Against Thebes* at the Frankfurt Schauspielhaus. See Fischer-Lichte 2005.

18. See Jauß 1970, Iser 1972 and 1978.

19. Grimm 1977.

20. The Meininger production used the translation by Wilhelm Rossmann. This was the first production of the *Oresteia* on the German stage and the only one of a Greek tragedy by the Meininger Theatre. Flashar 1991: 96f.

Greek and Shakespearean Plays in Performance: Their Different Academic Receptions

David Wiles

This volume testifies to the enormous interest which 'reception' enjoys within the discipline of Classics today, and more specifically the reception of performance. In this essay I shall indicate how scholars in a sister discipline have engaged in studying Shakespeare through the lens of performance reception, hoping that this will indicate both ways forward for Classicists and some dangers to avoid on the road.

To begin with definitions: as a theatre scholar, my impulse is to turn to the best available theatre dictionary, which happens to be in French. Patrice Pavis' semiological *Dictionnaire du théâtre* has a helpful entry on *réception* :

> The attitude and activity of the spectator confronted by the performance; the manner in which he uses the information supplied by the stage to decipher the performance.[1]

We can distinguish between the *reception of a work* by an audience (*public*), a period, or a given group, and the *reception or interpretation of the work by the spectator*. The first is the historical study of the *accueil* or welcome given to a work by a particular group in a particular period. The second is an analysis of the mental, intellectual and emotional processes of understanding the performance. Classicists tend to use the word in the first sense. Because I work in a theatre department concerned with the creation of theatre, I am normally engaged by the second problematic, how the spectator responds to the play. So the first difficulty in the project of this book lies in the way two different interpretive communities receive the word 'reception'.

Before we examine the academic work of Shakespeareans, it seems necessary that I provide some idea of Theatre Studies' mission to penetrate the processes of the spectator. Classicists who have preferred to sidestep this quest, because they have a different mission, have not been unwise, for the task of understanding the intangible and irrecoverable moment when something 'happens', when a particularly intense experience sometimes described as 'presence' is encountered in a performance, is a recalcitrant one. In Theatre Studies, I have observed four broad approaches to the business of analysing how an audience receives the performance.

Traditional theories stem from Aristotle's isolation of pity and fear, and more broadly his analysis in the *Rhetoric* of discrete emotions as states to be aroused by public speakers. These have fallen out of favour in the modern period as a means of analysing the effect of performance, although the notion of catharsis continues to fascinate, and Artaud is a latter-day apologist for one of the possible meanings of the Greek term *katharsis* (i.e. those which have to do with notions of purgation). The popular under-standing of the Aristotelian notion of catharsis bred as its logical antithesis the Brechtian *Verfremdungseffekt*, which grew out of both Marxism and Russian Formalism. Behind Brecht's didacticism lay the Renaissance tradition which in turn derives from Horace that the best drama should combine pleasure with instruction. There is also a theory generated in opposition to those like Brecht and Boal, which relates to Freud's assumptions about the human mind, and to Stansislavski's teach-ings in *An Actor Prepares*. When the dominant work of an actor shifted from representing human passions to creating a unique character, then the correlative audience response shifted from sympathy to identification and empathy.

In practice, many theatre analysts prefer to dispense with theory, instead adopting the more pragmatic approach of going straight to the primary evidence. Video recordings are inherently incapable of recording the transaction between audiences and performers, but the attraction of the recording is that it presents the performance as a finite, changeless and easily analysable object like a literary text. Newspaper reviews are often the basic tools of the trade, although contemporary reviews tend to be less detailed and useful than their lengthier nineteenth-century coun-terparts. One may consider artefacts that position the performance as a calculated object for consumption, including posters, programmes and interviews, or one may undertake direct observation of audience behav-iour,[2] or demographic analysis of box office records. It is also possible to interrogate typical spectators by questionnaires or focus groups, despite the inevitable difficulty of articulating feelings in other than a familiar received language.[3]

Over the last fifty years, many theatre scholars influenced by modern 'critical theory' have worked from the premise that the performance is a kind of 'text'. Once that manoeuvre is permitted, the apparatus of literary analysis opens fresh possibilities. The analysis of semiotic codes shaping different aspects of the performance made it possible to explore the para-linguistic competence of the spectator. The semiotic approach gained its momentum from the emergence of the director as *auteur*, imposing a coherent aesthetic form on the *mise-en-scène*, which stood in a creative tension to the classic text being performed. The spectator is assumed to be more or less competent in decoding correctly the 'language' used by the author, director, costume designer, etc. Reader response theory also focused upon the reader's (or spectator's) experience of the work. Susan Bennett published an influential book called *Theatre Audiences* in 1980, inspired by Jauss' work in the late 1970s. This line of enquiry has not been developed in recent years, and the metaphor of a level 'horizon of expectations' collapses when one takes into account the diversity of physical viewpoints in an auditorium. However, Bennett observes that she has little interest in 'the particularities of an individual spectator's response' and prefers to focus on 'the cultural conditions that make theatre and an audience's experience of it possible'.[4] This side-stepping of the immediate phenomenological experience of 'receiving' a play is characteristic of a critical generation preoccupied with culture and ideology rather than aesthetics.[5] Discourse Analysis, as used in Shakespeare studies, can be considered in an influential essay by Barbara Hodgdon, who analysed reviews of Lepage's *Midsummer Night's Dream* in order to demonstrate that the production was consistently read in relation to Brook's production. She aimed to divert performance criticism away from the director as *auteur* in order to analyse the way spectators talked about this production. Her comparative method owes something to Jaussian formalism, while her conclusions concern cultural identity, culture being conceived in terms of sign-systems.[6]

The problem with defining the *mise-en-scène* as a kind of text is the fact that spectators not only watch performances, but interact with them. Pavis is quick to acknowledge that the spectator is an active producer of meaning, but that is not the same thing as active participation, changing the work as it is constituting itself. Pavis refers to a tension in theatre practice between two aspects: the *sémiologique* and the *événementiel*, the second being unique and uncodifiable. Others have been less willing to concede that such a crucial part of theatre resists analysis. Richard Schechner, in partnership with Victor Turner, proposed that theatre should be understood in a continuum with participatory rituals, thereby making no conceptual distinction between actor and spectator. This school may be tempted to use the term 'communitas' as a synonym for 'catharsis'. European scholars such as Willmar Sauter, reacting against North American 'Performance Studies', have been reluctant to dissolve the aesthetic concept of theatre into a wider concept of 'performance', and examine how phenomena like play and festivals relate to the artistic event. These methods lead us away from the inner world of the spectator, towards social *interaction* rather than *reception*. The active nature of spectatorship is stressed by most contemporary theatre scholars,[7] though as Jacques Rancière has recently pointed out, the definition of 'active' may be suspect.[8]

Shakespeareans share with Classicists the reference point of the canonical text which they want to interpret, but they live in a society where

Shakespeare retains a dominant theatrical position. There is a complex symbiotic relationship between theatre practitioners who rely economically on spectators who study and or have studied Shakespeare at school and university, and pedagogues who use performances to animate their teaching. Students are soon taught to be wary of their personal, subjective responses, so what I have termed the traditional approaches to spectator experience are of limited utility. Accessing the director, on the other hand, is invaluable, because the director can be treated like a prestigious literary critic, offering a specific interpretation of the text that can be weighed, compared and contrasted. To interview actors is also a popular strategy because actors can be regarded as directors of their own particular character, and six volumes have now appeared in the Cambridge 'Players of Shakespeare' series.[9] The practical skills of analysing reviews etc. are all extensively quarried for the sake of getting to the performance as it *really* was. The anthropological approach is also popular because it serves to place Shakespearean performance as a cultural phenomenon, and allows Shakespeareans to deal with anxieties about the place of their potentially elitist, nationalistic and sexist discipline in the modern world.

Shakespeareans talk about the history of performance, but 'reception' is not part of their everyday vocabulary outside a limited literary-critical context. In Classics, on the other hand, it has become a prominent label. While the story of the twentieth century for Shakespeareans is one of continuity, Classicists had to endure the great cultural break that came with modernism. In an age of atonal music, free verse, fauvist colours, and moulded concrete buildings, it was declared that the past no longer mattered, only the future. Classics got swept out of mainstream education as a redundant link with the past, and Shakespeare as a denizen of 'English Literature' slipped into the educational niche that classical drama had vacated.

Classics had now to demonstrate that it was 'relevant'. Reception emerged, consciously or otherwise, as part of the struggle for survival by a threatened organism. A cynic might say that, since attack is the best form of defence, the Reception industry was a bold colonial enterprise, a means of bolstering a beleaguered empire. My own view is a more positive one: because modernism severed our cultural links with the past in often regrettable ways, knowledge of the Classics is essential if we are to find coherence in the cultural and intellectual history of the last five hundred years. The work of Hall and Macintosh has a clear focus on this project.[10]

While the work of Hall and Macintosh is rooted in cultural materialism, and positivist assumptions about the possibility of historical knowledge, postmodernism yields a different perspective, denying the possibility of either aesthetic values or historical certainties. Relativism became the most acceptable form of academic knowledge, once the last remnants of Marxist certainty had been discarded. Reception studies sit comfortably in a postmodern milieu, allowing Classicists to demonstrate that they know perfectly well their vision of the classical world is but a function of the eye of the beholder. Post-modern relativist rhetoric paves the way for two dangerous manoeuvres. First, a positivist historiography of, say, obscure nineteenth-century productions of Greek tragedy, may pass muster, whereas the same historiographic methods applied to antiquity will look moth-eaten. And in the second manoeuvre, a trawl through the multiple and contradictory interpretations of a classical text may easily be used as a rhetorical ploy to assert the timeless aesthetic values of the classical original. Relativism is all too often an act of camouflage

The exceptional aesthetic value of classical literature has long been held up as a justification for the study of classical drama. But post-war critical theory has left the idea of absolute aesthetic value in tatters. The upshot is well illustrated by Gary Taylor's discussion of Shakespeare's *Comedy of Errors*. From the point of view of Shakespeare editors, Taylor observes, the Plautine source is dismissed as cynical and amoral, while Shakespeare improves the structure so that one critic can liken it to a Bach fugue. From the point of view of classical editors of the *Menaechmi* looking at the afterlife of Plautus' play, Shakespeare wrecks Plautus by complicating and sanitising him. The consequence, Taylor comments, is that 'neither has proven anything. Tweedledum blasts Tweedledee.'[11] We love what we know best, and our point of view determines our values. Values become, in Taylor's view, a function of the historical frame within which classic plays are set.

Alongside the growth of reception studies in Classics, we can observe a performative 'turn'. Arthur Pickard-Cambridge's pre-war investigations of the physical conditions of performance led in a logical line of development to the work of Taplin, who demonstrated that readers of Aeschylean text needed to understand the grammar of performance in order to make aesthetic judgements. This performative turn was part of a wider cultural process embracing, not least, the emergence of Drama departments within the academy. In linguistics, sociology and anthropology, performance served as a convenient paradigm.

Which brings me to the convergence between the 'Reception turn' and the 'Performance turn'. Does the one logically imply the other? Or did the performance turn simply provide a new set of tools for reading plays within the terms of their own formal structures? I think performance and reception were necessarily implicated in each other as soon as Classicists looked beyond the amateur world of university drama to see what was going on in professional theatre. It was once possible to believe that theatre is theatre, and has certain immutable laws, so theatre practitioners will instinctively know how Greek theatre works. But greater awareness of the modern professional and international theatre necessarily brought recognition that the laws of theatre are constantly in flux. When the director as *auteur* replaced the actor-manager or star actor as the principal figure of theatrical authority, it became hard to conceive how the meaning of a

47

performance could ever be safely encoded in the script. Attention to the vagaries of reception sat comfortably with a newfound sympathy for the contingency of the performance event.

Now that I have sketched the context for studying 'reception' in different disciplines, I will pass on to examples of critical practice. In particular, I want to examine what happens when one play or performance is regarded as a reception of an anterior classic work. Since it is often easier to hold pictures in our minds rather than abstractions, I find it helpful to look at some of the metaphors that critics have used when trying to describe what is involved in this form of reception.

My first is from George Steiner's *Antigones*. 'As it comes to us from Sophocles' *Antigone*, "meaning" is bent out of its original shape just as starlight is bent when it reaches us across time and via successive gravitational fields.'[12] Modern versions of *Antigone* are thus different creative forms of distortion, and the original has by no means disappeared, nor is its brilliance in dispute. The Shakespeare scholar Barbara Hodgdon, citing Sonnet 116, likewise uses the metaphor of the 'pole star' to sum up what 'Shakespeare' meant to performance-oriented critics in the 1960s and 1970s: a reference point that never moves.[13]

Pantelis Michelakis, in a recent essay on Iphigenia, offered us the metaphor of the 'sacrificial substitute', the stag which Artemis produces as a surrogate for Iphigenia. 'The stag restores ritual and social order ... by *becoming* the sacrificial victim it substitutes ....'[14] In this metaphor, the classical original has now vanished. Michelakis cites a play by Racine, a critical edition, and a film as three exemplary surrogates which all *become* Iphigenia, invested as if by a goddess with cultural authority and efficaciousness. Michelakis draws his idea from modern performance theory, specifically from the argument of Joseph Roach, as modified by Bill Worthen, that live performances are surrogates which resist the status quo and generate written texts as a by-product, but in his critical work he confines himself to documents, and in this sense restores the ritual order of Classics as a discipline. Though he changes the terms of the debate, and undermines Steiner's notion of the original play as a fixed aesthetic object, he does not engage with the problematic of live performance any more than Steiner did.

Simon Goldhill adopts a postmodern stance, perhaps inspired by the attention which Lacan gave to mirrors. He explores how 'the reader of the past is constantly caught between two mirrors, as it were, caught between self-reflections'.[15] While his vivid account of Strauss' *Elektra* demonstrates how audiences see their Englishness or Germanness reflected back to them in such a play of mirrors, his postmodern metaphor causes him to worry also about his own 'pose of the disinterested and objective scholar'.[16] Notice another important metaphor here: the past is something that we are expected to 'read'.

Moving on from these three examples of Reception Studies in Classics, let me offer for comparison an extended metaphor used by an art historian concerned with the notion of 'influence'. For Michael Baxandall, the field of Art History is like a snooker table, Italian style without pockets. When the cue ball, which might be Picasso, hits a ball on the table, which might be Cézanne, then the whole configuration of the table changes. Rather than Cézanne influencing Picasso, Baxandall conceives of Picasso acting on Cézanne, shifting him closer to the main tradition of European painting, and changing for ever the way we can see Cézanne.[17] Goldhill maintained that the word 'reception' was 'too *passive* a term for the dynamics of resistance and appropriation, recognition and self-aggrandisement that make up this drama of cultural identity';[18] Baxandall likewise stresses the active nature of cultural reworkings, but his metaphor of a solid material table relates to his placing of the artist within the market-place, in an intellectual tradition that is Marxian rather than postmodernist, and he has no qualms about his own aloof role as the snooker player with an overview of the table. Baxandall's metaphor allows us to see very clearly why there are such difficulties in saying baldly that ancient drama *influenced* later theatrical practice. Returning to the *Iphigenia*, we might say that Racine and Cacoyannis did not simply substitute for a vanished Euripides; they rewrote performance history and changed the angle at which we now can see Euripides.

For my final metaphor I return to the Shakespeare scholar Gary Taylor, and his account of the relative merits of Plautus and Shakespeare. Where Steiner likened Sophocles' *Antigone* to a shining star, Taylor likens Shakespeare to a black hole: 'a point at the centre of a once vast, now collapsing star ... Light, insight, intelligence, matter – all pour ceaselessly into him, as critics are drawn into the densening vortex of his reputation; they add their own weight to his increasing mass ... He distorts our view of the universe around him.'[19] Taylor infuriated many with his insistence that Shakespeare traps critics in the gravitational well of his reputation, so no serious evaluation of his worth is possible. The only sensible analysis left to the critic becomes an analysis of cultural power. American New Historicism has generated here a counsel of despair, that risks yielding nothing but critical introspection. The analysis of contemporary performances of Shakespeare becomes a more intellectually secure activity than any attempt to write about the Bard himself.

Placing ancient theatre to one side now, I want to focus my attention on Shakespearean scholarship. Shakespeareans and Classicists face many of the same issues, though debates within Theatre Studies have made more impact on the former. Through seeing their own activity reflected in the mirror of Shakespeare Studies, Classicists may find some new light is shed on what they do, though they will not find any easy answers. Specifically, I am going to examine how performance reception is handled in twentieth- and twenty-first-century editions of a Shakespeare play. My choice of *Henry V* is essentially arbitrary, though I note that the rediscovery of the

'Chorus' in *Henry V* was an important twentieth-century development as it was also in scholarship on Greek tragedy. It is a received convention that editions of Shakespeare give substantial space to stage history, while it is still unheard of for editions of Greek plays do the same. In signs of the times, Donald Mastronarde concedes a page to chronicling modern adaptations of *Medea* which simply attest 'to the enduring fascination of the classic story'.[20] James Morwood in his 2007 edition of *Suppliant Women* references the APGRD website, but there is no hint that the productions on record might have influenced his thinking about Euripides.[21]

The 1903 Arden editor maintained that the interest of *Henry V* was 'epic' rather than 'dramatic',[22] which spared him any obligation to talk about performance. His main concern was to resist demeaning claims that Henry is less than heroic, or that the play might have been concerned with Ireland and thus topical rather than universal. John Dover Wilson struck a very different note in his Cambridge edition of 1947. Through witnessing Frank Benson's long-running production at Stratford, he declares, 'I discovered what it was all about',[23] namely that Henry anticipated Winston Churchill, and that Hazlitt's republican critique of the play (reflecting the ideals of the French revolution) was misguided. Dover Wilson also had a sense of the contingency of reception, noting the power of Benson's performance at the moment of Rupert Brooke. He praises the excellent and popular Olivier film as 'an encouraging sign of the times'.[24] Attached as an appendix to his introduction was a nine-page stage history, chronicling text amendments and curiosities such as the all-female version. The inspiration of Stratford-upon-Avon, in the later twentieth century, as the home of the Royal Shakespeare Company and the major international Shakespeare conference, would become the glue holding theatre practitioners and Shakespearean scholars together in a mutually convenient symbiosis. The professional theatre environment attracted academics, while the privileged place of Shakespeare on the educational agenda drew audiences to the Shakespeare Memorial Theatre.

The Penguin Shakespeares proved very popular with RSC actors because of their slim format, and pages free from the clutter of annotation, allowing the actors as it were direct access to the bard. The New Penguin *Henry V* of 1968, however, was deeply mistrustful of theatre. The editor remarks how the spell cast by performance brings about an 'anaesthetizing of the intellect' alongside an 'exhilaration of the pulse'.[25] The influence of F.R. Leavis can be discerned in the editor's quest for the felt life underlying the text. When Oxford University Press entered the Shakespeare market, Gary Taylor in his edition of 1982 set a very different tone. We discern some influence of Jauss when Taylor chooses to begin his introduction with a section headed 'Reception and Reputation'. He analyses the expectations of an audience in 1599, and concludes that this play must have disappointed those expectations. For Shakespeareans, however, it was not Jauss who served as prophet for a new era so much as John

4. Greek and Shakespearean Plays in Performance

Styan, with his book *The Shakespeare Revolution*, published in 1977. Styan cited an axiom of Dover Wilson that Shakespeare's plays were written not be read but as libretti for stage performance.[26] He then traced a line through Granville Barker and Tyrone Guthrie to Peter Brook, arguing that the rejection of illusionist methods in the modern period has brought us ever closer to understanding the score that Shakespeare had written for actors to perform; the modern scholar and the modern actor each shine light upon the other. Taylor, unlike Wilson, had had the opportunity to see productions of *Henry V* which rejected not only illusionism but also patriotism. Examining the protagonist, Taylor concluded: 'Postwar productions have done much to restore the complex and sometimes disturbing figure Shakespeare must have intended.' We hear the optimism of Styan in Taylor's assertion that 'the demotic, complicated Henry of these recent productions takes us closer to the play than has any production since the Restoration'.[27] We see no trace in this introduction of the postmodern pessimism summed up in his 1991 metaphor of the black hole. In 1982, performance could still provide a route back to authorial intention.

When Andrew Gurr brought out a replacement for Dover Wilson in the 'New Cambridge' series in 1992, he worked in the same vein as Taylor, though with a more conventional structure, starting with the play in 1599, and ending with an extended stage history. The stage history documented the twentieth-century transition from illusionism to anti-illusionism, and from patriotism to pacifism, without, however, explaining the correlation between dramatic form and ideology. Gurr, like Taylor, had witnessed a series of successful anti-war *Henries*, and he had seen Branagh's introspective protagonist in a film that contested the martial values of Olivier's version. Questions about reception were central to Gurr's introduction, and he argued that the play enjoyed its greatest success less in times of war than in times when British social cohesiveness was in question. Also, like Taylor, Gurr evinced a new interest in what used to be known as the 'bad Quarto', a text evidently written down from memory by a pair of actors. This now became a rather good Quarto because it provided insight into the processes of Elizabethan performance.

Tom Craik, in the third Arden edition published in 1995, took up the cudgels on behalf of tradition. It was no longer acceptable for a critic to present himself as anti-performance, so Craik evoked the readings and performances that had inspired him at his grammar school, and his introduction claimed to demonstrate how *Henry V* works as a stage play. Craik enjoys the Olivier film, exclaiming: 'how it makes one wish that one could see exactly how the play was performed by the Lord Chamberlain's men at the Globe', and was clearly fascinated and horrified by Bogdanov's leftist and anachronising production of 1986. This prompted a closing polemic against fashionable directors. Spectators, Craik argues, are 'entitled to witness a performance that is reasonably close to what that text demands'.[28]

As a textual critic, Craik counters the enthusiasm of Taylor and Gurr for the Quarto; while Taylor and Gurr discern elements of developmental process within the Folio text, Craik seeks to demonstrate that the Folio is indeed the definitive work reflecting the original performance.

2002 saw the publication of *Henry V* in the Cambridge 'Shakespeare in Production' series, which formalises the common ground between theatre historians and literary critics. For the editor, Emma Smith, the climax of her narrative was the 1999 Globe production, directed by the son of Laurence Olivier. This prestigious event, documented in a monograph by Pauline Kiernan, pushed the ideal of uncompromising authenticity as far as possible in matters such as costume and all-male casting. Embarrassingly, the Globe audience ended up hissing and booing the French. So Smith borrowed from Norman Rabkin the analogy of the duck-rabbit image, in which one cannot see both creatures at once. Either one perceives as rabbit Bogdanov's anti-war play, or one perceives as duck the patriotic play of the Oliviers; to see both in performance appears to the theatre historian impossible. Andrew Gurr was one of the principal intellectual consultants on the Globe theatre project, and he was much struck by the 1999 production, and by Smith's argument. He published in 2000 an edition of the Quarto text, maintaining that this simplified and patriotic version was the text actually performed by the Chamberlain's Men in 1599, and in 2005 he updated his New Cambridge edition, developing the case further, and interrogating his own editorial role. 'Transfixing a Shakespeare text as an edition in one version only for reading has to turn the naturally plastic stage script into marble, and the process of such editorial fixation incurs substantial losses. Fixity denies the flow from author's mind to staged event.'[29] Gurr's inference about *Henry V*, however, is – in his own words – 'rather alarming'. He suggests that Shakespeare was writing a version that he knew could not be staged; to grasp the essential 'duplicity' of the play, he concludes that we are better off reading the script than sitting in a theatre audience.[30]

This judgement is a remarkable outcome of the Globe Theatre project, and illustrates the perils of a quest to pursue ancient stagecraft, without questioning more than superficially the cultural context within which any performance then and now takes place, and without questioning the cultural arrogance of Styan's modernist vision, which implied we have achieved a more privileged and authentic view of the past than earlier generations could aspire to.

So what conclusions may be drawn by the Classicist at the end of this Elizabethan survey? The analysis of Performance Reception has been at the centre of critical discourse in Shakespeare studies for some thirty years. The move by Classicists into Performance Reception does not, therefore, manifest a desperate survival strategy by a beleaguered discipline, but is a response to intellectual currents of the present. Why, then, have editors of classical plays been slow to embrace this discourse? It may be argued that a further mediating layer, the translation, separates the classical text from the modern production, but I do not believe that this explanation has substance. James Bulman commented wryly in 1996 that performance criticism 'has even forced us to come to terms with a Shakespeare who can exist without his language'.[31] Arguably, the Shakespearean text is qualitatively different not because we perform the untranslated words, but because it exists in multiple versions. Gary Taylor and Stanley Wells brought out a new Oxford *Complete Works* in 1986 with the objective of presenting the text that was heard in an Elizabethan playhouse rather than the text which best reflects authorial intent. The classical editor of an Oxford text is not in a position to make such fine distinctions, even if scattered clues to the performance process can be found in corrupt passages of the *Iphigenia in Aulis*, or the ending of the *Seven Against Thebes*.

Far more important than the stability of the text, it seems to me, are institutional differences. Epidaurus and Delphi do not do the same cultural work, at least for Anglophone scholars, as Stratford and the new Globe. Classical scholars rarely make their first acquaintance with ancient drama through the theatre. Worthen insists that a performance does not simply render a text; it iterates, constitutes and gives cultural authority to a text. That is not an easy message for Classicists to accept, when brought up to assume that the text gives authority to the performance.[32]

Performance Reception is a central and vibrant element in Shakespearean critical discourse. It is also highly contested and riddled with intellectual contradiction. Charles Martindale charges Simon Goldhill with collapsing Reception into Cultural Studies,[33] and the same charge could easily be levelled at progressive Shakespeareans from the 'new historicist' stable, such as Barbara Hodgdon. Yet if this work on our own cultural identity is not done, we risk finding ourselves in the paradoxical position of Andrew Gurr, whose encyclopaedic knowledge of Elizabethan stagecraft led him finally to reinstate the authority of the reader. Desirous of restoring to Classics its leading role among the humanities, Martindale discerns in Jauss' *Rezeptionsästhetik* a route back to the aesthetic values of works, which solved formal and moral problems inherited from previous works. Since I work in a discipline which likes to combine theory with creative practice, I have much sympathy with Martindale's desire to restore the aesthetic dimension. My argument relates to his assumption about what constitutes the artistic 'work'. If we take the performance as the aesthetic object under investigation, and the text merely as the contingent verbal score – a position widely accepted by Shakespeareans in principle if not in practice – then we can talk about the formal aesthetic innovations of the work and the cultural job done by the work in a more fruitful juxtaposition.

The intermeshing of literary study and performance study in the Shakespearean field is an established and apparently irreversible fact. To think of Shakespeare as the author of Elizabethan performances leads inevitably to questions of reception because a Shakespeare script under Shakespeare's authoritative direction had multiple performances in diverse venues. Most conspicuously, the Quarto and Folio texts of *King Lear* relate to different performances with different aims, so the real *King Lear* eludes us. It is not possible to be sure whether Greek plays were written with a single performance in mind (and therefore be susceptible to a greater degree of critical essentialism), or whether the playwrights were aware that they would be revived in deme theatres and other locations. Still, the principle remains that an active reception by an Athenian public was part of what gave the play its historical meaning. Subsequent performances – not just in Athenian demes, but in neo-classical reworkings and in twentieth-first-century professional theatre – extend that unpredictable and undocumented initial reception in continuing to generate meaning.

But what did the play *mean* to any given individual spectator? Pavis in his semiological dictionary clearly believed that answers were available, but we have become rather less confident in our epistemologies, and those mental processes remain obdurately opaque. Since we cannot understand what theatre *does* to people, or what *happens* in the actor-audience relationship, we shall doubtless carry on developing such evasive strategies to avoid the unknowable as specifying material conditions and generalising about cultural processes. 'Reception' is an ever elusive goal. The unknowability of the spectator's response offers a humbling reminder that any critical pronouncement reflects the eye of the beholder. Since we cannot tell what goes on inside the spectator, we reach necessarily for something external, something of substance, something that is made. In practice, to speak of 'reception' is always to speak of remaking, or simply making: making contemporary productions, making film records, making punchy reviews, making scintillating conversations in the theatre bar. Though the word 'reception' continues to be useful in respect of, say, Thucydides, it is increasingly unserviceable in respect of drama/theatre/plays because of an ontological uncertainty about what constitutes the 'work' under investigation, and because reception is already inherently part of any live performance. Whatever the sell-by date of the term, no obvious substitute is yet on the market. Despite its unfortunate connotations of passivity, and of receiving a pre-existent message, the greatest advantage of the term is its reminder that we ourselves are receivers and implicated in any analysis we generate.

Notes

1. Pavis 1980: 329-332.
2. E.g. Mervant-Roux 1998.
3. E.g. Sauter 2000.
4. Bennett 1997: vii.
5. Cf. Knowles 2004.

4. Greek and Shakespearean Plays in Performance

6. Hodgdon 1996.
7. E.g. Paulus 2006.
8. Rancière 2007: 277.
9. Cf. also Holmes 2004.
10. Especially Hall and Macintosh 2005.
11. Taylor 1991: 396.
12. Steiner 1984: 206.
13. Hodgdon and Worthen 2005: 2.
14. Michelakis 2006: 220.
15. Goldhill 2002: 297.
16. Goldhill 2002: 298.
17. Baxandall 1985: 60-1.
18. Goldhill 2002: 297.
19. Taylor 1991: 410.
20. Mastronarde 2002: 69-70.
21. Morwood 2007: 26.
22. Evans 1903: xli.
23. Dover Wilson 1947: viii.
24. Dover Wilson 1947: viii, lv.
25. Humphreys 1968: 49.
26. Styan 1977: 33.
27. Taylor 1982: 50-1.
28. Craik 1995: 95.
29. Gurr 2005: 61.
30. Gurr 2005: 63.
31. Bulmann1996b: 8-9.
32. Worthern 1997.
33. Martindale 2006: 9.

Cultural History and Aesthetics: Why Kant is No Place to Start Reception Studies

Simon Goldhill

I

When our aestheticians never weary of maintaining, in favour of Kant, that under the spell of beauty one can view even undraped female statues 'without interest', we may, to be sure, laugh a little at their expense – the experiences of artists are in regard to this ticklish point 'more interesting' and Pygmalion was in any event not necessarily an 'unaesthetic man'.

Nietzsche, *The Genealogy of Morals*

The cover of Charles Martindale's fine book *Latin Poetry and the Judgement of Taste: an Essay in Aesthetics* reproduces James McNeil Whistler's celebrated painting *Arrangement in Grey and Black: Portrait of the Painter's Mother*. This may not be an obvious choice of image for a book on Latin poetry, but it goes to the heart of a Victorian row about aesthetics – and to the centre of Martindale's own work on aesthetics and politics. In 1877, Whistler sued John Ruskin, then the most distinguished art historian in Britain, because Ruskin had reviewed his painting, *Nocturne in Black and Gold (The Falling Rocket)*, in damning terms: 'I have seen, and heard, much of Cockney impudence before now; but never expected to hear a coxcomb ask two hundred guineas for flinging a pot of paint in the public's face'.[1] Artists may like to shock and to enjoy the publicity of outraged viewers, but the insulting combination of snobbery and dismissal from this critic was too much for the cantankerous Whistler. He had his day in court, won the case – though with derisory damages of a farthing – and revelled in the opportunity publicly to declare his credo, that he aimed at 'artistic interest alone, divesting the picture of any outside anecdotal interest which might have been otherwise attached to it'.[2]

The very title of *Arrangement in Grey and Black: Portrait of the Painter's Mother* highlights the paradoxes of Whistler's pose. The painting is indeed a coolly brilliant study of colour and shape, with the asymmetric undifferentiated mass of the woman's black dress set against the grey wall and floor, and set across the squared blocks of the ornate curtain, the picture on the wall behind the figure, and the footstool on which her feet rest. Whistler's painting anticipates a more formal abstract art in its technique, vision and colouring. Yet the specificity of the subtitle seems precisely to demand 'anecdotal interest'. This is a *portrait,* a title that in itself lays claim to the (anecdotal) narratives of identity and biography.[3] It is a portrait of the artist's *mother,* a relationship hard to divest of emotional and social significance, especially in a portrait. It is, however, a portrait which subordinates identity, the identity of the artist's mother, to a mere 'arrangement' of colour. Within the pious context of the Victorian family, how could such a gesture not be seen as a particular engagement with aesthetics – an engagement that shockingly allows the 'sacred ties of motherhood' to be bracketed as an experience of tint and shape? Whistler's insistence on including the subtitle for his painting keeps the tension between aesthetic response and psychological, social, cultural history firmly in view. The colon is integral to the question: what does it mean to call a portrait of one's mother 'an arrangement in grey and black'? Whistler may have declared, 'What can or ought the public to care about the identity of the portrait?',[4] but it is no surprise that the painting is most familiar under the far less challenging sobriquet *Whistler's Mother.*

The question of aesthetic value and the value of aestheticism was fought out in the courtroom as well as in the journals and newspapers of Victorian Britain. Wearing a green carnation may have lost its iconic terror today, and the financial reward of experimental art may have become a tired and clichéd public debate, but the relationship between art's beauty and its political and social impact continues to be as fiercely contentious as ever. Should Wagner's rabid anti-Semitism affect the reception of his music? When is the possession of a beautiful picture of a naked child a criminal offence, and why? Is artistic value a defence of violent or politically abhorrent films? Do books, films or other produced images have an instrumental effect on behaviour, and if so, is artistic beauty an integral factor – dangerous or preventative – on such instrumentality? In the literary academy, one surprising response to this continuing arena of contestation is an evangelical and polemical turn towards aesthetics and towards Kant, particularly his *Critique of Judgement* (*Kritik der Urteilskraft,* 1790, commonly known as the Third Critique) as a fountain-head for aesthetics, a turn which sets itself self-consciously against the prevalence of cultural and ideological criticism in the arts.[5] For reception theory and ancient poetry this aesthetic turn has been most powerfully articulated by Charles Martindale, for whom Kant and Walter Pater, a wilfully odd couple, emerge as special heroes; this chapter aims to explore this plea for aesthetics in reception, and the particular problems that are created when we turn to consider the reception of performance, the specific subject of this book.

I wish to essay two related arguments. First, I shall investigate the role of the individual in the current construction of reception theory. I shall suggest that the post-Enlightenment development of the concept of the bourgeois individual, together with its alter egos, the Romantic artist or Carlylean Hero, plays an integral role in the formation of reception studies in a potentially damaging, but markedly unappreciated, manner. Second, I shall explore what performance, as an idea, can bring to reception studies, and ask why it is so rarely part of reception theory, especially in its aestheticist guise. To anticipate my conclusion, I want to use the idea of performance to criticise the position of the individual in current theoretical thinking on reception, and to ask for a redrafting of what Sheila Murnaghan has called the mantra of current reception studies, namely, that 'meaning is always realised at the point of reception'.[6] My claim is that thinking about performance enables us to see the costs both of focusing on the individual artist as the scene of reception and of the corollary restriction of the elements of politics and history in reception theory; this enables us to see more clearly the tension between Rezeptionsästhetik and Rezeptionsgeschichte which the turn back towards Kant has encouraged.

I start with an insightful observation made by my graduate student Edmund Richardson. He notes that the phrase 'the classical tradition', in the sense of a privileged inheritance from ancient Greece and Rome, did not appear in the English lexicon until fairly late in the nineteenth century.[7] Before then, although rarely used, it seems to mean simply 'what usually happened in the olden days' – as in 'it was a classical tradition to offer sacrifices to the gods'. This should give us pause. Martindale writes: 'reception was chosen, in place of words like "tradition" or "heritage", precisely to stress the *active* role played by receivers'.[8] But what is at stake in the vocabulary of tradition or heritage, I would suggest, is not merely a question of activity or passivity. The new Victorian vocabulary stresses the *value* of classical texts and art, and does so in a way quite different from the Renaissance valuing of the classical, say (which privileges discovery and renewal rather than inheritance and preservation). The terms 'tradition' and 'heritage' imply a value which 'reception' does not necessarily invoke: even if one can mock tradition in the name of modernity, it is hard to dismiss heritage. Indeed, to lose one's heritage, is to imply a loss of self, identity, of one's place in the historical sweep of things. With that comes a parallel vocabulary of preservation, support, continuity: the fight to save the classics as a fight to preserve what is valuable about the past, *our* tradition, our *heritage*. This is the core of Victorian classics.

'Classical tradition' is invented as a term during the same years that 'heritage' becomes a vivid issue in Victorian society: this is the era of Ruskin, Morris, Octavia Hill (and others) starting societies committed to 'preservation'; when the listing of historic buildings starts; when there are campaigns to protect stretches of the countryside, starting with the Romantic mindscape of the Lake District at Thirlmere; when old churches are destroyed or preserved within a welter of arguments about the conflicting claims of aesthetics, and of past and future religion – when, in short, 'heritage' and 'preservation' and 'conservation' become signs of a battleground over modernity's relation to history, both at a conceptual level and at the level of practical political action.[9] The background to these debates is inevitably the often uncontrolled expansion of metropolitan London and the industrial cities, coupled with the uncertain boundary between booty and trusteeship in the Empire. The National Trust is formed in this period too; the name evokes the passionate Victorian sense of national identity, coupled with a sense of the value of the past as embodied in physical objects, and their connection with forms of law, banking, the fiduciary system ('trust' in all its senses). The invention of the 'classical tradition' brings Classics into this frame of reference, making it part of the necessary, privileged past for the self-definition of the British educated elite. It is a persuasive term belonging both to the argument about the role of Classics in education and in civilised self-formation and to the Victorians' understanding of themselves as living in an age of progress: whose past, what pasts, how to understand the role of the past?

Yet there is another way to think about the terms tradition and heritage. The nineteenth-century shift of meaning of tradition from 'what usually happens' to 'something valued and normative' activates the strong sense of *trado* and *traditio* in Latin: that which is passed on, handed down. So too 'heritage' – a word fraught with political implications in Victorian culture – cannot slip the shackles of *inheritance*. That is, both 'tradition' and 'heritage' are to be seen within the strong model of the household – the patrilineal, patriarchal household, as it inevitably appears – where property, passed on between generations of men, defines social status and constitutes value. As the seventh Duke of Devonshire inherits Chatsworth from the sixth Duke and passes it on to the eighth Duke, so each generation of scholars and gentlemen inherits the classical past and passes it on to the next generation as valued property; both the property and the act of handing it on define social or cultural identity. To be a man of property defines citizenship, in the sense of the franchise to vote, at least until the 1832 Reform Act; the connection between property and propriety and proper place is policed by education, by what you need to know. So the question used to be phrased not as 'Do you know Latin?' but 'Do you *have* Latin?'. Latin is a possession of the man of property.

At one level, the key figure for conceptualising inheritance in this era (as he still is) is Darwin, or, earlier, Chambers, who inaugurate what becomes an intermittently strident debate about evolution. How are human or animal characteristics formed, passed on through the generations, and, most frightening of all, how do they change? At another level, evolutionary history, attempted in different ways by McLellan, Maine, Bachofen, Tylor et al., constructed accounts of world history where all societies developed along similar lines from savagery up towards civilisation, or in Bachofen's case down from the sexual utopia of matriarchy to the horror of patriarchy. The classical world formed an awkward but necessary space in these arguments. The violent myths of classical antiquity drew it close to the savages, as the Victorians called them. But the Glory that was Greece and the Grandeur that was Rome remained privileged sources. So, in the case of Germany, where the German race was re-invented as the new Dorians, Greece provided privileged genetic and racial origins (and the 'savages' of the Teutonic past, thanks in part to Tacitus' idealising agenda, emerge as models of purity and natural nobility). Was Greece like the savage world of the Victorian anthropologists' historical models, or was it a gleaming white haven of the best that has ever been?[10]

At the sharpest end of this debate was the argument about Christianity, as Evangelicals, Tractarians, High Church, Low Church, Dissenters, Unitarians, Protestants and Catholics disputed the correct understanding of the Christian tradition. Was Jesus a classical figure? What role did the pagan world play in the image of Christianity? What is the role of the early church, or the church fathers, or the papal succession in authoritative religious dogma? In short, whose tradition is to be privileged? Here, too, thinking about classics and about inheritance overlapped in a potentially explosive way in Victorian culture.[11]

The phrases 'classical heritage', then, or 'classical tradition', come loaded with hefty ideological baggage, and are invested with Victorian intellectual and social anxieties. But, crucially, one unrecognised corollary of the *familial* language of inheritance is the strong emphasis on the *individual figure*: the man – or woman, though usually it is a man – who inherits: the heir. Thus, the standard model of reception has become Virgil reading Homer, or Martindale reading Virgil reading Homer, or Milton reading Virgil, and so on. We can play games with linearity: we can introduce a Bloomian swerve in the line of influence, or we can insist on the lines being dynamic, or two-way: Milton's influence on Virgil, as Martindale would put it. But the model remains (the) one person responding to (the) one person. Indeed, for Bloom all literature constitutes a Freudian struggle of sons and fathers. The theory of reception remains deeply indebted to the Victorian patriarchal family.

This is easy enough to demonstrate in the rhetoric of cultural tradition. One paradigmatic example comes from one of the most influential pieces in the field: T.S. Eliot's essay 'What is a Classic?', addressed to the Virgil Society in 1944, when 'European culture' was a most fragile construct. Eliot concludes that a mature poet necessarily 'preserves the essential family characteristics'. A poet is like the scion of a family of poets who inherits and passes on those family traces through his work as a poet (and not as a passive genetic inheritance). The use of the word 'preserve[s]' indicates that there is a heritage to be observed in and by the new poet, a kind of Family Trust. Eliot, expanding his idea of maturity to societies as a whole and to literature itself, requires the metaphor of the individual human being: 'A society and literature *like an individual human being* do not necessarily mature equally and concurrently in every respect'.[12] This organic image finds its roots both in Hegel's now infamous declaration that Africa was a child-like society and in Plato's use of the human body as a model for society. Eliot's modernism here is fully beholden to the Victorian family metaphors of inheritance and evolution.

This model helps produce what is least satisfactory in current work on reception: the list of authors, often pleasingly unknown, who have written a work in response to a classical text or figure. The style has become relentlessly familiar. Here is a single example, a paragraph, chosen almost at random from the *Blackwell Companion to the Classical Tradition*:

> The Greek text of Aristotle's *Poetics*, which expounded the principles of classical drama, was first printed in the 1508 Aldine edition of *Rhetores Graeci* (Greek rhetoricians); but it was only 40 years later that Italian theorists turned their attention to ancient Greek tragedy, producing a vast series of treatises in Latin and Italian on poetics. After the appearance in 1548 of the *Explicationes* by Francesco Robortello (1516-67), the next decades saw the publication of Latin and Italian translations and commentaries on Aristotle's treatise by Berrnardo Segni (1549), Bartolomeo Lombardi and Vincenzo Maggi (1550), Piero Vetori (1560), Lodovico Castelvetro (1570), Alessandron Piccolomini (1575), Antonio Riccoboni (1585), and Lionardi Salviati (1586). Mediated by works like Julius Caesar Scaliger's Latin *Poetices libri septem* (Seven books on poetics) (1561) and Jean Vauquelin de La Fresnaye's versified *Art Poétique* (1605), neo-Aristotelian standards shaped the French tragedies of Corneille and Racine (Weinberg 1961; Schmitt 1983).[13]

Martindale would recognise in this paragraph an example of what he dismisses as 'positivist history, often of a rather amateurish nature', which all too often passes for Rezeptionsgeschichte.[14] The paragraph is certainly positivist, and, for all its learning, it is unwilling to ask any of the relevant questions. Why were there so many translations and commentaries on this text? Were they all asking the same questions in the same form or was there a debate about Aristotle? What social or intellectual needs were they addressing? Were they actually read? What was the mediation from Italy to France? How does a versified *Art Poétique* differ from a prose version? How do neo-Aristotelian standards differ from the translations of Aristotle, and why?

It is easy to be sniffy about such paragraphs, as it is easy to defend them on the grounds that 'at least they give you the material' (the last resort of the desperate positivist). Terence Cave's magisterial *Recognitions* shows that it is indeed possible to fuse the material of Aristotelian reception with searching analysis and historical nuance. But what links this sort of *catalogue raisonné* with the more sophisticated writers on reception is the *limitation* of focus produced by concentrating on the act of a single figure reading a single figure and then writing a text for us to read.

Now of course we can allow, if we want to, that Milton was an individual human being, as was Virgil, and Milton did read Virgil, and it would be hard to read *Paradise Lost* critically and intelligently without thinking about that relationship. Martindale is right to insist that seeing how

Milton reads Virgil can teach us about Virgil as well as about Milton. What worries me is what this focus on the engagement of the individual Milton with the text of Virgil leaves out. First, other texts are silenced. Milton read widely, and many voices other than Greek and Roman ones clamour for attention in the echo chamber of his creativity, from the Bible to now obscure pamphlets and poems. Secondly, the vertical relationship with a text of the past silences the horizontal connections with contemporary texts. Milton is writing in the context of religious controversy, which affects his language, rhetorical style, and narrative flow. A polemicist as well as a poet, he is engaged with contemporary argument (especially when?) writing through Virgil. Thirdly, as Heidegger put it, *Die Sprache spricht*: that is, every speaker of a language is spoken by it. Any critical reading needs to take account of the historical and ideological placement of a speaker in and by language. These three elements in comprehending a work of literature seem self-evidently basic.

Yet the strategic downplaying of each of these elements turns out to be a crucial move in Martindale's practice of reception theory, which embodies the current aestheticising turn. In *Redeeming the Text*, he investigates, for example, Titian's pictures of Diana and Actaeon and of Marsyas, which he painted as *poésie*, free poetic invocations, of scenes from Ovid, which he had read in the translation of Dolce.[15] Now Galinsky describes Ovid's story of Actaeon as 'glib' and lacking the seriousness the subject demands;[16] Martindale skilfully reads Titian reading Ovid, and uses what he finds in Titian's rendering to criticise Galinsky's version. He finds that Titian can bring out the darker elements of Actaeon's desires and Diana's punishment of him, and from this we can learn to see these grimmer colours in Ovid's text. What concerns Martindale in both cases is precisely the aesthetics of violence, how art makes pretty versions – in words or paint – out of grisly mutilations of the human form: 'Marsyas' pain is pain aestheticized, objectified, made the object of artistic vision.'[17] The aesthetic turn self-reflexively fixates on aesthetics itself.

This argument is an explicitly paradigmatic and programmatic exposition, from which we can learn much. But it is worth underlining what is left out, according to the three categories I have outlined. First, the discussion involves no other version of these myths that would have been in Titian's mental repertoire, no other versions of sexual violence or torture, no other contemporary interest in what Ovid might be doing, although the Renaissance was obsessed with Ovid and the classical past. All that counts is the blank Titian face to face with Ovid. Secondly, the paintings' treatment of aesthetics, gender, violence and Ovid is in not contextualised within Titian's contemporary world. Yet a contextualisation could address the difference Christianity makes to the aesthetics of pain, and what happens to these aesthetics in the Reformation/Counter Reformation. Or it could ask what such classical tales of violence meant within Renaissance culture, and the role of such art in a Catholic country.

Whom was Titian addressing and in what terms? This is, for Martindale, not interesting: the focus on the individual artist and his fellow individual artist from the Roman past excludes any audiences (but the modern critic). Thirdly, he neglects Titian's placement within the languages and techniques of art. Martindale knows Hope's discussion of this work as 'a manifesto for the art of painting',[18] but Hope is a mere foil for Martindale's own argument. When Martindale does observe 'the destabilization of space and viewpoint' in Titian's work, which might raise the issue of Titian's connection to artistic developments outside Venice, he declares: 'it matters little ...'.[19]

This particular reading, then, stimulating as it is, depends on the severe restriction of focus: an individual, decontextualised, artist responding to a decontextualised, individual, artist, a scene played out in the forum of modern critical readings of Ovid. The gain is in a newly nuanced perception of Ovid, as well as in the pleasure of viewing Titian with a perceptive viewer as guide. The loss is that our understanding of the semantics and emotional power of pain and its representation is impoverished because it does not take account of its historical conditioning; in particular, it silences the different relation between spectacles of pain and divine punishment that arise from the necessarily different cultural models of Titian and Ovid. The aesthetics of pain in Martindale's reading silences any historical or cultural specificity for the display of the anguish – the passion – of the body.

Are the strategies of reading that Martindale adopts in this example a required consequence of his theoretical position? I think that his more recent explicitly Kantian work makes this clear. Kant in the Third Critique demands that a principle of disinterestedness governs the contemplation of the art object. Since the nineteenth century, this text has been read to mean that the principle of 'disinterestedness', when it is taken to imply a separation from an interest in the good, demands a rejection of a concern with the political – and, indeed, a rejection of an audience's conflicted engagement with conflicting moral debate in their response to beauty (as Nietzsche wickedly underlines in my epigraph to this chapter). Judgment should be 'universal' (that is not historically or culturally contingent, but something that can be imputed to others across such contingencies), and 'purposive without purpose' (that is, should attempt to abstract itself from knowledge of the purpose of production), and 'necessary'; and this in turn constitutes how the object of studious attention is conceptualised.

Some modern criticism has tried to break down barriers between the political, the moral and the aesthetic in Kant's thinking. Martindale, aware of how variously Kant is read by competing aesthetic theoreticians, wants to show that a commitment to aesthetics need not be politically conservative, and is also firm that Kant's criteria are applied only to *aesthetic* judgment. Other judgements are also possible, which would involve ethical and political debate. He also offers some sharp criticism of what he terms contemporary 'ideological' and 'cultural' criticism, and its unwillingness to consider beauty, which it so often finds embarrassing. Yet in two crucial areas Martindale is inconsistent and less convincing. First, on the interaction of politics and art, he approvingly quotes Harpham to the effect that 'If the aesthetic is always already ideological, so, too ideology is always already aesthetic'; this seems to imply that the categories of the ideological and the aesthetic are at least mutually implicative, if not inevitably intertwined.[20] (So Walter Benjamin famously declared that fascism aestheticised politics, while communism politicised aesthetics.[21]) But Martindale also declares 'there is surely great virtue in keeping, with Kant, the two categories – politics and aesthetics – apart'.[22] It is not clear how Martindale would wish to reconcile those two positions.

It is, however, the second credo which Martindale most consistently attempts to maintain. He imagines a poem praising the Holocaust and comments 'we might decide not to read it on moral and political grounds, which would have no bearing on its aesthetic quality'. Even if one granted the theoretical possibility of a purely aesthetic response to a poem praising the Holocaust, it is unclear to me what the value of putting morality or politics in brackets would be, or what the criteria for such a decision would be, except an *ideological* commitment to the necessary privilege of an aesthetic response. Is a poem's beauty separable from its semantic content, its semantic content from its engagement with the world? Such a response would seem to be an unacceptably muddled reaction to the work of Leni Riefensthal, say, where to evade the politics of her art in the name of aesthetics is to grant the artist her own mealy-mouthed defence of a shocking complicity. Could one look with a pure aesthetic gaze at violent child pornography? It is an argument that the contemporary legal system (as well as contemporary psychiatry) would view without sympathy. Martindale wonders why we should care about particular works of art if we do not believe they have special aesthetic qualities. One might ask in reply why one should care at all about something that aims to be no more than a sophisticated self-pleasuring.

This leads directly to the second pressing issue of historicisation. What does the universalising claim of the Kantian do to history (an 'issue [which] is a complex one', as Martindale correctly notes)?[23] 'Works of art transcend their context', writes Martindale, 'in the sense that they continue to arouse a response in the viewer *now*'.[24] He cites Jeanette Winterson approvingly: 'All art belongs to the same period.' Indeed, it makes no palpable difference to Martindale's analysis in what century or city Titian painted in, or who his audience was. (This forms part of what he describes as his 'war against the determination of classicists to ground their discipline in "history"'.[25]) For sure, every critic is a figure of her own present; every reading is made in the here and now. But what are the implications of these evident truths? An aesthetic response is learned and trained. An aesthetic response to a representation of the human body, say, depends at least in part on socially determined ideals of beauty, as well as on conventions of representation.

5. Cultural History and Aesthetics

The tortured body of Jesus on the Cross, the fleshy nudes of Rubens, or a bearded grandee of the Victorian drawing room, may all be part of the repertoires of beauty in a modern viewer's horizon of expectation, but each image also plays its role by virtue of its perceived difference from and similarity to contemporary ideals. This sense of the otherness of the past is essential to any critical self-awareness of the contingencies of the present. The more nuanced and sophisticated our understanding of the past, which will always be a projection, the greater is the potential for a nuanced and sophisticated understanding of the *Jetzzeit* – itself also a projection or construction.

These two areas of concern lead, I think, to a tension in Martindale's project, which I do not see how to resolve. Martindale has often written eloquently against what he calls the naïve view that a text has an essence, something fixed and integral, to which subsequent generations respond. Rather, 'meaning is always realised at the point of reception'. Yet recently he has expressed a concern that the *value* of the classic texts is being downplayed, occluding the significant difference between Dante's *Comme-dia* and *Gladiator*. So, to recapture the virtue or value of a text, he exhorts us to look for 'the unique aesthetic character of an artwork'.[26] Can one propose a 'unique aesthetic character of an artwork' *without* supposing it has an essence, or something fixed and integral?

Furthermore, Martindale wants to emphasise the unique aesthetic character of the artwork of Plutarch because 'for some reader who dares to break through the *Zeitgeist*, somewhere, who knows? Plutarch might yet change the world again'.[27] That is, the focus on the so-called aesthetic character of art cannot escape the lure of the political – of changing the world, of doing something in the world, which needs a sense of history and of placement within history. How, therefore, can Martindale insist that there is nothing fixed and integral to a text? In fact, he fails to hold to the disinterested, aestheticist line in his own critical prose, because he is lured by the thought of texts having a real impact in and on the world.

Modern reception theory, as embodied for classicists most intelligently in the work of Martindale, focuses too restrictedly on a model of individual authors responding to individual works: Martindale on Milton on Virgil. This model, indebted to a Victorian construction of the past as an inheritance, brings with it ideological values associated with passing on the property between generations of landed gentry (even in Martindale's more dynamic system). The aesthetic focus on an individual artist, face to face with an artist of an earlier generation, is instrumental in down-playing reception as an embedded, political, and historical process, where art is located in history, and has an effect in and on the world, and is constructed within multiple audiences over time, and the mem-ory of those audiences. The aesthetic turn turns out to depend on the dodgy ideological image of the heroic individual artist and his Doppel-gänger, the heroic individual critic.

II

In asserting that words do things in the world, this chapter has already utilised one fundamental idea from performance studies: the idea of the *performative*. I now want to show how thinking about performance can help us escape from the negative aspects of the face-to-face individual model. I use as my example a performance I have already written about at length, Strauss' *Elektra* in London in 1910, in order to draw out some precise theoretical observations in line with this book's objective of exploring the theory of performance reception.[28]

A crucial factor is the collective or the multiple nature of each part of the process. A performance as an event embodies (at least) three different levels of reception. First we have the artwork itself, which is responding to an artwork of the ancient past (*Elektra* is a multi-dimensional re-working of the Sophoclean tragedy, *Electra*); second, the audience response to the artwork (the London audiences' and the critics' responses to *Elektra* as a modern opera and as an engagement with the classical past); third, our response, as critics or historians, to the artwork *and* to the audience's response, which are both part of the performance. Each of these processes is a form of reception, and the meaning of the artwork is enacted in the relations between these three levels of reception.

Let us explore each of these levels in more detail. Strauss' *Elektra* is called *Strauss' Elektra* because he wrote the music, and wonderful music it is too, fiercely modern, precisely violent and perversely sexual, searing and thrilling. But the words were written by von Hofmannsthal, whose play *Elektra* had already been a *cause célèbre* seven years earlier in the German-speaking world. The libretto is a reduced reworking – a reception, as it were – of this earlier drama. As Hofmannsthal re-wrote his masterpiece, he adopted many suggestions made by Strauss. We could discuss how this text responds to Sophocles: its approach to rewriting locates Hofmannsthal within a set of early twentieth-century German-speaking intellectual and cultural concerns, re-composing the privilege of Greek culture in a shockingly provocative way. But while such an analysis could contribute to performance criticism, it would not in itself be performance criticism.

The music was conducted by Thomas Beecham, already a star in his own right. His interpretation of the score was crucial to the performance, and the first-night audience presented him with a laurel wreath in recognition. The lead role of Elektra was sung by Edyth Walker, and any performance of the opera depends for its success on this massive and brilliant diva role. Her performance was central not just to the musical triumph of the piece, but also, thanks to her wild staring eyes and unmatched violence, to the public perception of the opera as an anti-classical Greek tragedy. The sets were designed by Attilio Comelli, based on recent archaeological discoveries at Mycenae, and were discussed in the press, including a double-page spread in the *Daily Mirror*, as a specific response to new versions of the ancient world. One could go on: the artwork in performance is a collaborative project, where the performance is constructed out the work of many individuals, interacting. Performance is impossible to reduce to a singular product of a single individual (which is one reason why in British law you cannot copyright a performance).

The second level of reception, the audience, is equally complex. Obviously, audiences are made up of many individuals. But there is also a collective dynamic that is crucial. There is a dynamic of crowds and power which is more than the sum of the individual responses. But our understanding of an audience should also include the reviewers of a work, privileged figures who publish critiques or encomia of performances, thereby both directing future audiences and redrafting previous audiences' responses. Audiences change their minds about what they saw after reading a review. They formulate opinions in discussion with friends or in response to an ongoing debate. They bring different knowledges and ignorances to bear on the artwork: different awarenesses of Sophocles, say, in the case of Strauss, or different appreciations of Wagner. There is a temporal frame to audience reaction that goes beyond the time of performance itself. The meaning of a performance spreads, develops, formulates and reformulates in an ongoing response, which may grow more rich or more simplified over time. The mantra of reception studies, '*at the point* of reception', is better phrased as '*in the process* of reception'.

The third level of reception involves us, the critics and historians, reconstructing our versions of the performance, blinkered by our contemporary rows, concerns and ambitions, trying to be self-conscious about our own biases while being aware (or in extreme cases denying such historical conditioning altogether in the name of objectivity). The more one recognises the institutional, intellectual and historical embedding of scholarship, the harder it is to defend the disinterestedness of the aesthetic gaze of the critic, except as a theoretical projection. And how could one not worry about the self-interest of such a projection?

So, performance raises a fundamental problem for Rezeptionsästhetik in its current form, which privileges the individual artist and text. Theatre and opera rarely appear in this aestheticising scholarship; when they do, as in studies of Shakespeare's use of classical sources, the analysis remains relentlessly *textual*. The artwork in performance is a collaborative response to the art of the past from the artists and the audiences of the present. Indeed, investigating the audience to a performance highlights one of the central difficulties for reception theory: should reception studies concentrate on a culturally defined, historically located norm of response, or rather on an individual's particular response? Are we interested, that is, in what links the multifarious responses to the past (an Edwardian view of Sophocles, as it were)? Or in a specific artist's or audience member's response (Hofmannsthal on Sophocles, or Shaw on Hofmannsthal, as it were)? It would be easy and correct to answer immediately that reception is best understood in the relation between the two – between the individual and a more socially or culturally normative framework. The hard work begins in trying to articulate this relation carefully and in detail.

My second point on performance and reception theory concerns how we look at the meaning of performance in history. The grounding question is this: what makes a performance significant? Taking Strauss' *Elektra* again as my example, I would like to summarise some of the frames relevant to the question of the significance of its performance in London in 1910.[29] We need, first, to take account of Hofmannsthal's script in relation to Sophocles: this cannot be merely a recognition of how the librettist adapts specific lines or scenes. The self-conscious work of rewriting engages sharply with the Victorians' pious image of Sophocles, and does so through a thorough-going modernism.

Second, Strauss' *music* needs to be understood within the context of British and European opera, where Wagner is the Master against which Strauss is writing as much as he is the Master through which British audiences are struggling to respond. Again, as we saw above, there is a formal element to this analysis, at both the scenographic and musicological levels; but the reception of Strauss' music, the perception of how he was responding to the ancient world, was also mediated through the public critical arguments between Ernest Newman, Shaw and others about the place of Strauss' musical modernism in British culture.

Third, the staging, set and costumes need to be placed within the conventions of dress and set design of the period. It was shocking for the audience to see Electra, a classical heroine, dressed in black rags with wild, unkempt hair and singing such violent music; or Clytemnestra in modernist, decadent guise. The visual element is basic to the reception of the past in performance. Fourth, the response to the opera was implicated in the performance of nationalism: only four years before the First World War anti-German feeling was much manipulated in the press. Indeed, the response of the media to the performance, before, during and after the run, was manipulative, answering to their own needs of circulation and scandal, as much as to an analysis of the opera. But the audience at the first night had already had the opportunity to read much about it and to have prepared its views. The reaction to Strauss in London was an English response to a great German's music.

Fifth, reactions were tied up with the modern discipline of psychology. Reviewers agreed that Electra's psyche was laid bare, but the way in which they discussed the psychology of the performance was quite different. In Austria the debate tended to proceed through the new and trendy work of Freud; in England, especially from the older reviewers, a response was framed in out-of-date psychological language. And, of course, Edwardian stereotypes of gender inevitably informed responses to Electra's screaming and murderous rows with her mother.

5. Cultural History and Aesthetics

A performance is an event in history and to understand its significance we need a full historical analysis. The study of reception in the sphere of performance requires extensive skills including archival research, and a willingness to spread one's intellectual net widely. I therefore willingly embrace the charge laid against my work by Charles Martindale that I want to take reception studies closer to cultural history: I do, because I see a performance as an embedded event in culture and in history, and therefore see culture and history as the necessary routes to understanding the significance of a performance. Can a rigorous Kantian aesthetics, with its commitments to disinterestedness, the purposive without purpose and the necessary, have anything to say to the inevitable contingency and cultural embeddedness of performance?

Looking at performance history as a field of reception studies reveals, then, two specific difficulties with the aesthetics that we have traced in the work of Martindale. First, it becomes apparent that the diffuse, collaborative, multi-levelled nature of performance as an event cannot be reduced to the model of an individual artist nurturing an aesthetic response to an artwork, or responding to the ancient world through an artwork. Second, and more contentiously, we can see how aesthetics tends to write out the performative. Or rather, art may have an aesthetic effect on an individual (in that sense it is performative) but as soon as this effect becomes an effect on society, a *political* effect, it becomes no longer purely aesthetic.

The final question is this: can the cultural historical view of reception theory essential for performance studies be brought together with the aesthetic approach underlying Martindale's reception studies? For once, I don't think there *is* an evident Hegelian *Aufhebung* to this opposition. The best cultural history can read texts in as sophisticated a way as possible, attuned to their aesthetic value and to their textuality, and aware of the way that literature can be – must be – about itself. It is also possible to write history without being a naïve empiricist. But I am not sure how the current strong claims of aesthetics, with its intellectual roots in Kant, can rebuild any significant history, politics and social impact back into their model. Hence what I described as the unresolved tensions in Martindale's current work, where politics and the social impact of art seem to slip back into the analysis, against the express theoretical aims of the pursuit of the 'pure judgement of taste'. For performance history as a branch of reception studies, therefore, it seems to me that Kant is the wrong place to start.[30]

Notes

1. Merrill 1992: 136. In general, see MacDonald 2003. Martindale 2005: 111-13 discusses the trial within his own argument.
2. Merrill 1992: 144.
3. See Brilliant 1991; Pointon:1993; Jordanova; 2000.
4. Whistler 1967: 128.

5. Exemplary are Eagleton 1990; de Bolla 2001; Martindale 2005; each with extensive bibliography.

6. Murnaghan 2006. See also Martindale 1993: 3.

7. Richardson 2008.

8. Martindale 2006: 11.

9. See Mandler 1997; Dellheim 1982; Ritvo 2007; Swenson 2007.

10. A huge bibliography could be given: but do see Secord 2000; Detienne 1981; Stocking 1987.

11. See from a huge bibliography Wheeler 2006; Vance 1985; Chadwick 1970; each with many further references.

12. Eliot 1945: 12, 14.

13. Marsh 2007: 215-16.

14. Martindale 2006: 9.

15. Martindale 1993: 60-4.

16. Galinsky 1975: 66-7, 102-3, 195.

17. Martindale 1993: 64.

18. Hope 1980: 133.

19. Martindale 1993: 62.

20. Martindale 2005: 26.

21. Benjamin 1992: 234-5.

22. Martindale 2005: 129.

23. Martindale 2005: 26.

24. Martindale 2005: 27.

25. Martindale 2005: 29. One might wonder what the inverted commas add to that remark. Is there a real history out there that classicists don't know about? Is the past for classicists different from the past of historians? Are historians too committed to 'history' only?

26. Martindale 2006: 10 – what Pater calls the 'virtue' of a text.

27. Martindale 2006: 11.

28. Goldhill 2002: 108-77.

29. For a far fuller account, see Goldhill 2002: 108-77.

30. Thanks to Charles Martindale, for many years' inconclusive discussion of these issues, and to Edith Hall, for performing the paper at the conference when I was unavoidably prevented from attending, and for helping to edit my too long chapter down to this length. No jokes, thus ... and the notes are deliberately minimalist.

Performance, Reception, Aesthetics: Or Why Reception Studies Need Kant

Charles Martindale

On a sudden the imagination feels itself free –
Walter Pater, 'Winckelmann'[1]

Let us suppose Milton in company with some stern and prejudiced Puritan, contemplating the front of York Cathedral, and at length expressing his admiration of its beauty. We suppose it too at that time of his life, when his religious opinions, feelings, and prejudices most nearly coincided with those of the rigid Anti-prelatists. –P. Beauty: I am sure, it is not the beauty of holiness. –M. True; but yet it is beautiful. –P. It delights not me. What is it good for? Is it of any use but to be stared at? –M. Perhaps not! but still it is beautiful. –P. But call to mind the pride and wanton vanity of those cruel shavelings, that wasted the labour and substance of so many thousand poor creatures in the erection of this haughty pile. –M. I do. But still it is very beautiful. –P. Think how many scores of places of worship, incomparably better suited both for prayer and preaching, and how many faithful ministers might have been maintained, to the blessing of tens of thousands, to them and their children's children, with the treasures lavished on this worthless mass of stone and cement. –M. Too true! but nevertheless it is very beautiful. –P. And it is not merely useless; but it feeds the pride of the prelates, and keeps alive the popish and carnal spirit among the people. –M. Even so! and I presume not to question the wisdom, nor detract from the pious zeal, of the first Reformers of Scotland, who for these reasons destroyed so many fabrics, scarce inferior in beauty to this now before our eyes. But I did not call it good, nor have I told thee, brother! that if this were levelled to the ground, and existed only in the works of the modeller or engraver, that I should desire to reconstruct it. The GOOD consists in the congruity of a thing with the laws of the reason and the nature of the will, and in its fitness to determine the latter to actualize the former: and it is always discursive. The Beautiful arises from the perceived harmony of an object, whether sight or sound, with the inborn and constitutive rules of the judgement and imagination: and it is always intuitive.

Samuel Taylor Coleridge[2]

Coleridge's fable re-enacts an old battle, but its particular expression follows in detail one of the most up-to-date versions of aesthetics available to him, that of Immanuel Kant's Third Critique (he is exactly following the passage about the palace in §2). Recently I have argued for the importance of Kant in theorising reception; it is significant that in his famous inaugural lecture of 1967 (a founding text for reception) Hans Robert Jauss called not for the kind of reception history widely practised today in Classics but for an Aesthetics of Reception (*Rezeptionsästhetik*). In this essay I will respond to criticisms of the model of reception advanced in *Redeeming the Text* (with its subsequent Kantian gloss)[3] made by Simon Goldhill in a challenging paper presented (*in absentia*) to the conference from which this book derives (published here in much revised form) and by Edith Hall in a provocative and sparkling article that first appeared in the journal *Arion* and is reprinted, in a shorter form, at the beginning of this volume.[4] I will argue (against these criticisms) that this model, in the main, can work just as well for performance reception as for the reception of literary works.

My particular interest is in the reception of texts – I will come back to that word in a moment – that have, in Kantian terms, been judged 'beautiful', or, as people tend to put it today, have been assigned positive aesthetic value. These texts are often, but not necessarily, works of high art (as we now see the matter). In general I am much less interested in texts in which I find little or no aesthetic quality (although these may be of considerable sociological or ideological interest), texts that is which do not produce *in me*[5] the complex and pleasurable interplay of the mental faculties involved in our experience of beauty as described in the Third Critique. The *Iliad* was produced in the past, but it is valued, or not, in the present, and the student of reception, if she is not to be a mere antiquarian, must be attentive to both aspects. If we are dealing with texts of this kind, it would be wrong to bracket out questions of aesthetic value. Indeed I would argue that there is a sense in which reading aesthetically does have a kind of priority over other ways of reading (though this is in no way an entailment of Kant's analysis). A worthwhile ideological reading of Beethoven's late quartets (or of Strauss' *Elektra*, to use Goldhill's example) would have to follow on, or at least be simultaneous with, an aesthetic one, if it is not to mistake the character of the object with which the critic has to do (though that of course is not in itself an aesthetic matter, for the reasons that Kant gives). Works of art as it were invite us to make the Kantian judgement of taste ('this is beautiful'),[6] and to ignore that invitation is thus somewhat perverse (as though one were to grind up Michelangelo's David, and then use it as hardcore for the garage floor). And if that is true, we cannot afford to neglect the founding text of modern aesthetics.

Hall argues that *Redeeming the Text* will not help much with performance reception, because 'it explicitly puts the *reader* at the centre of Reception' (see Hall, above). And Goldhill complains that I figure reception as an encounter between the heroic individual author and the equally heroic critic. Throughout the book I used the word 'text' with a particular poststructuralist inflection of the 'objects' concerned. A text in this usage means 'any vehicle of signification', so that 'a mosaic, or a marriage ceremony, is a "text" as much a book'.[7] Or, I might have added, a perform- ance – and indeed I several times use musical performance as a good way of thinking about reception more generally. A 'reader' in this discourse is someone who encounters a text, responds to it, reaches an understanding of it (or fails to do so), and indeed is herself figurable as a text, a locus of innumerable intertextualities (poststructuralists often expressed this thought by means of scare-quotes, so 'Martindale' for Martindale[8]). As Roland Barthes puts it, 'This "I" which approaches the text is already itself a plurality of other texts, of codes which are infinite or, more precisely, lost.'[9] Even if the text is a book, a reader is on this view never alone in the room with a book; there are always numerous other readers there with her, even if she is unconscious of them, all those other receivers who have left their traces in the text and helped to determine how it is read. That's why the phrase 'the lone scholar' has always struck me as so peculiar; the scholar keeps excellent company with a cloud of witnesses from the present and from multiple pasts. Reception as I conceive it necessarily involves the collaborative; the reception critic collaborates with other receivers – and you certainly don't have to be in a theatre or a cinema or an opera house to do this. In her keynote address to the conference, Erika Fischer-Lichte argued that a performance is an event, not an artwork, and that it always belongs to the here-and-now (see Fischer-Lichte in this volume). That provides a point of contact with the Kantian judgement of taste which tells us nothing about the nature of the object judged (for example, what sort of a thing a palace is), and is always a direct response by the subject in the present (you can listen to the symphony again, but it will be a new judgement, a different singular experience). Wolfgang Iser writes tellingly of Walter Pater's aesthetic thought (which derives from Kant), 'There are no longer any aesthetic objects with an existence of their own – there are only aesthetic potentials in the empirical world which must each be realised individually.'[10] A poem, just as much as a play or an opera, can be thought of as an event in time rather than as a thing; reading it (where there is a different encounter on every occasion) is to that extent like listening to a piece of music. In short, Hall's distinction between reception in performed and non-performed media, between text and per- formance, though a founding one in classical performance reception, is one that can, and should, be deconstructed. This is a crucial point, and I shall soon be returning to it.

What I did posit, in seeking to avoid any crude reification of the text, was an *active* reader, who plays an important part in the making of meaning. In my genealogy of reception, one key work is Roland Barthes' 'The Death of the Author'. In the symbolically significant year of 1968 Barthes proposed a dramatic, indeed revolutionary event, the death of the Author (with a capital A) and the birth of the reader (with a small r). Despite its shortness and clarity, the essay is frequently misrepresented.

Barthes is of course not saying that books are not written by people who have intentions; rather he is protesting against the idea that 'the *explanation* of a work is always sought in the man or woman who produced it, as if it were always in the end ... the voice of a single person, the *author* "confiding" in us'.[11] Barthes starts with a quotation from Balzac's *Sarrazine*: 'This was woman herself, with her sudden fears, her irrational whims, her instinctive worries, her impetuous boldness, her fussings, and her delicious sensibility', and comments:

> Who is speaking thus? Is it the hero of the story bent on remaining ignorant of the castrato hidden beneath the woman? Is it Balzac the individual, furnished by his personal experience with a philosophy of Woman? Is it Balzac the author professing 'literary' ideas on femininity? Is it universal wisdom? Romantic psychology? We shall never know, for the good reason that writing is the destruction of every voice, of every point of origin ... As soon as a fact is *narrated* no longer with a view to acting directly on reality but intransitively ... this disconnection occurs, the voice loses its origin, the author enters into his own death, writing begins.

(There is a nice pre-emptive strike on the narratological notion of 'focalisation' here, if that is used as a way of fixing rather than complicating interpretation.) That 'a text's unity lies not in its origin but in its destination'[12] – a better formulation perhaps than 'meaning is always realised at the point of reception' – does not imply that readers are the final arbiter of a text's meaning (that would be just another version of the Author-God). A reader is 'simply that *someone* who holds together in a single field all the traces by which the written text is constituted'. Barthes also warns us against discovering 'beneath the work' the Author's 'hypostases', which include 'society' and 'history'. History (or ideology) is thus no advance on the Author as a closural move. Historicists who profess to give us a text's meaning through historical contextualisation (rich as that may be) are not thereby escaping 'the Author-God'. Rather the birth of the reader means that 'in the multiplicity of writing, everything is to be *disentangled*, nothing *deciphered*; the structure can be followed, "run" (like the thread of a stocking) at every point and at every level, but there is nothing beneath: the space of writing is to be ranged over, not pierced'.[13] We have left the world in which there is a final signified, in which meaning is closed. That is what is meant by the birth of the reader, not the licensing of the all-powerful Critic.

Goldhill also introduces a red herring when he maintains that current models in reception derive from Victorian concerns with inheritance. He starts with a move much beloved of historicists, appealing to the 'fact' – if fact it is, given the necessary provisionality of dictionaries – that the phrase 'the classical tradition' was first used in its current sense in the late nineteenth century. He moves from there to the position that our idea of the classical tradition was invented by the Victorians. The Victorians

74

certainly invented many things, including many valuable things, but if we were not fixated on particular words and phrases it is surely clear that there has been no time since antiquity itself when there have not been those for whom certain Greek and Roman texts have not been accorded special and exemplary status (in certain limited cases, Virgil, for example, without any significant break). The very name of our discipline – Classics – continues to register this long-held view; and that sense of the word 'classic' was already established in the Renaissance from a passage in Aulus Gellius.[14] In Renaissance grammar schools education consisted almost entirely in the study of Latin; there was thus no need for a separate subject called Classics, the matter was taken for granted.[15] By the nineteenth century there were various educational alternatives to the study of antiquity, not least the sciences. So perhaps the need to identify a specific 'classical tradition' increased; this would then reflect a loss rather than a gain in privileged status. Moreover the Victorian period could just as well (and perhaps more accurately) be figured as the time when that tradition (to reify for a moment) was made available to much wider audiences, with the formation of working-class reading groups and the dissemination of classical material in popular cheap editions such as the Bohn Classical Library.[16] The point only matters because in locating the idea of the classical tradition in the late nineteenth century Goldhill is trying to give it a negative 'Victorian' image. What we are offered in this opening section, it seems to me, is a reductive culturalist account of 'the Victorian', with its emphasis on such ideologemes as 'Victorian social anxieties' and the other usual suspects. If you try replacing the word 'classical' by the word 'medieval' throughout Goldhill's text, you will get an equally cogent narrative; in other words we are dealing with *idées reçues* too generalised to serve as serious history – rather, all this seems to me a pretty pure instance of ideological self-positioning.

Hall, as we have seen, draws a sharp distinction between performed and non-performed media. Within performance reception studies, performance is often reified in this way. But criticism can always be attentive to the performance element in anything. And a 'performance' might be many things: Winckelmann showing an ancient sculpture to a group of visitors; or a musician with a score experiencing in real time Wagner's *Ring* 'in his or her head'; or a parent reading a novel by Dickens to a family; or a critic performing an interpretation of a poem to an imaginary audience in an essay or an actual one in a lecture. Hall explicitly excludes visual art from performance. What, then, about art exhibitions, or museum displays, often attended by thousands, in which the art works are as it were 'staged'? An exhibition typically results from 'collaboration' among artists by juxtaposing their work (or by putting works by the same artist but from different historical moments in the same space); and it involves not just the viewer but curators, designers, technicians, bureaucrats. For that matter a book involves collaboration between author, editor, designer and others. Author and reader are never alone.

In general aesthetic experience and aesthetic criticism can themselves readily be figured as performative. Hall has many interesting things to say about reception, but what she doesn't do, in my view, is to offer a distinct 'theory' of 'performance reception', as she herself virtually acknowledges at the close, when she describes her approach as 'theory ordered *à la carte*'. A theory of performance reception would need to show why we need a different theory for those things that are traditionally designated 'performance arts' – and that is likely to involve a concealed Platonic aspiration, a commitment to some notion of the essential nature of drama (or whatever). In contrast to Kant, who concentrates on the mind of the receiving subject, Hall is making the mistake of Clive Bell and other aestheticians who suppose that the classification of the object is crucial for the type of analysis to be employed – in Bell's case, what makes something a work of art or not,[17] in Hall's, whether it meets the conditions she defines as constituting performance. (Certainly within the Kantian aesthetic what a thing is (ontologically) doesn't matter – that is not the kind of knowledge that the judgement of taste bestows, or that constitutes its content.) At all events the different art forms cannot be reliably differentiated as involving few people or many. And if we need a special theory of performance reception, why not a special theory for lyric reception, or epic reception, or for any other genre or mode (these themselves are, of course, construable as forms of reception)? An approach of this kind almost always eventuates in setting up a hierarchy of art forms and in all those faintly absurd and definitely pointless discussions about the relative value of these different art forms – so Hall and Goldhill tell us in effect that in certain respects performances of plays and operas are 'better' than the experience of poems as a result of the interaction between performers and audience (the myth of the possibility of full presence seems to be lurking here). Thus Hall claims that a compelling theatrical experience can leave a deeper impression on the memory than the printed word or painted image. But that will depend not only on the individual works but on the individual receivers, who may well be responsive to one art form more than another (one thinks, for example, of the Stendhal syndrome). Again Hall says that the libidinal response to great acting 'is, by any account, simply not the same type of encounter as that experienced by a reader with a Penguin Classic in her study'. Well! most Penguin Classics are fairly unexciting things, but studies can be sexy places too, when, for example, the right poem meets the right reader.

Moreover when Goldhill and Hall write about performances, they don't – as yet anyway – break out into radically new ways of doing business. And, like other performance critics, they have to face one particular difficulty. A problem about a *past* performance of a work of art is that in one obvious sense it longer exists, and is thus particularly difficult to write about effectively. In such cases what performance critics actually have at their disposal are written or visual texts about performances, not the performances themselves. To bring such lost performances to life requires exceptional skill. As a result performance histories can be quite dull and unilluminating. It is true that Winckelmann was mysteriously able to intuit the aesthetic qualities of Classical Greek sculpture without ever having seen an example, but his was a rare gift. Here at any rate Goldhill may be right to say that aesthetics has no role to play in performance reception. We cannot become part of the original collectivity except by imaginative projection. Kant would not allow that the judgement of taste was being made in the strict sense because there is no direct encounter ('I must present the object immediately to my feeling of pleasure or displeasure, and that, too, without the aid of concepts'[18]). We could receive and respond aesthetically to some of the documentary evidence (an engraving, a photograph, a record on film, for example). The photographs of Wieland Wagner's productions of Wagner's operas are indeed, in my view, beautiful. But clearly this is a different kind of experience from viewing the original performances. In short there is only an indirect and roundabout way of making the judgement of taste in such cases, and we are left with logical judgement based on evidence, not with response. I confess to finding this kind of thing in the main fairly tedious. In Goldhill's threefold model for performance reception, the performance in the more ordinary sense of the word tends to disappear. The first level is the work of art (in this case Strauss' *Elektra* as a reworking of Sophocles); the second is the response of the audience and critics at the time of the first performances in London; the third is 'our' response to those responses (that is, those of Goldhill himself and other scholars today). At all three levels the focus of attention thus turns out to be written texts; the performance as performance is largely left out. At all events, it is certainly worth seeking alternatives to the kinds of performance histories that Hall and Goldhill and other practitioners of classical performance reception typically offer.[19] These might include a practice-based approach through recreating past performances, or the investigation of what kind of audience a work might be said to configure – the audience could then be brought in as a key player in the making of meaning. Or we could use the evidence to imagine what the performances might have been like, and try to respond to that (though the dangers are obvious).

Both Hall and Goldhill also have a Marxising and to my thinking sentimental preference for collective responses over the responses of individuals (always, of course, to be stigmatised as male bourgeois subjects). You find this preference in Walter Benjamin (in contrast to Adorno), and it always disturbs me. We should not get dewy-eyed about the collective. And the preference is not infrequently combined, in the performance reception practised by classicists, with an analogous sentimentality about popular culture. Now popular culture is a particularly inexact category. Whether something is popular or not is a purely empirical matter: Dickens' novels or Shakespeare's plays have, in particular times and places, been extremely popular.[20] If you count up your audiences over the centuries *Hamlet* may well have been received by more people, and a greater variety (and wider social spectrum) of people, than *Gladiator* or the most popular Hollywood movie. I do not know on what basis Hall claims that the Ovid of the *Metamorphoses* 'has been enjoyed by far more individuals in theatres and opera houses than he ever reached via textual study';[21] it seems unlikely, given that the poem was a school text from the Middle Ages onwards. Collectivities do not have to be confined to one time or place. If we leave on one side the issue of popularity, Adorno's critique of the shortcomings of the kind of mass culture produced by consumerist capitalism remains telling:[22] too often its productions are politically and culturally reactionary (the same might be said of pre-capitalist popular culture as well, which, because of its traditional character, is often highly conservative). Does one prefer the high art works of Oscar Wilde or the popular culture of the mass-circulation newspapers which developed at the end of the nineteenth century and which crowed over Wilde's downfall and even in one case hoped for his death? Of course there are also many precious works of popular culture; it all comes down to the particular case. Another positive feature of the Kantian judgement of taste is precisely its concern with the singular – 'this poem which I am reading is beautiful' is the form of the judgement, not 'this kind of thing is beautiful', let alone 'works of high art are more beautiful than the products of popular culture' (a view sometimes attributed to Kant which is wholly at odds with his whole system).

There are good and bad collectivities, good and bad audiences. A bad audience might be one in which the whole group is manipulated into a shared experience which is morally coercive. An obvious example would be a Nuremburg Rally, where there is certainly 'a dynamic of crowds and power', to use Goldhill's phrase. More controversially the operas of Wagner have been seen as designed to produce responses of this kind. An audience that combines to laugh at a Beckmesser is not necessarily an attractive entity. On the other hand, the universal communicability of aesthetic response posited by Kant would be an excellent example of a good collectivity (*Critique of Judgement* § 40). The 'universality' of the judgement of taste does not mean that the judgement is not historically or culturally contingent, as is so often said; Kant is not claiming that in practice people do agree (that would be a merely empirical matter) or even that they should. It means rather that the maker of the judgement 'imputes', while not necessarily getting, the agreement of others. The judgement of taste is thus something worth talking about. It is different with the judgement of 'the agreeable' (where you like spinach, and I don't); here there is little more to be said, since there is nothing serious at stake worth disagreeing about. Indeed we may say that disagreement is in fact needed within the aesthetic (the judgement of taste is subjective as well as universal). We are not forced to agree, but we can talk with others about judgements that are open to contention. There can be no final resolution, since there are no proofs of beauty (if there were, you wouldn't have to read a poem in order to be able to judge it beautiful – you could simply identify it as falling under the appropriate rule or not). As a reception critic I engage, at least potentially, in contention with all the other readers of a text, including the author. Disinterest helps this whole process – I try to set aside purely personal interests in making the judgement of taste. I may judge a palace beautiful even if I strongly disapprove of palaces, or in general don't particularly care for that kind of thing (this is Kant's own example, and returns us to Coleridge's fable with which we started). Disinterest increases the possibility of a fruitful discussion, which can be impeded where the discussants have opposed personal interests which get in the way of dialogue. Someone who approaches, say, *Paradise Lost* in this spirit through the critics and editors of the eighteenth century and the responses of the great Romantic writers and all the other fine readers of the poem throughout the last 300 years has at her disposal just such a good collectivity, richer I would say than your average theatre audience, and certainly more varied and potentially larger. Still more would this be the case if we were to take, say, the Bible.

This is the kind of reception I would advocate. Goldhill ends up arguing for what sounds like a rather traditional form of contextual, historicising criticism. That's fine on its own terms – though I have my reservations about it[23] – but it's not really reception, and it is comparatively inert. As regards his account of Strauss' *Elektra*, I would say that what he wants to do is to give a 'thick description' of the first English performance.[24] This could indeed be an interesting project, a project I would say in 'New Historicism' more than in 'Reception'. For what Goldhill is not really very concerned to do is to consider the opera as a reception of Greek tragedy: Strauss and Sophocles, or more complex cross-temporal receptions of related texts, are not used for *mutual* illumination. He does not ask, for example, if Sophocles' *Electra* might be different after Hofmannsthal and Strauss. Mieke Bal in *Quoting Caravaggio: Contemporary Art, Preposterous History* is one of many reception theorists to quote a famous sentence from T.S. Eliot's essay 'Tradition and the Individual Talent': 'Whoever has approved this idea of order ... will not find it preposterous that the past should be altered by the present as much as the present is directed by the past' ('preposterous' here means 'utterly absurd', but also glances at the word's etymology, 'topsy-turvy').[25] For this reason for my *Cambridge Companion to Virgil* I put the chapters on translation and reception first, preposterously; in Bal's words, 'this reversal, which puts what came chronologically first ("pre-") as an aftereffect behind ("post") its later recycling is ... a *preposterous history*'.[26]

Goldhill by contrast is only interested in one time period, or any rate only one time period at a time. Marxising criticism tends in this way to be opposed to the transhistorical. However we can operate across temporal boundaries, and there is nothing inherently conservative or objectionable in so doing. In *Redeeming the Text* I have a short discussion in which I attempt to read a story of Ovid through a painting by Titian, rather than reading either in its original context, to show the possibilities of this different kind of analysis.[27] I do not of course claim that this is a complete or final account (indeed I do not believe that such a thing is possible), simply that it may allow for insights of a different kind. Goldhill criticises this account as comparatively decontextualised, and calls for proper and full contextualisation. There is the usual assumption here that context equates to original context, or a context within a single time-frame. In fact what is to count as legitimate context is a tricky matter; contexts are constructed, not merely found lying about. So unless the conditions of relevance and the rules for what constitutes a context are specified, a call to contextualise is simply an ideological gesture. Contexts have no logical limit (part of the context of the 1910 London performance of Strauss' opera is what the singer performing Elektra had for breakfast, but it may not be deemed a relevant part). There is a similar problem about how long an 'original' context lasts. Critics have tried to locate Marvell's political stance in 'An Horatian Ode Upon Cromwell's Return from Ireland' (1650) by locating it in its precise historical moment. But exactly how long does that moment last: a week, a month, a day, a year? Paterian history by contrast is vertical as well as horizontal, allowing such judgements as this on 'the true character of Michelangelo':

> That strange interfusion of sweetness and strength is not to be found in those who claimed to be his followers; but it is found in many of those who worked before him, and in many others down to our own time, in William Blake, for instance, and Victor Hugo, who, though not of his school, and unaware, are his true sons, and help us to understand him, as he in turn interprets and justifies them.[28]

Such judgements may be transhistorical, but (at least in Pater's way of handling them) they are not ahistorical, as classicists tend to assume. Works of art were never merely 'of their time' in the first place;[29] one context in which artists are always conscious of working is that of the transmitted practice of their art, which necessarily takes them out of their own time.

I want to establish an alternative, more dynamic model in which texts and receivers can engage in a freer sort of dialogue across time that is not organised in a hierarchy (temporal or otherwise), one in which in Eliotic fashion the present can affect the past as well as the past the present. Texts from different periods can mutually illuminate each other, suggesting interpretative possibilities without closing discussion down. Whatever may be the case with the Victorian classical tradition, Walter Pater's 'House Beautiful' is neither patrilineal nor patriarchal. The 'House Beautiful' is, in Pater words, continually being built 'for the refreshment of the human spirit' by the 'creative minds of all generations – the artists and those who have treated life in the spirit of art', that is non-instrumentally, as an end in itself.[30] Commenting on Pater's conception, the great E.R. Curtius wrote: 'We have no use for a warehouse of tradition, we want a house, in which we can breathe.'[31] The builders of the House come from every century, they may be either men or women, and within the House they live in a state of equality. Anyone to whose work value has been accorded at any time is an inmate of the House. The inhabitants occupy the same space, but that does not mean that they exist outside history or atemporally – though certainly we are operating with a different temporality from that presupposed by positivistic historians. Rather, in Wolfgang Iser's words, within the House 'the changeability of history' is 'preserved and rendered contemporaneous'.[32] Any inhabitant of the House can talk to any other, backward or forward in time. Above all, to that extent in sharp contrast to Eliot's Tradition, there is no hierarchy in the House.

This is the model of reception I want to promote for all art forms whether or not they are regarded as performance arts. Putting Strauss' *Elektra* into fruitful conjunction with Sophocles' play and other texts from different centuries *ad lib.* (including performed versions of those texts) can produce what Kant calls 'aesthetic ideas'. Aesthetic ideas are ideas that do not involve immediate closure or strict determination of the form 'this text is an instance of Victorian patriarchy or elite male anxiety'. So any notion that as an aesthete I wish to avert my gaze from the messy business of politics and history, or any other messy business for that matter, isn't quite right, though I do want to say that the judgement of taste is not a judgement of the same kind as the judgement of practical reason, and we would do well to keep the two judgements apart. This is not to deny that many judgements of works of art are in practice contaminated (and sometimes as a result woolly), merely that in any instance it is worth knowing which judgement we are making and what the difference is. When Goldhill accuses Pater and other aesthetes of 'sophisticated self-pleasuring',[33] he replicates the criticisms made by conservative critics of the 'Conclusion' of *The Renaissance* on its publication (criticism which often had a homophobic edge), and, like them, he confuses the 'beautiful' with the 'agreeable'. The close attention to the object in the judgement of taste is not perhaps usefully characterised as masturbatory (and what model of the erotic is Goldhill working with here?). Interestingly aesthetics seems not to have lost its power to shock and irritate, because it goes against some of our most deeply ingrained habits. However, as Elizabeth Prettejohn puts it, 'to contemplate something "for art's sake" ... is not to prejudge its meaning or value within Western (or any other) society. It is, though, to free ourselves from the relentless instrumentality of our ordinary habits, if only for moments, and only "for those moments' sake".'[34]

Furthermore, I do not think there is an inconsistency between my commitment to reception (which implies that a work of art doesn't have an 'essence') and my commitment to aesthetic value (which, according to Goldhill, implies that it does). Actually it is Goldhill who turns out to be something of an essentialist. He treats *Redeeming the Text* and *Latin Poetry and the Judgement of Taste* as constituting a single, seamless, universal discourse, without any attempt to historicise or contextualise either. 'The Victorians' are essentialised throughout (they turn out to include some Germans, but never, interestingly, anyone French), and in one striking passage described in the historic present ('this is the era of Ruskin ...'). The character of Strauss' music can be unproblematically described ('fiercely modern, precisely violent and perversely sexual, searing and thrilling'). In his remarks on Plutarch Goldhill appears to imply that the potential for political efficacy has to be an inherent, unchanging feature of a text. And he concludes that 'the cultural historical view of reception theory' is 'essential' for performance studies.

That a work of art has, in a particular reception, a 'virtue' in Pater's special sense[35] – a distinctive aesthetic character which makes *for me* a concerto by Bach or an opera by Strauss what it is while I listen to it and not something else – doesn't mean that it has an essence or a fixed identity. You don't ever step twice into the same river, and the experience of listening to the concerto, even to the same performance on a record, may differ on every hearing. We are talking about how I respond to something at a particular time and place, not about a property of the object. Only I can say whether I experience pleasure and encounter beauty when I listen on any particular occasion (I may, of course, lie about the matter). But I can, while I am having the experience of beauty, try to be as precise about what that experience is for me, and that can be the basis for discussion with others, for universal communicability or for contention. What the outcome will be is not knowable in advance, but it just might change the world – whereas the ideology critic typically tells us what he already knows, that the Victorians were patriarchal, or in some way fail to live up to our enlightened standards. Goldhill thinks that if I talk about changing the world I am moving from aesthetics to politics. But that is to have a diminished sense of what the world is or how it might be changed. I agree with Pater that the enemy here is habit, the stock predetermined response from which the free judgement of taste offers us, to a unique degree, the possibility of escape. In his first published essay ('Coleridge's Writings') Pater observes of the artist, 'What constitutes an artistic gift is first of all a natural susceptibility to moments of strange excitement, in which the colours freshen upon our threadbare world, and the routine of things about us is broken by a novel and happier synthesis'.[36] In the 'Conclusion' to *The Renaissance* he movingly writes of the potential benefits of aesthetic experience for the receiver:

> In a sense it might even be said that our failure [in life] is to form habits: for, after all, habit is relative to a stereotyped world, and meantime it is only the

roughness of the eye that makes any two persons, things, situations, seem alike ... Not to discriminate every moment some passionate attitude in those about us ... is, on this short day of frost and sun, to sleep before evening ... What we have to do is to be for ever curiously testing new opinions and courting new impressions, never acquiescing in a facile orthodoxy, of Comte, or of Hegel, or of our own.[37]

By contrast non-aesthetic criticism (at least as currently practised) tends to homogenise and not infrequently to suggest that we know better than the past:

> We think our fathers fools, so wise we grow –
> Our wiser sons, no doubt, will think *us* so.[38]

In his encounter with 'the Victorians' Goldhill writes from a position of rather too evident ideological superiority. I seek instead an aesthetic encounter between equals, in which – for at least that utopian moment – for once there need be no hierarchy.[39]

Notes

1. Pater 1980: 146.
2. Wittreich 1970: 209.
3. Martindale 1993, 2005, 2006, 2007.
4. Hall 2004a.
5. This formulation is Paterian. Goldhill is wrong to call Kant and Pater 'a wilfully odd couple'; Pater was exceptionally well informed about German philosophy which he taught at Oxford. The same cannot be said of Goldhill; for example, it is quite false to say that in the Third Critique 'Kant demands that a principle of disinterestedness governs the contemplation of the art object'.
6. For us a judgement usually involves hierarchy (this is better than that). But for Kant a judgement occurs when you put together something given by the senses with conceptual activity. Examples of judgements would be 'this is a table', 'this is an instance of injustice', 'this is beautiful'.
7. Martindale 1993: 13.
8. Goldhill asks what the inverted commas add to what I describe as my 'war against the determination to ground their discipline in "history" ' (Martindale 2005: 29). 'History' here means 'what they figure as history'. There are, of course, many versions of history. A joke I like to make is that I have nothing against 'history', simply that I seldom encounter any; much 'history' would be better redescribed as ideology. Our own historicisms (through what Bal 1999: 19 calls 'parontocentrism', the assumption that 'one's own position is normal, the standard, beyond questioning, hence, universal and transparent') often become as ahistorical as the most unreflecting universalisms; they presuppose a position as it were outside history and with no history from which the facts about the past can be revealed. Jauss' 'aesthetics of reception' can thus be seen as more, not less historical than its rivals, only differently so.
9. Barthes 1974: 10.
10. Iser 1987: 64.
11. Barthes 1974: 126.

12. Barthes 1974: 129.

13. Barthes 1974: 129.

14. See Lianeri and Zajko 2008: Introduction.

15. The point is well made by Lyne 2006: 177-8.

16. See Rose 2001; Hall 2008a.

17. Bell 1914.

18. *Critique of Judgement J* § 8; Kant 1952: 55.

19. Michelakis 2008a calls for greater methodological awareness in classical performance reception, noting that the emphasis has been on the accumulation of historical data.

20. Two other excellent examples are Kipling and Puccini, both of them frequently patronised within the academy.

21. This passage (which appears in Hall 2004a: 59) has been cut from the version of that article that appears above in this volume.

22. Adorno 1973 and 1992, especially 'Commodity Music Analysed': 37-52.

23. See Martindale 2005: ch. 5.

24. For his full account (exemplary in its way) see Goldhill 2002: ch. 3.

25. Bal 1999: 1.

26. Bal 1999: 6-7.

27. Martindale 1993: 60-4.

28. Pater 1980: 76.

29. Mason 1977 is good on this point.

30. Pater 1913: 241.

31. Curtius 1953: 396.

32. Iser 1987: 82.

33.The reference to Pater was explicit in the earlier version.

34. Prettejohn 2007: 281.

35. Pater 1980: xx-xxi. 'To him [the aesthetic critic], the picture, the landscape, the engaging personality in life or in a book, *La Gioconda*, the hills of Carrara, Pico of Mirandola, are valuable for their virtues, as we say, in speaking of a herb, a wine, a gem; for the property each has of affecting one with a special, a unique, impression of pleasure ... And the function of the aesthetic critic is to distinguish, to analyse, and separate from its adjuncts, the virtue by which a picture, a landscape, a fair personality in life or in a book, produces this special impression of beauty or pleasure, to indicate what the source of that impression is, and under what conditions it is experienced.' The virtue is of course subjectively experienced (the effect *on me*) and not an objective property, though it is potentially communicable.

36. Quoted Prettejohn 2007: 257.

37. Pater 1980: 189.

38. Pope, *Essay on Criticism*, 438-9.

39. I would like to thank David Hopkins, Elizabeth Prettejohn, and Vanda Zajko for their help with this essay – as well as Simon Goldhill and Edith Hall for prompting my thoughts on this issue.

From *à la carte* to Convergence: Symptoms of Interdisciplinarity in Reception Theory

Zachary Dunbar

The term 'multidisciplinary' crops up in reception theory with unacknow-
ledged frequency. What is meant by it? It would seem that wherever two
or more disciplines gather in the name of shared intellectual and cultural
kinship (and with a let-live policy regarding methodology), there you will
find multidisciplinary scholarship. Edith Hall's oft-quoted 'menu' for
theorising performance reception ('*à la carte*' – see above, p. 27) is symp-
tomatic of this style of research. Her discussion cites eclectic and wide-
ranging sources such as Giambattista Vico, German classical-romantic
idealism, and poststructuralist theory, which in themselves represent
multidisciplinary impulses.[1] In *Dionysus Since 69,* published in the same
year as the first version of Hall's article, a broad spectrum of theatre
practitioners, historians and classicists juxtaposed views, theories and
commentary about *why* Greek tragedy is 'particularly special to our specific moment in human history'.[2] The argument for the interrelatedness of
socio-politics, gender, performance aesthetics and cognitive philosophy
implies that complex topics such as Greek drama require a network of
analytical responses and procedures, a polyphonic dialogue rather than a
hegemonic tone of specialist research.[3]

The multidisciplinary approach has clear paradigms outside reception
theory. From the biological investigation of emotions to Chicano studies,
from global climate change to musical creativity, from understanding time
to the causes of Burnout, fields of knowledge converge to increase, enrich
and possibly convert specialist knowledge in order to understand the full
measure of complex phenomena. As a practitioner in musical theatre, I
would find it impossible to theorise my work outside a multidisciplinary
framework. The current perception in research-led postgraduate performance training in music theatre is that the performer is part of a network
of disciplines (singing, acting, dancing) around and through which composing, directing, and designing simultaneously reinforce *versatility* and
adaptability, two qualities crucial to a profession rapidly expanding and
changing in several directions.

Within studies of the performance history and practice of ancient Greek
drama, the discussion of, for instance, the tragic chorus, has revealed a

growing multidisciplinary account. This represents a seismic shift away from a structuralist, Aristotelian sum-of-parts approach (the one that informed the analysis of stagecraft and of ancient texts),[4] toward viewing Greek theatre as an interwoven discourse of dance, music, costume, media, adaptation and configurations of theatre space. For example, spatial and archaeological concerns merged with modern stagecraft to form the centre of the revisionist research by hybrid academic-practitioners such as Rush Rehm in *The Play of Space* (1997), David Wiles in *Tragedy in Athens* (1997) and *Greek Theatre Performance* (2000), as well as Graham Ley in *The Theatricality of Greek Tragedy* (2007). The reassessment of the tragic chorus alongside new approaches to ancient *mousikê*,[5] and its performative rebirth in the twentieth century alongside modern dance, have attracted dance theorists and musicologists as the newest voices in this polyphonic discourse. The productions of modern practitioners such as Schechner, Suzuki, Pasolini, Woody Allen, Lars von Trier, Koun, Terzopoulos, Marmarinos, Grüber, Stein, Schleef, Castelluci and Mitchell, to name but a few, have made the multiple discourses of interculturalism, anthropology, film studies, gender studies and postmodern theatre relevant for reception studies on the chorus. Based on the frequency and intensity of multiple approaches to Greek drama, multidisciplinarity is a condition of analysis and a criterion of research particularly suited to understanding *why* classical Greek drama happened in fifth-century BCE Athens, and *why* we are still concerned about it now in the modern era. So why do we need to theorise it?

The call to theorise within the prevailing multidisciplinary context signals a critical research mass achieved through over a decade of robust cross-disciplinary archiving of historical materials, prolific publications, colloquia, conferences and electronic symposia. As we become 'self-aware and self-questioning',[6] are we detecting shifts in our multidisciplinary framework? The frequent reference to a 'turn' – as in experiential *turn*,[7] textual *turn* (Perris, this volume), performance *turn* (Wiles, this volume) – seems to address, if not an anxiety, at least a prognosis of shifts in the present state of reception. In our self-questioning mode, are we noting, as Julie Klein pointed out in her seminal work on interdisciplinary research during the 1990s, a strain in shared epistemological assumptions?[8] Furthermore, is reception theory undergoing a process of restructuring knowledge systems, or integrating and synthesising knowledge in new ways? Nick Lowe's analysis of the relationship between classical reception and performance included amongst the key questions it defined one that asked whether the reception bubble will eventually burst.[9] If present conditions are alerting us to an emerging theory, what are those conditions and what sort of theory might complement a post-multidisciplinary discussion of performance history and practice?

The history and meaning of interdisciplinarity are much too complicated to unwrap in a short essay. In the discourse of interdisciplinarity there is already a veritable twenty-first-century *Nachleben* of concerns about taxonomy, etymology, language, and legitimacy.[10] I offer Joe Moran's recent definition. Influenced by Barthes, Moran states that 'interdisciplinarity is always *transformative* in some way, producing new forms of knowledge in its engagement with discrete disciplines'.[11] I find Moran's definition appropriate because the discourse of the 'transformative', whether as theory *de jour* in performance reception (as Fischer-Lichte suggests in this volume), or as a descriptor of current expectations in the call to theorise (as I will argue below), has acquired a currency in the discussion of reception theory.

Moran further suggests that interdisciplinary activity creates undisciplined or ambiguous spaces that form at the interstices between fields of knowledge.[12] Over time, out of frequent and intense dialogue, new hybrid fields form out of these ambiguous fields. Outside reception theory there are examples such as *bioinformatics* which formed out of biology and information technology, *ethnomusicology* out of anthropology and musicology, *postdramatic theatre* out of poststructuralism and performance aesthetics, *evolutionary theory* from agricultural breeding programmes, geology and biology, and *interbehavioural psychology* which sprang from general systems thinking, naturalism and behavioural psychology. The parent field of classical reception studies, at various stages and junctures, related to cultural studies, literary criticism, theatre studies and classical philology. Over time, a common lexicon has gained descriptive and explanatory currency, so that metaphors or analogues such as *Zeitgeist, afterlife* (or 'Nachleben'), *energy, reception, diaspora,* or *transformation* and so forth create meanings that telescope from practice to critical theory and vice versa. Klein points out that 'the communicative competence needed for interdisciplinary work is inextricably bound up with problems of language'.[13] Crucially, the present call within reception to theorise may be an attempt for some in-house interrogation of these metaphorical or analogical accretions. Under the reception theory umbrella, do classicists and theatre practitioners understand *diaspora* or *energy* to a degree consistent with disciplinary procedures?

There are other processes to be observed at work during the interdisciplinary *turn*. One is that when disciplines (in dialogue) confront complex subjects, they can change, and change radically. Tradition-clad theories, conventional data-gathering, and strict protocols of validation come under stress within disciplines when encountering new data and phenomena. When this happens, binary postulates may collapse, convergence occurs in the form of new theories (or axioms), or a call goes out for the discipline's language to adapt to the new discourse. We have over the last century, and also quite recently, observed these changes to attitudes and to methods within specialist disciplines. I give three examples.

Modern-day physics constitutes a synthesis of, on the one hand, classical principles established in the Newtonian-Laplace era, and, on the other, new theories promulgated by Einstein and Heisenberg. Both positions collapsed in a paradoxical convergence: in theory, that an observer could not simultaneously measure the location and also the momentum of a subatomic particle. Subjective and objective experience, once distinguished in a Cartesian spatio-temporal field, were necessarily re-conceptualised as inseparable events. In order to render the subatomic world coherent and predictable, Heisenberg and Bohr formulated the new language of quantum physics.[14]

Music scholarship also experienced an interdisciplinary turn over the last twenty years. Musicologists and performers once naively asserted the authorial intentions of the composer based on the structure and function of the music score's main elements (melody, harmony and rhythm). Under the pervasive influence of modern critical theory, studies in historicism and performance practice research, musical analysis is now to the core an interdisciplinary enterprise, and may even appropriate the language of theatre to explain and describe the multivalent processes that occur inside and in between music and performance.[15]

In a manner analogous to shifts in the study of music, the revivification of classical scholarship correlated with an encounter of philological practice, literary criticism and the performance history and practice of Greek drama. Converging methods tested epistemological assumptions in classical studies and acknowledged new ways to *see* old knowledge. For Taplin, a convergence of hermeneutics and heuristics could help to answer such riddles as the dramaturgical but also historical construct of the place where Oedipus' roads meet in Daulis.[16] Jauss, in *Rezeptionsästhetik*, sensed that 'intersections' formulated between describing and examining an artwork created the point of meaningful reception between the reader/viewer and the text.[17] The authorial voice of the text had no context on its own. One of the fortunes of revived scholarship is the shared skills and protocols of research which has opened up coherent and formal dialogue between theatre performance and Classics, and also created hybridised academic and practical research.

In the rest of the chapter, I briefly identify symptoms of interdisciplinarity which indicate a prominent binary formulation (e.g. Martindale opposite Hall/Macintosh/Goldhill) in the multidisciplinary framework. Alongside binary formulations are calls toward convergence (e.g. Wiles and Griffiths). In other cases, an interdisciplinary voice may promote a closer or systematic integration of complementing disciplines which leads to reconceptualisation of theory and terminology. I include Hardwick and Budelmann in this category. I have chosen these theorists not because they represent mainstream interdisciplinarity. Rather, they implicitly problematise the present mode of multidisciplinary scholarship and describe transitional phases ahead in the way we define, research and discuss performance history and practice of ancient Greek drama. Whether these phases lead to a more 'joined up way of thinking' (Easterling), or a Classics 'truly of the future' (Martindale), remains to be seen.

7. *From* à la carte *to Convergence*

A bifurcation in classical reception theory ambulates about the 'point' of reception. In the Martindale camp, an epistemological relationship is 'simultaneously constitutive of both' reader and text, the point of meaning being a cognitive event during which the 'text comes alive as the consciousness of the reader'.[18] There are distinctive or essential qualities that are actualised at that conscious point, and Batstone amplifies modern linguistic theory in the exposition of this reader-text axis. The act of reception incorporates a sliding scale between past-/present-/future- (im)perfect tenses. The transferred meanings embodied between text and reader are identified as having aesthetic properties, and the shared experience of these properties transfers diachronically through history, becoming localised in specific cultural arenas through skills-based methods in disciplines like Classics. If the 'Love that moves the sun and other stars' (Martindale) is experienced in literature as the primary aesthetic point of reception, intellectual relativism and historical materialism can but be secondary coefficients in the making of that point.

For the cultural/historical faction (which among others include Hall, Macintosh and Goldhill), the aesthetic 'point' of Martindale and his allies telescopes out to the interconnected fields of aesthetics, ethics, psychology, culture and socio-politics. Diachronic and synchronic paths are generated from moral and intellectual history. For Macintosh, Freud and the nineteenth-century star system of the French theatre constitute a significant meeting point for cultural reception in the case of Sophocles' *Oedipus Tyrannus* before the First World War. The intellectual links continue into the latter half of the twentieth century where Berkoff's methods (with Freudian overtones) meld with French philosophy and drama (Artaud, Barrault and Lecoq) to produce his East End *Oedipus,* entitled *Greek.*[19] The relentlessly driven lyric iambics, anapaests and Ionics *a minore* in the choral text of Aeschylus' *Persians*, which underscore universal woe in times of war, may be the reason for its enduring aesthetic appeal in modern times. But according to Hall, pervasive remodernisations of this ancient Greek drama, especially during the westerner's late twentieth and early twenty-first-century experience of war against Muslim countries, and especially of terrorism, diachronically telescopes from the 'Greek's struggle against Achaemenid Persia [to] the Christian West's adversarial relationship with Islam'.[20] Goldhill generally contends that to understand the point of reception – and to a larger extent 'why we need Classics' – one ought to know the intellectual and cultural provenance that makes us receptive to the Classics in the first place.[21]

Having briefly described the bifurcation in reception theory, I now ask whether there is scope for interdisciplinary transformation; that is, are new forms of knowledge about to emerge through critical engagement with discrete disciplines? A kind of détente has come about with both camps acknowledging the complexity of text, and seeking to avoid the complacent prejudices and self-ignorance of the past. But is such a détente a condition for interdisciplinarity? The future, perhaps, will disclose not so much a convergence but an *emergence* of sub-units of reception theory. With Martindale and his allies, it may turn out to be the case that the experiential 'point' of reception, through repeated experiences and transfers, accrues increasingly localised and exclusionary knowledge; note the call for Classics to have once more 'a *leading* role among the humanities'.[22] For Goldhill's camp, an increasingly multicultural and multidisciplinary society of reception (or as the sociologist Jerome Bindé puts it, 'knowledge society') may result in heavier trafficking in appropriated metaphors. Marilyn Strathern, an interdisciplinarian theorist from sociology, may well ask of performance reception whether it is enough simply to provide the multidisciplinary space and allow terms to transfer from one discipline to another 'as metaphor, *façon de parler*'.[23] If the multidisciplinary scholarship of reception theory is modulating into an interdisciplinary study, it may also take place in the 'undisciplined or ambiguous spaces' between theatre practice and formal analysis. For some theorists, the condition of liminality between scholarship and performance is central to convergence.

Two publications, one a book by Wiles (2007) on the tragic mask, the other an article by Griffiths (2007) on tensions between practice and theory in reception scholarship, discuss the binary paradigms within research of Greek drama from Classics and Theatre Studies and make calls for convergence. For Wiles, the mask constitutes a major focal point for binarist constructions of the modern self which contribute to a misapprehension in theatre performance of the ancient mask as an artefact of concealment rather than as an agency of revelation. The book's final chapters evidence the influence of anthropology on Wiles' thinking. The ancient mask requires transforming conventional reference points from our culture, which is rooted in a monotheistic value-system, to one that peers from behind a polytheistic framework, such as the Dionysian world of the fifth-century BCE Attic tragedians. Refracting simultaneously both multifaceted modernity and polytheistic antiquity, the tragic mask, in scholarly and practice-based activities, challenges us, as Wiles does, to go in search of a language that can articulate a nexus of experiences. How one might quantify and qualify the ephemeral *affect* of theatrical performance has relevance to Classics and performance reception equally. This relationship prompts Griffiths' recent survey of methodologies (2007). Her conclusion is that performance is a polyvalent subject-matter which shapes the research and methods of performance reception; performance analysis, theatre history and literary criticism are drawn together in versatile and open-ended ways. Classical reception is also conversant with these networks of critical analysis. The confrontation is enacted elsewhere, in the 'spaces' between first- and third-person scholarship – the 'emancipatory episteme of the subjective voice and the formalist attitude that favours the objectivist detachment of third-person scholarship'.[24] For Griffiths, the polarisation need not exist. Fastidious objectivity based on a closed system of traditional methods, and experiential insight grounded on the open system of the performance event, together offer the multiple frames of reference operating in the field. Both Wiles and Griffiths call for a workable vocabulary, or re-conceptualisation, that can negotiate terminology without incurring the wrath of scholars and/or practitioners. To that end, Hardwick and Budelmann offer possibilities.

Lorna Hardwick pursues a systematic theory of reception influenced by hermeneutics in literary, cultural and post-colonial theory. Her use of terminology, with no specific hierarchy of definitions, such as 'acculturation', 'foreignisation', 'transplant', etc., informs modes of perception, interpretation and legitimisation in the reception of tragedy.[25] 'Diaspora', in its post-colonial resonances, has proved a fertile linguistic model for Hardwick, so that discussions of Athol Fugard's *The Island* or Fémi Òsòfisan's *Women of Owu* can cope with dialogic relationships (or map 'collisions') between multilingual and intracultural theatre. The term 'diaspora' displaces the way metanarratives of reception may exert notions of progress and enlightenment in the reception of classical literature. As an interdisciplinary tool, the 'diaspora' model can create spaces 'for the remapping and reevaluation of the theory and practice of Greek drama', in both its past and future life.[26]

Modern cognitive science(s) constitute an interdisciplinary field of study and Budelmann argues in this volume that this can help us think about reception studies in terms of theory. Cognitive science has undergone a re-conceptualised understanding of binary opposites such as the Cartesian duality of mind and body, the ontological divide between objectivity and subjectivity, and the nature via/versus nurture debate. The hypothetical convergence of science of the mind and of classical philology offers a fresh perspective on cultural, gender-based or socio-political constructs. In Budelmann's view, classical Greek drama may have developed elements of a counter-text, or metanarrative, concurrently with the knowledge and experience of ancient medicine. Modern audiences feel, imagine or commiserate with the pain of the tragic protagonists – the pus-swollen foot of Philoctetes, the bleeding orbs of Oedipus, or the agonies of Hercules, writhing in his toxic robe – because they too have experienced related symptoms and pathologies. While not arguing explicitly for interdisciplinarity, Budelmann acknowledges that the paradigm of binary convergence in science is reflected in synchronic (concerning performance) and diachronic (concerning reception) aspects of our own theorising. Performance yields the experiential turn, while reception reveals the propensities of the human mind that use multiple strategies in order to explain and describe trans-historical processes at work.

In an age of increasing proliferation and extinction of hybrid disciplines, the main attraction of interdisciplinary scholarship is its potential to cause traditional disciplines, such as Classics, to reflect upon and to question their own methods, epistemology and analytical tools. Multivalent scholarship also solves or explains complex problems that single disciplines on their own cannot. Self-questioning, in view of the uses and abuses of reception, has led to valuable critical analysis. But as a method in its own right, interdisciplinarity has had to face its own demons, as well. One problem with calling research 'interdisciplinary' is that there is nothing intrinsically unique about interdisciplinary scholarship that is not already a characteristic of disciplinary work. Disciplines routinely debate 'ambiguous' cognitive spaces, renegotiate terminology, and reach critical research mass, all of which may result in the creation of sub-disciplines. Also, interdisciplinary fields set up a space for comparative modes of research, preserving a state of criticality among disciplines as the process toward institutional success or legitimacy.[27] Each discipline keeps its research house in order in much the same manner.

Another important problem concerns the far-reaching eclecticism in interdisciplinary work, which requires extensive reading and authoritative conversation with several fields. The resulting research cannot be so easily distilled into neat expositions, and this factor inevitably encourages what at times are short-handed if not superficial explanations. That is, it can result in less vertical and more overarching analysis. One of Nick Lowe's questions is whether classicists can be 'masters of other professional disciplines'. This question can as appropriately be asked of interdisciplinarians who grapple with multiple points of reception. When attempting to understand the current debates, theories, and lexica of various disciplines, an arithmetical gradient of research easily turns into an exponential trajectory. In current reception publications, uneven conversance with a specialist language (in a discipline such as music, for instance) inevitably results in uneven brush strokes. I highlight briefly two examples.

The stated aim of the distinguished performance reception scholar Marianne McDonald, in *The Living Art of Greek Tragedy*, is a 'balanced overview, adequately covering both performance, or text, or textual analysis'. This panoramic approach to music entails, however, rather sketchy sound bytes; in the account of Stravinsky's *Oedipus Rex*, for example, Oedipus' passages are simply described as 'whining' and Jocasta's arias as 'regal'.[28] McDonald's interpretation of the music and the chorus also seems slanted towards a quasi-ritualistic reading, which does not include a discussion of the neoclassical discourse that is so central to musicological and theatrical influences in Stravinsky's interwar years. Peter Brown, in his chapter on opera, in *Dionysus since 69,* admittedly treats the materials as a reference list.[29] Yet without reference to influential schools of composition (e.g. the Second Viennese School immigration to the United States; the Boulanger-Messiaen influence in Europe; the formation of the Columbia-Princeton Electronic Centre and its counterpart in Paris), or perhaps to science and aesthetics (e.g. stochastic theory and extensions of serialism), his 'list' short-changes the intellectual provenance which shaped the idiosyncratic reception of Greek drama in the works of representative composers such as Iannis Xenakis, Luigi Nono, Harrison Birtwistle and Jacob Druckman.

If *à la carte* theory transforms into interdisciplinarity, the process is valuable as long as the merging disciplines remain internally rigorous and productive.[30] This means that balance of vertical analysis and horizontal exposition in scholarship will have to find some means of being adjudged rigorous, citeable and valuable to an academic discipline. A paradox nonetheless remains for a possible interdisciplinary turn in reception theory, one raised by Stanley Fish, a critic of interdisciplinary research. In moving toward a theory, will the intrinsically multidisciplinary scholarship of performance reception be negated by the kind of 'routinisation or institutionalisation' that characterises the normative voice of traditional disciplines?[31] Turning reception theory into a discipline, interdisciplinary or not, may annul its unique attribute – its receptivity toward many points of view.

Notes

1. During the Enlightenment, Vico warned against the excesses of specialist knowledge and appealed on behalf of a broad educational curriculum. Nineteenth-century German idealism represented the will to synthesise knowledge in the arts and sciences. In the twentieth century, the post-structural thinkers paved the way for diachronic analysis among disciplines.

2. Hall, Macintosh and Wrigley 2004: 4.

3. Kristeva: 'If language is a dynamic process then the subject is a dynamic process' (2002: xviii).

4. Webster 1970; Gardiner 1987; Scott 1984. Examples of this research resonated with the works of notable classicists such as Oliver Taplin. for whom 'Greek tragedy is a structure of parts' (1977: 50). Taplin himself was paying tribute to the post-Second World War formalistic thinking of H.D.F. Kitto's *Form and Meaning in Drama* (1956) and John Gassner's *Form and Idea in Modern Theatre* (1956). Since then, Taplin, Hall and others have been instrumental in creating a higher tolerance among Classicists of theatre practitioners, and *vice versa*.

5. *Mousikê*: a wide network of traditional and innovative performance practices regarding song and dance in ancient Greece (Murray and Wilson 2004).

6. Goldhill 1994: 553.

7. Griffiths 2007.

8. Klein 1990, 1996.

9. Lowe's aptly titled 'Oedipus at the Crossroads' was the keynote lecture to the reception 'faithful' distilling the current state of research in classical reception theory, at the recent *Current Debates in Classical Reception* Conference (Open University), 18-20 May 2007. His lecture was built around ten questions including whether 'practice had outpaced theory' and whether the 'performance tail was wagging the reception dog'.

10. Marilyn Strathern gives an overview of recent debates in interdisciplinary practices to be found in the human sciences in 'Interdisciplinarity: Some Models from the Human Sciences', *Interdisciplinary Science Reviews* 32.2 (June 2007): 123-34. For historicism and foundational principles, see Klein (1990 and 1996). For

supporters and sceptics, see multiple contributions in Carlo Ginzburg, James D. Herbert, W.J.T. Mitchell et al., 'Inter/disciplinarity: a range of critical perspectives', *The Art Bulletin,* vol. 77, no. 4 (1995), 534-52, and the multi-authored work 'Defining Interdisciplinarity', by Timothy R. Austin, Alan Rauch, Herbert Blau et al., in *Publications of the Modern Language Association of America,* vol. 111, no. 2 (1996), 271-82. Sociologists such as Grix, Nicolescu, Gibbons, Bindé, Fish and Strathern have all added to current interdisciplinary discourse. A recent university conference (Birkbeck, University of London) hosted discussions on crossing disciplinary boundaries that interrogated the 'naivety' in interdisciplinary rhetoric: http://www.bbk.ac.uk/crs/news/interdisconf (accessed 01.08.08).

11. Moran 2002: 16 (my italics). See also Weiss and Wodak 2003. Moran draws his influence from Barthes and the notion that fields of knowledge are never stable or constant, but fluctuating.

12. Moran 2002: 15.

13. Klein 1996: 217.

14. See Cropper 1970.

15. For music and interdisciplinarity see Kramer 2007: 41-51. For appropriation of theatre models, see Whittall (2003) who uses the Apollo-Dionysus dichotomy; Cross (1998) for Peter Brook's four kinds of theatre: Deadly, Holy, Rough and Immediate.

16. Taplin 1989: 11.

17. Jauss 1982.

18. Batstone 2006: 17.

19. Macintosh 2004: 315, 318-19.

20. Hall 2007: 13.

21. Goldhill 2002.

22. Martindale 2006: 13 (my italics).

23. Strathern 2004: 36.

24. Griffiths 2007: 75.

25. Hardwick 2003: 7-8.

26. Hardwick 2006: 204-5.

27. Klein's seminal work *Crossing Boundaries* (1996) specifies 'institutional success' and 'critical interdisciplinarity' as prerequisites of interdisciplinarity.

28. McDonald 2003b: 67.

29. Brown 2004: 285. A forthcoming book, *Ancient Drama and Modern Opera,* (ed. Peter Brown), may expand on these aesthetic issues in music.

30. Or as Strathern advises, 'interdisciplinarity works as rhetorical evidence for disciplinary success'. See Strathern 2004: 80. Strathern's background in sociology accounts for notions of 'flow' and ownership in her understanding of knowledge.

31. Klein 1996: 170-1.

8

Archiving Events, Performing Documents: On the Seductions and Challenges of Performance Archives

Pantelis Michelakis

'What – if anything – can one learn about performance through archiving performance?' asks Linda Cassens Stoian in a recent issue of *Theatre Research* devoted to archives and archiving.[1] And she continues: 'Theatre has its script, dance its Laban notation, music its score, while the documents of performance lack the ability to gather, represent and thereby conserve the genre's own quintessence.' The notion that performance is an event, rather than an object, which vanishes as it unfolds, is a persistent theme in performance criticism. Archiving performances, the argument goes, is different from archiving other artworks in that performances cannot be placed in the documentary archive directly in the way that paintings, manuscripts or film prints can. The transience of performance has found some of its strongest supporters among those who believe in its transformative potential and political power: unlike other art forms, performance challenges the object-status often attributed to artworks, resisting its full subjection to the principles of a culture of commodities. An obvious objection to the notion that performance vanishes is that it is in conflict with the empirical realities of its often powerful and life-changing impact on the world of the spectators. How else can we explain the cultural distrust of mimesis, and more specifically the anti-theatrical bias which has accompanied stage performance for most of its history in Western culture?[2] And why theatre censorship has such a long history and why even after its abolition the regulation of live performance remains an issue today?[3]

As Rebecca Schneider has argued in an influential article entitled 'Performance Remains',[4] the problem with the argument about the transience of performance is that it casts performance in a role which, while emphasising its uniqueness, also underscores its loss and disappearance: performance cannot be what it is without ceasing to exist. By not giving in, at its own cost, to the logic of a culture that values the production, circulation and collection of objects, performance ends up delimiting itself and therefore facilitating what it purports to disrupt.[5] 'Disappearance is not antithetical to remains', argues Schneider, but a condition of them.[6] Death results 'in the paradoxical production of both disappearance and

95

remains'.[7] The issue, therefore, is not whether the polarity between the disappearance of performance and its remaining can be transcended but *how* its remains, both material and immaterial, can do justice to what is lost without belittling its status and significance.

Conventional notions of the archive have always held a strong appeal for the theatre historian. Views of the archive as a sheltered, protecting space where written documents and other artefacts are collected and saved from destruction or oblivion are deeply embedded in historiographical practices and discourses. Holding the promise of the return to a past which can be reconstructed and recovered, such views of the archive are associated with the attribution to its contents of the authority of documentary sources and of the aura that Walter Benjamin has associated with the cultural value and limited accessibility of traditional artworks.[8] A widespread interest in the workings of the archive in recent years has both expanded and complicated this picture. Jacques Derrida's *Archive Fever* (1996) has shown how archives are characterised by a double impulse to totalise and to destroy: processes of descriptive and encyclopaedic collection and keeping are inevitably implicated in mechanisms of control and regulation as well as of random exclusion, fragmentation and distortion. Michel Foucault's *Archaeology of Knowledge* (1976) has defined the archive in more abstract terms, as a dematerialised, discursive domain: 'not as the repository of shared knowledge, but as a "general system of the formation and transformation of statements" of a culture'.[9] As a site for the production rather than preservation of knowledge, the archive resembles a performance event: rather than storing information, it makes the acts of reading, writing, and remembering appear and disappear. At the same time, the performance event can be seen as a form of discursive archiving, creating as it does a space for the reflection, development, and articulation of social expression.[10] This essay engages with the notion that the archive can provide a productive framework for thinking about performance, and that performance itself can help to investigate the workings of the archive. To substantiate this claim I will draw on a set of examples which include theatrical ephemera, stage props, play-scripts, and theatrical anecdotes. Exploring the performative nature of documents and the documentary value of performance raises a range of issues which include the complexities of witnessing, the paradoxical workings of censorship, the blurring of the distinction between commodity value and symbolic value, and the status of cultural detritus on the theatrical stage.

Theatre posters are among the most common and prominent artefacts in theatre archives. Instead of wordy descriptions, pictorial posters communicate essential information in ways that captivate the attention of the viewer. For instance, the poster of Katie Mitchell's production of Aeschylus' *Oresteia* for the National Theatre, performed in London in 1999-2000, touches upon a series of issues thematic to the production and the trilogy (see Fig. 1). It does not simply establish the identity of the spectacle

Fig. 1. Poster for the production of the *Oresteia* by the Royal National Theatre, London, directed by Katie Mitchell, 1999-2000. Designed by Michael Mayhew, photograph by Ivan Kyncl. Reproduced by kind permission of the Royal National Theatre Archive.

through the details of its title, playwright, translator and production company. The young girl's dress on the wet sand conjures up associations of absence and lost innocence. It engages with the sacrifice of Iphigenia in the background of the trilogy and with Aeschylus' 'motif of cloth and clothing and the weaving of fabrics',[11] thus preparing for their prominence in the production. The sense of loss conveyed by the poster was articulated in the production through Iphigenia's introduction as a ghost-like figure hovering over the action. The dress itself was linked to two significant moments in the production: the carpet scene in which Agamemnon treads on a cloth which 'is made up of dozens and dozens of little girls' dresses' and the scene of the display of his slain body, where the dress of the poster is 'draped over the edge of the bath in which Agamemnon lay dead'.[12] Another feature of the poster that prepares for the production and its interpretation of the *Oresteia* is the typeface which is used for the title, which imitates the font of an old manual typewriter. Like the young girl's dress, this aspect of the poster returns in the production when one of the war veterans of the Chorus of the *Agamemnon* records the onstage events with the help of a typewriter on a little tray by his wheelchair. Lest the links between the poster and the production do not receive their due attention, the programme features on its cover the picture of the poster and on the inside the typewriter typeface which accompanies pictures of other 'items of clothing tagged and bagged like evidence at a murder trial'.[13]

The question I want to address here is not how a performance event can possibly be thought of as vanishing when it leaves behind such material traces. Nor how a sheet of printed paper, whose primary function is to be used for publicity purposes, transcends its ephemerality, and outlives the theatrical spectacle for which it was produced. The question I want to ask is at once more specific and more paradoxical: how can a poster be the trace of an event that does not take place for weeks, if not months, after its production and circulation?[14] The poster of Mitchell's *Oresteia* draws on witnessing material and techniques and thematises the issues of evidence and testimony. The black-and-white photograph and the typewriter lettering have a documentary quality which invites the spectator to think of the production as evidence for a murder trial. The education work-pack of the production underscores the historical grounding and overtones of this interpretation: 'At the time of the production, the Bosnian/Kosovan conflict was at full throttle. The civil war nature of the conflict, as well as its geographical relationship to the *Oresteia*, influenced the production.'[15] As well as conveying a sense of documentary objectivity and authority, the greyscale print of the picture and the typewriter lettering perform another function: they 'constitute … a nostalgic act which attempts to bypass the perceived virtuality of the postmodern condition'[16] and promise the return to a 'more embodied, physical past era different from our own'.[17] Absence is embedded not only in the emptiness of the little girl's dress but also in the aesthetic strategies of the poster's graphic design. The poster promises that the production, like the war veterans-turned-witnesses of the Chorus of the *Agamemnon,* will provide access to what has been lost. This is tied in with conventional notions of the archive and with its drive to recon- struct the past and to reveal its hidden truths. But it also points in the direction of the archive as a murder trial. Can theatre provide evidence for – or act as – witness to history and its crisis? Can Aeschylus' trilogy be seen as testimony for familial and communal violence brought about by the historical collapse of social order in the Balkans of the 1990s? If the poster invites us to think of the production of the *Oresteia* in a legal or courtroom context, this has implications for the poster itself. The historical value of the poster, like the historical value of Mitchell's production and Aeschylus' trilogy, is not only cognitive but also performative. What the poster provides is not evidence, but a crisis of evidence which awaits a verdict to be resolved. The poster is not a survivor of the performance event – it does not provide an account of it based on first-hand experience. Rather, it is mediated in a way that blurs the distinction between testi- mony and representation. Its relation to the event of the performance is only tenuous, and its effectiveness is contingent upon its participation in the courtroom drama of interpretation. Theatre historians who want to explore the mediated and performative nature of the traces that the theatrical event leaves behind have much to gain from the extensive theoretical work on the relation between mimetic representation, witness- ing and testimony.[18]

My next example comes from a silent film entitled *The Legend of Oedipus.* The film is now lost, and its documentation through the processes of publicity and censorship raises historiographical questions not dissimi- lar to those of a theatrical performance. The film was made in France in 1912 by Gaston Roudès, and it was released in several countries in Europe and North America.[19] One of the most valuable pieces of information we have about the film comes from the censorship records of Germany. The censorship entry for the film is brief but illuminating. No less than six scenes had to be cut for the film to gain permission for screening: Oedipus' killing of his father, his killing of the Sphinx, his cutting off of her head, his display of the severed head in Thebes, Oedipus' discovery of Jocasta's hanging body, and Oedipus' blinding of himself.[20] The temptation to recon- struct the narrative of the film from the scenes that were censored is difficult to resist. However none of these scenes were part of the film as it was screened. They may have left some traces in the film's censored version but they were not part of its narrative. The reason that we are aware of their existence is precisely because of the documentation of their exclusion from the film by the system of censorship. The paradox of this process of regulation and repression is twofold. On the one hand it records loss, and provides insights into the moral and ideological preoccupations which justify the truncation of the narrative body of the film. On the other hand, the 'waste' this process produces outlives any other aspect of its

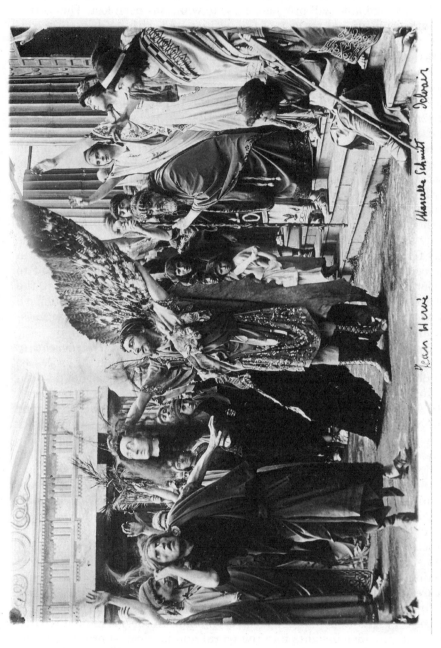

Fig. 2. Oedipus (Jean Hervé) displays the head of the Sphinx to the Thebans in *The Legend of Oedipus*, directed by Gaston Roudès, France 1912. Reproduced by kind permission of Bibliothèque Nationale de France.

contribution to the making, or the undoing, of the film. Without the destruction brought about by censorship, our understanding of the film would have been much more limited than it currently is. By granting incomplete but unconditional access to what the original audience of the film was forbidden to see, the censorship records enact the simultaneous destruction and preservation that Derrida identifies as distinctive of the experience of archivisation.

One of the few surviving production stills of the film sheds light on what made such scenes disturbing. Oedipus arrives at Thebes and displays the head and skin of the Sphinx to the people of the city (see Fig. 2). The right-hand side of the composition is dominated by a triumphant Oedipus framed by jubilant Thebans. The left-hand side is occupied by the head of the Sphinx and a spectator who stares at it transfixed. The distortion of his head and his bodily posture do not simply reflect his horror but embody and re-enact the violence inflicted on the Sphinx. The performative em-bodiment of emotions by the spectator is precisely what critics of representational art from Plato to the German censors of the film have adduced as evidence for its communicative power, for its corruptive poten-tial, and for the need to control and regulate it. The still, however, was in all likelihood part of the publicity strategy of the company that produced the film. It sought to reinvent Oedipus as an invulnerable hero of popular fiction and to situate the film within the generic parameters of a cinema of action and special effects.[21] Within this framework of film promotion, stimuli of shock and surprise were not to be avoided but actively pursued, even at the expense of the narrative development of the film. Publicity may have a different agenda from censorship, but it is equally dependent on a process of archivisation which regulates what the spectator sees: if censor-ship limits what can be seen, publicity promises more than the film actually delivers. As a still frame, the picture can be seen as standing for the larger narrative of the scene from which it comes. At the same time it can be seen as being severed from that larger context. The still is like the head of the Sphinx: it can be used for display, as proof for the body of a film that is no longer in existence, and as basis for speculation over what the missing body of the film might have looked like. Or it can be used to reflect on the violence of the process through which such evidence has been produced: for the still image to be available as proof, it had to be detached from a narrative of moving images or shot independently from the film, with the help of a photographic camera. To say that the difference between still and moving images is only quantitative and that the former stands for the latter is to ignore the profound gap that separates cinema and photo-graphy, movement and stillness, life and the death.[22]

Derrida has projected onto the etymological origin of the word 'archive' his own preoccupation with the power of the law, associating the Greek 'archeion' with 'the residence of the superior magistrates, the archons, those who command'.[23] Historians who have studied the emergence of record-keeping in classical Athens have exposed a different archive, where written records were recorded on non-permanent materials such as papyrus or wooden tablets rather than stone or bronze, they served as copies rather than originals, and to a great extent they depended on their oral transmission.[24] Greek theatre confronts us with aspects of an archival logic which are different from but no less important than the ways in which early twentieth-century cinema or late twentieth-century theatre are characterised by the contradictory drives of preservation and destruction.

The protagonist of Sophocles' *Ajax*, frustrated by his failure to win Achilles' weapons and humiliated by a fit of madness which makes him take his revenge on a herd of animals instead of the leaders of the army, cannot be reintegrated into the society of the Greek army while he is alive. Ajax plays out the logic of entering the discursive archive of his culture at the cost of his own life. In casting his death as an act of resistance and revenge, he inflicts on his own body a fatal wound that bears all the hallmarks of archival violence. Putting things in the archive of Sophocles' theatre has physical, bodily implications for those involved. It turns Ajax's body into a repository of value which literally contains Hector's sword, but at the same time it scars it and reduces it to an object. Ajax becomes himself through his self-annihilation. He defines who he is and fixes his identity through his disappearance. In this he enacts the language of disappearance of performance, with its political promise and simultaneous submission to the laws of the archive. If the protagonist of the play defines the process of archivisation in conventional terms, as a process of hiding or sheltering, this hiding is far from simple or straightforward. In Ajax's deception speech, Hector's sword is presented as no longer threatening and harmful. Its concealment in an 'untrodden place' deep in the earth, out of human sight (657-9), is similarly presented as a ritual practice of appeasement and atonement.[25] With Ajax's suicide, however, it becomes clear that the Trojan earth 'in which he fastens his sword is as hostile to him as ever' (819, 1208-9),[26] that the sword is still dangerous and that its disposal is far from harmless. The objects which enter modern archives or museums acquire symbolic value at the expense of their use value. To become archival objects, they trade one kind of value for the other. Unlike modern archival objects, the symbolic objects of the Sophoclean stage do not lose their use value. In Sophocles' text, the sword is not objectified and decontextualised as a result of entering the archive. On the contrary it is endowed with the agency of an actor. Ajax calls the sword 'the slayer' (815), and attributes to it a leading role in a macabre performance which results in his suicide.[27] The sword is not a randomly chosen sharp weapon but a weapon whose history as a gift from his now dead enemy comes back with revenge. The ironies of Ajax's cryptic language become the dangers of the archive: Hector remains a deadly enemy after his death, and Ajax's body does not stop being problematic and divisive until several hundred lines after Ajax's suicide.

102

In the ancient reception of Sophocles' *Ajax*, the tag 'slayer' is attributed not only to the sword of the protagonist but also to Timotheus of Zacynthus, whose convincing re-enactment of Ajax's suicide won him his reputation as an actor. The anecdotal evidence for Timotheos the Slayer can be found in an ancient comment on line 846 of Aeschylus' *Ajax*: 'The audience must believe that he falls on his sword, and the actor must be strongly built so as to make them imagine Ajax, as is said of Timotheus of Zacynthus, who so captivated and enthralled the spectators with his acting that they called him Sphageus [the Slayer].'[28] The passage has often been interpreted as evidence of the sensationalism of the Hellenistic stage, but recently it has been recuperated as evidence of the growing sophistication of professional acting,[29] and as an example of an increasingly realistic method of tragic performance.[30] In the context of archive violence, the anecdote can be read in a different manner. It marks the transition from the agency of the sword to the agency of the actor, from an archive of objects (stage props) to an archive of embodied practices (performance techniques), and from the authoritative repository that is Sophocles' text to the repository of heterogeneous and unauthenticated anecdotes that constitute the ancient comments in the margin of his text. Ajax is killed not only by a sword with important history but also by an actor with the appropriate mimetic skills. The fixity of identity and the preservation of archival objects of Derrida's archive give way to the performative repetition and body-to-body transmission of Foucault's discursive archive. However there are also continuities between them. Sophocles' archive of stage props is no less performative and animated than Timotheus' archive of bodily postures perfecting the art of falling upon a sword. Conversely, the fixity of identity pursued by Ajax beyond his death and into the cultural archive of Sophocles' theatre, is also pursued by Timotheus into the textual margins of Sophocles' manuscripts.

If Sophocles' *Ajax* provides insights into the complex relation between archives of objects and archives of performance practices, the play by the German playwright Heiner Müller entitled *Despoiled Shore Medeamaterial Landscape with Argonauts* (1981) enables us to look at the relation between performance and the archive as detritus.[31] Müller's play takes place in a polluted wasteland littered with garbage, debris, human fluids and limbs. As the playwright puts it in his introductory note, the gruesome and realistic imagery of his text 'presupposes the catastrophes which mankind is working toward'. At the same time, the text is noticeably non-prescriptive as to how it will be staged. Müller writes that *Medeamaterial* can be shown in 'a mud-filled swimming pool in Beverly Hills or the bathing facility of a nerve-clinic', and directors of his work have responded to his challenge with a wide range of stage configurations. Now, archives and landfills are usually seen as occupying opposite ends on the spectrum of attitudes towards things past. Archives are sites where remains of the past are organised and preserved, whereas land-

103

fills are sites where remains of the past are mounted up and left to decay. Assman speaks of 'a reverse affinity' between archives and rubbish dumps: 'archives and rubbish are not merely linked by figurative analogy but also by a common boundary, which can be transgressed by objects in both directions. Objects that are not confined to archives end up on the rubbish dump, and objects occasionally cast out of archives, due to shortage of space, likewise end up there.'[32] Assman draws on Krzysztof Pomian who argues that 'the sequence "object – waste product – object of symbolic value" applies to most objects "which constitute the repository of our cultural legacy"'.[33] As discussed above, Sophocles' text uses Hector's sword to resist the neatness of this sequence from use value to symbolic value. Heiner Müller's work on Medea, on the other hand, looks at landfills not as a transient phase in the life cycle of material objects destined for the archive but as a metaphor for their whole trajectory. If the archive is conventionally seen in terms of an edifice where each single object is protected and classified under the benevolent gaze of the archon, Müller turns it into an alternative archive, a post-apocalyptic or 'dis-pastoral'[34] space without boundaries, a detritus of the modern consumer culture. Instead of the totalising tendency and the promise of order and control of the conventional archive, Müller presents the reader and the spectator with an archive which consists of cross-cultural images and texts of Western history from its origins to nuclear destruction[35] and which resists easy categorisations and frustrates 'attempts at "analytical and rational understanding"'.[36] Müller's work revisits not only what is monumental and therefore worth archiving but also what has been disposed of, what has been rejected as redundant, fragmented, degraded, and what has survived by accident. This alternative conception of the archive as mélange, which can be found in surrealism, in the arts of collage and pastiche, and in the historiographical turn in cultural studies, enables Müller to turn the character of Medea and Greek tragedy and myth into the liminal space of a despoiled shore.

Like other modern playwrights and directors, Müller uses as organising principle for his work not the plot or the characters but the frame provided by the theatrical setting (inverting Aristotle's hierarchy of tragedy's qualitative parts).[37] The language itself of the text reflects the setting: it becomes a collection of disconnected words, cries, narrations, and dialogues piled up one after the other without apparent order and without punctuation, re-enacting at the level of the verbal structure the destruction thematised in its subject matter. Müller's text provides a grotesque account of a culture of consumerism, with the end result of the production process being obliteration rather than valuable commodities. He does not simply invert the process of labour as outlined by Karl Marx in the first volume of his *Capital*.[38] He also collapses the differences between commodity value and symbolic value, subjecting Greek tragedy and the dramatic character of Medea to the uses and abuses of objects in the marketplace of commodities.

Opting for the story of the Argonauts, a foundation myth of Western imperialism, Müller uses the despoiled shore as the point for the violent encounter between classical theatre and the origins of modern colonialism: 'European history began with colonisation' as Müller puts it.[39] The play performs on the body of classical myth and drama the violence that the history of colonisation performs on the colonised body of Medea. The title *Medeamaterial* shows how the protagonist herself loses her individual character to become raw material. However, as a newly-coined compound, the title also suggests that this process of destruction and dispersal into the theatrical landscape is inseparable from the theatre's creative imagination. It is a process of violent objectification which nevertheless results in a collage composition open to various performative possibilities rather than in an item for safe storage in the archive. 'Medea is not a character, but the sum effect of the discourses, images and screams distributed across the text. For Müller, this abstraction of the woman's body or subjecthood has been accomplished not by the playwright, but by the appropriative historical and political practices that he stages through his representation of this originary myth.'[40] By the end of *Medeamaterial*, Medea who could previously speak of herself only as the 'slave', 'tool', 'bitch', 'whore' owned by Jason, reclaims the identity of 'the barbarian'. As the avenging angel of history (in a new take on Walter Benjamin's allegorical figure of redemption[41]), she kills her children with 'the newfound power and violence of the non-European, the barbarian, the Third World'.[42]

Harriet Bradley speaks of the 'intoxication of the archive'[43] and Helen Freshwater of the '"allure of the archive" as in part voyeuristic pleasure and in part the sense of accessing authentic material'.[44] Müller's *Despoiled Shore Medeamaterial Landscape with Argonauts* presents theatre as an archive in decay. Müller does not define decay as a central part of the nutrient cycle of life, as modernist poets often do.[45] The detritus of the stage is presented as a symptom of the decay and impoverishment of the world of the spectators rather than as an antidote to it. The contamination of the mythical archive and the theatrical canon by the cultural and historical archive is not far away from Derrida's concept of 'archive fever' or Antonin Artaud's comparison of the theatre to the plague.[46] There is of course no straightforward correlation between Derrida's archival contradictions of the impulsive and destructive desire of origins and Artaud's plague-like symptoms of the theatre whose crisis is 'resolved either by death or cure'.[47] But both of them, like Müller, focus on mechanisms for the transmission of knowledge centred around the materiality of bodily contact, often unwilling and violent (compare the violent deaths of Iphigenia, the Sphinx and Ajax), and on channels of physical communication which cannot be controlled or contained (Iphigenia's return as a ghost in Mitchell's production, horror in *The Legend of Oedipus*, madness in Sophocles' *Ajax*). A more comprehensive discussion of the archive and performance would include the archivisation of other performance arts such as dance and opera; or the performativity of other media associated with the conventional archive, such as those related to moving pictures, or to digital and networked information and communication technologies.[48]

The purpose of this essay has been to complicate the relation between archives and performances, plotting the ways they work with the help of narratives from Greek tragedy. The usefulness of the archive does not need to be confined to its ability to ensure the supposedly neutral, objective, and authoritative documentation of the theatrical past. Similarly, the value of performance does not need to be limited to its politically driven but problematic promise of disappearance. The transformative effect of documentation and the material or immaterial traces of reality on the theatrical stage open productive paths for a reconceptualisation of both the archive and performance as processes involved in the encounter between past and present.[49]

Notes

1. Cassens Stoian 2002: 128.
2. Barish 1981.
3. Freshwater 2002.
4. Schneider 2001.
5. Schneider 2001.
6. Schneider 2001: 104.
7. Schneider 2001: 104.
8. Benjamin 1992: 'The Work of Art in the Age of Mechanical Reproduction'.
9. Benstein 2007: 7 quoting Foucault 1976: 130.
10. Freshwater 2002: 52.
11. Taplin 2001.
12. Taplin 2001.
13. Llewellyn-Jones 2001.
14. The question is raised by Reason 2006 in relation to performance photography.
15. The education work-pack of the production is available electronically at the following address: http://website-archive2.nt-online.org/?lid=1707 (accessed 20 March 2009).
16. This is a formulation by Hainge 2005: 1 which refers to the process of writing by hand but which also applies to nostalgic fonts such as 'Mom's typewriter'.
17. Hainge 2005: 6.
18. The relevant bibliography is extensive but consider, for instance, the work of Cathy Caruth, Shoshana Feldman, Geoffrey Hartman, Dominick LaCapra, Michael Rothberg, Gary Weissman, and James Young.
19. The relevant information is collected in Michelakis 2008b.
20. Birett 1980: 209, 341.
21. Michelakis 2008b. On the cinema of attractions in the context of the emerging modern visual culture, see the influential work by Gunning (e.g. Gunning 1989) and more recently the essays collected in Strauven 2006.
22. On photographs and the methodologies of using them as evidence for theatre performance, see Hodgdon 2003.
23. Derrida 1996: 2.
24. See, for instance, Thomas 1992; Sickinger 1999.

25. Ringer 1998: 42.

26. Segal 1981: 123.

27. Ringer 1998: 41. On the agency of the sword see Segal 1981: 132 (Ajax), 135 (Tecmessa, 906-7). On the sword as a product of demonic technology (Teucer, 1034-5), see Segal 1981: 132.

28. Translation by Easterling 1996: 222.

29. Easterling 1996: 222; 2002: 327-8.

30. Lada-Richards 2002: 398.

31. Published in English in Müller 1984.

32. Assman 2002: 71.

33. Assman 2002: 71, quoting Pomian 1990: 43.

34. Fuchs 1996: 188.

35. Marranca 1996: 47.

36. Campbell 2008: 101, quoting Wilke 1999: 285.

37. Fuchs 1996: 188; Marranca 1996: esp. 34-48.

38. Marx 2004: esp. 283-306.

39. Quoted in Case 2007: 124.

40. Case 2007: 125

41. Hell 2006: 80.

42. Teraoka 1996: 119, cf. 117.

43. Bradley 1999.

44. Reason 2003: 84 referring to Freshwater 2003.

45. Elder 2000.

46. Artaud 1958: 15-32.

47. Artaud 1958: 22.

48. On the reception of Greek tragedy in dance and its recording on film, see Michelakis 2009.

49. I am very grateful to Edith Hall and Kostas Valakas for stimulating discussions and generous help with this essay.

Bringing Together Nature and Culture: On the Uses and Limits of Cognitive Science for the Study of Performance Reception

Felix Budelmann

The study of performance reception within Classics is currently dominated by two activities. One is documentational and archival work, the patient assembling of information about performances past and present. The other is cultural history in a broadly constructivist vein, a historicism that emphasises discourse and is circumspect in the claims it makes about reality: we analyse performances of ancient drama as part of the political, social, literary or gender discourses of the relevant periods and places. This combination of documentation and fine-tuned attention to cultural discourse has been, is, and will continue to be immensely successful.[1]

Inevitably, this programme of research, like any other, cannot do everything. One topic it has relatively little to say about is the trans-historical and cross-cultural reach of ancient drama. The survival and remarkable influence of Greek tragedy in particular has much to do with cultural circumstances, both with the high status of classical antiquity in the West in most periods since the Renaissance and with a host of locally and historically specific factors. But it is far from clear that this is all there is to be said. Earlier generations of critics had a different explanation. Rather than pointing to circumstances, they appealed to our shared humanity. The success of ancient drama, as of Shakespeare, was ascribed to the way it reflects and speaks to human nature. Nowadays we have become suspicious of unproven assumptions about a constant and universal human nature. Justified and necessary as these suspicions are, they leave us with a problem. We find it much easier to point to the many *different* reasons that make ancient drama appeal to different people, than to answer the question of what all these people have in *common* when they are attracted to ancient drama. If an unchanging human nature is the wrong answer, what is the right one?

A second and equally difficult issue that is left unaddressed by the constructivist focus on discourse is experience. People's experience – in writing, rehearsing, performing, watching or reading ancient drama – is something that cultural history finds hard to analyse with the tools at its disposal. We have learned that studying the subjective experience of persons past or present is a hazardous endeavour, and more often than not we wisely avoid the topic. At the same time, though, the burgeoning work on the emotions in various humanities disciplines, including Classics and theatre studies, as well as new empirical work on audiences suggests that this is not for lack of interest.[2] Experience is an elusive subject, but one of undeniable importance for a rounded account of performance reception.[3]

These issues – universality, human nature, experience – are extremely challenging, and are likely to remain so. The aim of this chapter is not to provide lasting answers, nor indeed to take issue with current approaches. Rather it is to draw attention to a body of work that can offer us new perspectives as we grapple with these challenges. This body of work is cognitive science.

Cognitive science is not so much a discipline as an interdisciplinary field of study. Some authors prefer the plural 'cognitive sciences' or the term 'cognitive studies', and others put 'science' in inverted commas to make clear that not all of it is science in a narrow sense. Cognitive science brings together researchers from neuroscience, artificial intelligence, psychology, linguistics, philosophy and other fields. Their shared undertaking is research into the workings of the mind. Cognitive science has strong historical roots in computing, and the model of the mind as a processor of information remains prominent. However, over the years much cognitive science has come to understand 'cognitive' not to be thinking as opposed to feeling. *All* mental activity is within the remit of cognitive science, including for instance emotions, memory and aesthetics.

Cognitive science has been notably successful, not just in the discoveries it has made but also in reaching out and contributing to other disciplines. Anthropology, the subject that has given many humanities disciplines their cultural models, has sprouted a branch called 'cognitive anthropology', there also are a 'cognitive archaeology' and a 'cognitive musicology'; aesthetics does cognitive work, and over the past ten years literary scholars have also started drawing on cognitive science.[4]

What makes cognitive science particularly interesting to reception studies, and not least reception studies in the field of drama, I want to suggest, is its reassessment of various binary opposites.

The most obvious pair to begin with is *mind and body*. Attacks on 'Cartesian dualism' are commonplace in cognitive science.[5] There is considerable debate over exactly how the mind relates to the brain and how fully mental states are reducible to biological phenomena. But there is agreement that mind and brain are closely related. Moreover, recently there has been considerable emphasis on the mind as an embodied mind: in cognitive science, mental activity and bodily activity are looked at as inseparably intertwined.[6]

Secondly, *objectivity and subjectivity*. Cognitive science has an obvious objectivist dimension. Especially at the neuroscience end, research is into objective, hard facts about the brain, such as the neuronal activity made measurable by brain imaging technology. On the other hand, the emphasis on the mind bars simple positivism. Cognitive science studies the mind as it represents the world, and hence has a distinctly constructivist streak.[7] This juxtaposition of objectivist and constructivist paradigms has prompted a good deal of epistemological discussion within cognitive science.[8] For instance, one of the most high-profile philosophical works in the cognitive science tradition, George Lakoff and Mark Johnson's *Philosophy in the Flesh*, argues for a philosophy that breaks with traditions of both subjectivism and objectivism and instead argues for what it calls a philosophy of embodiment.[9]

This chapter is structured around a third binary pair, which maps partly onto the other two: *nature and culture.* Like the other pairs it has a long history, reaching back at least as far as ancient Greece. Today, the subject can produce highly emotive and politicised debates, for instance in matters of child development or criminal justice.

Two points above all emerge, it seems to me, from discussions about nature and culture in cognitive science. The first is a refusal to think about the two as irreconcilable opposites. Cognitive scientists regularly suggest that it makes little sense to try to work out whether behaviour is driven just by genes or just by the environment. Steven Rose, for instance, bemoans 'that tired old hangover from nineteenth-century dichotomous thinking, of nature and nurture, genes and environment'.[10] One of his examples is smiling. Babies learn to smile at the age of about one month even if they are blind, which suggests a strong genetic foundation. But sighted babies soon learn to smile socially in a way that blind babies do not, and obviously different cultures will produce different regimes of smiling. There is no sensible answer to the question: is a baby's smile genetic or cultural? And the same is true for many different types of behaviour. The title of a recent popular science book sums this up memorably in the formula *Nature via* (rather than: 'vs') *Nurture.*[11]

The second issue obvious from even a quick perusal of the cognitive science literature is that any global approach to the nature-culture interaction will fail. This point is a central claim of Geoffrey Lloyd's 2007 book *Cognitive Variations.* Lloyd runs through various debated aspects of cognition, such as colour perception, emotions and the self, and argues that the respective roles of nature and culture need to be looked at for each topic on its own terms.[12]

From these two points I draw what will be the main claim of my chapter: I will argue for the value of analysing various aspects of performance reception not just in terms of culture as we so often do, but by looking at the interplay of nature and culture; and by doing so separately from case to case.

Case Study 1: Pain

I will look at three topics, moving from the more to the less obvious. My first example is pain. It is the most obvious in so far as in this area several humanities disciplines are already looking at the nature-culture interaction.[13]

Terry Eagleton writes as follows about Philoctetes' pain. 'It is surely true that to ask, say, why we feel sympathy for Philoctetes is a pseudo-problem bred by bogus historicism. We feel sympathy for Philoctetes because he is in agonising pain from his pus-swollen foot. ... There is nothing hermeneutically opaque about Philoctetes' hobbling and bellowing ... As far as his agony goes, we understand Philoctetes in much the same way as we understand the afflictions of those around us.'[14] The context of Eagleton's statement is the explosion of work on the body in the humanities. Eagleton complains that much of this work talks about the body as something socially or culturally constructed, more or less ignoring its biological side, which he sees exemplified by Philoctetes' pain. Similar points have been made by scholars in other humanities subjects, including theatre studies.[15]

The particular relevance of this work to reception studies lies in the historically unchanging nature of the basic make-up of the human body. Pain is a good illustration. As Eagleton says, pain is a universal phenomenon. The biochemistry of pain is fundamentally the same in everybody and will have been the same for over a hundred thousand years. Eagleton's point is both right and important.

Yet this is not the whole story, as Eagleton himself would probably be the first to say and as he has pointed out elsewhere.[16] From the perspective of reception studies, one obvious objection springs to mind immediately. The varied reception history of *Philoctetes* shows that discourses about pain change. In the eighteenth century, for instance, several French theorists complained that the screams Sophocles gave to his Philoctetes were intolerable on the modern stage, and the first modern play based on *Philoctetes*, Chateaubrun's 1755 *Philoctète*, came close to editing out the fits of agony. By contrast, several late twentieth-century versions and productions have pulled out all the stops in expressing pain.[17]

Ronald Melzack, one of the biggest names in pain research, writes as follows in the entry on 'pain' in the *Oxford Guide to the Mind*: 'In recent years the evidence on pain has moved in the direction of recognizing the plasticity and modifiability of events in the central nervous system. Pain is a complex perceptual and affective experience determined by the unique past history of the individual, by the meaning to him of the injurious agent or situation, and by his "state of mind" at the moment, as well as by the sensory nerve pattern evoked by physical stimulation.'[18]

Clearly, the simple model of tissue damage producing predictable and universally identical pain signals is too simple for anybody dealing with pain, including medical practitioners and brain scientists. The best-known example of a complicated connection between tissue damage and experience of pain is the well-researched initial absence of pain reported by soldiers seriously wounded in battle. Another is phantom pain in an amputated limb. Less drastic but also significant are cultural differences. Many comparative studies show that both the experience and the expression of pain are to a degree affected by cultural conditioning. One upshot of all this is that the environment affects the very experience of pain. It affects not just cultural constructions or discourse, but also subjective sensations. It is clear, therefore, that the best way to talk about pain is with as interactionist a model as possible, a model in which biology and environment go together rather than oppose one another.

With that in mind I return to Philoctetes. The way Sophocles makes him express his pain is influenced by cultural contexts. Philoctetes' description of his suffering reflects Greek notions of the self and of bodily sensations insofar as pain is described as an outside agent attacking the body: 'it comes towards me, it approaches' he says (787); 'I am being eaten up' (745). Similarly, Heracles' pain in *Trachiniae* 'jumps up' (1027) and 'darts through' his body (1083). It is obvious that such expressions are usefully placed in the context of the Greek conceptualisation of disease as invading the body from outside.[19] Interestingly, though, this is not the only relevant context. Recent work in medicine and anthropology as well as literary criticism shows that recourse to metaphor is not particularly Greek but is common.[20] Like other internal and hence invisible sensations, pain can be described in concrete terms only by metaphor. Many of Philoctetes' and Heracles' specific metaphors are comparable to those used today. We too can speak of 'devouring' or 'darting' pain. The point is made eloquently by the McGill questionnaire, the standard tool doctors use when they ask chronic pain patients to describe their pain (see Fig. 3). Heracles' 'jumping' pain reappears here identically (group 2); Philoctetes' sense of 'being eaten up' finds a correspondence in the questionnaire's 'gnawing' pain (group 5), and further parallels could be drawn.

The point at issue, then, is one of *translatability*. As a consequence of the interplay of nature and culture, Sophocles' experience and conception of pain are different from mine (as mine are from those of anyone else's), but at the same time eminently translatable. Enough is recognisable in Philoctetes' pain, when written on the page and especially when embodied on stage, for people with different experiences of pain to activate these experiences and to feel justifiably that they understand Philoctetes because of what they share with him as human beings. Cognitive science does not fundamentally change Eagleton's claim, but it adds precision, detail and a more robust theoretical foundation.

112

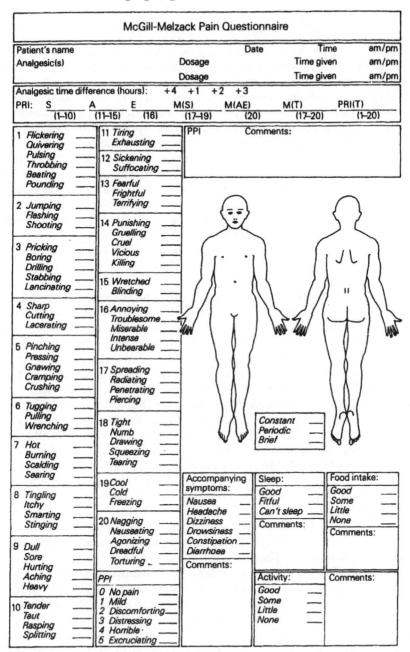

Fig. 3. The McGill-Melzack Pain Questionnaire. Reproduced by kind permission of Professor Ronald Melzack.

113

Case Study 2: Conceptual metaphors

My second example aims to show that even in an area that is less clearly a matter of nature, there is much to be gained from thinking about the interaction of nature and culture.

Metaphor is no longer the exclusive domain of literary scholars. Since the 1970s, two disciplines in particular have developed wide-reaching non-literary programmes of research into metaphor. In the wake of Lévi-Strauss, cultural anthropologists have looked at metaphor along with other tropes for the insights they give us into a culture.[21] For them, metaphor is not literary artifice but can express a culture's beliefs and thought patterns. The other discipline, which has had less impact among classicists, is cognitive linguistics.[22] Since the publication in 1980 of George Lakoff's and Mark Johnson's book *Metaphors We Live By*, a large body of work has steadily built up.[23] Like Lévi-Strauss and his followers, cognitive linguists attach major significance to metaphor. Yet while anthropologists use metaphor as a means of access to a culture, Lakoff and Johnson argue that it gives access to the mind.

At the heart of their theory is what they call 'conceptual metaphors'. Metaphors are conceptual when they draw on deep-seated connections between two conceptual domains in the human mind. Sometimes the term 'embodied metaphor' is used to stress that these connections derive from the bodily experience of the world. A much cited example is the many metaphors based on the mapping between the concepts 'anger' and 'heat'. We speak of 'a heated exchange', 'blowing one's top', 'hot under the collar', and 'hot temper'. Lakoff and Johnson argue that the mapping between anger and heat, which underlies all these expressions, derives from our bodily experience of blood pressure and body temperature rising when we are angry. What is more, they argue, such metaphors do not just ultimately *derive* from this bodily experience of getting hot when angry, but are also mentally *processed*, consciously and unconsciously, by recourse to our embodied experience of feeling hot when angry every time they are used.

These are the bare bones of conceptual metaphor theory, with numerous controversies left to one side.[24] Before moving on, one methodological issue needs to be pointed out. Throughout this section I use the term 'theory' to refer to Lakoff's and Johnson's work. Their overall case, many people (including me) believe, is a strong one, but even the longest list of metaphors based on 'anger as heat' does not amount to a *proof* that either these metaphors or the underlying notion of 'anger as heat' draw on bodily experience in origin and/or in mental processing. In the past decade cognitive psychologists have devised tests trying to prove exactly that,[25] and recently there has been a call for neurobiological research too,[26] but this work is still in its infancy. Hence it is important not to overplay one's hand in this field but to admit the inevitable element of speculation.

9. Bringing Together Nature and Culture

The conceptual metaphor I will use as my example as I now turn to Greek tragedy is another frequently discussed one, that of life as a journey. English has 'arriving in life', 'going through life', 'departing life', 'the life span', 'being without direction in life', and so on. Ancient Greek too uses this conceptual metaphor extensively,[27] and nowhere is it more prominent than in *Oedipus at Colonus*.[28] Oedipus is characterised as a wanderer (3) who has arrived at the holy ground that is his final destination (45). The chorus say to him, *ep' eschata baineis*, literally 'you're walking towards the final/extreme things' (217). Words from the root *hodos*, 'path' / 'journey', appear throughout the play. The life-journey metaphor culminates in the powerful moments in many performances when the blind Oedipus leads the other characters off stage (1542, 1547-8).

Now, the life-journey metaphor does not as obviously relate to bodily experience as that of anger as heat. However, there are good reasons for believing that it, too, reflects something fundamental about the nature of human cognition. First, 'life is a journey' is widespread. The *Odyssey*, *Gilgamesh*, *Job* and *The Pilgrim's Progress* all use it, and it is not confined to the West, but is used also for instance in Chinese.[29] Secondly, there is the broader point that it is common for languages to express time through space. As John Lyons puts it in his semantics textbook, 'temporal expressions, in many unrelated languages, are patently derived from locative expressions'.[30] Striking English examples include 'coming to know' and 'going to sleep', and in a different way the phenomenon is illustrated by timelines in history books. It would seem, then, that the frequency of the 'life is a journey' metaphor is something to do with people's use of their concrete experience of space and movement in space to grasp the much more abstract and intractable notions of time and time passing. (Why exactly that is so, still escapes our knowledge.)

There are two consequences for the study of performance reception. The first relates again to translatability and cross-cultural reach. There is much that is specific about how every culture and indeed every person uses metaphors.[31] The notion of life as a journey would have a rather different meaning for classical Greek audiences of *Oedipus at Colonus*, with their knowledge of, for instance, mystery cults, than for spectators in a broadly Christian culture, who may (or may not) think of Jesus' journey to the cross. As ever, nature and culture blend. Yet at the same time, in so far as the metaphor takes recourse to something fundamental in the human cognitive system – the tendency to conceptualise time as space – it is just as translatable into different spectators' different individual worlds as is Philoctetes' pain.

The second point one can derive from work on conceptual metaphor concerns the way metaphor operates in the theatre. One way of looking at metaphor is to regard it as an add-on for the purpose of illustration: *Oedipus at Colonus* is about Oedipus' troublesome life and his death, and the metaphor of the journey is a poetic and theatrical way of visualising this theme. However, if conceptual metaphor does indeed express pre-linguistic perceptions of the world, then an alternative way of looking at metaphor is to regard it as just as fundamental as anything on stage. On this view, Oedipus' journey is not added as an illustration on top of the primary meaning. Rather it is an example of what our minds do all the time: think about movement through time as movement through space. If this is along the right lines, then conceptual metaphor theory helps us to adumbrate the considerable affective power of the moment when Oedipus departs the stage unguided.

Case Study 3: Characters' minds

My final case study will focus on characters' minds. It will become clear that (as far as I can see) in this area the scope for interdisciplinary work drawing on cognitive science is at present more limited.[32] I have chosen this less rich example because I want to suggest that even where there is less scope for engagement with detail, cognitive science can be provided a valuable structuring framework for the comparative and inter-textual work that is the bread and butter of reception studies.

I shall start by introducing a term used in a range of different disciplines with cognitive interests: 'theory of mind', conventionally abbreviated ToM. The roots of its importance to cognitive science are usually traced to a 1978 article on primate cognition by primatologists David Premack and Guy Woodruff.[33] ToM is, to cite that article, the ability to 'imput[e] mental states to [one]self and to others', where 'mental states' should be understood comprehensively to include 'purpose or intention, as well as knowledge, belief, thinking, doubt, guessing, pretending, liking, and so forth'. To put it differently, ToM is the capacity for reading minds (with more or less success).

The question Premack and Woodruff posed, whether and to what degree primates have such a ToM, remains a live research topic today,[34] but what has given the concept wide currency is its application to the minds of humans.[35] So-called 'false-belief tests' were devised to investigate at what age children typically develop a ToM. The design of these tests is as follows. An object, say a marble, is placed under a cup in view of both the child that is being tested and another person. Then the other person leaves the room, and the marble is placed under a different cup. The child is asked under which cup the other person will say the marble is after coming back into the room. Most children after the age of four will rightly point to the first cup (under which the marble no longer is), realising that the person who left the room is bound to hold a false belief about the marble since they did not see it being moved. Younger children will usually point to the second cup. ToM has been important to developmental psychologists mostly because of disorders like autism: most autistic children fail false-belief tests and are often thought not to have the same faculty for ToM as the rest of their age group. Brain scientists too have made progress in understanding which parts of the brain are involved. In addition, research into ToM has an evolutionary component, with various theories on offer about how humans evolved this capacity. All these lines of research reflect the conviction that ToM is central to understanding what it is to be human. ToM is seen 'as no less fundamental than the faculty of language', as 'crucial for many of those phenomena that are most characteristic of our humanity', and as 'our natural way of understanding the social environment'.[36]

It is obvious that ToM is relevant to drama. Developing notions of characters' minds is something that the characters do themselves in a play, that the actors and directors do in putting on a performance and that the spectators do in watching it. Drama functions by drawing on the human propensity to read minds.

This may seem little news beyond new terminology. That the characters' minds do not simply exist but need to be constructed has often been stressed.[37] Compared to both pain and metaphor, ToM is a rather thin concept: it buys its universality at the expense of richness. Yet I believe ToM research can nevertheless be helpful in studying performance reception, especially that of Greek tragedy.

Greek tragedy repeatedly encourages spectators to think about the characters' states of mind. Medea's anxious deliberation about the right course of action is probably the most famous example, but comparable moments occur in all surviving plays. Pat Easterling recently made a case for believing that the frequent emphasis on characters' minds may be one of the reasons for Greek tragedy's current wide-spread popularity in many different cultures: it appeals, she argues, to an age like ours that is so deeply interested in the human mind.[38]

Easterling's attractive argument can be pursued further by thinking about ToM. The universality of ToM would suggest that the interest in mental states is one of those characteristics of Greek tragedy that have always helped it travel both cross-culturally and trans-historically. Earlier periods may not all have had the same intense interest in the mind, but implicit and explicit mind-reading is, like pain and (apparently) conceptual metaphor, such a basic aspect of human nature that Greek tragedy's focus on characters' consciousness is easily translated from one context to another.

How can one marry this kind of universalist recourse to human nature with the blatant influence of cultural contexts? Character portrayal underwent enormous changes across periods, with for instance Brechtian *Verfremdung* reacting against the psychological intimacy of nineteenth-century drama, and both differing greatly from what we find in Greek tragedy.[39] Moreover, the related notions of self and person are hardly universals, as Christopher Gill demonstrated at some length in the case of ancient Greece.[40] Changes in performance practice (outdoor *vs* indoor theatre, masked *vs* unmasked actor, more or less formal acting styles) also change the way spectators read minds.

In this context of enormous change in many dimensions, ToM can perform an important function. It gives us a concept around which to structure trans-historical or cross-cultural discussions. The cognitive anthropologist Maurice Bloch recently wrote about taking the false belief tests of Western psychology to a village in Madagascar.[41] His focus is on the way bystanders interpreted the false-belief tests they were witnessing. Two things emerge that are relevant here: first, Bloch stresses the fundamental similarity of the villagers' interpretations with those of Western ToM research, giving further support to the notion that the ability to read minds matters to different cultures. Secondly, he then develops a rich reading of how ToM is integrated into the broader culture of the village in Madagascar, talking for instance about how it is seen as a major political skill in a way that it is not usually in the West.

Evidently, ToM work gave Bloch a useful *point of comparison* between different cultures, and this is what it can give also to students of performance reception. We can ask how the intensity and frequency with which Greek tragedy stimulates our ability to explain and predict actions is manipulated in the various different performances and performance contexts, and we can then for each type of context develop the kind of rich analysis that Bloch developed in Madagascar.

Of course there are other concepts which one could use and which indeed have been used successfully as points of comparison: 'personality', 'self' or 'character' are all relevant. The advantage of 'ToM' I suggest is its obvious grounding in basic human cognition. Thanks to this grounding, one has to do a great deal less work than with 'personality', 'self' or 'character' to identify what the underlying something is that one compares in the different cultures. Like pain, ToM is at the nature end of the nature-culture scale and is something that is regarded as characteristic of our humanity. Hence it offers a simpler foundation on which to base cross-cultural or diachronic comparisons than many culturally richer rival terms.

This leads to a broader point. Only few people would deny the existence of human universals altogether. Rather, many scholars interested in culture assume that some universals exist but that they are 'too abstract or insubstantial'[42] to permit interesting cultural analysis. The fact humans are universally born with two legs is unquestionable but not particularly interesting for most kinds of cultural analysis. I want to suggest that even the more etiolated of universals can have enormous benefit for reception studies in that they give us something to hold on to when we jump from culture to culture.[43]

Instinctively a belief in comparability and underlying human nature informs most cross-cultural and diachronic research: the cultural specificity that we emphasise would not be interesting if we thought we did not share anything with ancient Greeks or Elizabethans. One thing cognitive science offers us is the concepts for working those unexpressed instinctive beliefs into our scholarly discussions.

118

Conclusion

Cognitive science touches on many aspects of performance reception. In this chapter, I chose three examples to give a sense of the range. Other areas one could explore include gestures, emotions, humour, genre, memory, narrative, the rehearsal process or the frequent recurrence of certain themes – the list could easily be extended. By way of conclusion to this essay, however, I shall sketch briefly what I believe are the most important *general* issues that have emerged in the course of the discussion.

I begin with some thoughts about limitations inherent in the project of using cognitive science for the study of performance reception. One kind of limitation that one comes up again almost constantly is the many gaps in our knowledge. Cognitive science is moving apace, but even so there is much less that we know than that we do not know. Even pain, the subject of a major, well-funded field of research is by no means fully understood. Many of the things we would like to know about how the mind responds to dramatic performances have not been studied so far, or have been studied only by cognitive linguists or philosophers but not by empirical brain scientists. Secondly, there are the practical problems posed by the fact that cognitive science is a vast and complex field. Mastering it is close to impossible for a classicist or a theatre historian. Even though I very much hope that my accounts of cognitivist research in this chapter have not been misleading, they are bound to have failed to do full justice to the complexity of the issues and the debates. Thirdly, many research programmes in cognitive science, especially those with a natural science focus, aim at generalisation. In the humanities, 'reductionism' is usually a term of abuse; in various aspects of science it is a goal. As a result, the interest in particularity and complexity that is characteristic of humanities scholarship will not always be satisfied by what cognitive science has to offer.

These are serious limitations that should caution against over-optimistic assessments of the likely impact of cognitive science on the humanities in years to come. Yet that said, there can be no doubt that scholars of performance reception have much to gain from engaging with cognitive science. Above all, I have suggested, cognitive science focuses our attention onto the intersection of nature and culture that is the mind. This focus is productive in various ways. At the most general level, it permits us to maintain all the insights and techniques of cultural analysis while taking into account the indubitable influence of facts of nature on all aspects of performance reception.

Going back to my opening paragraphs, I would emphasise in particular two aspects of bringing together nature and culture in this way, one synchronic, concerning performance; the other diachronic, concerning reception. First, the intersection of nature and culture is a good place for catching at least glimpses of the difficult but central issue of experience, without going back to what today is felt to be unreflected positivism and without ignoring the ubiquitous variation that nobody can deny. Of course, inward and variable thing that it is, experience will always remain elusive, but I would like to think that my examples suggest that cognitive science helps us both in framing questions about experience, and in carrying out analysis about them.

Secondly, the intersection between nature and culture can have a productive role in studying reception history. Different models of writing reception history blend different selections from the same list of factors in different ways. Most prominent on this list are: the ancient work, the new work (which in the context of this volume may be a production of the ancient work), the intervening acts of reception (which in turn affect the new work), the producers of the new work (poets, painters, directors, actors), the readers or spectators of the new work, the various contexts of the new work. Cognitive science gives us one further factor: the cognitive propensities of the human mind. Adding this factor to the blend, I have suggested, helps us structure arguments that involve cross-cultural and trans-historical comparisons since unlike all the other factors it is at work both in antiquity and at the point of reception.

The argument of this chapter is probably best characterised as exploratory. Only the future will show whether there really is enough potential in bringing cognitive science to bear on performance reception for scholars to take it up. This essay has achieved its objective if it has managed to suggest that we should at least try to find out.

Notes

1. The Oxford 'Archive of Performances of Greek and Roman Drama', which organised the conference that formed the basis of this book, is a good example: it combines the creation of a database of performances with the study of these performances in their various cultural contexts. Within Classics, the most outspoken proponent of an alternative model of reception studies is probably Charles Martindale, who emphasises aesthetics: see esp. Martindale 1993, Martindale 2005 and the introduction to Martindale and Thomas 2006 as well as his chapter in the present volume. Michelakis 2006: 218-19 has helpful remarks on the methodologies of performance reception in British Classics.

2. Outstanding recent work on the emotions in Classics includes Harris 2001, Braund and Most 2003, and Konstan 2006. For emotion in the theatre see especially Konijn 2000. Empirical work is well established in theatre and performance studies; see for instance Schoenmakers 1992, Bennett 1997: 86-94 and Ang 2001.

3. States 1985: 378 (in a discussion of phenomenological work on theatre) laments 'the sheer poverty of scientific language in the face of subjective experience'. McConachie 2001 reviews humanities scholarship on experience and its shortcomings (with reference to theatre and performance); some related points in Crane 2002.

4. Scholarship using cognitive science in literary studies: Johnson 1987, Lakoff 1987, Turner 1991, Gibbs 1994, Turner 1996, Spolsky 2001, Tsur 2003, and three special journal issues: *Poetics Today* Spring 23 (2002) and Summer 24 (2003), and *Journal of Consciousness Studies* 11.5-6 (2004). Introductions to the field are

provided by Stockwell 2002, Hogan 2003, Gavins and Steen 2003 and (humanities rather than just literary studies) Slingerland 2008. Richardson and Steen 2002 is an excellent overview. For an annotated bibliography see: http://www2.bc.edu/~richarad/lcb/bib/annot.html (accessed 22 March 2009).

Theatre and performance have received less than their fair share of attention, but see Crane 2001, Sugiera 2002, McConachie 2002 and especially McConachie and Hart 2006. McConachie 2008 was published after completion of this chapter. Cognitivist approaches to classical literature have centred on oral poetry, especially in the work of Egbert Bakker, Michael Clarke and Elizabeth Minchin, but note also Lowe 2000.

5. Accessible high-profile discussions include Edelman 1992 and Damasio 1994.

6. A good starting point is the introduction of Gibbs 2006.

7. A point made by Smith 2005: 4.

8. For an overview see the relevant chapters in Foley 1997.

9. Lakoff and Johnson 1999. The philosophical literature relevant to my topic is of course immense and I make no attempt to provide an overview.

10. Rose 2005: 59,135-6.

11. Ridley 2003.

12. Lloyd 2007. Similar approach in Hacking 1999.

13. The most detailed discussion of pain in the theatre is Carlson 2002. On pain in Greek tragedy see Budelmann 2006.

14. Eagleton 2003: xiv, where he also makes relevant comments on the body in recent scholarship. Hall 2004: 63 draws on Eagleton's point.

15. In theatre studies: Fischer-Lichte and Fleig 2000, Fischer-Lichte, Horn, and Warstat 2001, McConachie and Hart 2006.

16. See Eagleton 2000: ch. 4 ('Culture and Nature').

17. On changing attitudes to Philoctetes' pain, including documentation of the instances mentioned here, see Budelmann 2007.

18. Melzack 2001: 86-7. For accessible general works on pain, covering the material in the next paragraph, see Melzack and Wall 1991, Wall 1999 and, from a cultural perspective, Scarry 1985 and Morris 1991.

19. Padel 1992.

20. E.g. Melzack and Wall 1991: 36-44; Bending 2000: ch. 3.

21. Of fundamental importance are Lévi-Strauss 1966 and Lévi-Strauss 1969. Fernandez 1991 is a more recent collection, and for an overview of metaphor research up to the 1990s see Tilley 1999.

22. The best introduction to cognitive linguistics is Croft and Cruse 2004.

23. Lakoff and Johnson 1980. Particularly important works: Turner 1987, Lakoff and Turner 1989, Ortony 1993, Gibbs and Steen 1999, Barcelona 2000, Fauconnier and Turner 2002. Overview in Kövecses 2002 and relevant chapter in Croft and Cruse 2004. Examples of applications of this work to literary analysis: Freeman 1993; Freeman 2000; Stockwell 2002: ch. 8; Crisp 2003; Hogan 2003: ch. 4; application to issues of theatrical space: McConachie 2002, Hart 2006.

24. Gibbs 2006: ch. 4 gives a good sense of the controversies.

25. Earlier experiments summarised in Gibbs 2006: 182ff., with references. More recent work: Wilson and Gibbs 2007.

26. Gallese and Lakoff 2005.

27. Becker 1937: index s.v. 'Lebensweg'. On metaphors of journeys in Greek texts see also Giannisi 2006.

28. On journeys in *Oedipus at Colonus* see Easterling 2010, and Becker 1937: 197, 209-11.

29. Yu 1998: 117. Cole 1997, a book about ageing in America, has much to say about this metaphor. Cole gives further references to (non-linguistic) discussions of it in the introduction.

30. Lyons 1977: vol. 2, 718-24, quotation from 718. Cross-cultural examples are collected by Alverson 1994. Note, however, that Alverson assumes the invariance of human cognition of space, which has since been challenged by Levinson 2003. See also Kövecses 2005: 49-51 on the universality of the passage of time conceptualised as motion.

31. First-generation work on conceptual metaphor often assumed universality. In the past ten or fifteen years there has been much more interest in the role of culture, partly as a result of criticism from anthropology: see Fernandez 1991 (especially the article by Quinn), Kimmel 2004 and the other articles in the special issue of the *European Journal of English Studies* 8.3 (2004), and Kövecses 2005 (pp. 125-6 on 'life is a journey').

32. Scope, that is, in the context of the particular concerns of this article. Otherwise, for literary work drawing on the kind of cognitive material that I use in this section see Zunshine 2004, Rokotnitz 2006, and especially Zunshine 2006. Blakey Vermeule has announced a book entitled *Making Sense of Fictional People: A Literary and Cognitive Project* on her Stanford website.

33. Premack and Woodruff 1978: quotations taken from 518. The term 'theory' is potentially misleading: there is considerable debate over where on the scale between a fully reflected theory and a pragmatic understanding ToM normally sits: see in particular Carruthers and Smith 1996 and Gallagher 2001.

34. Recent work is reviewed in Whiten 2000 and Call and Tomasello 2008.

35. On the work summarised in this paragraph see the items in notes 33 and 36. More recently, see the three papers on ToM in vol. 1 of Carruthers, Laurence, and Stich 2005-7.

36. Quotations from: Sperber 2000: 6-7 (who is writing about the capacity for 'metarepresentation', under which he subsumes ToM); Dunbar 2000: 242; Baron-Cohen 1995: 4.

37. For discussion of these matters as regards Greek theatre see Easterling 1990.

38. Easterling 2005; Budelmann and Easterling 2010.

39. Which is not to say that Greek theatre is in no way susceptible to later approaches: see Lada-Richards 2005.

40. Gill 1996. On more recent Western theories of the self see in the first instance Seigel 2005.

41. Bloch 2006.

42. Foley 1997: 17, describing the views of Clifford Geertz.

43. Different arguments for the use of cognitive science in writing history are presented by McConachie 2006 and Nellhaus 2006 (the former touching on ToM, the latter on metaphor).

44. Such over-optimistic assessments can be found for instance in Carroll 2004 and some of the essays in Gottschall and Wilson 2005.

Does a Deleuzean Philosophy of Radical Physicality Lead to the 'Death of Tragedy'? Some Thoughts on the Dismissal of the Climactic Orientation of Greek Tragedy

Freddy Decreus

1. Theatre and physicality

This chapter addresses theatre and physicality – not just the use of the body in contemporary theatre, but the radical representation of physicality, a phenomenon that started some decades ago, soon after the political and economic earthquakes caused by the Vietnam war and the Parisian May Revolt, a period described by Edith Hall as one of 'seismic political and cultural shifts marking the end of the 1960s'.[1] One may single out as a pivotal moment *Dionysus in 69*, Richard Schechner's famous performance in the Performing Garage in downtown New York, with its explicit use of the body – remember the 'Total Caress Sequence' recalled so fondly by Froma Zeitlin[2] – but ever since, hundreds of other tragedies, dramas and performances have been deeply influenced by the increasing attention paid to the body. In this paper, I address the impact of this paradigm on the interpretation of Greek tragedy, a shift that takes us from the world as text to the world as performance,[3] from the modernist and essentialist 'holy body' (Artaud, Grotowski, Brook) to the postmodern, culturally and ideologically encoded body,[4] from the 'discursive' to the 'visceral body',[5] from 'representation without presence' to 'presence without representation'.[6]

My story of the increasing use of physicality on the stage symbolically starts in the year 1981, when an Italian company in Cesena led by Romeo Castellucci (the company consists of the brothers and sisters Romeo and Claudia Castellucci, Chiara and Paolo Guidi) embarked upon a new investigative programme of theatrical language and produced a series of rather nightmarish productions under the banner of 'iconoclasm'. In the view of this company's members, theatre had to overthrow traditional plays and touch all the senses, the whole nervous system and ideally the subconscious of the audience. Like their Renaissance hero, Raffaello Sanzio, better known as Raphael, they wanted to elaborate the close relationships

Freddy Decreus

between art, nature and science, and understand the physical world (especially anatomy) through art. More specifically, they borrowed his name, because 'in the perfection of his compositions, the body bathes in metaphysics'.[7] These were noble statements and objectives, but they resulted in revolutionary theatre which left nothing whatever intact of traditional theatre.

In the same period can be situated the first important productions of The Wooster Group (1975), Jan Fabre (1980), Jan Decorte (1982), La Fura dels Baus (1983), Theodoros Terzopoulos (1986), Einar Schleef (1986), Robert Wilson (1986) and The Needcompany (1987),[8] none of which could be called tragedies, since they consisted of patchworks of heterogeneous materials, such as citations, cries and whispers, textual and iconic fragments, acoustic climates, paratactic and simultaneous constructions, bodily presences and atmospheres, in fact a series of 'performances' stitched together into a new 'open form' of dramaturgy. From the 1980s onwards, many traditional tragedies have been staged in a 'postdramatic' way, focusing upon diverse types of auto-sufficient physicality and featuring an obsessive attention to the here-and-now experience rather than the referential materials. [9]

Over the last three decades, some major transformations have certainly taken place on the stage, questioning all our traditional (western) categories of watching, understanding and participating. They are exemplified by some hundred really outstanding productions all dealing with aspects of tragedy and the tragic, in which actors, directors and artists have integrated radical forms of physicality into new forms/formats of theatre. Yet the question arises about the place they occupy in the cultural history of western theatre. As Helena De Preester observes, 'the official version of modern western philosophy has been a philosophy of reason'.[10] The acceptance and birth of a philosophy of the body was a slow and complex process[11] that testified to the global distrust felt by ideologies and religions of the West towards that threatening and corrupting instrument called the 'body'.[12] During recent decades, however, a new interdisciplinary combination of philosophy, psychoanalysis and neuroscience has witnessed the resurrection of this body. It was in the 1970s that theoreticians initiated what can be called 'the first wave' of research into a more energetic presence of bodies on stage, no longer formulated in terms of a theatre of mimesis and representation, but in terms of a totally new type of interaction between actors and public, looking and breathing, male and female identities. A 'theatre of energy' was born,[13] heralding 'the end of humanism' and resulting into an apparent 'theatre of chaos',[14] in fact a multiplicity of theatrical forms that in one way or another relied upon Artaud's idea of 'theatre as plague'.

Antonin Artaud (1896-1948), himself a physical sufferer, inspired numerous artists and writers to attempt various major experiments in anti-representational performance. He was one of the first to delineate a

124

new concept of the body, most famously (especially after his death) included in which was the notion of the 'body without organs', a body that no longer occupied a real physical and organic entity, but withdrew as much as possible from colonisation by forms of representation and ideological inscriptions. Artaud used this notion for actors who did not rely upon the transcendental authority of author or text but instead deeply expressed the play from within themselves in an attempt to merge with all participants and to experience life unmediated. *The Theatre and its Double*, a collection of texts written between 1931 and 1937 (published in 1938), expressed a totally new vision of theatre (immediately labelled *Theatre of Cruelty*), not based upon positivist definitions, but variously and poetically defined as plague, alchemy or Balinese dance and to be experienced as a bombardment of sounds, lights, colours, masks and gestures.[15]

The origins of this radical change in attitude are also often traced to Roland Barthes' *The Pleasure of the Text* (1973) and his plea that the body should activate its own ideas. Barthes shifted the focus from processes of rational interpretation to moments of pre- or even unconscious sensations, as they happen during so many other aesthetic or artistic experiences. The experience of 'pleasurable reading' at which he was aiming immerses the reader so deeply in the text that s/he feels lost within it, a cathartic moment situated at the edge of communication and thriving upon the elusive and puzzling nature of reading.[16]

In the same year, Jean-François Lyotard expressed his preference for 'flux' over 'focus' in the analysis of the body, in which it is not the fixation of signs and meaning which holds the most central position but their infinite perturbation. Theatre was no longer conceived as an institution where representation and interpretation were governed and produced by a series of signs coded and transmitted in a fixed manner and thus patronised by the forces of tradition and the ideology of the west. Theatrical practice, he argued, should not rely upon the endless repetition of the same old traditional stories. On the contrary, it had to break with ideas of mimesis, opening up the possibility of representing everything on stage through what was registered on performing bodies as they executed already known categories of thought, narration, gestures and genre.[17] In 1977, Lyotard proposed a 'somatographic' analysis of performance, a methodology that describes the weight and impact of the performance on the body. Theatre was no longer to be conceived as a mediation of signs, but to be felt and translated in terms of energy streams and libidinal forces. For this, the body should stand outside signification in order to become a stream of energy in an endless, elusive series of flows.[18]

However, the most elaborated version of the recognition of physicality was developed by two other French philosophers, Gilles Deleuze and Félix Guattari, shortly after the events of May 1968 in Paris, as part of their new vision of philosophy. Deleuze's books *Difference and Repetition* (1968) and *The Logic of Sense* (1969) prompted Michel Foucault to declare that 'one day, perhaps, this century will be seen as Deleuzean',[19] and much later, Bonta and Protevi even proclaimed 'that Deleuze – once his work is fully understood – can be the Kant of our time'.[20] The reason for such perhaps excessive praise is that a Deleuzean philosophy can be seen as a systematic attack on and inversion of all traditional metaphysical categories. What he proposes is nothing less than a philosophical alternative to the Cartesian subject of knowledge (cf. Foucault's criticism of the Cartesian unity of the subject and its monolithic *cogito* in his *Les mots et les choses,*1966) and an exploration of how this person turns into a decentred subject that brings along his/her physicality and the consciousness of the whole body in the processes of thinking, perceiving, experiencing.

It was especially the two books he wrote in collaboration with Félix Guattari, *Anti-Oedipus* (1972) and *A Thousand Plateaus* (1980), which brought Deleuze worldwide fame in the 1980s and gave him a place among the most influential thinkers of the twentieth century. These books have provoked a new 'nomadic' way of analysing psychoanalysis, philosophy and culture and also led to a fruitful reconsideration of the whole network of transcendental and essentialist underpinnings of western culture. Since my summary of the philosophy of Deleuze and Guattari is intended to better situate and understand Castellucci's theatre, I will focus on three important notions in these two collaborative works: the 'body-without-organs', the 'desiring machine' and the 'rhizome'.[21]

Anti-Oedipus, written in the afterglow of the May 1968 events in Paris, reads like a tourist guide for a new life. It develops an anthropology based upon psycho-energetic processes and is one of the first western philosophical treatises to stress the importance of energy as a guiding principle. As such, is it connected to the new awareness of bio-dynamics (or bio-energetics) that spread throughout the western world at that time, and drew attention to the use for more than 2,000 years by eastern philosophies, such as Buddhism and Taoism, of the notion of energy to construct their worldviews. Already developed in Deleuze's doctoral dissertation, *Différence et répétition* (1968), but now reappearing in elaborated form was a theory of intensities: a human being goes through all experiences of varying intensity, but these processes do not differ in essence from other processes that deploy forces in magnetic fields, acoustic waves or heat waves. Human experience, with all its gradations of temperature, spasms of pain and orgasms, is of essentially the same nature as other physical processes, difficult to represent in language, and only measurable by gradations of the sort indicated by thermometers and barometers, an 'explosion' of anger, a 'wave' of shame, a 'flood' of tears, a 'stream' of pleasure.

Fundamentally, a human person is a desiring being, a cluster of psychic-energetic processes that produce desire, a desire that continuously produces products, these being biological (like hormones), neurological (like emotions) and subjective reflections (like: 'I feel this').[22] Hence the idea of equating human productivity with machines: desire functions as a machine and all partial machines that constitute the human person are interconnected and can at any moment change their interaction. However, when one considers the way a breastfeeding mother proceeds (the breast of the mother produces milk, the mouth of the child sucks it), one understands how desiring machines not only produce a product (milk), but also produce a process of production (a child reacting to this). In order to create, within the human being, a state of consciousness that registers the functioning of all these machines at work, Deleuze and Guattari, paying tribute to Artaud, introduced their version of the 'body-without-organs'. This difficult notion, which is at the root of our experience of subjectivity and denotes the primitive situation of our experiences, merely coordinates the actions of the different machines, and introduces the distance necessary for the evaluation and interpretation of what has been going on between them. It consists of pulsations, zones of intensity, gradations and energy streams, and is both hypersensitive and extremely open. From this viewpoint, the human body is no longer considered the bipolar construction created and worshipped by Cartesian rationality, but a continuous and heterogeneous series of intensive processes, a series of gradually ordered forces that are generated, reach a climax, conflict with other series, and die. No special respect for that holy construction of Man is implied thereby, just a general perception. One remembers all too well the relativistic opening words of *Anti-Oedipus* concerning the functioning and meaning of Man:

> It is at work everywhere, functioning smoothly at times, at other times in fits and starts. It breathes, it heats, it eats. It shits and fucks.[23]

What Deleuze and Guattari actually introduced in their works was a new 'a priori-filter', a neurological filter, carrier of all processes of experience, not 'my body' made up of all its organs and limbs, but the experience of a neurological condition in its chaotic and preconscious existence, the streaming whole of prickles and tickles that are felt by the brain whenever organs, nerve signals or hormonal liquids are on the move. It follows that the definition of philosophy itself is supposed to be understood in a different way that fully engages with the body and which, contrary to the Freudian interpretation of the Oedipus Complex, does not refrain from desire nor has to fear castration.

Since desire is a constitutive force that animates man and fulfils him, there is no reason to investigate the hypothesis of the tragic condition, which typically has been interpreted as a situation of loss ('gap', 'Kluft', Zäsur'[24]) and an anti-affirmative and anti-vitalist enterprise.[25]

In *A Thousand Plateaus,* Deleuze and Guattari illustrate concretely what 'energy' can mean to the western citizen who is not used to think beyond the dichotomy between mind and body. An important notion introduced here is the 'rhizome', a term conceived to function in a way diametrically opposed to a traditional arborescence model, also called the 'tree-structure'. Rhizomes make us think of the way the unconscious functions, in an endless series of affirmations and additions ('like and ... and ... and ...'), like the floods of the river, or the fire ant, gossip, sexuality, the rain forest, any terrorist force, or the Internet.[26] Images that obey a rhizomatic rhythm force us to acknowledge that we cannot foresee and understand all phenomena, however strong the urge may be to situate everything in the world of representation. As Rosi Braidotti observes: 'In his *Nietzsche et la philosophie*, Deleuze describes the activity of thinking as life lived at the highest possible level of intensity. In this framework, ideas are events, active states that open up unsuspected possibilities of life. Faithful to his topology of forces, Deleuze argues that thought is made of sense and values and that it rests on affective foundations. In other words, beyond the propositional content of an idea, there lies another category: the affective force, the level of intensity that ultimately deter- mines its truth-value.' And as a most important conclusion, Braidotti holds that 'This intensive redefinition of the activity of thought entails in fact a vision of subjectivity as a bodily, affective entity.'[27]

It is obvious that nowadays this philosophy of the body, a radical new vision that challenges the one preached by patriarchal religion and phal- logocentric thought, is popular in feminist circles, and also in (post)modern art, especially in the type of cinema that thrives upon fluidity and a Bergsonian conception of time.[28]

As an example of the transition from 'visceral philosophy' to a 'visceral presence on the stage' or from 'conceptual thoughts' to 'corporeal logics',[29] I analyse below the *Tragedia Endogonidia* of the Socìetas Raffaello Sanzio, the 'iconoclastic' theatre company directed by Romeo Castellucci. A Deleuzian-Guattarian philosophy of the body proves useful in under- standing the epistemological and aesthetic principles operating in their radical theatre.

2. The Socìetas Raffaello Sanzio: 'Pilgrims of Matter'

Castellucci's *Tragedia Endogonidia* consisted of eleven 'Episodes' staged in ten different cities, with Cesena as start and finish (twelve phases of 'Crescita' from 2002-2005, and eleven parts of the 'Film Cycle'). It was a major work of art created over a period of three years (2002-2004; some parts are still being performed as I write in 2007), and honoured with many prizes. It provoked a sustained discussion about contemporary tragedy, both as an artistic and aesthetic message on stage, and a series of critical discussions in the elaborate theoretical articles published in the eleven programmes,[30] gathered together in a volume called *Idioma Clima Crono. Quaderni dell' Itinerario*, 2000-2004. At the same time, a film cycle, *Video Memories*, made by Cristiano Carloni and Stefano Franceschetti,

128

was presented at most locations, as well as a series of installations, called *Crescite,* an *Atlas Room* and an open laboratory, *Vox in Tragoedia.*[31]

At first sight, there seems to be in these eleven productions no mediation or solution, no apparent story to be told, no unity to connect acting characters, no chorus to offer ancestral wisdom, no *polis* to show the corpse of the local hero, no actors to incarnate roles. What is offered instead is universal fragmentation, episodes that do not obey any logical or causal construction (first you see the blood, only then the murder), enigmatic figures in various phases of transition or metamorphosis, dimensions that elude any easy understanding, scenes that evoke terrifying cruelty and horror but at the same time reveal, in visually impressive and grandiose scenes, forms of an extreme beauty. You see landscapes halfway between the innocence of a fairy tale and the violence of a horror film, you experience shudders and shivers on the edge of the unmentionable, beyond the representational character of theatre. A newspaper review of the London Episode staged in 2004 wrote that Castellucci is 'a director whose unsettling, astonishing, enraging theatre is often as difficult to watch as a train crash, but cannot be easily ignored' (see Fig. 4, overleaf).[32]

This preliminary analysis also reveals that the company challenges several important western attitudes towards life, replacing the traditional teleological vision of the work of art (based upon order, plot, verbal materials) with one that focuses more on its reception by an audience. It substitutes a closed totality of semiotic signs and chains with the efficiency of stimuli (to be received by a public), privileging not the syntactic and semantic organisation of a work of art but rather a more pragmatic dimension that focuses on a climate of intensity and physicality, on shivering and trembling.[33] Fundamentally, these changed perspectives replace the thinking head with the powerful presence of the experiencing body, or, put in other terms, they replace the question of a rational interpretation with that of a physical and affective one. As was the case with a Deleuzean interpretation of the paintings of Francis Bacon (1981) and the many films analysed in *L'Image-Temps* (1985), the 'natural' succession of 'movement-images' is broken in favour of an ontology of bodies that incorporate and exhale elementary forces,[34] causing scenes, movements and language to become expressive rather then representative.

In the programme of the first Episode C. # 01 Cesena (2002), a series of assertions about contemporary tragedy were formulated: cosmopolitan cities no longer have links with the earth and with people, there is no *polis* that gathers people in a discussion about common values and norms, and there is no pattern of mythic narratives that guide modern consciousness, all assumptions leading to a reasonable conclusion of the 'contemporary impossibility of an authentic tragedy'. Throughout his career, Castellucci has retained a lively interest in the functioning and dominating presence of tragedy, despite his view that it is a *via negativa,* a road that leads to

Fig. 4. *Tragedia Endogonidia,* 2002-2005, directed by Romeo Castellucci. Reproduced by kind permission of Luca del Pia.

battle, that exhausts people, tears them apart and throws them back upon themselves, in an atmosphere of complete silence. In his opinion, the most interesting opposition to be treated is the one that opposes the notions *tragedia / endogonidia*. They represent two completely different worlds, since:

> -*tragedia* belongs to the human sciences and is a western invention indica-
> tive of our stubborn and unbroken will to detect meaning in this life and to
> defy the idea that the world as such might be devoid of meaning, and of our
> finite and vulnerable position in life;
> -*endogonidia,* on the other hand, belongs to the world of microbiology and
> studies the life of small organisms that multiply through self-reproduction,
> clearly a matter that belongs to the secrets of Nature itself.

The oxymoron created by the juxtaposition of these two notions is a splendid one: it refers to the oldest dichotomy possible, that of Culture vs. Nature, or the conflict between the suffering, tragic hero and creatures which, since they are the effect of a process of an everlasting self-reproduction of micro-organisms, stand totally outside passionate life. It is an oxymoron that opposes the strongest possible mortal efforts to escape death and a meaningless life to a process that occurs in Nature, self-repro-duction without suffering or sex within the existence of small immortal beings. This conflict reminds every classicist of the famous opposition in Vergil's *Georgics* IV, where Orpheus, the human and mortal lover, finds himself confronted with the ever regenerating life of bees, insensitive slaves to their instincts, and of nature in general.

In the following subsections, I touch upon a number of aspects of Castellucci's theatre, compare them to Deleuze's ideas and discuss the presence of some tragic aspects. Although both Deleuze and Castellucci depart from an immanent philosophy, their attitudes towards tragedy largely differ. Deleuze is mainly interested in the tragic condition as a Dionysian affirmation of life.[35] Castellucci feels the distance, but cannot escape its attraction.

2.1. Mysterious beings in continuous transformation

What characterises *Tragedia Endogonidia* (hereafter *TE*) most is an anti-representational stage inhabited by bodies that elude any easy under-standing and dwell in grandiose landscapes governed by unnamable forces. In one way or another, the scenes are always pervaded by violence, threat and abject, disturbing forces in a cosmos where unknown principles rule. Nobody in the audience feels safe in their seats, because, often unconsciously, they are aware of a general climate of tension and aggres-sion. Some examples: women trample upon the two stone tablets of law received by Moses, police officers are beaten, women openly masturbate, a gigantic tank rolls up onto the stage and for minutes faces and threatens the audience, an arrow-machine shoots arrows with precision, cars fall out of the sky, a little baby is left alone in the middle of the scene and cries at length, executioners and their victims threaten each other, Christ urinates in a plastic cube, animals take possession of the stage ... .

There appears to be no narrative filter that governs our gaze and understanding in *TE*, nothing that would allow us to order our thoughts. Rather the *TE* obliges us to leave behind our traditional selves and pass through another filter, to experience a neurological one that liberates us from all culturally determined visions and interpretations and creates a 'nomadic' body that dares to react to the presence of bodies on the stage, unhindered by imposed interpretations. This is why Castellucci's characters on stage are called 'pilgrims in matter', merely presences going astray, since on the stage there is only flux and a fluidity of bodies, only rests of signification, bits and pieces of stories, dark fragments and relicts from former tragic and mythic stories, often presented in a reversed sense. These are blind spots that make us reconsider and remember the silences in and the incomprehensibility of Greek tragedy, that trap where you can easily lose yourself.

Apparently, the characters are often just bodies moving in and out of primary matter, created right after the moment of their collective genesis, just breathing and trusting in the rhythms of their breath. On the one hand, the dramatic and literary part of the characters seems to fade away or to obey (still) unknown principles of transformation; on the other hand, one has the feeling of being in the presence of breathing organisms that have direct contact with our own nervous systems, inspired by an immediate trust in life, in the rhythms of life, illustrating the principal Nietzschean affirmation of life. This is a theatre where the familiar categories of western representation fall into the abyss that turns out to be a desperate feeling of the unknown, a strange mixture of fascination and anxiety, of satisfaction and pain.

Between whatever is happening on the stage and whatever is taking place within the neurological perception of the spectator, there is some indefinite and indistinct circulating going on, halfway between stimulus and response. In these spheres of constant uneasy transitions, tragic characters cannot tell their stories, though many of the feelings and tensions they evoke can be called tragic. In the eyes of Romeo Castellucci, the *TE* cycle is 'an organism on the run', comprising events that leave no time for intelligence or interpretation, only immediate response, immediate reaction from the brain and the flesh.

The *TE*, then, does not want to restore tragedy to the status of a treasure held in common by all Europeans. It merely explores it as a field of unstable and threatening intimacy, where people get in touch with hitherto unknown dimensions of being, not as rational persons but as 'bodies-without-organs' who become attuned to other ways of living. The message seems to be: do not follow exclusively the neo-cortex and its Apollonian regime of imposing order, teleology and climactic scenes, signifying and semiotic chains. Go also with the flow of your limbic brain, seat of sensations and emotions, even allow your reptile brain to be engaged, as illustrated in many productions of Theodoros Terzopoulos.[36]

2.2. Origin of life

Many productions staged by the Socìetas Raffaello Sanzio have dealt with the actual origins of life itself, in their treatment of what can be considered mythic roots, aspects of genesis and becoming, as expressed by the mythic stories of *Inanna* (1989), *Gilgamesh* (1990), *Iside e Osiride* (1990), *Ahura Mazda* (1991), *Lucifero* (1993), *Orestea* (1995), *Giulio Cesare* (1997) and *Genesi* (1998). Some themes in *TE* suggest the same preoccupation. Take, for instance, the letter machine. This is a mechanical device alluding to old information boards of the kind found in train stations, with their rattling letters of the alphabet. In fact, it presents only the basic elements of which letters are made up, mostly not words that lead into language or representational characters. In this mechanical device, language is broken down into its smallest components, suggesting that in the beginning there was a moment when there were only letters, provoking a search for a new and purer language, more appropriate for these decades. This utopian vision has been elaborated since the company's early productions in the early 1980s, when they were engaged in the construction of a private kind of language called *La Generalissima* ('The Very General One').[37]

Secondly, the alphabet also refers to the twenty letters used as abbreviations for the amino acids (such as L for Lysine, R for Arginine and H for Histidine), the twenty elementary building blocks of nature that 'through their almost unlimited recombination ... produce numberless proteins'. These are elementary forms of energy that live completely in the 'silent darkness made up by the inside of a body', biological proofs of the deeper life we all share.[38] But why precisely the amino acids? Instead of focusing on the text of the tragedy, which no longer expresses the norms and values of contemporary society, Castellucci overtly (re)introduces the goat, the tragedy's dark origin. 'Now the time has come that the eponymous animal takes back what belongs to it', he says, replacing the closed dimension of a written text with the larger one of the living presence of the goat, and the abstract and narrative dimension with one that connotes real danger, an operation that goes from the text to the testicles, a 'text-testicle'.[39] His idea was to replace a cultural artefact, the song of a goat, with the goat itself, changing a combination of sounds and letters for a combination of amino acids, substances that characterise organic processes. It was exactly the same step that led from *Tragedia* to *Endogonidia*, since certain protozoic formations have both male and female gonads and do not reproduce sexually but exclusively by means of division. As pointed out by Céline Astrié in the 'Programme of the Brussels Kunsten Festival des Arts, 2006' (on the occasion of M. # 10, Marseille), among the most revealing aspects of tragedy are explosion and revelation, the birth (in a Nietzschean sense) of a new gaze that always leads to new forms of life:

> In the heart of tragedy, ... (e)verything explodes in order that a new always and still to come world be born, unformed, impossible to formulate, containing all possibilities, generating the power of fleeing, a vital trajectory full of strength, promise and positivity. It's not about admitting defeat, about man's impossibility of fulfilling himself, but an affirmation, of the unheard-of point where we finally touch Life, a Life that resembles Death, a Life that we aspire to and dream of endlessly and that never stops making us die.[40]

Like Artaud's metaphor, this theatre thrives like the plague and functions as an organism in continual flux: the eleven episodes reproduce a life split up by fission, creating eleven episodes or 'micro-organisms' that are separated from each other and develop into other parasitic forms called *Crescite*, installations or smaller performances developing some aspects of one of the Episodes. Formulated in Deleuzean language, this means that every major action planned in one of the ten cities develops into 'heterogeneous flight-lines' and 'nomadic presences'. These constitute links between the episodes in all other cities, like recurring elements that contagiously spread from one episode to another destabilising the images and the production (for example, the white clown with long red ears that pops up here and there, or the baby that crawls around).

For the theatre of Castellucci, the impenetrable dark chaos constitutes the kernel of our human existence on earth, doomed as we are to face processes and situations with no apparent meaning. After all, we are made out of cosmic dust and react as microcosmic particles that are unaware of major macrocosmic dimensions. The tragic impulse that emanates from the *TE* is the urge to convince us, physical beings, to explore the hidden (and hence dark) aspects of life inside us and to accept that we are at the mercy of large invisible forces. All eleven 'Episodes' confront us with our limits and stage aspects of chaos within ourselves that we do not want to confront. But, as the examples of the petrified Sphinx and the tired and urinating Christ show in the Parisian Episode (2003), as well as the pietà who unsuccessfully squeezes her breasts for more than twenty minutes, the cultural examples and icons from the Hebrew, Greek and Christian traditions no longer work. They are out of time, out of joint, but they continue to pursue us, since we are bound to think, feel and behave according to the worldview in which we were raised.

3. Conclusions

In Castellucci's opinion, Nature should always be part of a considered life because it obliges us to rethink what really is at the core of our existence. His theatre invites us to free ourselves from (all) imposed cultural identities and necessities and to consider the consequences of the type of existence we are living. Deleuze, for his part, has drastically reformulated the aims of philosophy, redirecting it towards more practical fields in order to produce new devices and generate new questions. Both Deleuze's philosophy and Castellucci's *Tragedia Endogonidia* offer excellent opportunities to reconsider the mental limits we have created in the West and help us become the creatures that we actually are. Among the interesting questions that can be generated in this context, one may cite these: are the tragic and the Christian messages the most valuable ones, or should we not move further on and develop in other and better directions? Have we not been colonised too long, physically and mentally, by notions like guilt, shame and fear of sexuality, affecting and poisoning our visions of the body and the female? The message disseminated by Deleuze is that philosophy, instead of looking for ultimate and foundational onto-theological categories (Truth, God, mimesis), should create ways of conceiving of ourselves anew, fully situated as we are in a world that does not resent multiplicity. Finally, the message of the *Tragedia Endogonidia* is that we should never forget that, however mighty and attractive the tragic hypothesis may be in the West, we always remain attached to the mysteries of Nature, life and our bodies.

The political importance of the Deleuzian-Guattarian project can be gauged by their wish that everyone, in the end, should 'become minor'. In their opinion, there is always a fundamental tension between all those who think of themselves in terms of 'being' and holding a consolidated position in whatever field of experience, and those who 'are' not, but are 'becoming'. Frequently, the position of 'becoming' leads to a deep questioning of previous acts of empowerment, especially those that have led to the creation of the self-conscious white male of the occident. It follows that the major acts of becoming are the ones of 'a becoming-woman', 'a becoming-Indian', and 'a becoming animal'. Mental and social positions like these have to be conceived as alternatives for traditional contexts that, ultimately, only function as false forms of freedom. As part of their philosophical project of decentralisation, or 'deterritorialisation', of the human subject, Deleuze and Guattari constantly exhort us to examine submerged dimensions of equality and justice and promote nomadic thinking that cuts across the boundaries of the state and traditional identities. In their opinion, philosophy should think 'prior to' such current values and structures and conceive of them only as possible manifestations of political organisation.

Contrary to a number of postdramatic productions that merely alienate the spectator from classical and Hegelian forms of representation, both Deleuzean-Guattarian nomadic philosophy and Castellucci's 'pilgrims in matter' appeal for the forging of radical new identities. Their political programme is one that, in the wake of the activities of the Italian *enfant terrible* Carmelo Bene, both believes in the power of dismantling collective identities and in the creation of new ones. Finally, the philosopher and the artist call upon us never to forget that life is, as Rosi Braidotti in her 'nomadic' philosophy says, 'a flow of intensity', always 'capable of carrying the affirmative power of life to a higher degree'.[41]

Notes

1. Hall 2004b: 1.
2. Zeitlin 2004: 55.
3. Fischer-Lichte 1998 and 2008.
4. Butler 1993.
5. Lorraine 1999: 165-91.
6. Van Houtte 2002: 46-7.
7. Bleeker et al. 2002: 217.
8. See Lehmann 2006: 23-4.
9. Fuchs 1996.
10. De Preester 2007: 350; see Welton 1999.
11. Le Goff and Truong 2003; Foucault 1976-1984.
12. Decreus 2005.
13. See the 'energetic theatre' of Lyotard 1977.
14. Schechner 1982 and Demastes 1998.
15. Bermel 2001; Crombez 2008.
16. Ungar 1983.
17. See Van den Dries 2002b.
18. Lyotard 1977: 88; see Van den Dries 2002a.
19. Deleuze 1995: 88.
20. Bonta and Protevi 2004: VII.
21. See Holland 1999; Colebrook 2006.
22. Bogue 1989: 83-106.
23. Deleuze and Guattari 2005: 1.
24. See Hertmans 2000 and 2007.
25. This world-view, best expressed in the adage, traceable to *Ecclesiasastes* as well as Theognis and Sophocles (see Hall 2010: 11), can be summarised as 'it is best not to be born, next best to die young'. As Steiner points out, this is 'transparent shorthand' for the view that 'human life per se, both ontologically and existentially, is an affliction' (Steiner 1996: 535-6).
26. Bonta and Protevi 2004: 136-7.
27. Braidotti 1994: 113.
28. Bogue 2003; Pisters 2003.
29. Lorraine 1999.
30. Novati 2006.
31. Castellucci et al. 2001.
32. Lyn Gardner in *The Guardian*, 15 May 2004.
33. Crombez 2005.
34. Decreus 2008.
35. See his interpretation of Nietzsche, in Deleuze 1962.
36. Decreus 2009.
37. Novati 2006: 25-6.
38. Guidi 2002: 3.
39. Castellucci 2002: 3.
40. Astrié 2006: www.kunstenfestivaldesarts.be (last accessed 28 March 2009).
41. Braidotti 1994: 112.

Generic Ambiguity in Modern Productions and New Versions of Greek Tragedy

Helene Foley

The essential achievement of modern art is that it has ceased to recognise the categories of the tragic and the comic or the dramatic classifications, tragedy and comedy, and sees life as a tragicomedy.

Thomas Mann

The combination of opposites, and the tragic and comic above all, is the fundamental principle of modern drama.

F.W.J. von Schelling

Very few eras have produced drama that scholars and critics would define as 'tragic' in either the Greek or Renaissance sense. George Steiner prominently declared tragedy dead in numerous languages, and many have argued from various other perspectives that composing 'tragedy' for the modern stage is impossible. They may attribute the problem to a culture's unfamiliarity with a vital earlier literary and mythic tradition, to the religious and social disunities of the modern audience, or to the problem of producing meaningful heroic protagonists in a context where serious dramatic characters range widely in social status, and perform in a context where realistic acting conventions and less poetic and distanced language predominate. As one scholar put it, 'Any attempt to write tragedy today is likely to produce melodrama instead.'[1] By contrast, comedy as a literary mode is alive and well in both dramatic and non-dramatic contexts;[2] tragicomedy, which has appeared in various incarnations since the Renaissance, remains a vital and evolving theatrical form arguably still alive on the modern stage in the work of playwrights such as Beckett, Ionesco, Dürrenmatt, and others who are sometimes characterised as writing the theatre of the absurd;[3] even the often-despised melodrama, which separates its good and evil characters according to their deserts, manages to update itself respectably upon occasion.[4]

Contemporary theatrical audiences inevitably bring to their viewing of both Greek tragedy and other serious new plays their powerful experience of later theatrical forms, from Greco-Roman New Comedy to melodrama or tragicomedy. And many recent performances of both the original Greek tragedies in translation, and adaptations and new versions, have responded to these expectations by blurring 'traditional' generic boundaries. When reviewers of Greek tragedy throughout the past hundred or more years have repeatedly complained that the plays should be read, but also that they often fail to be performed successfully on the modern stage, especially in productions that aim to be 'authentic', generic issues are in my view often at the heart of the problem.

This essay will argue that studies of the reception of Greek tragedy on the stage must account more fully for the generic expectations that audiences, directors, and playwrights bring to the theatre in different eras. My discussion and examples will be drawn from the contemporary western world, but the principle should apply to other periods and contexts as well. A very brief review of some prominent current views and controversies about tragedy and tragicomedy that are relevant to theatrical approaches derived from them will set the stage for various case studies.

George Steiner's case (shared by others), that tragedy 'is synonymous with the bleakest form of metaphysical pessimism'[5] and human estrangement, represents one pole that makes any performance of tragedy that solemnly promotes this view on the modern stage problematic. American democratic ideology resists fatalism and favours rewarding the human effort to repair and remake the world. Bertolt Brecht criticised such putative tragic pessimism as promoting resignation and passivity in the face of powerful historical and social forces. Greek views of a divinity that often seems arbitrarily to distribute pain and favour can also be incompatible with the hopes of a Christian audience. Even Freud's case for a modern tragic sensibility based on the permanence of psychological conflict and unsatisfied desire often meets resistance in a social world turning to ever new therapeutic approaches. And while many recent performances of Greek tragedy can be coloured by a popular psychology derived from Freud and his followers, a slide into soap opera can distort the original plays beyond recognition. Although a number of recent scholars have made a case for the renewed relevance of this kind of bleak tragic perspective for a modern world facing issues beyond the limits of human understanding and control, this perspective has not, in so far as I know, been embodied in any 'pure' form on the modern stage.[6]

On the other hand, performance of Greek tragedy is clearly undergoing a modern renaissance, and is hardly dead.[7] A backlash against universalising or philosophical interpretations of tragedy formulated in various ways from Aristotle onward has opened other avenues of interpretation that can emerge as well in performance. As Goldhill among others has argued, tragedy did not aim primarily to promulgate a universalising world view.[8] As a genre, its struggle to represent conflicts and contradictions through drawing on the entire Greek poetic tradition did almost from the start generate a broader panhellenic interest. Fifth-century Greek tragedy also evolved to avoid engagement in specific political controversies. Yet tragedy was shaped by and responded to the political and social realities of both Attic democracy and its festal institutions. When modern performances focus on questions of leadership, on gender conflict or tensions and confrontations between family and state, on what are now defined as racial issues lurking in tragic tensions between native and foreigner, on collective catastrophes (found in tragedies on the fall of Troy), they respond to a genre that explored, sometimes rather episodically, irreconcilable social and ethical issues. Here the focus is not on the struggles of an heroic, existential individual to confront fate that is enhanced by Aristotelian recognition, negative reversals, and a unified plot designed to produce pity, fear and catharsis, as in tragic theories overly attentive to plays like *Oedipus Tyrannus*, but on an open-ended and evolving tragic confrontation with communal problems that require responsible reactions regardless of their unmanageability. When productions do aim self-consciously to create catharsis, as in the case of the well known gospel version of Sophocles' *Oedipus at Colonus*, *The Gospel at Colonus*, the production can have a Christian colouring.[9]

The range of tragedies performed on the modern stage has recently expanded considerably, and efforts to define the tragic by excluding plays represented in our already highly selected and perhaps misleading corpus will not only shut us off from responding to its broader reception on the modern stage, but distort the status of the original plays in context. It seems clear, for example, that from the fourth century BCE onwards, both revivals of plays by Aeschylus, Sophocles, or Euripides and the selection of plays for longer-term preservation and canonisation split individual tragedies from the tetralogies for which they were designed. The acting tradition also modified the plays, reduced the choral role, and, as Jennifer Wise has argued, very probably favoured plays that could best serve as a vehicle for famous actors.[10] Theatre practitioners now, while aware of and at times responsive to the Aristotelian and post-Aristotelian interpretive tradition, also justifiably choose to approach each play on its own – that is, far more open – terms.

In addition, recent classical scholarship has renewed interest in those elements of Greek tragedy that can strike at least a modern audience as verging towards the 'comic'. Greek tragedies (Euripides' late plays like *Helen, Iphigenia Among the Taurians*, or *Ion* especially), comedies, and satyr plays could all generate plots that in some respects anticipated Greek New Comedy by concluding with full or partial dramatic resolutions, rather than simply falls into suffering. Lower-class characters in Aeschylus like the Nurse in *Libation-Bearers*, who catalogues the baby Orestes' digestive habits, or the guard's self-interested calculus in *Antigone*, have always been recognised as bordering on the comic, as has the battle between the monstrous chorus of Erinyes and Apollo in *Eumenides*.[11] The tone of scenes involving noble figures have proved more controversial, as in the case of the pugnacious and class-conscious arguments between Teucer and the Atridae in the second half of Sophocles'

Ajax, the Cadmus-Tiresias scene in Euripides' *Bacchae* or the recognition scene in his *Electra*, which refers pointedly to that in Aeschylus' *Libation-Bearers*.[12] Yet many would agree that Euripides' appropriation of domestic themes, his references to physical detail, the self-consciousness of his treatment of the formal elements of tragedy, his use of distancing and possibly metatheatrical gestures, his competitive allusions to earlier tragedies, or his radical transitions in tone tend to push a nevertheless always evolving genre in new directions that appear in other forms in Old or New Comedy, yet are not necessarily incompatible with serious drama in later ages.[13] The question is whether, as Bernd Seidensticker usefully argues in his book *Palintonos Harmonia,* these 'comic' elements reinforce the tragic effect, mutually enhance both genres, or prove to be more disconcerting and difficult to categorise.[14]

Finally, it is important to remember that we cannot reproduce from texts the tone of performances of the original plays. Considering tragedy serious or *spoudaios,* as our ancient sources agree that it is, does not mean that tragic *performance* necessarily precluded additional elements of humour, parody or satire. And if Aristophanes in plays like *Frogs* apparently plays on or perhaps tries to define a sense of the decorum about tragic performance, he also suggests, even if he comically distorts his case, that Euripides regularly violates it; in any case, his accusations proved sufficiently convincing that they became part of the later reception of the genre.

I noted earlier that the sheer prestige of tragicomedy and/or theatre of the absurd as forms of serious modern and post-modern drama that wrestle with important metaphysical issues inevitably conditions both the reception and performance of Greek tragedy. As defined by Verna Foster, 'a tragicomedy is a play in which the tragic and the comic both exist but are formally and emotionally dependent on one another so as to produce a mixed, tragicomic response in the audience'.[15] Renaissance tragicomedy was a logical if not consciously historical outgrowth of late Euripidean-style drama in a period where tragedy itself also flourished. The struggle of its high-status characters, in a largely private world, with the meaning of existence in the face of suffering, is ultimately affirmed, and disaster averted or transcended. By locating potentially tragic characters in an eventually benign universe, the performance invites a degree of pity, fear, and awe tempered by laughter and ironic detachment; in this context, absurd behaviour does not ultimately undermine tragic dignity.

By contrast, modern tragicomedy often self-consciously rejects tragedy and comedy as distinguishable genres and can draw as well on melodrama, farce, burlesque, satire, and romance. Among dramatists, Dürrenmatt and Ionesco both insisted that tragedy and comedy are the same thing (both play on the discrepancy between what is and might have been) and that tragicomedy has now 'subsumed tragedy'.[16] Beckett's lower-status protagonists often become comic figures in a tragic, absurd, or unknowable universe that denies them dignity of meaning or escape. Here the characters respond not with despair or a move to transcendence, but endure in the face of incomprehensible reality; this process is facilitated by and often arises from laughter. At the same time, the tragic can emerge more shockingly from a comic context, like an opening of a sudden abyss, for an audience resistant to it.

Dürrenmatt argued that tragedy was no longer possible in the modern world because there are no more tragic heroes, 'only tragic events on an enormous scale perpetrated by faceless bureaucracies; tragedy presupposes individual guilt and responsibility, but these qualities have been eroded; tragedy, finally, is predicated on an audience that is already a community, and this, too, no longer exists. Comedy, unlike tragedy, does not need a preexisting order. For it typically creates form out of chaos, and comic invention can shape its own audience. Comedy, too, can still reach us because it is attuned to the "grotesque" (the expression of the "paradoxical") that is so much part of the world of the atom bomb.'[17] Tennessee Williams, on the other hand, argued in a 1974 interview for the integration of comedy into tragic action because his audiences were 'too wary' to take it seriously in an unadulterated form.[18]

Recent productions of Greek tragedy, whether of the Greek originals in translation or new versions, have aimed to revitalise the form for a modern audience, for better or worse, in part by exploiting or introducing generic ambiguity in various ways. The use of metatheatre and other forms of sometimes comic post-Brechtian dramatic distancing invite audiences to be self-conscious about tragic form and its ironies, even while sometimes enabling its representation of suffering in the process. At its best, generic ambiguity and especially comedy can protect and empower a form vulnerable to anachronism. At worst, it can deform a play by obscuring its larger social, political and philosophical issues.

My examples begin with a performance of Euripides' *Bacchae*, a play in which classical scholars have argued for both 'comic' moments in the Cadmus-Tiresias scene and the 'toilet scene', in which the cross-dressed Pentheus is tended mockingly by Dionysus and awkwardly attempts to imitate maenadism, and for a series of arguably metatheatrical gestures by the god of theatre, Dionysus, in disguise as a mortal.[19] The version of this play by David Greig (based on a literal translation by classicist Ian Ruffell)[20] premiered at the King's Theatre, Edinburgh in August 2007 in a co-production between the National Theatre of Scotland and the Edinburgh International Festival (see also Hardwick in this volume). Directed by John Tiffany and starring Alan Cumming, it takes self-conscious note of (and expands on) this potential to the point that the play retains an intergeneric, close to black comic, tone until the final scene where Agave returns with the head of Pentheus.

In Euripides' prologue, the god Dionysus announces that he will appear in human disguise and that he will send his chorus of maenads to try to persuade King Pentheus and the Thebans to accept his worship. Greig's version follows the argument of the original prologue fairly closely, but sets an insouciant tone ('I spin words playfully', Dionysos says later[21]) adopted by the now pointedly androgynous and often camp god throughout. Themes involving disguise are common to many forms of theatre and easily move towards the comic, as does the playful conversation developed by Dionysos in his opening words to the audience:

> So, Thebes.
> I'm back.
> Dionysos,
> You do know me.
> Semele
> Was my mother,
> Zeus my father,
> Lightning my midwife.
> I am, of course a god.
> But if you saw
> Me as I really am – divine –
> Your eyes would burn out of their sockets
> So
> For your benefit I appear
> In human form. Like you. Fleshy.
> Man? Woman? – It was a close run thing.
> I chose man. What do you think?
> ...
> So Thebes, you will acknowledge me
> Whether you want to or not,
> You will acknowledge me
> And love me because I am
> Dionysos.
> I am the Scream.[22]

The metatheatrical tone of the opening was then partly enhanced in performance by the chorus, a group of black Motown-style (a mixture of gospel and R & B) singer-dancers dressed in red who come across as 'foreign' (eastern in Euripides), more because their identity is entirely linked with the world of stage performance than because of their skin (see Fig. 5). Furthermore, the play repeatedly reminds its audience that the players are performing a script, a game that even Pentheus tries to join:

> Dionysos:
>   I'll pay, but you'll pay too, my friend,
>   A fine for failing to applaud
>   A theatrical god.
> Pentheus:
>   He's bold,
>   This Bakkic actor from abroad.
>   He's learned his lines – I'll give him that –
>   But now I'm in charge. I'm writing the script.[23]

Fig. 5. *The Bacchae*, National Theatre of Scotland, 2007. Alan Cumming as Dionysus with Chorus. Reproduced by kind permission of Geraint Lewis.

Some lines move the text itself even more fully into the range of the comic by offering a more explicit level of sexual innuendo than would normally be thought appropriate for a tragedy.

> Pentheus:
>   You met him then,
>   This Dionysos?
> Dionysos:
>   In the dance,
>   His spirit enters us.
> Pentheus:
>   Enters you –
>   Sounds nice – at night?
> Dionysos:
>   In broad daylight.
> Pentheus:
>   From the front? Or from behind?[24]

The performance becomes Dionysos' until the moment he exits to take Pentheus to his death. He dazzles the audience by appearing from above, making flowers pop up from his mother Semele's grave, causing real flames to burst from tubes lining the walls, or suddenly producing a series of dresses for Pentheus to try. 'No trouble', he remarks, 'it was too, too easy really'.[25] This production's Pentheus (Cal MacAninch) was not the poten-

143

tially pathetic, near-adolescent youth of Euripides' play, but a more mature, rather stiff man whose comeuppance the audience was repeatedly invited to enjoy. As Bergson notes, rigidity of body and mind is always potentially comic.[26] Pentheus' rigidity (physical as well as mental) appeared in multiple scenes before the toilet scene, where Pentheus simultaneously looked better in this 'drag act'[27] than before and could not imitate the proper role. Although Dionysos repeatedly reminds the audience that Pentheus is heading towards tragedy, that possibility tended to be distanced by the performance style.

With the possible exception of the mad Agave's grotesque hope to *eat* the head of her captured lion/her son (a detail considerably exaggerated from the original),[28] the realistic, serious style of the final scene – the painful exchanges between Agave and Kadmos and the now powerful god's cruel return – thus came as an even greater shock and transition than in the original. Arguably, this performance's continuous flirtation with comedy and metatheatre was meant to enhance the 'tragedy' in the final scene for an audience hard to surprise or shock in a fashion similar to what Seidensticker argued for some comic moments in Greek tragedy generally. But it also, in New York at least, puzzled audiences and reviewers, who despite enjoying Alan Cumming's extraordinary *tour de force* as Dionysos, were left uncertain as to what point was being made overall – except perhaps about the power of performance itself.[29]

My second example, a production which moved from Dublin's Abbey Theatre to London to the USA from May 2000 to 2002, involves a translation that closely follows the original, but was performed in a fashion that produced repeated laughs before concluding with another descent into horror. *Medea*, directed by Deborah Warner with Fiona Shaw as Medea and Jonathan Cake as Jason, set the play in an unfinished suburban backyard designed by Tom Pye, replete with a wading pool, cinder blocks, and scattered children's toys. The chorus consisted of five neighbourhood women who arrived with offerings of casseroles and other food; the Nurse and Pedagogue were young, naïve, and emotional caretakers of two lovely children; costumes were modern and casual. In this pointedly domestic setting, Jason and Medea's highly sexualised warfare opened the way for a performance that bordered on soap opera. The fairly colloquial translation by Kenneth McLeish and Frederic Raphael permitted (but did not require) the tone that the virtuosic performance of Fiona Shaw produced. I shall therefore concentrate here on the use of her voice and body on stage to produce a tragicomic mix.

Jonathan Kent's 1992-94 *Medea*, starring Diana Rigg and translated by Alistair Elliot, produced laughs from its audience,[30] particularly when the script highlighted gender conflict explicitly. On the basis of a large range of recent performances and new versions, it seems clear that Jason and Medea's competitive accounts of their differences easily lure an audience to recognise in these scenes a sophisticated domestic spat. At the same time, Shaw's style domesticated her role from her first appearance. She arrived in a somewhat revealing housedress, dark glasses and sneakers, announcing: 'Corinthians, I'm here.' The audience laughed (I lost count of how many laughs there were throughout the play, both during my original viewing at Brooklyn Academy of Music and a second time on tape at the Lincoln Center Library for the Performing Arts). Shaw gave her first 'feminist' speech holding a child's dinosaur, her arms flailing awkwardly and hips thrusting to underline a point; feminism was lost. In her speech after the scene with Creon, which was marked by rough handling by the king, she ate a bit of a chorus member's cake with an aside about its being good. While contemplating revenge, she played with a toy stethoscope and doctor's kit (hardly underlining her potential magical powers). She took off her sweater, looked at her arm muscle, flexed it, then sat down defeated, having tied the sweater around her waist. Later, she did not seem to get the Athenian king Aegeus' Delphic riddle about relieving his childlessness, as Euripides' heroine surely did. She could barely resist Jason's repeated physical attempts to win her over at any point. Shaw imagined killing the princess while holding a toy bear on her lap, which she then lit and threw into the pool. When she finally took out her knife, she appeared increasingly demented, as well she might, since she seems to have had no larger issues in mind than jealousy and feelings of abandonment that could explain her choice to kill her children.

The audience for this performance would have found it hard to believe that this half-mad, entertaining housewife was capable of the destructive magic of a granddaughter of the Sun, and indeed she failed to produce magical power on stage. The final scene found Medea listening in stunned, half-mad fascination to the story of the princess' horrific demise – indeed almost identifying with it rather than enjoying her revenge – and then turning wildly to infanticide, chasing her children behind the illuminated glass patio doors of the house to the accompaniment of frightening electronic sound and an hysterical chorus, until a splat of blood appeared on one door. In Jason's presence she then brought out the children's bodies to the pool in which two boats still pathetically floated, and washed them before returning them within. She gave a speech that is delivered by Euripides' quite sane heroine from the stage machine usually exclusive to gods, which permits her escape to Athens with the bodies of the children and excludes Jason from any possibility of action.[31] But in this play, the children were inches away from Jason and Medea never left.

At the final moment, after a feeble attempt to wash the blood from her white jacket, she began to flick water, perhaps madly, perhaps flirtatiously, at Jason, who was hunched in misery on two cinder blocks stage right. The original stages an issue about power and justice; Euripides' androgynous Medea, at great cost to herself, nevertheless triumphs and exacts agony from a now feminised, lamenting, humiliated Jason. Shaw's Medea had not an heroic, magical, or even foreign bone in her body. Her

performance was virtuosic and compelling to many in an audience prepared by their own theatrical experience to appreciate tragedy as high
class soap opera/domestic comedy turned disaster; indeed many seem not
to have noticed the disjunction between Medea's words and actions in this
final scene.[32] But the focus was on the spouses' ultimately irresolvable
erotic and spectacular confrontations (the refusal of an ending was perhaps a touch of the theatre of the absurd), not on issues with important
public implications (for example, contradictions in epic representations of
heroism or the importance of oaths sworn by the gods). In this case, then,
intergeneric play enhanced the stage experience, but radically distanced
the play from central issues in Euripides' original.

A version of Sophocles' *Women of Trachis* by Kate E. Ryan and directed
by Alice Reagan for Target Margin Theater's Hellenic Laboratory at New
York's Ohio Theater in January 2007 used tragicomic effects to address
the problem of representing violence on the modern stage. I quote from the
Program Note:

> If tragedy shows excess (of violence, of temperament, of fate), it also promises
> the audience that in death lies a sense of realization. In *Trachis*, such
> realization is cut short because the husband and wife who bring so much pain
> on one another never meet. Their high noon remains suspended. Out of
> balance, this is a tragedy without security blanket. Suffering is what you
> learn.
>
> In our production, we wanted to explore what it means to stage a theatre
> of catharsis at a time when tragedy has become inflated everyday news-time
> that has exhausted our ability to empathize. In adapting the text, we wanted
> to focus on the gap and allow the clash between the old and the new, rather
> than smooth over the oddities of Sophocles' play. If watching tragedy unified
> a community in Hellenic Times, the role of displaying suffering in our society is
> far murkier. Our adaptation asks how we can still relate to Deianira's and
> Herakles' excess of pain, so embellished with all things monstrous and mythical.
> What are our responsibilities, as an audience, when watching pain?

This rarely performed drama depicts the tragic error made by Herakles'
long-suffering, largely abandoned wife Deianeira, who attempts to use a
love charm to win back her long-absent husband Herakles after he has
sent a mistress home to await his return. She commits suicide when she
learns that the charm was poison, and Herakles is brought back in agony.
When he understands that he is being killed with poison from his own
arrows in the blood of a centaur who tried to rape Deianeira, he asks his
son Hyllus to arrange his funeral pyre on a mountain top and to marry his
mistress Iole. Hyllus refuses to light the pyre, but reluctantly agrees to the
latter. The adapter's additional problem, in a cut (one hour) but fairly close
version in modern prose, and with characters in modern dress, was how to
make the naïve Deianeira's error credible in a modern context.

I wish to comment only on two dramatic choices here. As in the Edinburgh *Bacchae*, the production relied on a shift in tone to the serious shock

of the final scenes from scenes that included humour – the teenage, back-pack carrying Hyllus was full of himself, and Herakles' messenger Lichas was played as a pretentious celebrity hunter. This version's biggest change to the original script was a chorus of easily distracted picnicking country girls dressed in pink dresses and flowery bracelets. Sophocles' chorus is composed of naïve young virgins, but this chorus took its role to extremes, substituting childhood tales and experiences and pop songs for the chorus' original myths, and bromides for the Greek chorus' turns to collective wisdom. In the company of these vacuous moderns, the once fairly worldly and successful, but now desperately isolated Deianeira (an excellent Heidi Shreck) had nowhere to turn. Unlike *Bacchae*, then, this production (success-fully in the view of Jonathan Kalb, *New York Times*, 24 January 2007) employed generic shifts to protect its representation of suffering.[33]

My next example draws on a two-hour, highly ironic and anachronistic version of Aeschylus' *Oresteia* by David Johnston, performed by Blue Coyote Theatre Group and directed by Steven Speights at New York's Access Theater in February 2007.[34] Each of the three original plays adopted a different tone, but I wish to comment only on its treatment of *Agamemnon*. The audience in this black box theatre entered past a sleep-ing watchman, whose struggle to stay awake for the beacon from Troy was soon interspersed with a vision of a radiant Iphigeneia dressed in bridal garb, and a glimpse of a naked Clytemnestra and Aegisthus making love within the palace. The beacon, Clytemnestra's orgasm, and Iphigeneia's sacrifice occurred simultaneously. The next scene opened with a blood-stained Iphigeneia lurking in the background, while a mousy Curator of the Argos Cultural and Historical Society began to expound on objects from the royal household of Tantalus. Three women (who later became the Furies) interrupted from the audience, asking whether Tantalus' bowl, for example, was used to serve his son Pelops to the gods. In the next scene, a herald returned, leading a ragged Cassandra on a choke chain. Agamem-non, a 'simple' man who claims to do what he says, acted in the name of Faith and Freedom to punish Troy (a probable Bush parody was thinly veiled). Clytemnestra had the Furies roll out the red carpet for an Agamemnon who was stymied by her manipulation of the public context (the use of this device for film stars has problematised it even for more serious productions). She then openly announced her murder plans to Cassandra, who could not persuade the Curator of what she (and the audience) had heard or of the presence of the sacrificed Iphigeneia in the background. Cassandra then reluctantly left for death with only the hope of being remembered. A display of the dead bodies of Agamemnon and Cassandra, with Clytemnestra standing above, axe in hand, was meant to be deliberately reminiscent of Brian DePalma's *Carrie*. Clytemnestra defended herself to a Curator now losing hope in his attempt to rescue the royal family's image, and the play closed with the appearance of Electra to greet her father, only to encounter his corpse.

The Curator, to say nothing of the play's continuous metatheatre, made clear that this *Oresteia*'s audience was experiencing a dialogue with (not a parody or burlesque of) a museum piece about to explode out of its original form into something else that drew in part on horror flicks with laughs. And in fact, the play's adoption of the original's display of off-stage violence only did succeed in being gripping in this new context, and, despite all the new version's anachronisms, the original's serious issues and its plot sequence remained pointedly central to the script.[35] Overall, Johnston seemed to suggest that we need to view Greek tragedy through the distancing filters of later theatre (and even film) history in order to appreciate its full impact.

Especially in the late 1960s and 1970s and again very recently, Euripides' *Orestes* has invited performances through the lens of the theatre of the absurd in both in performances of the original in translation and in new versions. As interpretations of *Orestes* by classical scholars indicate – even the ancient hypothesis calls the ending of the play 'rather comic' – this approach is less of a stretch than might be imagined. Euripides' lurching plot, with its continuous self-conscious, implicit, at times argu-ably metatheatrical, references to earlier dramatic versions, temporarily leaves the myth behind. The maddened matricide Orestes begins the play in a sickbed tended by Electra. He fails to save himself with arguments from previous plays in a world where bringing his issues to court appears to have been anachronistically available. Condemned to death by the Argives in a failed assembly, the hero and his sister have no means of escape; incited by Orestes' friend Pylades, they decide to kill Helen, who has recently returned to Argos with Menelaus. Yet her off-stage shrieks do not, as would be expected, indicate a death reported by an incoherent singing Phrygian slave messenger (messengers normally do not confuse the audience or sing). The play seems to have reached a stalemate. As Orestes stands with Electra and Pylades on the palace roof preparing to set it on fire and kill Menelaus' daughter Hermione, the god Apollo intervenes from the machine, accompanied by a now divine Helen; but this final scene offers from a human perspective an entirely artificial resolu-tion. Metaphysically speaking, *Orestes* is operating in a vacuum, and indecorously obsessed with mundane detail and survival; the radical shifts in tone from one scene to another take on the speed of tragicomedy.

I do not know of a single American production of *Orestes*, from the 1968 and 1973 productions at Berkeley (directed in the Berkeley Greek Theater by Jan Kott) and Stanford (directed by John Chioles), to the 1981 perform-ance of Adrienne Kennedy's double bill of *Electra* and *Orestes* at New York's Julliard School directed by Michael Kahn, that has not been at least partly absurdist or post-modern. From a modern perspective, it seems almost impossible to do otherwise. Kott set his play against a photographic image of Washington, D.C. which burst into flames at the conclusion. A Pylades in black leather arrived on a motorcycle to greet his fellow alienated hippies Orestes and Electra; a call-girl Helen swung across the stage on a trapeze.[36] New versions, such as that of Charles Mee, which interspaces modern texts into versions of the play's scenes already close to hysterical action, and has received far more productions from 1992 than Euripides' play, or Theodora Skiptares' 2007 *The Exiles*, a version at New York's La Mama, Etc. that mixed actors and puppets, have simply taken performances of the original a step further into absurdity.[37] Mee's version, for example, closes with a meaningless intervention by Apollo, accompanied by a blow-up doll Helen, who uses the voice of the current American President but has no meaningful effect on the stage action; Skiptares' Apollo was a huge gold lamé puppet whose features reminded one reviewer of Donald Rumsfeld.[38] In a stab at the presentation of justice on the media, Orestes' trial in Mee takes place on stage, but is drowned out by three Nurses/Furies discussing their sex lives on a radio talk show.

Euripides' *Phoenician Women*, my second example in this category, is less obviously amenable to this kind of interpretation, although equally replete with allusions to earlier versions. In Euripides' action-packed play, the blind Oedipus and Jocasta have survived to confront the battle between their sons Eteocles and Polynices over ruling Thebes. The prophet Tiresias demands the sacrifice of Creon's son Menoeceus to save the city from Polynices' attack. Menoeceus ignores his father's advice to flee and kills himself. The brothers twice resist being reconciled by Jocasta and slaughter each other. Jocasta kills herself over their bodies; Creon then prevents Antigone from burying her brother and play closes with the departure of Antigone and Oedipus for exile, an event that normally occurs earlier in the myth and leaves this textually corrupt play without an ending (it may have had a different one).

In Steven Gridley's *Post-Oedipus*, performed at New York's Flamboyan Theater at the Clemente Soto Velez Cultural and Educational Centre in 2004,[39] the family of Oedipus – Jocasta, Oedipus, and their four children – attempted and failed to avoid their fates. The narrative loosely followed Euripides' original but echoed its repeated refusals to achieve a coherent storyline and meaningful conclusion. Jocasta, who opened the play with one of endless futile attempts to re-formulate the family story through photographs, memories, and awkward interventions, repeatedly resisted her family tree, which had been deformed through incest. Her favourite self-portrait represented her lamenting, but she can never quite imitate it properly. 'It's odd, but when I look back on it my life is actually much more fulfilling than it feels', asserted Jocasta in a hopeful moment.

She closed the play crowned in maternal glory, with the limp bodies of her family draped around her. Each has just repeated a characteristic 'loop' before their final collapse. The blind, endlessly bleeding Oedipus carried around a tape recorder filled with inspirational sayings, such as 'when you lose, don't lose the lesson'; he is trying to save the family fortunes and reconcile with Jocasta by building gum ball machines. Antigone obsessively worried over and tried to reconcile her brothers, cared for her father, and periodically re-read an old love letter (by Haemon?) stashed in her pocket. Ismene, ignored by all, played the recorder; she finally adopted the sacrificial role of Menoeceus in order to put herself in the picture. The two brothers performed a hilarious, childish verbal duel that echoed their Euripidean debate over sharing power. The pipe-wielding Polyneices sulkily favoured equity, and the secret wanker Eteocles insisted that neither reality nor the gods ensure anything but inequality. Eventually, after many attempts to divert the outcome, the brothers slaughtered each other just as Oedipus proclaimed the success of his gumball machine. The play's multi-purpose messenger constantly failed to establish a suitably tragic tone to events, as did bursts of classical music. Characters fell into their fates like puppets and then sprang up to try once again to escape their destinies. The play constantly introduced moments in which large picture frames literally reframed the family group, snapshots were taken, and cameras and slide projectors were used as weapons: all to no avail. 'Without memory, we would have nothing but the present. And the present is always disappointing.'[40] Or, as Eteocles commented on his father's fate: 'The Truth – is Not – Your Friend. Search for Me. And Find Your Ruin'.[41] This post-modern version clearly appropriated the clichés of tragic metaphysics in tragicomic style.

This essay lacks the space to take on other major trends in new versions of Greek tragedy that began with the burlesques following nineteenth-century tragic performances discussed by Edith Hall and Fiona Macintosh in their *Greek Tragedy and British Theatre 1660-1914*, and has evolved into drag and cross-dressing close versions of the original plays that satirise without losing a certain grandeur and poignancy.[42] Whereas some post-Renaissance eras were uncomfortable with Greek revenge tragedies, both these modern burlesques and other intergeneric versions can invite their audiences to revel, if sometimes only temporarily, in the violence of the plays. A large number of recent performances, often influenced by the work of Charles Mee, have used various versions of pastiche to splice alien texts into productions of the originals that range from horrific to comic and satirical. Alternatively, large sections of a tragic text can be embedded in modern contexts that comment on the originals, but surprisingly do not undermine their tragic force in ways that might be expected.[43]

This essay has argued that when assessing modern performances and new versions of Greek tragedy, it is important to look not just at current theories of tragedy and other dramatic genres that have developed since the fifth century BCE, but also at performances, translations and scripts. Tragedy is comprehended and defined differently through performance than on the page, and performance offers a living laboratory for exploring a genre prematurely declared dead.

11. *Generic Ambiguity in Modern Productions of Greek Tragedy*

Notes

1. Foster 2004: 117.
2. Silk 1998 stresses this point.
3. See among many other studies, Hirst 1984; Orr 1991; Foster 2004. Playwrights from Ibsen (especially *The Wild Duck*) to Pinter or Shepard have been included in this category of plays.
4. Felski 2008: 7. She argues that this is especially true when it retains a sense of 'impossible contradictions'.
5. Felski 2008: 4; Steiner 1961 and 2008.
6. For discussions of views recuperating tragedy for the modern era, see Felski 2008.
7. The bibliography is too extensive to cite here. For a good introduction, see Hall, Macintosh and Wrigley 2004.
8. Goldhill 2008. For useful works discussing tragedy as a genre see Felski 2008; Lambropoulos 2006; Poole 2005; Eagleton 2003; Williams 1966; and for Classics, Sommerstein et al. 1993; Silk 1996.
9. The play opened in 1983 at the Brooklyn Academy of Music and received multiple revivals until 2004 at New York's Apollo Theatre. See Breuer 1989 (introduction).
10. Wise 2008 with earlier bibliography.
11. Herington 1963.
12. See Barnes 1964; Knox 1970; Seidensticker 1978 and 1982; Foley 1980 (revised in Foley 1985); Gibert 2000; Goff 2000; or the sceptical views of Gregory 2000. On generic boundaries between tragedy and comedy in the fifth century see Taplin 1986 and 1996; Goldhill 1991; Segal 1995; Zacharia 1995; Wright 2005; Most 2000; or Foley 2008.
13. See further Mastronarde 2000.
14. Seidensticker 1982. The last of these questions is my own.
15. Foster 2004: 11.
16. Foster 2004: 13.
17. Dürrenmatt 1982 and Foster 2004: 31.
18. Quoted in Foster 2004: 149.
19. Foley 1980 raises this possibility more cautiously than Segal 1982.
20. Greig 2007. I saw the play in New York at the Lincoln Center Festival in summer 2008.
21. Greig 2007: 31.
22. Greig 2007: 7.
23. Greig 2007: 29.
24. Greig 2007: 26.
25. Greig 2007: 38.
26. Bergson 1956.
27. Greig 2007: 58.
28. Greig 2007: 72.
29. Eric Grode, *New York Sun*, 7 July 2008 and Charles Isherwood, *New York Times,* 5 July 2008. Both reviews found the final scene unconvincing. Grode thought the production misunderstood Greek views of religion and nature.
30. I speak from my experience of the New York production in April 1994.
31. As Goldhill 2007: 23-4 points out, the missing vertical dimension in this play undermined its point.
32. In the case of the New York production, John Lahr, *New Yorker*, 23 and 30

December 2002, Alisa Solomon, *Village Voice*, 9-15 October 2002, and Ben Brantley, *New York Times*, 4 October 2002 all offered enthusiastic reviews that particularly responded to the production's high level soap opera. Brantley compared her to a figure out of the *National Enquirer*. Solomon, the only critic to note the changed ending, thought the chorus an impediment to this style of performance.

33. The audience for this play grew night by night by word of mouth and my students and colleagues at Barnard and Columbia were generally enthusiastic about it. I am grateful for a copy of the script and an interview with Alice Reagan.

34. I am grateful to David Johnston for a copy of the script. The *Eumenides* is published in Denton 2006: 125-38.

35. The audience on the night I attended loved the first two acts. See reviews by Jason Zinoman, *New York Times*, 2 February 2007 and Robert Davis 2002: 86-90.

36. See Arnott 1987: 367-8 and *New York Times*, 17 February 1968. For reviews of Kahn's production, see Marilyn Stasio, *New York Post*, 16 April 1981, *Soho Weekly News*, 22 April 1981; Robert Massa, *Village Voice* 22 April 1981.

37. See Mee 1998: 87-158. Anne Bogart directed the play at the Saratoga International Theatre Institute (SITI) in 1992; Robert Woodruff directed it at the Mandell Weiss Theatre in La Jolla, California in 1992; Tina Landau did an En Garde Arts Production on New York's Penn Yards (on the waterfront) in summer 1993; James Keene directed it for the Annex Theatre in Seattle, May 1995; Ellen Beckerman of Lightbox Theater staged another version at New York's Here Arts Center in 2001; Michael Patrick Thornton directed it for the Gift Theater Company in Chicago, 2002; a second Here Arts production by Jose Zayas for the Intermediate Theatre Company took place in April 2007. For further discussion on Bogart, see McDonald 1993a; on the Landau production, see Andreach 1996, Jonathan Kalb, *Village Voice*, 13 July 1993, and D.J.R. Bruckner, *New York Times*, 30 June 1993. There have been several university productions as well. Among other post-modern efforts were Michael McClure's 1985 *Vktms: Orestes in Scenes* (directed by Judith Malina for The Living Theater in New York, 1988) and 'Orestes: "I Murdered my Mother"', adapted and directed by Jeff Cohen for Rapp Arts Theater Company at New York's Worth Street Theater in 1996 (reviewed by Ben Brantley, *New York Times*, 30 July 1996).

38. Honor Moore, *New York Times*, 28 March 2007.

39. Directed by Jacob Titus and Steven Gridley, the play received two earlier workshop productions at One Arm Red in DUMBO, Brooklyn and at HERE Arts American Living Room Festival. The script was published in 2006. New York reviews were relatively positive.

40. Gridley 2006: 36.

41. Gridley 2006: 62.

42. For further discussion see Foley, 'Bad Women: Gender Politics in Late Twentieth-Century Performance and Revision of Greek Tragedy' in Hall, Macintosh and Wrigley 2004: 77-112.

43. I will offer examples of all these trends in a forthcoming study derived from my 2008 Sather Classical Lectures at Berkeley.

Revising 'Authenticity' in Staging Ancient Mediterranean Drama

Mary-Kay Gamel

> If Aeschylus had lived today
> he'd have to write a different play
>
> Tony Harrison, *Prometheus*

1. Theory

In 1955 Jean-Louis Barrault staged a production of the *Oresteia* which received high praise. The production made use of ritual elements inspired by Barrault's participation in religious rites on a trip to Brazil.[1] One audience member, however, was not enthusiastic. Calling it 'an ambiguous spectacle' full of 'confusions,' Roland Barthes criticised its mixture of acting styles (physical theatre, psychologised naturalism, rhetoric), costumes (Minoan, classical, *'grand couturier'*), and the treatment of the chorus (movement at times gymnastic, at others anarchic, speech at times declamatory, at others conversational) and concludes that these mixtures are the result of an 'inability to choose among opposing claims'.[2] He also criticised the director's and actors' failure to commit fully to the concept: 'If you set about to create a theater of participation, you must go all the way. Here the *signs* no longer suffice: what is required is a physical commitment from the actors ... a few twirls, a syncopated rhythm in some choral speeches, a little stamping on the floor are not enough ... Wishing doesn't make the witch doctor.'[3] It is fascinating to see the great semiotician insist that signs are not enough, and the critic who privileged the 'writerly' text (open, plural, indeterminate) call for greater clarity, one of the qualities he later defined as 'readerly' (closed, single, defined) – to be sure, *S/Z* was still fifteen years in the future. Barthes asks questions which every modern producer of ancient drama must answer: 'Are the Greek plays to be performed as of their own time or as of ours? Should we reconstruct or transpose? emphasise resemblances or differences?' Yet 'performance never helps us answer these questions'.[4] Indeed, performances do not proclaim their aims and methods; instead they put them into action, inviting audience members to respond in their own intellectual and emotional terms. The subtext of Barthes' statement, that performance needs theory, is the central focus of this collection.

Theorising the performance reception of ancient Mediterranean drama requires an understanding of the theoretical matrices both of those who create performance and of those who respond to performance. As a member of both these groups I have found theory, particularly questions about authenticity, helpful. In the case of artifacts from an earlier time, such questions quickly expand beyond the obvious ones about forgery and plagiarism. What is the status and value, for example, of items originally used for a culture's practical or religious purposes, but now created specifically for the tourist trade? Still more questions arise when presentation and performance are involved. Should Shakespeare's sonnets be printed in their original Elizabethan spellings, even if contemporary audiences cannot understand their meaning? What happens when the 'Elgin Marbles' are moved from their original location and displayed in a gallery to be viewed in a different way by a different audience? (To be sure, even if the Marbles were still in their original location their audience and meaning would be drastically changed.) Do reconstructed 'living' archaeological and historical sites such as Celtica in Wales and Colonial Williamsburg in Virginia have value, and if so, as what – archaeology? museums? theatre?[5]

Debates about authenticity have been pursued most actively concerning the performance of music, and these debates can inform the less well-developed theoretical discussion of performance reception of ancient Mediterranean drama.[6] Some argue that performers of earlier music should try to recreate the exact conditions of a first performance, including using original texts; researching the composer's intentions in creating the work; reconstructing early instruments; developing historically accurate techniques for playing them; and studying the cultural conditions of performance and audience reactions. Some performers and scholars have argued that such 'historically informed' performance is the only valid performance of early music.[7] Conductor Raymond Leppard, however, points out that a too narrow concept of authenticity 'arrives at the dubious but inevitable conclusion that there is only one way perfectly to reveal a piece of earlier music'.[8] The most polemical critic of historically informed performance, musicologist Taruskin, calls it not authentic but 'authentistic'. He attacks 'the notion, so widespread at the moment, that the activity of our authentistic performer is tantamount to that of a restorer of paintings, who strips away the accumulated dust and grime of centuries to lay bare an original object in all its pristine splendour. In musical performance, neither what is removed nor what remains can be said to possess an objective ontological existence akin to that of dust or picture. Both what is "stripped" and what is "bared" are acts and both are interpretations.'[9] Kivy, a philosopher who focuses on music, thoughtfully concludes, 'I am a friend of any authenticity, or any mix of authenticities, that withstands the only relevant test there is: the test of listening'.[10]

It is important to understand the *historical* and *contingent* nature of the concept of authenticity. As Wiles says, 'Most directors who engage with Greek drama feel a) that they have touched on something *authentically* Greek which is worth bringing to the present, and b) that there is something in the present which they would like to bring to the ancient text.' However, 'the element of authenticity keeps shifting – the circular auditorium, the use of the mask, uncensored Aristophanic obscenity, the message about war. What seems authentic to one generation seems stilted, ill-researched and irrelevant to the next.'[11] Moreover, authenticity becomes a value, and a problem, only when alternatives become available. The concept of 'live' performance, for example, came into being only with the advent of recording technologies: as Auslander says, 'The very concept of live performance presupposes that of reproduction ... the live can exist only within an economy of reproduction'. Hence 'the ancient Greek theatre ... was not live because there was no possibility of recording it'.[12] Benjamin was able to devise his influential concept of the 'aura' possessed by 'original' 'unique' works of art only because mechanical reproductions existed. In the ancient evidence, by contrast, there is no concern for authenticity in performance. For textual accuracy, yes, for good vocal projection and acting – but no sign that a production might be considered unfaithful or inappropriate, no concept of a fixed 'original.' We must remember, *pace* Aristotle, that few ancient spectators would have had the opportunity to read a script, or to compare script to performance.[13]

Those moderns who are familiar with scripts both in Greek and Latin, with translations, with live performances of various kinds, and with recorded performances in various media, need to define the relationships between these phenomena and to estimate their different claims. What criteria can we use to decide what makes for a valid 'subsequent performance' (Jonathan Miller's term)? Classical scholars, relying on their knowledge of the scripts and their ideas about the impact of the original productions, often idealise, explicitly or implicitly, the 'original form' of ancient drama, and find contemporary productions wanting.[14] Philosophers concerned with authenticity ask such questions as: What did the art work mean to its creator? How was it related to the cultural context of its creation? To what established genre did it belong? What could its original audience have been expected to make of it? What would they have found engaging or important about it? As Wiles says, however, there is no unmediated access to the past: 'We can only understand what Greek theatre was like in the past by looking through the eyes of the present.'[15]

Dutton distinguishes between 'nominal authenticity' ('the correct identification of the origins, authorship, or provenance of an object') and 'expressive authenticity'. The latter has 'to do with an object's character as a true expression of an individual's or a society's values and beliefs', and involves 'committed, personal expression, being true ... to one's artistic self'.[16] The formulation of 'expressive authenticity' seems to rest upon (though Dutton does not say so) ideas about personal authenticity (vs. 'bad faith') as self-definition through self-awareness, free choice, and commit-ment, ideas articulated by Sartre and others.[17] Citing Tolstoy's distinction between manipulative and sincerely expressive art, Dutton argues that examples of the latter 'are *meant* in a way that many examples of the former cannot possibly be: they embody an element of personal commit-ment',[18] and the *Oresteia* actors' failure of 'physical commitment' according to Barthes might be considered expressive inauthenticity. Presumably, then, a theatrical performance possesses 'expressive authenticity' in pro-portion to the 'truth' of the author's expression of his own values and beliefs; the participating artists' understanding of, and personal commit-ment to, the performance they are creating, and audiences' commitment to engaging with and evaluating that performance.

It is difficult, however, to apply this formulation to theatrical perform-ance. First, identifying an author's 'individual' values is always questionable, especially difficult in the case of a playwright, and even more difficult in the case of ancient playwrights, about whom little is known. Moreover, many more factors and personnel of different kinds are involved in theatrical than in musical performance – spoken word, architecture, visual aspects (set, costumes, masks, lighting, props), movement (gesture, dance), possibly music, and questions of translation, not only verbal but visual, theatrical, sonic. Connor calls theatre 'a radically impure form of art' which involves 'divisions which complicate, diffuse and displace the concentrated self-identity of a work of art ... Theatricality is the name for the contamination of any artefact that is dependent upon conditions outside, or other than, its own.'[19] Finally, how can we define a 'true expression' of a society's values and beliefs? Significantly, Dutton focusses on the art of small tribal groups, not of complex modern societies. None-theless, there may be ways in which the concept of personal authenticity via self-definition and commitment may be applicable to theatrical produc-tions, as I will suggest below.

Dutton further suggests that works of art possess 'emergent value' and that thinking about authenticity involves attention to 'the larger artistic potential' of a work.[20] 'An authentic performance of a piece of music,' he continues, might be defined as 'one in which the aesthetic potential of the score is most fully realized.' Such a formulation is obviously applicable to theatrical production; Dutton argues that Shakespeare would have chosen women to play the parts played by boys if he had had the option. Miller goes further, arguing that a great play's meaning begins to be fully appreciated *only* when it enters what he calls its 'afterlife'[21] and that such a play has 'the capacity to generate an almost infinite series of unforesee-able inflexions'. Shakespeare continues to be performed, he argues, because we are still looking for the possibility of unforeseen meanings'.[22] Indeed, 'it is precisely because subsequent performances of Shakespeare's plays are interpretations, rather than copies, that they have survived'.[23]

There is another fundamental objection to the concept of formal or nominal authenticity. Like the now outmoded concepts of 'influence' and 'the classical tradition,' such a concept assumes that the meaning of ancient artefacts can be determined, that it does not change over time, and that later adaptations are inevitably inferior imitations of the 'original'. Such a position has been seen by Hardwick as a kind of 'colonisation' and the move away from it as liberation.[24] I would add that artists working with these texts are also liberated; instead of being in a position of subjection to the past, they are free to seek expressive authenticity by exploring emergent meanings and being true to their artistic selves.[25]

There are few discussions of theatrical authenticity; most focus on Shakespeare.[26] The increasing number of studies of the performance reception of ancient Mediterranean drama have so far rarely addressed the question of authenticity. The result is a wide array of vague terminology: productions are called 'realist', 'modernist', 'experimental', 'conceptual', 'deconstructed', 'revisionist', examples of *Regietheater*, or Eurotrash, directors classified as 'conservative', 'liberal' or 'radical'. Meanwhile, the idea that a production can provide unmediated access to the past is hardly dead: the announcement of a 1996 Dutch production, for example, proclaimed:

> We emphasize the importance of an accurate approach of the text so that our audiences can experience genuine Greek drama … We aim at authenticity with regard to the theme as well. Every performance is inevitably an interpretation, no matter how hard we try to be authentic. But we want to play *Antigone* with a maximum of respect for its author. We find that an interested audience with some affinity with classical culture is able to appreciate Sophocles' ideas and we want to be no more than the medium through which his story reaches the public. We are not trying to make anything artificially attractive to a modern audience by adding some 'juice' of contemporary hot issues. For example, in our production nobody will find a homosexual Haemon who uses the conflict about Antigone to extort some degree of acceptance of his sexual orientation from his father.

Here as elsewhere, theoretical discussions of authenticity often lack an important element. The 'receivers' are conceived as authors and performers, with little attention to the audience's role. Yet the final 'reception' of performance is performed by the audience, who are not passive but central to realising the performance. This dimension of performance reception draws on analogous movements in literary theory such as the Konstanz School of *Rezeptionsästhetik* in Europe and reader-response criticism in North America.[27] Thom agrees with Taruskin and Dutton that concepts of authenticity are always defined in opposition to something else: 'What is done authentically is done because it has lately not been done. Authenticity is a reaction against a supposedly corrupt tradition of execution. It involves an attempt to overthrow one performative tradition and restore another. In this sense, authenticity is a matter of degree'.[28] As his book's title *For an Audience* suggests, Thom recognises the centrality of the

audience's role: 'Performance is action for an audience' and 'a good audience can take up certain opportunities for substantive interpretation that are
implicit in the very nature of the performing arts'.[29] Since audiences exist in
history, it is essential to consider the audience of particular performances and
their expectations. Altena stresses that theatre artists 'must know their
audience; know how to involve the spectators both rationally and emotionally,
and know how to shock in order to please them'.[30]

Evidence about ancient audiences and their reactions to performances
is woefully thin, so we must rely on anecdotal observations about what
those audiences experienced,[31] but we are more informed about the conditions of production. First, ancient theatrical performances were structured
according to *conventions* well known to their audiences, including such
items as a consistent playing space, alternation between speech and song,
use of the mask, and stereotypical characters. These conventions allowed
audiences to understand the differences between predictable and unpredictable elements in a particular performance. Second, ancient Greek and
Roman drama offered their audiences a *mixture* of elements, some familiar, some strange. Athenian tragedy combines mythical settings and
fifth-century dilemmas; Old Comedy mixes Athenian characters and allusions with surrealistic plots; Roman comedies written in Latin feature
Greek characters and settings. Such mixtures made different interpretations inevitable. Third, theatre in Athens and Rome was not an
antiquarian venue for presenting 'classics'. Revivals did occur, but audiences were usually seeing works for the first time. Even if they were based
on traditional stories, playwrights had great freedom in changing events,
portraying characters in new ways, and introducing new themes. Because
so few ancient performance texts have survived, we tend to experience
them as unique 'originals'. Ancient audiences, however, saw them as part
of a continuum, and evaluated them in light of the other versions they
knew. The latest version could differ from previous versions, as Euripides'
Electra explicitly contradicts Aeschylus' *Choephori*, and his *Phoenician
Women* contradicts Aeschylus' *Seven Against Thebes*. The older version
was not more authentic than the new, or vice versa; each was part of a
complex and ongoing dialogue.

The evidence suggests that audiences were attentive to both form and
content. They scrutinised dramatic performances for their ethical, social
and political implications, and responded vigorously – intellectually and
emotionally – to what they saw. Cicero says: 'In theatrical speeches, every
single passage in which something said by the author seemed to refer to
current events was either noticed by the entire audience, or the actor
himself made it clear.'[32] Athenians wept when the playwright Phrynichus
presented a play about the Persians' destruction of Miletus, a Greek city
in Asia Minor, and fined the author.[33] They grumbled when a character
expressed an unpopular idea, until the playwright himself stood up and
advised them to wait and see what happened to the character.[34] Contradic-

tory speeches in Athenian tragedy and comedy reflect the debates of the assembly and lawcourts, with the audience as jury. Plato reflects the deep connection between theatre and democracy in Athens when he says disdainfully: 'Whenever the masses gather in the assembly, in courtrooms, at the theater ... they voice their approval or disagreement always in excess, producing constant uproar with applause or protest.'[35]

2. Practice I

Dutton's category of 'nominal authenticity' is similar to the 'historically informed' performances of early music. A production which fits this category is the 1985 New York Greek Drama Company *Medea* directed by Peter Steadman, in which actors in masks and chitons spoke Greek in pitch accents. One male actor designated as the deuteragonist played all the secondary roles including female ones, and the chorus sang as they embodied choreography inspired by Greek vase paintings, accompanied by music tonally similar to ancient Greek music, played on an oboe, the modern instrument most similar to the *aulos*.[36] This production was intended to strike its modern audience as 'strange', declares William Arrowsmith in a foreword on the videotape, and that strangeness is 'the chief reason for producing this play in the first place' (a fascinating statement from one of the greatest twentieth-century translators of Greek plays into English). A modern audience must find this production alien – those who saw it live probably even more than viewers of the video, to which English subtitles are added.[37] Such alienation between performance and audience – not a momentary *Verfremdungseffekt* but a fundamental distance – is quite different from ancient audiences' relationship to the performances they saw.

Such a production can evoke admiration in its contemporary audience, but its focus on formal elements often undercuts its ability to communicate. When the chorus perform the first choral ode (410-45), for example, there is no obvious connection between the text of the chorus' song, which attacks male betrayal and expresses support for Medea, and their choreographic movement. The production's fundamental alterity prevents most spectators from bringing an engaged, critical perspective to bear on the issues involved. Dutton argues, moreover, that if La Scala were to lose its local and European audiences, and be frequented only by tourists, such audiences could not 'make the sophisticated artistic discriminations that we would associate with traditional La Scala audiences'. The result would be 'the loss of a *living critical tradition* that an indigenous audience supplies for any vital artform'.[38] Here is the 'catch 22' of nominal authenticity: the closer a modern production approaches the formal conditions of its original production, the stranger it will be to a modern audience. The stranger the effect on a modern audience, the more different their reactions will be from those of the original audience.[39]

159

If there is a kind of authenticity focussed on the audience, then, what should we call it? 'Aesthetic' in its original sense (perception via the senses) would work, but since Kant that term has pertained to the criticism of the beautiful or to the theory of taste. 'Phenomenological' has similarly become associated with a particular philosophical trend. For the moment I propose 'inductive', which I define as 'intended or likely to arouse effects on the audience'. In the case of 'subsequent performances', engaging the audience members via 'inductive authenticity' means trying to engage them as the original productions might have done. Modern productions and adaptations which may seem radically innovative, unfaithful, subversive, even parodic or satiric, but which provoke critical and emotional responses in their audiences, more closely resemble ancient performances in their *effect*.

How might a 'subsequent performance' be evaluated in terms of its 'inductive authenticity'? First, instead of total 'strangeness' like that of the *Medea* production, it might offer a mixture of the familiar and the strange. One challenge which all modern producers of ancient Mediterranean drama face is their audiences' unfamiliarity with the genre. There are various ways to deal with this, such as providing information in the programme or staged prefaces, or using familiar figures and situations analogous to those in the ancient script.[40] Another consideration is political impact. Athenian comedies make explicit comments on contemporary politics, while many tragedies contain more subtle allusions.[41] The political dimension of ancient plays offers a way to create inductive authenticity, to avoid censorship or to refer to contemporary political situations.[42] Another consideration is the social relationship between a theatre and its audience. Various aspects of drama at Athens identify it as a *community* theatre. It is likely that many members of the Athenian audience could recognise individuals among the performers, as well as many in the audience. Hence modern productions staged in local venues and campus theatres more closely resemble the social context of Athenian performance than do professional productions in large cities.[43]

3. Practice II

Aristophanes' plays challenge later producers because of their profusion of Athenian topical allusions. Substituting allusions to those a modern audience can understand, I would argue, is the only way to create inductive authenticity. Culture Clash's 1998 *Birds* successfully transposed the two protagonists into an African-American and a Latino trying to escape from Southern California's oppressive white culture. In 2000 I staged a version of *Thesmophoriazousai* called *The Julie Thesmo Show* in which the women's religious festival became a women's daytime TV talk show.[44] As I write, a version of *Peace* by Callie Kimball is playing in Washington, D.C. in which a father who has lost a son in combat heads off from Tennessee

to Mount Olympus to demand answers from the gods, with explicit references to current American political debates.[45]

Aristophanes' *Wasps*, though rarely produced, is relevant to the Ameri-
can political climate of the last few years, with an unpopular war and a
President widely criticised yet still in power. Aquila Theater Company in
New York City produced a version called *A Very Naughty Greek Play
(Utopia Parkway)* in 2005, and in spring 2006 I staged a version called *The
Buzzzz!!!!*, a title which attempted to evoke the sharp edge and excitement
of current political discourse. I set it at our own little city-state on a hill,
the University of California, Santa Cruz, a relentlessly leftwing, politically
correct campus. *Wasps* is not agitprop; both central characters Philokleon
and Bdelukleon are fallible, and though Philokleon gets the final dance it
is hardly clear which view triumphs, so it was important to let both sides
have their say, while poking equal fun at both. Bdelukleon became a
professor of History of Consciousness (a real department at UCSC), while
Philokleon became his redneck mother who has come to live with her son
after losing her raisin farm in California's Central Valley. This character
is loosely based on Victor Davis Hanson, an ancient historian and right-
wing pundit who was an undergraduate at UCSC, but a female Philokleon
'raises the stakes' (as theatre people say) by increasing the inappropriate-
ness of her vulgarity, drunkenness and lust. 'Maw' embarrasses 'Sonny' by
participating in rightwing political action, so he barricades her in the
on-campus house of a college Provost and has two of his slaves/graduate
students guard her. The production, staged at the actual Provost's house
with the audience seated on the lawn, included many local and national
political allusions. In the first song, two UCSC graduate students sing
their dreams to a pseudo-folk tune:

> Somewhere, out in the future
> the world will be what it ought to be
> We won't always treat each other
> with fear, with greed, with hostility
>
> Races, classes, and nations can
> get along if we only try
> to understand each others' views
> we can see clearly eye to eye
>
> But this doesn't mean that anything goes
> there are some things we can't stand:
> hierarchies, phallocrats,
> intolerance must be banned!
>
> Abortion rights are crucial, and
> we must uphold the right to die
> but anyone who says they are
> pro-death penalty's gonna fry!

> Open dialogue is the answer
> we're quite ready to hear what you say
> but once you hear our analysis
> we're sure you'll see things *our* way!

Here is the conclusion of Maw's speech during the *agon*, which roughly corresponds to Philokleon's speech 546-630:

> And thank God George W. Bush was president when those terrorists attacked us on 9/11! Because of his leadership, the American people pulled together and fought back, and now we're bringing democracy to the Middle East! Now that all three branches of government are working together, we can really make some progress!
>
> Yes, the future is bright, but there are still dark forces at work, both here and abroad, which could take away our liberty. We must remain ever vigilant! Watch out for dissidents! Listen to their phone calls! Examine the issues carefully! Vote! And if we don't like what the press, the courts, or our representatives are doing, buzz in and sting 'em! Democracy is hard work, but no one else is going to do it for us!

This is followed by a song which stands in for the choral response 631-47, in this case delivered by a double chorus of right-wing 'Jurists' and left-wing 'Slugs' (banana slugs, the proudly non-aggressive UCSC mascot):

> You're the greatest, Maw! Waa-hoo!
> Better than Roberts or Alito!
> Anything he says you'll veto,
> just paint over his graffito!
> He can't buzz! He's just a mosquito!

Now Sonny responds:

> Taxes have been cut, but who's benefiting? The average American family gets a few dollars, while the richest 1% get millions. Meanwhile, health care, social services, environmental protection, the arts and education are being starved! Just look at this 'public' university – it's being run more and more like a corporation, with huge salaries for the top administrators, and peanuts for the staff! Instead of being taught critical thinking, students are being made into cogs in the corporate wheel!

Maw loses, and Sonny offers her the chance to be the 'Chief Justice' in her own home, and the dog trial follows. In the case of comedy, I suggest, shared laughter from the audience may be considered a sign of inductive authenticity.

4. Practice III

Ritual and religion are crucial to ancient Greek drama, yet rarely included successfully in subsequent performances. References to Christianity creep into many translations and productions of ancient drama, when Hades becomes 'Hell' and 'crime' becomes 'sin'. Others like Barrault make gestures towards ritual, but these are often timid, not least because the producers have no strong ritual tradition on which to draw. My next example of expressive and inductive authenticity is *The Gospel at Colonus* by Lee Breuer and Bob Telson. *Oedipus at Colonus* is rarely staged, since it contains almost no action, and many of its central issues, such as pollution and hero-cult, are foreign to contemporary audiences. In Breuer and Telson's Christianised production, the play becomes a religious service in an African-American Pentecostal church, with the story of Oedipus as the 'lesson', the choir as the chorus, and the audience as the congregation. Roles are doubled between actors and singers, with Oedipus acted by the church's main preacher and sung by well-known gospel singers Clarence Fountain and the Five Blind Boys of Alabama. The script, including song lyrics, is based on the Fitzgerald translation (deeply cut), with some lines from *King Oedipus* and *Antigone* added. The theatrical techniques used in *Gospel*, like those in ancient Greece, are not naturalistic, and the use of a specific, living American religious and musical tradition provides a structure and conventions familiar even to non-church-goers among the audience. Breuer has stated that he is 'interested in a way into an American classicism'; his goal is not fidelity, but emotional and spiritual truth. He defines catharsis in terms of Nietzschean ecstasy: dissatisfied with the 'conceptual coolness' of the experimental theatre world, he felt that 'if you go one step further with cathartic theatre you might find pity and terror turning into joy and ecstasy'.[46]

There are both gains and losses in this adaptation. The civic dimensions of the Sophocles text are lost. In the Christian ambience of *Gospel*, where (as in Fitzgerald's translation) 'Zeus' is often rendered 'God', motives and actions are understood in terms of Christian ethics. Theseus' decision to take in the outcast, for example, is not an astute political choice based on self-interest, but an individual act of charity.[47] At times the fit is awkward: Oedipus' self-defence that his crimes were committed in ignorance fits a Christian context; his rage and refusal to forgive his son Polynices do not. And what might an audience unacquainted with the Furies make of the references to 'daughters of darkness' and 'those great ladies whom we fear'?[48] The most radical change comes after Oedipus' disappearance, when the choir sings 'I'm crying hallelujah – I was blind, but he made me see – Lift him up in a blaze of glory – with a choir of voices heavenly' and Oedipus (all five of him) rises from the dead! This adaptation's syncretism is obviously questionable; a cynic might consider it a way to get a middle-class white audience into a black church without having to take the leap of faith.[49] But many of the performers in *Gospel* were Christians, some of them members of established gospel choirs, and when asked whether performing in a pagan play contradicted their faith, they replied that they considered it an extension of their ministry. *Gospel*, then, may be considered an example of Dutton's suggestion that commitment on the part of the performers creates expressive authenticity.

Another aspect which makes *Gospel* expressively and inductively authentic is the race of performers and audience. The number of recent productions based on ancient plays tragedy, created by African-American artists and other artists of colour is remarkable.[50] Breuer and Telson, however, are white, leading some critics to question their 'colonising' a black art-form. In 1996, at a time when 'colour-blind' casting was high on the agenda, playwright August Wilson famously argued that African-American performers should involve themselves only in artifacts created by African-Americans. It is certainly true that for many years African-American creativity has been massively appropriated by white artists, but in this case I think the charge is not only wrong but once again over-emphasises the *origin* of this artifact rather than its use and reception. What audiences experience in *Gospel* is African-American performers to whom it gives great roles, and racially mixed audiences, most unusual in American theatre. What the artists express and what audiences experience in performances of *Gospel* and other ancient Mediterranean dramas is a powerful statement about African-Americans' experience – their suffering, anger, resilience, triumph, and above all their eloquence – qualities which make an unusually powerful connection with the themes of Athenian tragedy.

Perhaps most important to *Gospel* is the powerful central role of music. Ley, who refers to the ancient playwrights as 'composers', argues that choral song and dance are the heart of their plays and the tragic experience.[51] When song and dance are interwoven with spoken dialogue, the performance shifts to a different register and communicates on a different level, creating a dialogism or heteroglossia similar to that between characters, between individual and chorus, and between visual and verbal aspects.[52] There are important connections between European opera and ancient drama – the first composers took their inspiration from this drama, many operas are based on classical texts, and the contemporary staging of earlier operas raises the same issues as does that of ancient drama.[53] A modern production which does not include music and dance is not nominally, expressively, or inductively authentic, yet many studies pay little attention to these aspects. At least half of the *Gospel* performance, however, involves music. There is no formal dance, but at high points individual performers dance spontaneously and the chorus sway and clap their hands as they sing. Overall the production offers the alternation of speech and song like that of Athenian tragedy, and the music greatly increases the emotional power. For me the high point is the 'jubilee' welcoming Oedipus:

```
Chorus:    We will never
           No no never
           Drive you away
           We will never drive you away
           From peace in this land
Oedipus:   I stood a wanderer
           On life's journey
           At the close of the day
           Hungry and tired
           And beaten by the rain
           Lord here is my shelter
           A sacred resting place
Chorus:    We will never
           No no never
           Drive you away
           We will never drive you away
           From peace in this land
```

The communal emotional response from the racially mixed theatre audiences of performances of *Gospel* I have attended is unique in my experience of modern productions of ancient drama.[54]

Returning to Barthes: his response to Barrault's mixtures and 'confusions' is that 'a choice had to be made: either the voodoo rite or Marie Bell'. Everything, he insists, must be unified ('of a single nature and a single effect'), and clear.[55] This demand relates to the emphasis on *choices* which many theatrical performers today consider central to the rehearsal process. Barthes notes that a modern production of the *Oresteia* comprehends the epochs of the myth, of Aeschylus and of the spectator respectively, and that one of these three levels of reference needs to be chosen and adhered to. Since the *Oresteia* is the product 'of a specific period, of a definite social condition, and of a contingent moral argument', it is not a 'classic' or 'universal' work, but a 'profoundly politicized work'.[56] Fifty years later, we can see this statement as an acute early example of the now familiar 'historical turn'. But there are problems too. First, the original production of the *Oresteia* comprehended two levels – that of the myth and that of Athens in 458 BCE – so the original production was not, and could not have been, 'of a single nature and a single effect'. Second, Barthes' strong note of Marxist idealism ('the growing assurance that man possesses, in himself alone, the remedy for his ills') seems just as monolithic as ahistorical ideas about the drama's 'universality.' Finally, Barthes does not specify how he thinks a theatrical production might give to an ancient drama, as he demands, 'its precise figure ... not an archeological figure but a historical one ... progressive in relation to its own past but barbarous in relation to our present' because 'the new gods it sought to establish are gods we have conquered in our turn'.[57] And how could such a production be 'clear' and 'unified'?

5. Practice IV

My final case study is a production which tried to give a historical figure to the conclusion of the *Oresteia*. This figure involved three different histories – fifth-century Athens, and the United States in both the 1950s and the 1990s. In spring 1992, two UCSC feminist Theatre Arts majors were upset with what they saw as the masculinist portrayal of justice in *Eumenides*. Together we devised *The Furies*, designed to raise questions about the agenda of the 'new gods' in that play who were, in our view, far from 'conquered'. The historical moment was crucial: only a year after the first Gulf War, Bush 41 was president, and the USA was twelve years into a massive turn to the right. Our production consciously invoked issues such as environmental pollution, Gulf War propaganda, the abortion gag rule, and rhetoric about 'family values'. But we located it in the American fifties (identified primarily by the costumes) with Apollo and Athena as corporate lawyers, the Furies (dressed in black) as beatniks and proto-feminists, and the chorus as middle-class Americans. The text remained close to the Greek, but passages such as the following (based on *Eumenides* 683-706) inevitably took on contemporary implications after the hearings which assessed Clarence Thomas' worthiness to serve on the Supreme Court:

> Athena: Respect this court, for there will always exist
> an institution to decide what justice is.
> Reverence for the court and its decisions
> will keep the nation free from crime and fear.
> Provided, that is, the citizens do not try
> to change the laws and create innovations.
> Don't let clear water be polluted with mud.
> Keep in mind the founding fathers' intentions,
> don't go too far to the left or to the right.
> And don't get rid of fear entirely. If
> a man fears nothing, can he be truly just?
> A just fear for the court breeds law and order
> such as no other nation on earth can show.
> This place of deliberation will be free
> from any thought of profit. No bribery here.
> No hint of corruption will ever taint this court.

In a metatheatrical framing device appropriate to an academic setting, an actor welcomed the audience to 'Dr Aeschylus' lecture on the birth of modern justice in ancient Athens', explaining that the professor could not make it but that she, his teaching assistant, would stand in for him. She then showed slides with strongly slanted commentary on the events of the first two plays of the *Oresteia*, glorifying Agamemnon and denigrating his 'evil wife' before the Furies burst in pursuing Orestes.

After Orestes' trial ended with his acquittal, the Furies threatened Athens to a backdrop of slides of natural disasters such as dust storms, toxic waste, acid rain, and – most appropriate for Santa Cruz – earth-quakes. There is textual support for the idea that when Athena convinces the Furies to give up their hatred for Athens, they change costume into the scarlet robes worn by metics participating in the Panathenaia as a visual demonstration of their new status.[58] Most scholars find that the conclusion of the play offers a confirmation of Athens' moral, judicial and political excellence, and in his well-known 1980 production of Tony Harrison's translation at the National Theatre in London (the only complete *Oresteia* on videotape), Peter Hall made this a momentous celebration: the audience were asked to rise as the transformed Furies, led by Athena, proceeded up the central aisle to a beautiful hymn and out of the theatre. From a feminist perspective, we found the dissenter Vellacott's view interesting – that *Eumenides* is 'a statement of conflict and warning of defeat', the trial of Orestes 'not a civilized alternative to murderous revenge' but 'an inadequate and corruptible substitute for a positive and humane moral standard', and that 'what appears on the surface as a celebration of national unity and confidence is, on a deeper level, an ironic enactment of the most comprehensive tragedy of all, the moral tragedy of Athens'.[59] So we tried to suggest 'Athena's mixture of misrepresentation, threat, and bribery'[60] in lines based on *Eum*enides 851-69:

> Just try going to some other country;
> then you'll really appreciate this place.
> This land has a glorious future ahead of it,
> and you can have a part in that. Not only
> women, but men too, will give you respect.
> Just don't try to stir up trouble, twisting
> adolescents' guts with craziness, or turning
> men into fighting cocks, tearing into each other.
> No! Our wars must be against some foreigner,
> someone who's trying to make a name for himself.
> This is the deal I'm offering you: stay here
> in this great land which has God on its side,
> be good, do good, and we'll be good to you.

As she spoke, slides of 1950s consumer goods appeared, demonstrating what domesticated women desired, and female chorus members appeared offering the Furies 'sweetheart' dresses with tight waists and full skirts. Convinced, the Furies went offstage and returned wearing the dresses, pumps, and white gloves, and their demeanour was now appropriately feminine and submissive. The play ended with all singing to the tune of 'God Bless America':

> Bless us, Athena
> Goddess we love
> She trusts us
> for justice
> and turns night into light from above.

From Delphi
to Athens
to all lands
let us sing
Bless us Athena
Let justice ring

Bless us, good Goddesses
daughters of Night
they have turned from
nasty vermin
into girls shining good, shining bright

Orestes, Apollo and finally Clytemnestra, smiling, reappeared and joined in the song, the reconciliation, and the happy ending.

The production, which radically destabilised of the 'classic' status of the script, aimed not to parody *Eumenides* but to use theatrical means to raise questions about the meaning of justice, social progress, and the construction of female roles by masculinist institutions (including the theatre). The *content* was changed, but the *objective* (to raise significant issues in a theatrical form) was, we believed, very much what Aeschylus was doing.

The case I am trying to make for the authenticity of theatrical mixtures and hybrids such as *The Buzzzz!!!!*, *The Gospel at Colonus*, *The Furies* and others, is congruent with contemporary thinking about culture. Appiah's recent book, influenced by ancient Mediterranean ideas (Stoicism, Terence) includes a section called 'in praise of contamination' where he asks 'what makes a cultural expression authentic? ... Trying to find some primordially authentic culture can be like peeling an onion'.[61] Quoting Salman Rushdie, he celebrates 'hybridity, impurity, intermingling, the transformation that comes of new and unexpected combinations of human beings, ideas, politics, movies, songs. It rejoices in mongrelisation and fears the absolutism of the Pure. Mélange, hotchpotch, a bit of this and a bit of that is how newness enters the world ... Cultural purity is an oxymoron.'[62] As Hall has noted, ancient drama, 'more than any other Greek or Roman material, is now a worldwide phenomenon, an aesthetic language understood throughout much of the global village'.[63] Members of the global village understand this language because they *translate* it into their own linguistic, cultural and theatrical terms.[64]

Notes

1. See Barrault 1961: 64-84. As a disciple of Artaud, he had long been involved with primitivism and ritual; see Innes 1993: 95-107.
2. Barthes 1972: 59. As a Sorbonne student, in 1936 Barthes co-founded an ancient theatre group which staged *Persians*; he later wrote many articles on theatre; see Barthes 2002: 35-45, 306-29, 147-55.

3. Barthes 1972: 61.
4. Barthes 1972: 59.
5. Pearson and Shanks 2001: 101-19.
6. See Hall 2004a: 52.
7. E.g. Lawson and Stowell 1999.
8. Leppard 1988: 74.
9. Taruskin 1988: 205.
10. Kivy 1995: 285.
11. Wiles 2000: 179.
12. Auslander 1999: 54, 51. See also Fischer-Lichte 2008: 67-74.
13. Aristotle, *Poetics* vi.1450b28, xiv.1453b14.
14. See for example Golder 1996: 199; Goldhill 2007: 44; Rehm 2003: 17.
15. Wiles 2000: 179.
16. Dutton 2003: 259, 267.
17. Trilling 1971 influentially applied philosophical ideas about authenticity to literature. Interestingly, in his capacity as a playwright and writer on theatre Sartre put little emphasis on the playwright and performers' 'good faith' (Sartre 1976: 68).
18. Dutton 2003: 271.
19. Connor 1997: 142.
20. Dutton 2003: 267, 266.
21. Miller 1986: 23.
22. Miller 1986: 34-5.
23. Miller 1986: 55.
24. Hardwick 2005: 109.
25. On postcolonial theory and the classics see Goff 2005; Hardwick 2005; Hardwick and Gillespie 2007; Goff and Simpson 2007.
26. See, for example Barish 1994; Bulman 1996a; Hartley 2001; Marowitz 1978; Miller 1986; Orgel 1987; Worthen 1997. Wiles' contribution to this volume suggests how Shakespeare studies can provide models for the study of ancient performance reception.
27. Bennett 1997 and Blau 1990 offer thorough discussions of the modern theatre audience.
28. Thom 1993: 81.
29. Thom 1993: 172, 205.
30. Altena 2005: 488.
31. See Csapo and Slater 1995: 286-330 for the ancient evidence. See also Pickard-Cambridge 1988: 263-78.
32. Cicero, *Pro Sestio* 118.
33. Herodotus 6.21.
34. Seneca, *Epistulae Morales* 115.14-15.
35. Plato, *Republic* 492b.
36. A small polemic: print is not an adequate medium for discussions of performance. A possible solution is offered by Kapilow 2008, who has created a website of examples to illustrate his discussions of music.
37. I have seen this production only on video.
38. Dutton 2003: 269.
39. We might compare the performance of No drama in Japan, which maintains as closely as possible its fourteenth-century performance conditions. See Smethurst 1989.
40. A production of *Frogs* at UC Berkeley projected explanatory footnotes onto

the scrim behind the stage, and a 2001 staging of *Iphigenia at Aulis* by Shotgun Players in Berkeley prefaced Euripides' drama with a kind of satyr play which introduced the Atreus family history.

41. The political dimension of Athenian tragedy has been extensively analysed; see recently Carter 2007.

42. See Calder 2005 for a discussion of an East German production of Aeschylus' *Prometheus* and Hall 2005b on *Iphigenia at Aulis*. Rampell 2008 notes that Aeschylus' *Persians* 'has been produced about thirty times over the last five years,' often in McLaughlin's version.

43. Peter Sellars, who has periodically engaged with Greek drama (*Ajax* 1986, *Persians* 1993), in 2003 staged Euripides' *Children of Herakles* in order to foreground the worldwide plight of refugees. Although this was an international tour, he worked to engage with the communities in each locale, using local refugee children.

44. For details see Gamel 2002.

45. For a review see Nelson Pressley, 'A Modern-Day *Peace* with Classic Arrows', http://www.washingtonpost.com/wp-dyn/content/article/2008/09/04/AR2008090403292.html (accessed 31 March 2009).

46. Rabkin 1984: 49, 48.

47. 'He has asked for grace'. Breuer 1989: 24.

48. Breuer 1989: 12-13, 11.

49. McDonald 2001: 159-77 provides a description of the show. Wetmore 2003: 102-18 includes criticisms of the production; see also Green 1994: 58-66. The thoughtful analysis of Goff and Simpson (2007: 178-218, 213) questionably insists that the play presents a model of reconciliation between black and white Americans, and over-emphasises Sophocles' script at the expense of performance; they even refer to theatrical representation as 'sleight of hand' (2007: 204)! I suggest they consider the effects of performance as event discussed by Fischer-Lichte 2008: 161-80.

50. I have seen productions of scripts by Alfaro, Carter, Culture Clash, Dove, Power, and Smith-Dawson; Wetmore 2003 discusses many more; see also Svich 2005. There have been many African productions; see Wetmore 2002, and many of the contributions in Hardwick and Gillespie 2007 and Hardwick and Stray 2008.

51. Ley 2007: 202.

52. The terms 'dialogism' and 'heteroglossia' are Bakhtin's, although strangely he does not use them to discuss the theatre.

53. See Ewans 1982 and 2007; McDonald 2001; and Sutcliffe 1996.

54. I have seen *Gospel* twice in the theatre and viewed it numerous times on videotape.

55. Barthes 1972: 62, 64-5.

56. Barthes 1972: 63, 61, 65.

57. Barthes 1972: 66.

58. *Eumenides* 1028.

59. Vellacott 1977: 118.

60. Vellacott 1977: 122.

61. Appiah 2006: 106-7.

62. Appiah 2006: 112-13.

63. Hall 2004b: 82.

64. I am most grateful to the organisers of the conference, to David Jacobson and Michael Walton, and especially to Tom Vogler, *sine quo non*.

Towards Theorising the Place of Costume in Performance Reception[1]

Rosie Wyles

1. Theatre as a theatrical and cultural activity

The reception of a play cannot fairly be described as simply the reception of a text; it is the reception of the theatrical and cultural activity embodied in the performance of a piece of theatre. The performance of a play thus has much to tell us about both the nature of theatre itself, as well as the culture which produces it and for which it is produced. The play as a theatrical activity is distinct from the play as a cultural activity; the *Oresteia* at its first performance in 458 BCE may therefore have been in certain respects a milestone in theatrical history, while as a cultural activity it may have deviated little from the established role taken by theatre in that society.[2] In other cases, it is possible for the nature of a tragic performance as a cultural activity to vary radically from the original; attempts at 'historically accurate' performances of Greek tragedy, verging on historical re-enactments, are one example of this. When we consider the performance reception of an ancient play we need to look at it both as a cultural activity and as a theatrical activity in the receiving culture. Above all, it is essential to treat the reception of a play as the recreation of, variation on, or rejection of, an *experience*. Costume is a key index to the theatrical and cultural statement made by a performance (and the *experience* of it), and as such, this particular performance element deserves special attention in the task of theorising performance reception.

First, costume, as a visual element in the performance, is susceptible to *semiotic* analysis. The shared foundations of semiotics and reception theory make a semiotic approach particularly valuable in the analysis of a production in a way that is oriented towards performance reception.[3] Costume, of all the semiotic elements in a production, is immediately accessible and one of the most direct means of setting its 'tone', the historical period, mood and so on.[4]

Secondly, costume is inherently *metatheatrical* and therefore offers a key index through which to access the nature of a production as a theatrical activity. 'Costume, or what it can easily stand for, impersonation – the actor's pretending to be a fictional character – is the most basic element of theatre.'[5] Theatre could not exist without costume – it is set apart from other performance elements in this respect, since 'theatre' or a 'theatrical event' might still take place even without an elaborate set or lights, for example. Costume therefore, as one of theatre's basic elements, offers one of the primary means by which a playwright can invite the audience to reflect on theatre and the nature of this performance as a theatrical activity; hence, for example, the 'death clothing' costumes in Euripides' *Heracles* can be used to reflect on the performance of tragedy as a cultural act of bringing the dead back to life.[6]

Thirdly, costume is capable of representing a play, standing as a symbol for it, and embodying it as a theatrical experience. Therefore, as the work of Carlson and Sofer suggests, the 'stage' life of an iconic costume or prop (i.e. its appearance in plays subsequent to the original production), can in fact be considered to be one means through which a play is re-performed: an example in ancient theatre is Heracles' lionskin.[7] Costume therefore offers an independent means of tracking the performance reception of a play as a theatrical experience, rather than a text; i.e. by observing the re-appearance of an iconic costume over a given period.

2. 'Translating' costume

The costume and costuming strategy of a play both require 'translation' just as the words of the play-text might. The distinction here, between costume and a costuming strategy, is as follows: costume is the design and outward appearance of the characters' outfits, while a costuming strategy is the way in which these outfits are manipulated (both verbally and physically) in a play in order to create meaning.[8] The translation of each must be treated as distinct in the analysis of a production, since the same approach is not necessarily taken to both; so, for example, Katie Mitchell in her production of *Women of Troy* deviated from the original in her translation of the 'costume', but was true to the general principles of its 'costuming strategy' (see further below).

There are several factors that need to be considered in analysing this 'translation'. An *a priori* issue concerning the translation of the costuming strategy is that we can never have a complete knowledge of the original. A playwright may create meaning through the verbal or physical manipulation of a costume.[9] But while the verbal manipulation of costumes is preserved, embedded in the text, we can only know of such physical manipulation as was also given verbal emphasis. There must have been some physical manipulation, unmarked in the text, that contributed to the strategy and the meaning it produced. Therefore the costuming strategy, of which a subsequent playwright or director is faced with the translation, is from the outset only partial. There is a difference here between the analysis of performance of ancient plays and the reception of plays which have been performed in more recent times, where the range of source

materials, such as for example critical reviews, may allow a fuller knowledge of the costuming strategy.

Another issue is that the ancient play is 'imported' into the existing
theatrical tradition of the receiving culture. A production cannot be
treated in isolation from this tradition which informs the response to, and
reading of, what appears on stage. This in itself has four implications for
the translation of the costuming strategy. First, the meaning of the
costume, and the interpretation of its design, is dependent, to a large
extent, on theatrical precedent; the audience's decoding of the language of
costume depends on this past experience. Elements of costume therefore
each have a theatrical history, or stage life, which adds layers of meaning
to the material object. Sofer explains how: 'As they move from play to play
and from period to period, objects accrue intertextual resonance as they
absorb and embody the theatrical past.'[10] This 'layering' might be a limiting factor on the translation, or it might create new possibilities of
meaning. But it is clear that there can never be an exact equivalence with
the costume in the original ancient Greek production, because of this
difference in the material object's theatrical history.[11] Furthermore, elements of costume may also have a different cultural history, outside
theatrical usage, which limits how far it is possible to 'translate' the
meaning originally created by a costuming strategy. The new theatrical
and cultural context of the costume must therefore be taken into account.

For example, where a costume, or an element of it, evokes a specific
theatrical precedent (rather than a general pre-existing theatrical meaning), then it may result in the 'haunting' of the performance by a previous
iconic production in the theatrical tradition of a given society; a concept
which has been recognised by the theatre theorist Carlson.[12] This 'haunting', whether deliberate or not, will affect the way in which the audience
read the costume and it offers a new facet to the costuming strategy (which
might alter its overall meaning radically); thus an ancient play might be
'read' in performance 'through' or against the backdrop of a 'modern'
production. 'Haunting' might also have an impact on the audience's cate-
gorisation of tragedy (as a whole) as a theatrical activity – if a costume
from an iconic production of a Shakespeare play were used for example,
then it might set up Greek tragedy, in the audience's mind, in the tradition
of Shakespearean theatre.

There is, moreover, a possibility that an item of costume may impose
itself on a 'translation' through the pressure of theatrical traditions; this
kind of convention in costuming creates audience expectation which may
present another limiting factor on the freedom of a translation. This
phenomenon, where a piece of costume, after being used in an iconic
production, may become embedded in the performance tradition of a play
(even if this piece of costume had not formed a part of the original
production or was not historically accurate), is discussed by Hollander.[13]
She uses the example of the 'Juliet cap' originally worn by Theda Bara as

173

Juliet in 1916, which through Bara's success, became embedded in the performance tradition for the costuming of this character (despite being historically inaccurate). Hence performance-based expectations on costuming imposed themselves on the translation of Shakespeare's costuming strategy, and could even be said to have forced the equivalent of what a textual critic would term an 'interpolation', into the strategy.

An additional point is that the theatrical tradition in the West is generally one of 'unmasked' theatre. This produces another limiting factor on the 'translation' of a costuming strategy, since the familiar face of a well-known actor may change the way in which the costume is read; this issue of 'celebrity' and semiotics has been explored by Quinn.[14] So far as costume is concerned, then the actor's face may limit the extent to which the costume may be viewed as the character's clothing – the presence of the celebrity means that the costume in part remains just that, a costume.[15] So, for example, we do not see Hecuba dressed in rags but Vanessa Redgrave dressed in rags playing Hecuba. In ancient productions, the use of masks allowed the costume to belong absolutely to the character rather than the actor.[16]

The way in which costume is read in a performance depends on the semiotic experience of a culture – that is, the way in which they 'read' the visual element, and especially costume, in other performance arts and visual culture generally. In ancient Rome, the experience of watching pantomime performances, for example, may have changed the way of responding to a costuming strategy in a Greek tragedy. It is not therefore just a question of considering the theatrical context, i.e. the other types of theatre that are being performed alongside a production, but also the impact of, for example, film on the reading of costume. Furthermore, the exhibiting of theatre costume, or even film costume, in museums also potentially has an impact on the response to it in performance; it may, for example, be approached as a static work of art rather than a dynamic aspect in the play.[17] There is, relating to this, also the impact of the celebrity of the costume designer and whether the costume is going to be read in light of ('haunted' by), his/her previous work.

Our perspective of a costuming strategy is different, since we may consider it as a part of a system. This enables the costuming strategy of an ancient tragedy to be read and understood in light of any other extant Greek tragedy, regardless of chronology; so that, as in the example of *Molora*, it becomes possible to exploit the costuming strategy of later plays to create meaning in the production of earlier ones. Thus the meaning of a costuming strategy may be changed, even unintentionally, merely through our knowledge of later tragedies. Equally our understanding of a costuming strategy may be limited by the preceding and contemporary plays which we do not have knowledge of.

The issue of 'authenticity' is unavoidable in the 'translation' of costume. The stance on authenticity is immediately apparent from the costuming of a production. Ironically the costumes which seem the most 'authentic' are not necessarily those which are the most historically accurate. The notion of authenticity depends on the state of beliefs of a society. Therefore in trying to analyse the costume in a production and how 'authentic' it is intended to be, it is essential to be aware of the society's state of knowledge about the ancient world and the major sources influencing the society's understanding and construction of it. For costume, perhaps two of the most influential publications in this respect are: Thomas Hope's *Costumes of the Ancients* (1809, republished 1812 and 1841, reprinted in 1962 as 'Costumes of the Greeks and Romans'), and Iris Brooke's *Costume in Greek Classic Drama* (1962).

Finally, a specific characteristic of costume in Greek tragedy makes its translation rather different as a proposition from, for example, costume in Shakespeare. Costume in ancient tragedy seems to have exploited the model of 'the past is a foreign country'. Battezzatto has made a persuasive case for this, in his argument that the tightly-fitted sleeves, through their 'foreign' association, might have been used to evoke and construct a past world.[18] He identifies the conceptual model, which enabled this type of cultural 'reading' of the 'foreign' elements in tragic costume, in Thucydides (1.6) where the 'past is a foreign country' (so that Greek society could imagine its own past through its view of contemporary barbarian cultures). Thus any 'authentic' production now which tries to evoke the dress of ancient Greece in its costuming, both follows and deviates from the original – it follows it in evoking the past but, importantly for us, this is the past of a different culture (whereas in ancient Greece it is the different culture used to evoke the past!). It is possible, therefore, that where the Greeks are viewed not as a different culture but as our own past, then this 'authentic' costuming comes closer to the original experience.

3. Test cases

Some of the considerations that have been explored here can be illustrated by case studies which analyse a production and its costuming from the viewpoint of performance reception. The costuming employed in Katie Mitchell's production of Euripides' *Women of Troy* (National Theatre, November 2007), for example, offers an example of where the costume deviates from the original (is non-'authentic'), but the costuming strategy remains the same in certain respects. Mitchell explains her reasons for choosing not to use 'authentic' costume: 'There's something about dressing actors in tunics and Jesus sandals, or about an attempt to do a reconstruction with masks,' she says, 'which I think distances the viewer from the reality contained in the material. You go "Thank heavens we don't behave like that now."'[19] The women in the production were therefore dressed in modern evening wear. This communicated to the audience how the attack of the Greeks had come in the middle of the Trojans' precipitate celebrations at the war finally ending; the evening dresses hence became symbols evoking *pathos* throughout the performance. However, this costume also took on a sense of being located in a relatively past era when the women started to dance the 'quickstep' to music evoking the culture of a few decades ago. This, of course, allowed within the production a terrible and beautiful sense of nostalgia to be created, yet it also put a spin of the 'past' on the women and allowed the production to engage in the animation of the past, just as the original productions of Greek tragedy did. Furthermore this was truer to the original experience in that it evoked *our* past rather than another culture's past. Therefore while Katie Mitchell rejected 'authentic' costuming lest it should distance the play from the audience, nevertheless the costuming strategy offered a close translation of the original in this important respect.

My second case study, Yael Farber's *Molora* (Oxford Playhouse, June 2007 – see also Hardwick in this volume), is an adaptation of the *Oresteia* set in South Africa, and another production which used non-'authentic' costume. But here, too, we can see that elements of the costuming strategy engaged nevertheless with the principles of the ancient Greek tragic language of costume. The use of Wellington boots in the costuming of the production was particularly striking: while the chorus were barefoot, Klytemnestra (played by Dorothy Ann Gould) wore a pair of Wellingtons with her red dress. Even more strikingly, the death of Aegisthus was represented by a pair of Wellington boots (standing alone on stage) being struck down. The symbolic significance of these boots can be understood by reference to the play's setting. The action of the play is presented as a crime, performed under Apartheid, brought to a hearing at the Truth and Reconciliation Commission. Wellingtons, or 'gumboots', had been standard issue for workers in the gold mine in the time of Apartheid (since it proved cheaper than draining the mines of infected water), and gained iconic cultural status in this use with the emergence of the 'gumboot dance'.[20] These boots then could be used in the production as an effective and poignant symbol evoking the time of Apartheid and the general context of suffering which the crime presented in this production might embody.

These boots also raise the interesting issue of how far the language of costume in modern productions can be regarded as 'universal'. The design of this production, with its South African setting, used symbolism from that culture. The semiotics of this could be correctly interpreted where the elements of costume did not have a strong independent symbolic association for the audience, so the 'traditional' blankets of the chorus could be 'read' without a problem. But the Wellington boots carry an independent symbolic association in British culture, which is at odds with what was intended in the performance. Despite the probable awareness of the audience member that the intended allusion was not to this British symbolism, it is nevertheless difficult to prevent this symbolic association from interfering with the 'reading' of the costume. The other obvious problem here is that if the audience is unaware of the cultural status and associations of the gumboot in South Africa, then it is impossible for them to 'correct' their reading (a symbol can only 'mean' what an audience can understand it to communicate); there is the same general problem with the semiotics of dance: 'when moved onto a Western stage, traditional dance in South Africa loses its context and thus loses much of its meaning'.[21]

These boots, then, offer an example of a semiotic unit in the language of costume, set in a different historical and cultural context, taking on new layers of meaning. In a broader sense, however, these boots, as *boots* rather than Wellington boots, may also bear some relation to, and gain meaning from, the costuming strategy of the original. In Aeschylus' *Agamemnon*, much attention is given to the removal of Agamemnon's boots at precisely the point where he is about to walk into the palace and to his death.[22] Their removal spells his death and therefore the boots, like other items of costume in the *Oresteia* trilogy, seem to have a special symbolic status; they stand for Agamemnon's prime characteristic and in fact may be a symbolic embodiment of him as a character.[23] When we see Klytemnestra in *Molora* appear in boots, if they evoke and are 'haunted' by this moment in the *Agamemnon*, then one way of reading them is as a reminder of her murder of Agamemnon and also as an expression of her usurpation of his role and power. She has become the man and the ruler – the incongruity of her boots worn with her dress makes sense, if viewed in light of the ambiguous combination of masculinity and femininity seen in her Aeschylean characterisation (see Fig. 6).

We might go further and say that the boots represent her appropriation not only of his power but his identity. Indeed the use of costume to express the idea of 'identity theft' is suggested as a possibility in Sophocles' *Electra* (267-9), where Electra complains of how terrible it is to have to see Aegisthus wearing the very robes that her father Agamemnon had worn. This, as I have argued elsewhere, suggests the possibility that Sophocles dressed Aegisthus in a costume which evoked the costume of Agamemnon in the *Oresteia*, as a very clear way of showing that Aegisthus had stolen his identity.[24] If we read the boots in *Molora* with the Sophoclean costuming strategy in mind, then Klytemnestra is in effect doing exactly what Aegisthus had done in Sophocles' *Electra*; she wears the very boots which Agamemnon had worn and which had embodied his power.

Similarly, the use of boots at the death of Aegisthus in *Molora* can be decoded through reference to both the Aeschylean and the Sophoclean costuming strategy. The boots represent Aegisthus in the same way as they had represented Agamemnon in Aeschylus' play. Secondly, in standing for Aegisthus through Agamemnon, the boots may express the idea of identity theft which we have already discussed and which may have been exploited (and at the very least is suggested) in Sophocles' play. When the boots are struck down, symbolically representing Aegisthus' murder, we

Fig. 6. *Molora* by Yael Farber. Dorothy Ann Gould as Klytemnestra and Jabulile Tshabalala as Elektra. The Barbican Pit, London, April 2008. Reproduced by kind permission of Marilyn Kingwill/Arenapal.

178

are thus reminded of the reason for it (his murder of Agamemnon and usurpation of his power). At the same time, since the boots, on one level, may still represent Agamemnon, this moment re-enacts the original murder and represents this second murder as the repetition of the same crime (drawing attention to the cyclic nature of revenge killing).

The boots then offer an example of a deviation in costume design which nevertheless engages with aspects of the costuming strategy of both the original and another Greek tragedy, Sophocles' *Electra*. Although this play was composed later than the *Oresteia*, it can nevertheless be exploited in a production of the trilogy. This multi-layered engagement is unlikely to be consciously acknowledged by most audience members and may not even have been intended by Farber, yet I would argue that anyone with a knowledge of Greek tragedy benefits from being able to identify, even if on a subconscious level, some of the same principles of costume in operation. On a much more basic level, of course, even the use of items of costume to represent a character is a principle going back to the development of the language of costume in fifth-century theatre.

4. Future directions

Costume is a central part of any production and an essential element of theatre itself. The potential contribution that the analysis of costume may make to the study of performance reception should, I hope, have become clear. In order to profit fully from this potential, it is necessary to have a theoretical framework within which to undertake this type of analysis. This chapter offers, I hope, the beginnings of a framework, or at least highlights some of the theoretical issues involved. It seems to me that one of the most important potential contributions that such analysis may offer to the field of performance reception is a means through which the reception of plays can be thought of as the transmission of a theatrical experience rather than text; this is, after all, what sets performance reception apart.

Notes

1. This chapter builds on my doctoral research into the role of costume in the performance reception of three Euripidean tragedies (see Wyles 2007). I am grateful to Edith Hall and Helene Foley for their helpful comments on an earlier draft.
2. Elements of the production which made it a milestone include the use of the roof for the watchman's opening speech in the *Agamemnon*, and scattered entry of the chorus in the *Eumenides*, see the ancient *Life* of Aeschylus (Snell 2004).
3. See further Wyles 2007: 22-3.
4. The theoretical principles of a semiotic approach to the analysis of theatre were established by the Prague School theorists in the 1930s and 40s; the contributions of Bogatyrev and Honzl are particularly important for costume; for these

works in translation see Matejka and Titunik(1976). Elam (2002) is a helpful general introduction to the field.

5. Muecke 1982: 23.

6. Wyles 2007: 24-5, 152-3.

7. Carlson 1994a and 1994b; Sofer 2003; Wyles 2007: 7-20.

8. I use the term costume throughout to refer to garments or props – whatever is required by an actor to play the part of a character.

9. See McAuley 2000: 176 and Wyles 2007: 84-7.

10. Sofer 2003: 2.

11. Wyles 2007: 215-45. Even those aspects of the language of costume where there is seemingly continuity, e.g. black clothing to represent mourning, are not exact in their equivalence. In the case of 'black' it is far from exclusively associated with mourning in Western culture, in contrast to Roman culture where it retained its powerfully funereal air and was capable of causing serious disquiet if worn on the wrong occasion, see Heskel 1994: 141.

12. Carlson 1994a and 1994b.

13. Hollander 1993: 305-7.

14. Quinn 1990.

15. For the distinction between costume and clothing, see Wyles 2007: 42.

16. Wyles 2007: 18-20.

17. The Victoria and Albert Museum, London, holds a collection of more than 3,500 stage costumes and accessories. There are also one-off special exhibitions such as 'Jane Austen: Film and Fashion', organised by the Museum of Costume, Bath in 2004, which featured costumes from the BBC's 'Pride and Prejudice' and 'Sense and Sensibility'.

18. Battezzatto 1999-2000.

19. Taken from Jane Edwardes' interview, *Time Out*, Monday 12 November 2007: www.timeout.com/london/theatre/features/3819.html#articleAfterMpu (accessed 16 December 2007).

20. For the political overtones of the dance, see Snipe 1996: 70; 'the Boot dance of the gold miners in South Africa is a testament of the struggle these men face on a daily basis under the exploitative apartheid policy'; also Rani 2008: 126, 128. Health and safety in South-African mines was not controlled by legislation until the Mine Health and Safety Act of 1996.

21. Rani 2008: 126.

22. Aeschylus, *Agamemnon* 944-5.

23. Griffith 1988 and Wyles 2007: 108.

24. Wyles 2007: 11, 243 n. 53.

Performance Reception and the 'Textual Twist': Towards a Theory of Literary Reception

Simon Perris

If 'theory' means thinking about one's craft for the sake of improving it, then Aristotle is right to maintain that theory (*logos*) is a master-craftsperson (*architektôn*).[1] It is surely the contention of this volume – and of my own modest contribution – that theory and practice can and should inform one another, particularly in the sphere of *Rezeptionsästhetik*.[2] In that sense, theory and practice, or word and action, might co-exist in reception studies as mutually responsive phenomena; as Gadamer might put it, to understand is to implement.[3]

One practises praxis; one thinks, speaks, writes and reads theory. Despite the spectatorial origins reflected in its etymology,[4] theory (*theôria*, 'looking') is an essentially textual undertaking, and performance reception theory necessarily redounds upon text(s). In light of the theoretical, *reflexive* bent of this volume, I thus advocate a reassessment of the logo-centrism of Greek drama, while arguing at the same time that performance reception and literary reception are essentially distinct.

But first, a caveat. Like performances, texts have many lives, of the after- or former- variety. In a former life, this chapter referred to the 'textual turn' rather than the 'textual twist'. But theory is already *polutropos*, possessed of enough turns as it is: linguistic, performative, experiential, *Rezeptionsgeschichtlich*, etc. The suggestions laid out here do not claim the status of *turn*, but rather of a *twist* (or 'swerve', as Harold Bloom would have it) through which influence – with or without anxiety – might prompt redirection, not *volte-face*. 'Exercise moderation; everything in its right time.'[5] At the present hermeneutic moment, it is necessary to paraphrase Derrida and ask once more, at least of classical reception, whether there is anything beyond or outside the text.

The so-called performative turn in classical scholarship provides our first axiom:[6] *Performance of Greek drama in antiquity was/is important.* In contrast to previous eras, classical scholarship since the second half of the twentieth century has tended to treat performance as central to the interpretation of Greek drama, a phenomenon most famously evident in Oliver Taplin's *The Stagecraft of Aeschylus* (1977) and *Greek Tragedy in*

Action (1978). Taplin effectively secured for the performative turn a place in the methodological armoury of classical scholarship.[7]

From this first axiom I derive the following lemma: such 'grammars' of ancient stagecraft base themselves on textual cues needing to be *read*, metaphorically and literally.[8] 'The text, which is inevitably all we have, is no more than a transcript, a scenario. 'The play's the thing'; 'First of all we have to extrapolate the stage-directions and other signals from the text (or other evidence, if any is available)'; 'The *words* – which are, after all, almost all we have – contain and explain the visual dimension: there could be no play and no meaning without them.'[9] The text is merely a 'transcript', agreed. Nonetheless, it is almost our only source for specific stage-directions. (Archaeological evidence is of importance for the reconstruction of general praxis.) Despite its ultimate and ultimately successful goal of appreciating ancient drama *qua* performance, the performative turn is a textual tactic.

Our second axiom is that *Contemporary performance of Greek drama is important*. Whether from within classics, or theatre studies, or history, *inter alia*, scholarly interest in modern performance of Greek drama has increased in recent years: Helmut Flashar's *Inszenierung der Antike* (1991) pioneered what is now a well-established field of study.[10] The Archive of Performances of Greek and Roman Drama at Oxford (APGRD) is but one example of the ongoing institutionalisation of this field, another early indicator of which was the inclusion of a reception section in the 1997 *Cambridge Companion to Greek Tragedy*.[11]

My lemma to our second axiom concerns the material context of this enterprise. Analysis of performance reception, even of performances without dialogue, is grounded in texts: archival material, circumstantial documentation, reviews, articles, and so on. Ancillary textual evidence is most often the best means of engaging with performances which one has not personally witnessed, especially those which pre-date audiovisual recording.

An important type of archival material is the theatrical text, whether this takes the form of a published work (that is, a book) or a working copy (that is, a script). Analysis of what people say, sing, scream, or babble onstage is often bound to the interpretive reading of theatrical texts, *à la* Taplin. It is possible, indeed necessary, to *read* the texts (if such exist) of performed reception of Greek drama, particularly when these texts purport to translate ancient texts. When it comes to contemporary performance reception, theatrical texts may not be 'almost all we have', but they are nevertheless vital to what we do have.

The specific performative and civic-ritual-literary-historical-cultural-political context of Greek drama (for all its unfashionable, irremediable *Gegebenheit*) is precisely that which distinguishes its reception from any other matrix of reception. Not merely because Aeschylus is a different author from Shakespeare, or Ibsen, or Beckett; but because Greek drama enacts a specific milieu, through masks, chorus, performance space, theatrical competitions, and so on *ad infinitum*.[12] Without some recourse to antiquity, classical reception studies is theatre studies by another name.

Analysing, say, *Paradise Lost* without recourse to Homer, Vergil, Dante, and the Bible would constitute a naïve exercise in English literary criticism. Likewise, without some recourse to *Medea*, analysis of Müller's *Medeamaterial* would constitute a naïve exercise in theatre studies. If the classical reception inhabits some conceptual space (or matrix, or locus, or sphere of activity) involving ancient and contemporary forms of creative expression, then it is in some sense bound to the texts of ancient drama; this textuality is no conservative article of faith to be deconstructed, but a circumstance to be accepted and exploited. In other words, if one wishes to analyse a particular modern work in terms of its derivation from, relation to, or reaction against a particular ancient drama or dramas, then one key means of exploring that relationship is the text of ancient drama(s). You can't have your cake (that is, analyse reception of ancient Greek drama) and eat it too (that is, avoid ancient Greek dramatic texts).

Moreover, performance reception analysis applies textual semiotics to performance semiotics, producing further texts, in the form of papers, articles and books, rather than, say, mimes or radio plays.[13] As an inherently text-driven, logocentric enterprise, *Rezeptionsforschung* tends towards text rather than performance, towards the written word rather than the performing human body.[14]

Axiom number three: *Radical theatre does not embody a concern for 'text'*. In *Postdramatisches Theater* (1999, English translation 2006), Hans-Thies Lehmann identifies in contemporary theatre what he terms the 'post-dramatic': a tendency originating with Brecht and passing through Grotowski towards theatre which is non-Aristotelian, non-linear, non-mimetic, non-discursive, polyvalent, and so on, characterised in particular by the 'aesthetics of risk':

> [T]heatre does not attain its political, ethical reality by way of information, theses and messages; in short: by way of its content in the traditional sense. On the contrary: it is part of its constitution to hurt feelings, to produce shock and disorientation, which point the spectators to their own presence precisely through 'amoral', 'asocial' and seemingly 'cynical' events. In doing so, it deprives us neither of the humour and shock of cognition, nor of the pain nor the fun for which alone we gather in the theatre.[15]

The post-dramatic has indeed found noteworthy expression in performance reception of Greek drama. Schechner, Grüber, Terzopoulos, Suzuki, Castellucci and Kane, to name but a few, have developed performance modes which reshape, antagonise, or destroy Greek drama by treating it as something other than (merely) *words*: as movement, emotion, rhythm, community, ritual, or the phenomenological, experiential human body. 'The text has to be sacrificed in order to let the performance come into being,' writes Fischer-Lichte. 'Without the dismemberment of the text, there cannot be a performance of the text.'[16]

And yet, as Fischer-Lichte's comment above would indicate, the post-dramatic still tends to involve or implicate texts in some way, 'sacrificial' or otherwise. (To the aforementioned theatrical texts, we might also add: advertising and theatre programmes; text projected or inscribed in performance; and such so-called 'parasitic' texts as interviews and reviews.[17]) Even titles are texts. Take the title of Castellucci's *Tragedia Endogonidia*: this shorthand allusion to 'Tragedy' and to the theatrical canon is itself a sophisticated text, albeit of only two words, which invites sophisticated reading. Radical, violent manipulation of classical theatrical paradigms by practitioners such as Castellucci paradoxically tends to assume a familiarity with theatrical texts. Post-dramatic performance reception of Greek drama may be anti-textual; it is not *a priori* 'a-textual'.[18]

My fourth axiom is that *Radical literature does not necessarily embody a concern for 'literature'*. An analogous development concerns what we might call post-literary (*alias* postmodern) literature, characterised by non-linearity, pastiche, parody, intertext, reflexivity, deconstructed selves, multitudinous voices, and general relativity of expression. Such literature is paradoxically 'post-literary', seemingly less concerned with canonical norms of literary aesthetics than with the polyvalent potential of texts to embody meaning(s).

Axiom five: *Texts are not artworks but opportunities for aesthetic experience*. A more authentically 'post-textual' model of literary aesthetics is found in Wolfgang Iser's phenomenology of reading, which presents reading (*der Akt des Lesens*) as event, not object.[19] Note the similarity here between Iser's model and, say, a phenomenology of performance as temporal, experiential and never to be repeated (see Fischer-Lichte, above): the distinction lies not in a fundamental difference of *Rezeptionsästhetik*, but in the material context of production and the mode of aesthetic experience (spectating versus reading). Reading and spectating are related, distinct aesthetic experiences.

Various hermeneutic complications, however, arise from the interaction of these five axioms. The second and third potentially obscure the first by drawing attention away from ancient theatre. Secondly, the anti-textual and anti-literary tendencies of the third and fourth potentially obscure the textual foundations of the first and second. Description and analysis of post-dramatic *performed receptions* of Greek drama risk prescribing anti-textual *interpretations* of Greek drama (see Decreus below).

Such, then, are the facts of the matter as I understand them, leading to the following initial observation: (1) *Performance reception of Greek drama, and analysis thereof, is conducted through text(s)*. Even this is not without controversy. So Anne Ubersfeld: '[A] refusal to accept the text-performance distinction will lead to all kinds of confusion since the same tools are not used for the analysis of both.'[20] But given the diffuse nature of any text-performance distinction, given the textual nature of both performance reception and literary reception, surely that which leads to confusion is a refusal to accept the *literature/performance* distinction.

'A theatrical text is something of a literary paradox,' claims Michael Cacoyannis. 'It is written down, and yet it is not meant to be read.'[21] In my view, however, the paradox lies in the fact that theatrical texts can be, and are, both read and performed; many performance reception texts – that is, play-scripts of performed receptions of Greek drama – are published as literary works in their own right. In the introduction to his radio play *Homer's Odyssey* (2006), Simon Armitage makes the following trenchant observation:

> Although this version of the *Odyssey* was developed as a radio play [for the BBC] and is presented here in script form, it was always in the back of my mind that it should have a further life as a piece of writing. Not just something to be performed, but something to read. A book, in fact.[22]

'Not just something to be performed, but something to read.' Armitage here takes for granted what is in fact a fundamental assertion: books (published literary works) are not plays (theatrical performances); plays are not books. Of course, reading *and* spectating, writing *and* performance, are experiential, phenomenological, temporal, sensory, spatial, and essentially immanent. Both offer the opportunity for aesthetic experience, and thus for the concretisation of meaning. But reading and spectating (and listening, and viewing) occupy different loca within a matrix of aesthetic experiences. To restate what may seem tautological: performance texts differ fundamentally from published literary texts. Play-scripts are (a) provided to actors and other personnel for the purposes of performance, (b) presumably free of charge, and (c) potential sources for performance history. Published in their own right, however, such texts are (a) manufactured for the purpose of reading by an end-user, (b) usually exchanged for some form of payment, and (c) potentially canonical literary works in an author's *oeuvre*.[23] Scripts are liable to actors' revisions, authors' versions, marginalia and so on. Books, on the other hand, are relatively fixed: the expense of publishing printed material precludes frequent revision. (Except for occasional revision for an 'author's preferred edition' or selected/collected volumes, which are themselves fixed anyway.) Scripts are performed, and fluid; books are read, and fixed.

So, then, why publish theatrical texts as literary works in their own right? A common assertion made by poets is that poetry is 'to be read aloud', yet most contemporary poetry is still published in print rather than in some audio format. Publication, particularly with a prestigious publishing house such as Faber and Faber (as for Hughes, Heaney, Armitage, et al.), invites or at the very least suggests reading. Nor is the notion of a theatrical *readership* a new one: J.S. Peters observes this opposition between 'print and performance' already in Early Modern Europe.[24] (Crucially, this is not an opposition between *text* and performance.) To take a comparatively recent example, Tony Harrison's *Oresteia* not only forms an archival source for analysis of the National Theatre performance, but also, more than twenty-five years after publication, occupies a deserved place in the author's poetic canon, no longer reprinted separately but collected in *Plays: IV* (2002) and excerpted in the *Collected Poems* under the title 'The Ballad of the Geldshark'. The same is true of Heaney's *The Cure at Troy*, excerpts from which appear in the selected/collected hybrid volume *Opened Ground*. Yeats' *Collected Poems* set the precedent – with selections 'from *Antigone*' and 'from *Oedipus at Colonus*' – and I for one have trouble imagining 'A Man Young and Old' without the 'gay goodnight and quickly turn away'. Not to mention Gilbert Murray's 'The apple tree, the singing, and the gold' (*Hippolytus*); or Pound's 'What splendour, it all coheres' (*The Women of Trachis*).

If publication invites reading, it also necessarily implicates a text in literary history,[25] which is after all a story of texts talking with texts rather than performances talking with performances. Consider the history of Greek drama in translation. Murray's popular versions, for example, not only helped bring Greek tragedy to the English stage; they were read (or at least purchased) in great numbers.[26] William Arrowsmith's *Bacchae* was a primary source text for at least two well-known adaptations: Soyinka's *The Bacchae of Euripides: A Communion Rite* and Schechner's *Dionysus in 69*.[27] Publication subsumes even translations of performance scripts into literary history, inviting not only reading, but intertextuality, encouraging the processes of literary interaction (*à la* Eliot or Bloom).

Moreover, different modes of analysis pertain to the text as play-script versus the text as published literary work, even if applied to a single physical object. Books are susceptible to literary semiotics, scripts to performance semiotics. Crucially for our purposes, the so-called original texts of Greek drama, due to their unique status and historical provenance, have a foot in both camps as both book and script. (Likewise, for example, Heaney's *The Cure at Troy* is both book and script.) I thus distinguish two modes of reception: literary reception, which involves reading and writing, and performance reception, which involves spectating and performing. Consequently, I also distinguish between performance reception studies and literary reception studies.

But one might well argue that the immanent experiential reception of performance (spectating) is not formally different from the immanent experiential reception of text (reading).[28] But I am less concerned here with performance-*as*-text than performance-*of*-text, performance-*and*-text. Differentiating between literature and performance, I assert substantive differences in the circumstances of reading and spectating: class-based, social, material, phenomenological, and so on. A book is *not* a human body, nor is the human body a book.[29] Aesthetic experience of the performing human body differs fundamentally from aesthetic experience of the book, despite the critical horizons opened up by ideating the performing body as a text.[30] Spectators are physically implicated in what they are purportedly witnessing. Readers, on the other hand, do not write what they are reading. We participate in the *construction* of meaning when we read, but it does not follow that we are ourselves implicated in the *object* of aesthetic contemplation. Hyper-text might offer a marginal counter-example, but the popularity of Wikipedia, Google, and so on, does not necessitate the death of the book.[31]

As I contend, the reader and the spectator enjoy related but fundamentally different aesthetic experiences. This second observation may well be implicit in classical reception studies, but I consider it worth stating nevertheless: (2) *Performance (that is,* performed*) reception of Greek drama is essentially distinct from literary (that is,* written*) reception of Greek drama. Because spectating and reading are different modes of aesthetic experience, performance reception and literary reception (and filmic, musical, or artistic reception) respectively require different modes of analysis.*

An analogous distinction might be that between the APGRD on the one hand, and on the other, the Open University project on the Reception of the Texts and Images of Ancient Greece in Late Twentieth-Century Drama and Poetry in English. Such a distinction is necessary: Greek drama specifically has a contemporary performance dimension, unlike, say, Pindar. Literary reception involves more than the classical tradition (Highet) or motif analysis (Stanford's *The Ulysses Theme*). Rather, a concern for how (re-)reading and (re-)writing specific ancient texts constitutes a particular mode of creative expression and a particular mode of aesthetic experience, like but also unlike performance reception.[32] As Edith Hall, drawing on Eric Bentley, asserted in her article 'Towards a Theory of Performance Reception' (see the adapted version in this volume), people who study drama as literature and those who do the opposite have often censured one another, but quite unnecessarily. Neither 'script-alone' nor 'script-as-performed' is superior to the other: it is merely *different*.[33]

Such censure is indeed unnecessary, and the difference – *différance*? – is crucial. The published literary work ('script-alone') and the performance text ('script-as-performed') are different; so too are the film, the musical event, and the plastic artefact. Literary reception is but one *Nachleben* of Greek drama, one which is specifically subject to literary semiotics. We might talk also of filmic reception, artistic/plastic reception, and so on, which together fall within the wider remit of *Rezeptionsästhetik*, manifesting different modes of intertextuality in a matrix of possibilities.[34]

In its treatment of performance and text, this essay wilfully avoids the question of delimiting performance: there is a sense in which all text, film, music, visual arts, and of course theatre, is 'performance'. Indeed, I would argue that reading a theatrical text is also a performative activity in which

187

the reader 'directs' (that is, cognitively instantiates) a visualised performance by way of the reading experience. Nevertheless, Ubersfeld – in a book
entitled *Reading Theatre* (!) – strongly denies the autonomy of reading
theatre:

> Everyone knows – or accepts as truth – that you cannot read theatre. ...
> Whenever they ['ordinary readers'] take a stab at it, they realise the
> difficulty of reading a text that most decidedly does not appear to be
> intended for reading the way one reads a book. Not everyone is techni-
> cally versed in mounting a play, nor does everyone have the unique
> imagination needed to conceive a work of fictive performance. This,
> however, is what each of us does, and this private act cannot be justified
> either theoretically or practically ...[35]

This assumption is problematic for a number of reasons, not least inten-
tionalism, elitism, an unsubstantiated preference for performance, and a
concomitant unsubstantiated disparagement of the 'private act' of reading.
(Why should spectating outrank reading? Why should the collective outrank the individual?) Ubersfeld concludes with a rhetorical question which
I for one would rather see answered: 'Are we thus obliged either to give up
on reading theatre or to accept reading theatre as if it were some other
kind of literary object?'[36] Yes. Theatrical literature (like, say, poetry or the
novel) is indeed another kind of literary object. If, as Ubersfeld herself
argues, 'The theatrical text is a literary text',[37] then surely such texts can
be and are in fact read *qua* literature. Reading Greek tragedy is more than
possible, as is *Reading Greek Tragedy*:

> It is because tragedy is not reducible to a simple 'message', because these
> dramas are not played out or exhausted in a single reading or performance,
> that readers return again and again to ancient tragedy ... It is in reading and
> responding to the continually unsettling and challenging questions set in
> motion by these plays that Greek tragedy is performed and experienced.[38]

Not that I seek to reverse the performative turn. On the contrary, the
performative turn supports a subsequent (but not subsidiary) reappraisal
of the literary dynamics of theatrical texts. Indeed, semioticians have at
least established that theatre is a sign-system to be *read*, metaphorically
if not literally. But such theory tends to privilege 'reading' theatre as a
performative sign-system at the expense of reading theatrical literature
as a verbal sign-system, *qua* literature. So, for example, Aston and Savona
assert in *Theatre as Sign System*:

> In most academic institutions drama has, until relatively recently, been
> taught as a branch of literary studies, as dramatic literature and hence as
> divorced from the theatrical process ... At best, a student might be invited to
> become an armchair critic or to imagine a theatrical space in his or her
> 'mind's eye'. Rarely, however, did drama leave the written page.[39]

This otherwise innocuous polemic nevertheless smuggles its own brand of cultural politics into the discussion. Why should drama necessarily 'leave the written page' at all? Theatrical literature is equally able to 'remain on the page' through the act of reading. The authors conclude that 'The imposition of such approaches has proved singularly negative for the advancement of theatre studies, inasmuch as they fail to consider drama in its theatrical context: as a work which exists not only to be read but also to be seen.'[40] But this polemic likewise fails to consider drama in its literary context: as a work which exists not only to be seen but also to be *read* – whether Aeschylus, Shakespeare, T.S. Eliot, or Sarah Kane. To put it plainly: one may choose to attend the theatre or one may choose to read theatrical literature; either activity constitutes a valid aesthetic experience.

If, as I have argued, performance reception and literary reception of Greek drama represent different modes of cultural interaction, then performance semiology and literary semiology merely represent appropriately differentiated means of 'reading' that interaction. The textual twist is not a return to some doctrinal logocentrism by which text is sacred, performance profane, and 'words, not actions, rule humanity in all things' (Sophocles, *Philoctetes* 98-9), but rather an acknowledgement that: (1) *Performance reception of ancient Greek drama has a textual aspect*, and (2) *Analysis of performance reception of Greek drama is different from analysis of literary reception of Greek drama.*

All of which together constitutes the textual twist: engagement with the textuality of both performance reception and literary reception, while distinguishing different modes of aesthetic experience and different modes of analysis. And as with any theory, the foregoing is of use only inasmuch as it prompts, enriches, improves, and challenges praxis. To paraphrase Forrest Gump, theory is as theory does, with the point being not a theory of practice but the practice of theory. As such, I hope that a textual twist, swerve, or redirection can only leave us better readers and better spectators of Greek drama. Or as Aristotle might have put it, better craftspeople.

Notes

1. *Politics* 1260a 18-19.
2. Hall 2004a is 'theory ordered *à la carte*'; I intend to serve greater portions of select dishes without spoiling the broth.
3. *Verstehen ist Anwendung.* H.G. Gadamer, 'Wirkungsgeschichte und Applikation' in Warning 1979: 113-25.
4. Nightingale 2001; 2004.
5. Hesiod, *Works and Days* 694.
6. Contrast Lehmann 2006: 4-7, in which the 'turn to performance' is a historical shift in theatre practice away from *drama* and towards *performance*.
7. Earlier studies include: Nestle 1930; Hourmouziades 1965; Steidle 1968. Revermann 2006: 8-12 surveys the literature from Taplin 1978 onwards; Csapo and Slater 1995 collects and translates key primary sources.

8. Taplin 1992 likewise illuminates oral epic *qua* performance through exegesis of Homer *qua* text.

9. Taplin 1978: 1, 4, 5.

10. Flashar 1991.

11. Easterling 1997a. Reviewing the *Companion* in *JHS* 120 (2000), Jon Hesk noted that 'Part 3 [on reception] makes the volume distinctive and original by offering four chapters on changing patterns of reception, adaptation, performance and interpretation from antiquity to the present day.' Gregory 2005 includes essays on reception; cf. Kallendorf 2007; Hardwick and Stray 2007. Even the *Cambridge Companion to Lucretius*, Gillespie and Hardie 2007, includes a reception section.

12. Winkler and Zeitlin 1990.

13. E.g. Fischer-Lichte 1988; Aston and Savona 1991; Melrose 1994; Ubersfeld 1999.

14. Performance-assessed research qualifications in Theatre Studies do exist. For example, the Drama and Theatre department of Royal Holloway at the University of London (RHUL) offers practice-based MPhils and PhDs. Not that textuality has been effaced: 'The University of London offers the possibility of submitting MPhils and PhDs examined *partly by written thesis* and partly by the submission of practical work. The practical work may take many forms, but must be identifiable *as a piece of research* and not merely creative expression' (emphasis added). http://www.rhul.ac.uk/Drama/postgraduate/phd_mphil_research.html (accessed 01 November 2007). Research degrees examined *entirely* in performance would naturally counter my assertions to some extent.

15. Lehmann 2006: 187. Cf. Ubersfeld 1999: 6-7 §1.1.2.

16. Fischer-Lichte 2004: 343.

17. Sampatakakis 2004: 202. The review is a 'parasitic textual phenomenon' which nonetheless bears 'hermeneutical importance' by virtue of 'the coded ideological discourses it contains.'

18. Performance with no text whatsoever (title excepted) is arguably post-text, e.g. Robert Wilson's *Deafman Glance*.

19. Iser 1984. Cf. Fish 1980; Holub 1984 and 1995: 319-46.

20. Ubersfeld 1999: 5.

21. Cacoyannis 1982: vii.

22. Armitage 2006: vi; following his similar claim in the introduction to *Mister Heracles* 2000: ix, that 'virtually all stage instructions have been omitted ... this seems to me to be a production issue, and I didn't want to restrict the dramatic possibilities or to try to direct the play from behind the typewriter'.

23. On problems with defining 'the book': Patten 2006; Andrews 2007.

24. Peters 2000: 248 and 237-53 ('Making it Public') chart the early development of the readership of drama in Europe.

25. E.g. Jauss 1970, 1977; Hexter 2006.

26. Easterling 1997b; Hall and Macintosh 2005; 497-508 on *Major Barbara* and Gilbert Murray's *Bacchae*; Macintosh 2007. Also T.S. Eliot's essay 'Euripides and Professor Murray' in Eliot 1951.

27. Schechner 1970 and Soyinka 1973 cite Arrowsmith's translation. The copyright notice of Schechner 1970 explicitly acknowledges Arrowsmith's translation.

28. Fischer-Lichte 1988: vol. III.

29. A *locus classicus* for the 'people are books' metaphor is *Romeo and Juliet* I.iii.81-92, on which see Thompson and Thompson 1987: 165-70; Stern 2001:

213-14; also Thompson and Thompson 2005. Crucial to any metaphor is that, given the predicative assertion 'A is B', in reality A ≠ B. Cf. Knowles and Moon 2006: 3-4.

30. Melrose 1994: 210. On writing the (female) body: Cixous 1976; Jones 1981; Conboy, Medina and Stanbury 1997. Crucially, this is not a matter of *reading* the body. Iser 1984: 73-5; reading manifests 'das Nicht-Identische'.

31. Phillips 2007; Finkelstein and McCleery 2006: 483-525, 'The Future of the Book'.

32. Steiner 1984 is seminal; more recently, Hall 2008b.

33. Hall 2004a: 55, quoting Bentley 1975: 149.

34. Cf. Genette 1997; Hutcheon 2006; Sanders 2006. Hall 2004a: 61 refers to 'those of us ... for whom "Appropriation" seems to be a more suitable description [than "Classical Reception"]'.

35. Ubersfeld 1999: xxi. Contrast e.g. Veltrusk 1977; Melrose 1994: 50-1 on 'envisaging' future performances via reading theatrical texts; Bassnett and Lefevere 1998: 98-9 ('Drama as Literature'), 100-5 ('Reading a Playtext').

36. Ubersfeld 1999: xxi.

37. Ubersfeld 1999: 10.

38. Goldhill 1986: 286.

39. Aston and Savona 1991: 2.

40. Aston and Savona 1991: 2.

Negotiating Translation for the Stage[1]

Lorna Hardwick

Why is performing Greek drama still an attractive challenge for theatre practitioners worldwide? And why and how are different translations and versions created not only in each generation but also for different audiences and performance contexts? The persistence of these questions suggests that it is necessary to look to theatrical practice in conjunction with theory and scholarship in order to come up with some provisional responses that may help us to refine our theoretical models of translation for performance.

Translation is not only a means of communicating Greek material in non-classical languages, but also a significant means for transmitting understanding of the forms, conventions and idioms of the Greek theatre. In theatre, as in literature, translation is a catalyst for creativity. In this discussion I suggest that traditional polarities between source and target languages, and between concepts of 'translation' and 'rewriting', need to be reviewed, and that the sometimes under-researched roles of those involved in the different facets of 'translation' are worth examining; they are both receivers and generators of the continuously developing life of classical languages and culture.

Translation for and to the stage involves participatory relationships of various kinds – directors, designers, actors, musicians, choreographers as well as writers, readers and spectators. So the term 'translation' has to reflect the different kinds of activity that shape the move from the ancient text and understanding of *its* language and contexts to a new work that can be performed in the receiving language and is attuned to the semiotics and contexts of the receiving theatrical environment and *its* artistic and social traditions. Performances have to have an immediate impact; one cannot 'reprise' during live performance, and there is a process of 'creative misremembering' (to borrow the Shakespeare scholar Colin Burrow's phrase) that assimilates the performance into personal and group consciousness in ways that may be strongly divergent.

Yet performances also have their own histories – the narratives involved in their own creation and the histories of the individuals, groups, communities and traditions that have contributed (sometimes unknown to each other) to the generation and realisation of the performance. The academic as scholar may reflect in tranquillity on the origins and trajectories of the material that underlies the theatrical experience but (unless he or she is possessed of at least twenty brains and the necessary affective qualities) this is a different experience from that of spectating, when immediacy is likely to be the dominant sensation. Academic analysis does not easily map onto the practices and experiential aims of theatre. It is not possible to write about theatre aesthetics in the same way that one writes about a painting that one can at least revisit or even have as an image for reference.[2] So the starting point for my discussion is that translation provides a nexus between the ancient text and its reception in performance, and that the practices of translation (in the fullest sense) point to refinements in the theoretical models that have been developed both for translation and for performance reception.

I shall approach through discussion of two very different examples of 'translation' and the issues they raise. One translates an ancient work to the modern stage. The other makes use of translation techniques to create a new work. Both make distinctive use of Greek forms to focus the interaction between the verbal and non-verbal aspects of performance. At the end I will draw some preliminary conclusions about how the discourse used for conceptualising translations from classical languages might be reformulated. I agree with Edith Hall's premise in her 2004 *Arion* article (see above, Chapter 1), that there can be no totalising theory of performance. My contribution to the debate is to suggest that more refined models of translation will enhance understanding of both ancient and modern and thus contribute to theories of performance and reception. The examples will focus on ways in which translation shapes distinctive performance by interacting with other kinds of creativity.

How can translation be conceptualised as 'creative', you may ask? It is true that 'translations' of Greek and Latin poetry have sometimes created works that have taken on a literary life and status of their own (Douglas' and Dryden's translations of the *Aeneid* and Pope's *Iliad* are obvious examples), but this has been less characteristic of translations of drama, unless they have rolled far enough away from the source text to acquire new titles, theatrical contexts and identities (O'Neill perhaps). Two expectations have been dominant. The first is that translations of ancient drama can and should be judged according to the 'faithfulness' of their relationship to a linguistically, culturally and sometimes ideologically dominant source text.[3] Such criteria immediately raise problems for performance translation because 'fidelity' and 'accuracy' in terms of the ancient conditions of production would never be possible. This paradox is reflected in the second expectation, that drama translations have a limited performance life, needing retranslation for each new theatrical generation (to say nothing of each generation of scholarly interpretations). They are caught at a particular moment in the tension between history and modernity.

Greek drama is now big business in the commercial theatre. New work has to bear the stamp of leading practitioners – writers, directors, actors.

A recent trend has been the trend for 'star' dramatists (including those who have little or no knowledge of the ancient languages) to use 'close' or 'literal' translations, prepared by classicists. These may be commissioned 'to order' – as with Fionnuala Murphy's translation of Euripides' *Hecuba*, used by Frank McGuiness as the raw material from which he created the acting script for the 2005 production, or Ian Ruffell's *Bacchae*, prepared for David Greig's play that was at the centre of a recent triumph at the 2007 Edinburgh Festival. Alternatively, an older scholarly translation may be used by the dramatist – as with Seamus Heaney's use of Richard Jebb's late nineteenth-century *Philoctetes* and *Antigone* for his plays *The Cure at Troy* (1990) and *The Burial at Thebes* (2004).[4] Tony Harrison and Anne Carson are two of the few dramatists of international stature who are also classical scholars and work direct from the ancient texts and contexts. Those who are classical scholars but not poets or dramatists tend to fall foul of the critics on both sides – a past example is Gilbert Murray, who was criticised both for 'popularising' and for his outmoded (English) language.[5]

So theatre practice questions simple distinctions between source text and translation as 'dominant' and 'subaltern', and consequently challenges the associated hierarchies and aesthetic distinctions that adhere to it in the use of notions such as 'faithful' and 'accurate'.[6] In order to identify the key functions of translation it is also necessary to unlock the concept of 'creativity' and to see whether it can be used in a way that does allow the importance of translation to be recognised. To polarise 'translation' and 'creativity' seems to me to be a false opposition; it is more profitable to look at the relationship between the two.

The working definition I shall use is that of innovative combination. This allows, as part of the creative process, features such as imitation, allusion, quotation, parody and pastiche.[7] Literary, theatrical and aesthetic models that privilege metaphors of combination and recombination are important for classical reception theory (and of course re-combination may result from previous *sparagmos* ('tearing apart', like the body of Pentheus in *Bacchae*), suppression or simple forgetting).

Derek Walcott, for example, has developed the metaphor of ancient texts and civilisations as 'shards' that enable the archaeology of culture to be explored and to be reworked into new patterns.[8] Theorists such as Edward Said have built on the Latinate concept of invention (*invenire*) as an means of explaining the processes of cultural encounter, a feature which is always present in translation.[9]

The continuing role of classical texts as literary and theatrical catalysts throughout the twentieth century and into the twenty-first brings translation issues to the centre of both descriptive and evaluative debates. This is intensified by the way in which recent reception theory has located the creation of meaning at the point of reception and given a shaping role to the reader and spectator.[10] However, the role of the reader/spectator in the

194

construction of meaning applies not only to the 'end' reception of performance, but also to the role of the writer/director/designer/actor as herself a reader/spectator of the ancient text as well as of others that have influenced the process of performance creation. Translation is both a material link between these and a metaphor for the cultural and artistic processes. Materially, it not only translocates the text and context, but can also supply information that enables the reader or spectator, who may be ignorant of the ante-text and its context, to make sense of the dynamics of the new. In this sense, translation is an activity that is always pragmatic to some degree. Each translation has its own purpose and therefore has to take account of the target readership and spectators as well as of the special characteristics of the source text.[11]

Literary translation is an activity that may entail rich recombinations and rewritings.[12] The examples discussed here have been selected to demonstrate that the further step of 'translation to the stage' entails creating a collaboration between the verbal and non-verbal aspects of the performance.[13] This includes adapting to the impact of physical and cultural spaces as well as lexical innovation. Form may become as, or more, important as lexis. Finally, I want to push those arguments further to suggest that translation/invention, the creativity associated with input of the self-conscious literary or theatrical practitioner and the urgencies of cultural and political contexts can and do mutually enhance one another. Such encounters can be decisive in transforming awareness and understanding both of transhistorical themes and the particularity of contexts.

It is not always helpful to try to distinguish too rigidly between theoretical models for analysing 'translations' and 'versions'. The processes of arriving at an acting script and then realising this in performance show how porous the boundaries are. Nevertheless, the first example focuses on translation of a Greek play *per se*, including use of its formal structures and registers as the basis for variations. Two aspects are especially prominent: how translation prepared by a scholar acts as a mediating text between the ancient play and the modern acting script, and how theatrical semiotics actualise experience in the modern audience.

David Greig's version of *The Bacchae* was staged at the Edinburgh Festival in August 2007 as part of the new National Theatre of Scotland repertoire. The production, which subsequently toured in the UK and the USA, was directed by John Tiffany (who had studied Classics at the University of Glasgow and had previous successes at the Edinburgh Festival, notably with *Black Watch*). The production moved away from the 1960s 'flower-power' associations of the play, following the radicalising path signposted by Schechner's *Dionysus in 69*.[14] It provoked strong and sometimes divergent audience responses – one colleague referred to the impact on the Edinburgh audience of 'the energy and feeling of the divine and irrational erupting through the volcanic vent of Dionysus against the safe repression represented by Pentheus'.[15] She also reported that some members of the

audience felt that the ending was 'too explicit and 'modern'. They sus-
pected that it was tacked on to a more austere Greek ante-text (!).

Greig's acting script was prepared from a literal translation by the
Glasgow University academic Dr Ian Ruffell. In the Programme Notes,
Greig commented at some length on their approach. Ruffell worked from
the Greek, Greig from Ruffell's literal translation. But their transactions
were not narrowly philological. Greig was particularly interested in the
Athenian audience. Both he and the director were concerned with what the
ancient spectators might have been expected to experience when they
watched the play: 'they really stressed when we met [that] they wanted to
be authentic, they wanted to be faithful and they wanted to be as close to
the spirit of it as they could be ... what it would have been like to watch
Greek drama without it being an archaeological activity'.[16]

This question of the positive and non-antiquarian implications of
'authenticity' was crucial to the creation of the production. Ruffell was
keen to inject into the acting script 'the flavour of the play's word-order
and line structure'. Greig was conscious of the orality of Greek culture –
'These plays were written as poems to be spoken and heard. It is not simply
a question of trying to render the meaning: you have to rise to the poetic
occasion.' He did not wish to change the 'units of meaning' and this was
one way in which the play was intended to be 'performance-friendly'.[17] This
raises the whole question of how the Greek theatre conventions and
dramatic forms persist into a modern version and what they bring with
them. It also points to how the production aimed to exploit the synergy of
authenticity and radicalism: 'they [Greig and Tiffany] were very anxious
that it would get trashed by classicists in some ways. There was a certain
sense that they wanted a "clean bill of health" ... or at least if they were
going to get into trouble for it then it was for things they were prepared to
get into trouble for.'[18] This care, not only with the text and the conventions,
but also with questions of meaning, meant that the production could
demand that attention be paid to its overt radicalism and that it should
take the spectators 'back beyond expectations' as Ruffell put it, especially
in its association between disruption of gender stability and sexuality and
religious and political implosion.[19]

Greig and Ruffell identified particular aspects of the play that are
readily translatable into modern sensibilities, for example the character
of Pentheus and the relationship between repression and political and
physical power. This resonated particularly with the Scottish context,
which was the subject of early discussions between the translator and the
director: 'that was one thing that really did [carry] through to the performance – in terms of Scottish masculinity and what John [Tiffany] described
as quite conservative trends in Scottish culture'. Pentheus was characterised as representing 'very west of Scotland masculinity'.[20] In
performance this aspect was developed through accent, costume, gesture
and rigidity of physical stance, eroticised in the relationship between

Dionysus and Pentheus, especially in the seduction scene. It also underlay the metatheatrical reflections on the poetics of the play, drawn out in the sequence in which Pentheus resisted Dionysus' disruption of settled verbal and social norms:

> Enough, I'm sick of wordplay,
> This man mocks me and he mocks Thebes.[21]

In the 'Programme Notes', Greig pointed to the value of allowing Greek religion to speak as a counter-text to the (temporally) intervening dominance in the west of Judaeo-Christian morality. However, the question of the details and aetiologies of Greek mythology underlay an important difference between Greig's text and that of Euripides. Some of the references to Greek mythology were removed where it was felt they would confuse a modern audience because they are not part of modern cultural frameworks of orientation and understanding. This was particularly noticeable in the Prologue, a pared-down skeleton that omitted mythological details and instead addressed and involved the spectators directly by reference to their (assumed) world-view:

> 'So, Thebes,
> I'm back.
> Dionysos,
> You do know me.
> Semele was my mother,
> Zeus my father,
> Lightning my midwife.
> I am, of course, a god.
> But if you saw
> Me as I really am – divine – Your eyes would burn out of their sockets
> So
> For your benefit I appear
> In human form. Like you. Fleshy.'[22]

The prose translation by the scholar Richard Seaford has:

> 'I am come, the son of Zeus, to this Theban land, Dionysus, to whom the daughter of Kadmos once gave birth, Semele, midwived by lightning-borne fire. And having changed my form from god to mortal, I am here at the streams of Dirke and the waters of Ismenos.'[23]

Apart from the paring down of the mythological family tree and the removal of the specifics of mythological place, Greig's script gives much of the same information as would a scholarly translation. But the idiom and the directness of the diction anticipate aspects of the theatrical experience that the performance offered the spectators, especially the performative and expressive role of the body.

In Greig's Prologue, Dionysus becomes The Scream, picking up the Euripidean metaphor of the bull, what Dodds calls the Roaring God,[24] and relocating it in the context of modern celebrity culture (attuned to the image of the star actor Alan Cumming) as well as in the culture of psychoanalysis. I think there may also be a theatrical allusion to Peter Stein's *Exercises for Actors* (part of the Schaubühne Antiquity Project, 1974), in which the actors developed screaming as one of the features that explored how theatre is constituted by bodily action.[25] This thread is also developed in other areas of Greig's play-text, such as the closing Chorus. Dodds says in his commentary that a modern director would omit this, but here it is rewritten, eschews banality and plays didactically on the image of The Scream.[26]

As a theatrical event, the play and its special effects were stunning, especially in the ways in which body and words were brought together.[27] At the beginning Dionysus was lowered upside down onto the stage in a gold lamé dress that revealed all (well almost) – though as Joyce Macmillan pointed out in her review the metamorphosis was missing.[28] When the prison was destroyed there were dramatic lighting effects and a blazing fire (that almost singed the spectators' bodies, let alone their eyes). There was also extensive use of popular art forms. Cadmus and Tiresias played their encounter as a music-hall turn. The Chorus were red-robed soul singers (in the performance I saw, 15 August 2007, the *parodos* was applauded). They became backing singers as Dionysus seduced Pentheus and Queer culture was celebrated (in a sense substituting contemporary memories for mythological ones) (see Fig. 5 on p. 143). Yet the comedy and the entertainment also created in the audience a sense of horror at the consequences of failure to recognise Dionysian force. The comedic atmosphere in the first two-thirds of the play, heightening the transition to the violence and suffering at the end. In this production the change of mood and impact of the closing sequences rested on its violence.[29]

In spite of its imperfections, the production did integrate verbal, visual and physical in ways that translated ancient theatricality into visceral modern experience. This depended on the coherence of the different modes of translation – the scholarly mediating translation; the dramatist's acting script; the creation of the performances by director, designer and actors. These nuanced relationships in the interlinked processes of reception by scholars, theatre practitioners and audiences were activated by a sense of what Steiner has called 'interpretative tact', with the scholar as a mediator between ancient and modern rather than an arbiter. Although Ruffell described his mediating translation as 'the most footnoted translation in history' the acting script itself did not overtly signal the decisions made about reconstruction or interpolation.[30] Ruffell's role was to give the theatre practitioners as much information as possible rather than to make hermeneutic or aesthetic recommendations. The production as a whole showed how the mediating translator, the dramatist and the director saw the relationship between creativity, modification and authenticity. Their construction of the nexus privileged the interaction between translation and the categories of the body and the psyche (identified in Hall's chapter above) as central to theories of performance reception.

My second example is Yael Farber's *Molora*, which she created and directed as an adaption from the *Oresteia*. Body and psyche are also crucial but the production was primarily framed by other categories discussed by Hall – categories of memory, contingency, temporality and political potency. These brought the new work into a relationship with the Greek ante-text(s) that was less one of modification than of *aemulatio*. The framework was determined both by the Greek material and by the receiving culture and context. The focus was on how Greek narratives, figures, ideas and impressions were recombined and translated to the stage, rather than on detailed attention to the texts of Aeschylus or Sophocles. It might be described as an adaptation in which translation played a shaping role.

Farber is the founder and artistic director of the Farber Foundry, an independent production company based in South Africa. Its work ranges from personal testimonies, such as a biographical journey into female experiences under the Apartheid regime, to what the company describes as 'radical revisionings of the classics by way of reflecting modern South Africa'. Plays in the second category have included *Sezar*, an adaptation of Shakespeare's *Julius Caesar*, as well as *Molora* (which also has elements of the first type). The company looks to theatre to help South Africa through the process of creating a new nation after its emergence from the trauma of Apartheid – 'it is through theatre that our country has the capacity to help us transcend our shattered history by facing it head on through stories told. Theatre is a communal event that offers us a forum to heal from the past, and a canvas on which to envision the future'.[31]

The adapter and director Yael Farber has commented on why she chose Aeschylus:

> Coming from South Africa, the question of revenge begs enormous consideration in the light of the almost unfathomably peaceful transition to democracy. I long wanted to create a work that explores the cycle of violence and the compelling human impulse for revenge. It was on reading the ancient *Oresteia Trilogy* that I felt the potency of the classic texts as *metaphorical vehicles for expressing complex contemporary reality* (italics added). Here is an extraordinary epic family saga, passed down to us through the centuries, that unflinchingly articulates the spirals of violence unleashed in the pursuit of righteous bloodshed.

She added that:

> Notions of a Rainbow Nation gliding effortlessly into forgiveness are absurd. The journey towards forgiveness is never simple or easy. Yet it was not the gods … that delivered us from ourselves in the years following democracy –

but the common everyman and woman ... Molora is an attempt to grapple with the drive for revenge – and a celebration of the breaking of the cycles of violence by the courage of the 'ordinary' man.[32]

However, the resonances of the play are not confined to South Africa. The title of the play 'Molora' is the seSotho word for 'ash'. Farber adds that 'Our story begins with Orestes returning home with a tin full of ash [sc. what are supposed to be his ashes in the false story of his death]. It is the state from which we all come, from the concentration camps of Europe, the ruins of Baghdad, Palestine, Northern Ireland and Rwanda ... to the ash round the fire after the storytelling is done – it is a state to which we must all humbly return.'

Farber's approach explores recombination as a dramatic technique. She uses Aeschylus' *Oresteia* with some attention to Sophocles' *Electra* and Sartre's *Les Mouches*. The theme is of revenge and what it does to individuals and society. However, Farber's play makes very prominent those aspects of the *Oresteia* that explain Clytemnestra's killing of Agamemnon in terms of her outrage at his sacrifice of Iphigeneia to gain a fair wind for Troy. Farber's Klytemnestra also speaks of how she became Agamemnon's wife and how he killed her first husband and dashed out the brains of her first child before taking her back to Argos to become the mother of his children, a detail which she has found in Euripides' *Iphigenia in Aulis*. The result is to cast Klytemnestra as a victim as well as a root cause and perpetrator of violence.[33] Nevertheless, Klytemnestra was also played as culpable, both in the murder of Agamemnon and in her subsequent treatment of Electra (see Fig. 6 on p. 178). Equally, her grief at the false news of the death of Orestes is powerfully conveyed. This makes Orestes' agony as he decides to kill her even more telling.

However, there is an important change in the way in which Farber's play addresses the themes of the *Oresteia*. One might at first think that the *Oresteia* is not a good model for a modern treatment of how a society tries to come to terms with its suffering past, partly because of the theme of cycles of self-perpetuating revenge and partly because of its way of bringing about reconciliation in the *Eumenides*, with all the aspects that are so unsettling for modern audiences – a *deus ex machina*, a rigged vote, the apparent marginalising of female suffering on essentialist grounds of gender hierarchy and political pragmatism. Even though the *Eumenides* presents a society that is trying to move on, as must South Africa, the vision it presents is problematic and its 'solutions' to some extent over-ride the religious, moral and psychological complexities that are explored in the earlier plays in the trilogy.[34]

Farber's approach is to omit the *Eumenides*, other than by references to the Furies that will pursue Orestes. Instead, the court that figures in the *Eumenides* is used to frame the whole action of the play from the beginning. However, the court is not that of the Areopagus but the institution of the Truth and Reconciliation Commission in South Africa. The Pro-

Fig. 7. The Chorus of *Molora*, by Yael Farber. The Barbican Pit, London, April 2008. Reproduced by kind permission of Marilyn Kingwill/Arenapal.

gramme Notes give some background detail on the emergence of the Commission, whose first chairman was Archbishop Desmond Tutu. It was created from the efforts of the Government of National Unity to build 'a bridge between the past of a deeply divided society, characterised by strife, conflict, untold suffering and injustice and a future founded on the recognition of human rights, democracy and peaceful co-existence'.[35]

The Commission worked through three committees – Human Rights Violations, Amnesty and Reparation and Rehabilitation. So there was a strong aspiration towards restorative rather than retributive justice. Testimonies of victims and survivors could be taken in public or private. Amnesty could be requested for various categories of Human Rights violation (the former premier F.W. De Clerk was one of those who appeared before this committee).[36]

Farber's translocation was structured round the formal theatrical conventions of Greek tragedy, especially Chorus, *agon* and Messenger Speech. *Molora* opened in silence. The Chorus silently took their places on a row of chairs at the rear of the stage (which for the Oxford performances in 2007 was a thrust stage with audience on three sides).[37] To the sides were two wooden tables with microphones. Klytemnestra sat at one and her opening words were based on the Watchman's speech in Aeschylus' *Agamemnon*. Electra sat at the other table and initially functioned as a kind of judge/investigator/accuser. But she then left the table as episodes of the action of the *Agamemnon* and the *Choephori* were re-enacted.

The most stunningly effective aspect of the play was the Chorus (see Fig. 7). These were actors and musicians from the Ngqoko Cultural Group.

This is a group which preserves and transmits the indigenous music, songs and traditions of rural Xhosa communities in South Africa. It was first formed in1980 by a bow player and her daughter. Their instruments provided the live music for the performance. The instruments included the uHadi (percussion bow) and the inkinge (friction bow). Of the seven actors one was male; several of the others were grandmothers. In addition to their silent and finely observed witness, the Chorus also sang and chanted in the vernacular and played some active roles, for example as midwives assisting Klytemnestra when (in her dream) she gave birth to the snake that became Orestes. All these aspects represented a South African dynamic analogous to that of the Elders of Argos in Aeschylus, but going beyond it in the links to the Truth and Reconciliation Commission framework.

So the forms of the play involved inversions of chronology but preserved and elaborated on the Greek formal elements of Choral Ode, dance, debate and Messenger Speech. The African theatre and cultural elements brought back to the play some elements of Greek theatre that have become marginalised in the western theatrical tradition, and embedded the Chorus in the play as a force of cultural memory and practice that differed from the civic framework of the court and was thus able to view, participate and comment on it.

Three aspects of this production seem to me to be particularly important. First, this was very highly crafted performance which both drew on and differed from the 'workshop theatre' tradition which has been so important in South Africa. Workshop theatre has been perceived as an oppositional form that enabled groups and communities to articulate their sense of resistance and identity, and subsequently as a form that enabled participants to create new senses of community and shared experience.[38] Workshop theatre is made by a group of people as opposed to being written by a single playwright, so it is community focussed. It is created for performance and has more to do with life than literature. It often draws on traditional forms, especially oral ones, and combines music, narrative and dance. It sometimes also uses an ironic comic vision that challenges tragedy as a paradigm; since it grew out of the experiences of the townships in South Africa, it tends to be urban, although transmitting the rural cultural memory. The workshop form was used metatheatrically by Athol Fugard as a 'play-within-a-play' when he set a workshop performance of the *Antigone* in his play *The Island*. It has also been used by Mark Fleishman and others to develop Greek drama as a community resource in the context of Truth and Reconciliation and in the building of a new society. Farber's play does have affinities with some aspects of workshop theatre, especially in its conception of the Chorus as actors, spectators and commentators, and in its use of the vernacular.

Secondly, the play was built on multi-lingualism in performance. This has been a characteristic of South African adaptations of Greek drama, reflecting the multi-lingual nature of the country (which speaks no fewer than eleven official languages) as well as exploring the theatrical implications of a performance situation in which hardly anyone would understand everything that is being said. This has both a heuristic effect and also turns the attention of the spectators to the non-verbal aspects of performance. In the case of *Molora* this was intensified by the effect of silence at crucial points.

Raymond Williams has commented that in theatre, form is 'inherently multivocal', pointing to the way in which theatre can liberate from linguistic domination as well as from authorial authority.[39] In the case of tragedy, the conventions of the Chorus and the Messenger speech (in particular) gave a voice to the oppressed, marginalised and under-privileged.[40] Association between multi-lingualism and multi-vocalism is a major force in cross-cultural receptions of receptions of Greek drama.[41] It brings together diversity and critique. It also reveals and plays to faultlines in the understanding and orientation of the spectators. So the third important aspect of the performance, for me, was the prompt to think about the nature of the audience and how spectators might 'read' the changes from Aeschylus' *Oresteia*. This aspect raised in a particularly sharp way the question of the 'knowing' vs. the 'unknowing' audience.

Modern theatre is box-office orientated, whether in national venues or the most remote 'fringe' location. Changes in educational background and frameworks of cultural reference as well as the increasing diversity of audiences make it unsafe for producers to assume detailed knowledge of the ancient myths and stories, let alone of particular play-texts and Greek theatrical conventions. In addition, the assumed level of theatrical and classical sophistication, or ignorance, of the audience affects directorial decisions on language, set and lighting design, costume, acting style and gesture at all levels. Some directors try to create a common experiential starting-point for the audience that builds them into a community – for instance, Ariane Mnouchkine's *Les Atrides* (1990-1992) and Heiner Müller's *Medeamaterial* (1983) were both prefaced by exhibitions along the audience's route of entry. There are further questions about the pragmatic and transformative aims of performance and, in the case of close adaptations of ancient plays, of the extent to which a modern production aims to create an experience approximating to the dynamics of ancient audience response. I do not mean this in the literal sense of making the play part of a civic and religious institution in a democracy, as was the case in fifth-century BCE Athenian festivals, but rather in the sense of trying to ensure that the play 'matters' to the modern audience in a way comparable to how it might have 'mattered' to the audience in the source context.[42]

The question of how and why the relationship between ancient Greek and modern South African contexts in Molora 'matters' raises some problems. Spectators who were attentive to the performance but who knew nothing of Aeschylus' *Oresteia* or of the Truth and Reconciliation Commission would have been immersed in the play as an autonomous work.

203

Spectators who knew their Aeschylus but were ignorant of the South African context and the Truth and Reconciliation commission might have been thrown by the omission of *Eumenides* (and had to consult the Programme afterwards). Spectators who were familiar with the Commission but not with Aeschylus would have had to take a 'leap of faith' (or 'trust', as Steiner puts it) that the ancient play had something in it that was worth investigating. The classically knowledgeable but politically ignorant spectator might have had difficulty if he or she were seeking to judge the production in terms of its literal fidelity to the *Oresteia*. In the UK in 2007, most of the spectators probably had a smattering of both aspects of knowledge. Their understanding of the relationship depended on the aesthetic success of the play, and thus to a high degree on the translational techniques. In performances to spectators in South Africa, the balance of spectators' knowledge and their experiential engagement would be different again.[43] So Molora is a particularly good example of the need to revise the simplistic polarity between 'knowing' and 'unknowing' when talking about audiences. Recognition that there are mixtures of knowledge (and expectations) brings the need to analyse the whole production concept for how it embeds information and metatheatheatrical commentary as well as narrative.[44]

In the examples that I have discussed, translation is not opposed either to the historical authority and aesthetics of the Greek source texts nor to the creative work of the modern author. It is a natural extension of the former and an integral part of the poetic and theatrical imagination of the latter and thus an index of transhistorical value. There are consequent implications for the theoretical models of translation that might best describe such relationships. These may overlap with some previously influential models – for example, the first phase of George Steiner's outline of hermeneutic relationships emphasises trust in the value of the source text, while Kwame Anthony Appiah's concept of 'thick translation' brings into the discussion the layers of cultural and literary context that underpin translation practice.[45] Translation provides a hub for all the spokes of performance reception.

The trouble with many of the existing theories of translation is that most are conflict models, imaged in terms of acts of violence that either over-estimate the power of the target text and culture, or over-privilege the cultural and ideological authority of the source text. (The dystopic figure of Klytemnestra in *Molora* is a useful corrective.[46]) It is perhaps better to look for a constantly renegotiated relationship between translation theory and the theories that have been developed to accommodate readers and spectators in the construction of meaning. Reader and spectator receptions operate in several phases. The writers and dramatists who engage with the ancient material are often thought of as the first phase. They are, in the first instance, readers and spectators as part of their practice as writers. However, their roles overlap with those of the other theatre practitioners, especially the directors, whose involvement may have been prior, leading to the selection of the translator/writer. The readers and spectators who engage with the resulting recombinations of material constitute a further phase but they, as the assumed 'constructed' audience, will also have unknowingly influenced the initial approaches. Theories of translation, performance and reception all have to take account of these multiple relationships. It is possible to some extent to map the new material into which the ancient is interwoven and to identify accretions and repressions.[47] This map may include mediating texts and translations that have shaped the way in which new readers and spectators approach the modern work (and which influence how they regard the ancient). Some links and connections may be direct and marked in the palimpsest that is the new performance text. Others of course may prove to be discernable only with difficulty; some may have left no trace. Furthermore, because theatre is a lived experience, the comfort zones that might have been associated with notions of 'accuracy', 'faithfulness' and with the hierarchies associated with clear patterns of transmission through time and within genre are overlaid by the poetic and theatrical event. This event does not simply bring together ancient and modern. It is both enabled and constrained by how the relationship between the ancient text and the receiving context has been negotiated and by what *both* will bear at particular moments and in particular contexts. That is why the negotiations represented by and in translations can never be finite.

Notes

1. The stimulus for this discussion was the conference on Theory and Performance held in Oxford in September 2007. I am very grateful to the organisers and participants for their criticisms and suggestions.

2. This essay is a companion piece to Hardwick 2009b and 2010a, forthcoming, which concentrate on the reception of poetry.

3. This is even reflected in the categorisations made by J. Michael Walton, a scholar who is as sensitive to theatrical considerations as he is to philological. Walton 2006: 181-4, identifies seven categories, ranging from literal 'cribs' to 'translocations to another culture', uses words like 'fidelity' and 'licence' and attaches a defining importance to whether or not the (re)writer knows Greek. The valuable work done by Hutcheon 2006 is based on film rather than drama and does not address the specifics of classical reception performance.

4. Macintosh 2008 discusses the impact of Jebb's translations of Sophocles on W.B. Yeats' versions.

5. MacNeice 1935, reprinted in Heuser 1987: 7-10.

6. I do not suggest of course that these terms have no role to play in the history of scholarship or philology or education, merely that their rigid adoption may be inimical to the development of coherent theories of performance and reception.

7. For discussion of the history of this debate see Macfarlane 2007 and for its application to translation in and of poetry, see Hardwick 2009b.

8. Walcott 1998.

9. See further Steiner 2000: 13-53 and Said 1983: 126.

10. For explorations of different aspects of 'hard' and 'soft' reception theory, see the essays in Martindale and Thomas 2006.

11. Baker 1992.

12. Weissbort and Eysteinsson 2006 contains many examples, from antiquity to the present and includes material on translation as a poetic activity, for example in the work of Ted Hughes. See also Hardwick 2009a and 2009b.

13. Fischer-Lichte 1992.

14. Hall 2004b.

15. Source: Prof. J.W. George, personal e mail, 28 August 2007, referring to the performance of 18 August (the last night).

16. Source: Interview with Ian Ruffell for the Reception of Classical Texts Research Project, 3 April 2008. I am especially grateful to Dr Ruffell for discussion on these points.

17. Source: 'Hitting Your Ear', Interview with Andrew Burnet, Programme Notes.

18. Source: Interview with Ian Ruffell, 3 April 2008.

19. Source: Interview with Ian Ruffell, 3 April 2008.

20. Source: Interview with Ian Ruffell, 3 April 2008. Greig's unpublished *Oedipus* (2000) had already interrogated Scotland's imperial history (see Hardwick 2004).

21. Euripides, *Bacchae* 503-6; Greig 2007: 31-2.

22. Grieg 2007: 7.

23. Seaford 1996: 69. This translation has been successfully staged by Thiasos Theatre (2003-4).

24. Dodds 1960: lines 65-7, ad loc.

25. See the discussion in Fischer-Lichte 2004.

26. Tony Harrison also took up this trope in his play *Fram*. National Theatre, 10 April to 22 May 2008. In a scene in Poets' Corner, Westminster Abbey, he makes Gilbert Murray observe to Sybil Thorndike 'I'm convinced now that Greek tragedy had screams / to show the poetry that followed dealt with great extremes'.

27. It has, however, to be said that the proscenium arch and performing space at the Victorian King's Theatre in Edinburgh did not help.

28. *The Scotsman*, 13 August 2007.

29. By contrast, in Conall Morrison's *The Bacchae of Baghdad*, staged at the Abbey Theatre Dublin in 2006, the shift was experienced by at least some of the audience as chilling rather than incendiary. They perceived it as cultural and religious triumph of the dreadlocked Dionysus, who moved from being a spectacular pantomime figure to an icon for the overthrow of the western Christian fundamentalism represented by the American officer Pentheus.

30. Compare, for example, Arrowsmith 1959; Dodds 1960; Seaford 1996.

31. Source: Programme Notes from Oxford Playhouse production, 2007. There is further information in the introductory material in the published text, which also contains a note on the Greek plays and translations used. See Farber 2008: 16.

32. Source: Programme Notes, 2007

33. In recent years, productions of Aeschylus' trilogy or of the *Agamemnon* as a single play have tended to make the sacrifice of Iphigenia more prominent, either through the inclusion of mime in the chorus description of the sacrifice or by including additional material. Ariane Mnouchkine included material from *Iphigenia in Aulis* as a prelude to her production *Les Atrides* (1990-2). Katie Mitchell had the ghost of Iphigenia overlooking the action of *The Home Guard* (the first part of her production of Ted Hughes' version, 1999).

34. For a penetrating exploration of some of these problems, see Taplin and Wilson 1993.

35. Source: Programme Notes.

36. For detailed treatment of the relationship between the TRC and Greek drama in South Africa, see Goodman 2006 (which discusses the performative aspects) Steinmeyer 2007, and Van Weyenberg 2008. For further discussion of the South African context, see Van Zyl Smit 2010.

37. Performance reviewed, 14 June 2007.

38. Fleishman 1990; Steinmeyer 2007.

39. Williams 1994.

40. See Hall 1997 on the sociology of the Chorus. There is still work to be done on the mutually fruitful relationship between contemporary community productions of Greek drama and the Theatre of the Oppressed. For example, a version of the *Oresteia*, called *House of Murders*, directed by Peter Arnott and staged in 2004 at the Citizens' Theatre in Glasgow, gave an opportunity to a group of amateur actors, including asylum seekers to develop multi-faceted approaches to the problems of history, conflict and identity.

41. Hardwick 2007.

42. The question of 'mattering' is central to Kwame Anthony Appiah's theory of translation, Appiah 1993.

43. And of course Fugard's, Kani's and Ntshona's *The Island* moved from being a protest play in the South African context of the 1970s to being an international icon in the 1990s, with performances world-wide.

44. I hope to return in more depth to this topic in an essay 'The Problem of the Spectators, Ancient and Modern' (Hardwick 2010b, forthcoming).

45. See Steiner 1975; Appiah 1993 and for a model based on rethinking the humanities in terms of text, reading and 'the erotics of the discipline', Humphreys 2004: 25.

46. For discussion of the poverty of restricted notions of violence and 'victimhood' in approaches to translation and adaptation, see Hardwick 2008.

47. The nature and impact of repression is an under-researched area of classical reception, see Hardwick 2010b, forthcoming.

From Translation to Performance Reception: The Death of the Author and the Performance Text[1]

Eleftheria Ioannidou

Modern readings, adaptations and performances of the classical texts have recently found themselves at the centre of vivid scholarly interest which constitutes classical reception as a distinct area of both classical and theatre studies. The long and loaded history of classical literature poses a series of issues originally tackled by reception theory (*Rezeptionästhetik*),[2] such as the dialectical relationship between past and present forms, the impact of the historical context on literary production, and the active role of the interpretative community in rereading past texts. Yet recent discussions addressing the reception of classics tend to deviate into a celebration of adaptations and performances which overrides the clear foci of reception theory. While modern literary and theatre studies often lack the diachronic approach which is essential in analysing the process of reception, the adherence to the classical text advocated by classical scholars offers no satisfactory answer, presuming the use of theory to be altogether superfluous.

The turn to reception theory not only arises from the need to reaffirm the theoretical underpinnings of classical reception studies, but it is also necessitated by the particularities of classical reception itself. Unlike other forms of literary reception, the reception of the classical text usually involves the mediation of another text or the original text's transmutation into a different medium. The study of classical reception should therefore not be limited to analysing the appropriation of the classical text or to identifying the responses of certain reading communities or audiences to it (or its adaptation); instead, it has to pursue a complex process which lies at the interface between adaptation and response. It could be argued that, in this process, the receiving community has already conditioned the adaptation of the classical text before the actual moment it is presented with a new version or performance.

Performance encapsulates the process of the transformation and the communication of the classical text more than any other medium, due to the co-presence of the audience. In the theatre what is normally defined as the receiving community has a material presence. Being present as material entities, the spectators share the experience of the performance. Erika

Fischer-Lichte emphasises the reciprocal way in which spectators and performance affect each other. This 'autopoietic feedback loop', as she terms it,[3] entails the immediate confrontation of the aesthetic product with the horizon of expectations of the audience. Especially in the case of classical reception, this horizon is formed of specific ideas about the classical text and antiquity, depending on the different cultural context. As the most performed classical genre, Greek tragedy has reached large audiences, allowing them to play an active part in the performance reception. While the reception of Greek tragedy in performance is certainly affected by the ways the tragic texts are read, performances also affect the way in which texts are read, reread and rewritten. Thus the attempt to theorise performance reception should map out the channels through which text and performance communicate.

In this essay, I argue that the study of translation is crucial in establishing theoretical models with which to discuss the performance reception of the classics. I discuss recent translations of Greek tragedy which challenge authorial subjectivity and point towards collective forms of textuality. This translational practice would appear to be relevant to performance reception, because it demonstrates that the communal experience of reception is not simply a result of the performance context, but it is already embedded in the translated text. The collective element in translation is entwined with the collective medium of the performance as well as with the co-presence of the audience. Rather than a theoretical scheme, these parallels, I argue, are actively at work in performance, tightening the bond between the classical text and the contemporary audience in ways which reach beyond the level of signification.

A substantial number of late twentieth-century versions of Greek tragedy are characterised by what one could describe as 'a creative reading of the ancient text', which becomes evident when the plays are juxtaposed with their source texts. The translated lines correspond closely to the prototype (or a previous established translation), the *dramatis personae* are the same, and certain verbal conventions of ancient drama, such as lyric and choral elements, are reproduced.[4] Nonetheless, the playwrights make significant departures from the Greek text, varying from anachronisms and intercultural references to the interpolations of entire scenes in what is largely an unabridged translation. The fusion of two texts, which is endemic in every act of translation, here becomes a fully intentional translational tactic. Lorna Hardwick identifies the 'creative blurring of the distinction between different kinds of translations, versions, adaptations and more distant relatives'[5] as a major trend in the translation of the classics in the second half of the twentieth century. These versions of Greek tragedy form a dramatic corpus against which the conventional distinction between translation and adaptation can be tested.

The resemblances between (re)writing and translation, witnessed in the versions of Greek tragedy discussed here, bring to the fore one of the most prominent questions addressed by literary criticism in the later twentieth century, namely the question of authorship. If the translator rewrites and the (re)writer translates, then who is the ultimate producer and owner of the text? These plays recall Roland Barthes' displacement of the author and concomitant redefinition of textuality,[6] in which no text has a single meaning bestowed by the author awaiting decipherment by the reader. It is now the reader who creates the meaning in the process of a creative interaction with the text. The affirmation that there is no single meaning of the text seems to have influenced translation theory, as well as assigning greater liberties to the translator. If Barthes opened fire against the Author, aiming to eradicate the quasi-theological implications sustained in the idea of the Author as the originator of the text, translation studies have similarly abolished the notion of the 'sacred' text which is venerable and thus untranslatable.

If there is a genealogy for the recent hybrid versions of tragedy, Bertolt Brecht's *Antigonemodell*, performed in 1948, springs to mind as the twentieth-century ancestor. For rather than merely adapting the story, Brecht bases his version on Hölderlin's translation,[7] but intervenes in the dramatic structure so as to mould the play to recent political circumstances. The liberties taken with the text offer a reading of Sophoclean Thebes as an allegory of Nazi Germany.[8] Heiner Müller's refigurations of Greek tragedy, written some years later, demonstrate a Brechtian espousal of fidelity alongside interventionism towards their source texts. Manfred Kraus notes that Müller's *Philoktet,* written in 1965, neither a recreation nor a translation of Sophocles, provides a '*reworking* [*Bearbeitung*] in the strictest sense of the word'.[9] Yet, Müller's reworking treats the prototype text more freely than the more recent versions of Greek tragedy.

Recent versions of Greek tragedy engage with several issues which destabilise the idea of authorship: sometimes they rewrite the male hero, as in Ted Hughes' *Alcestis* (1999),[10] and Simon Armitage's *Mister Heracles* (2000); sometimes, as in *The Trojan Women* (1993), by the Irish poet Brendan Kennelly, translation redefines the insubordinate female, resisting the translational metaphor of the *belle infidèle*. Finally, and, most radically, the translational act can on the cultural plane resist authorial patriarchy, and celebrate collectivity in the reception of the classical text, as is the case in Wole Soyinka's *The Bacchae of Euripides: A Communion Rite* (1973).

My discussion here does not intend to assert the obvious truth that these hybrid versions of Greek tragedy resonate with recent theoretical ideas about text and textuality. Taking the counterarguments to poststructuralism into full account, I shall consider how these versions challenge the validity of the attack on authorship, and, in turn, necessitate a remodelling of the relationship between the author and text as well as the relationship between the text and the audience. The plays under examination demonstrate that the author does not produce a text in a vacuum, through the sole medium of language, but neither is the reader's experience of the texts exhausted in a self-indulgent individual *jouissance*.

Reception theory has, of course, pointed beyond the *jouissance* of early semiotic theory. But the more recent deconstructionist approach to theatre would also seem to be resisted by plays discussed here. Herbert Blau has repudiated the possibility of Victor Turner's *communitas* in performance, advocating an idea of the performance as an interplay between absence and presence, which is in principle divisive.[11] The recent adaptations of tragedy could hardly be viewed as the absent text that the performance tries in vain to embody; in marked contrast, the text itself already contains the core constituent of theatre: the collective element, which provides the *sine qua non* of both the production and the reception of the theatrical performance, permeating the production of the text itself. The collective element within the text, channelled through the collective medium of the performance, is not only emblematic of the reception of Greek tragedy as a communal experience, but seems also to enhance that communality.

In Ted Hughes' *Alcestis* and Simon Armitage's *Mister Heracles*, the critique of the supernatural hero is married with a translational practice that challenges the individual male author.[12] These texts oscillate between translation and adaptation; they follow the prototype closely, while taking significant liberties with it. In neither text does the departure from the ancient text merely serve the representation of Heracles; it relates more intrinsically to thematic concerns. While Heracles is criticised in both plays as superhuman hero, the hybrid form of the translations provides a critique of the notion of authorship. Indeed, the hybrid quality of these versions challenges established ideas about authorship and ownership of texts *per se*, in an era in which theoretical scrutiny of the Author has been implicit in the tenets of poststructuralist theory.[13]

The demise of the hero and the demise of the individual author are complementary in both Hughes' *Alcestis* and Armitage's *Mister Heracles*. Not only do these versions dispense with the quest for fidelity to text as the unique product of an Author, but they do so in order to question patriarchal structures and theological principles. In both plays the demise of the author is coincidental with the demise of god, as well as with a rupture of the superhuman male hero who is the substitute for god. Kathleen Riley's observation, that *Mister Heracles* is 'a comment on the way society construes masculinity and the cultural and political authorization of male violence',[14] could apply equally to Hughes' *Alcestis*. Albeit in broad terms a rewriting of Euripides' *Alcestis*, Hughes' interpolation of a middle section makes Heracles the protagonist of his version. Both plays dramatise the complete bankruptcy of the male hero by unveiling the discursive mechanisms which underpin the heroic ideal.

Both these versions of Greek tragedies come close to constituting what has been termed by one theorist as 'violent modernization'[15] of ancient texts, where contemporary references and archaic elements merge. In Hughes' and Armitage's texts the gods are replaced by technological triumph and nuclear power. The elimination of the references to the divine from the Greek text is not designed simply to make the prototype accessible to contemporary audiences, as in many other versions of Greek tragedy.[16] This translational choice here seems to dispute the commonly held view that tragedy is impossible in a godless world.[17] Reminiscent of Nietzsche's famous proclamation of the death of god, the second choral ode in *Mister Heracles*, originally a hymn to the gods, is dedicated to Heracles himself. In Hughes' *Alcestis* the emancipation of Prometheus by Heracles, enacted in the interpolated scene, marks the emergence of the sovereign human subject who has contempt for divine agency.

Metatheatrical interpolations occur many times in both versions. The metatheatrical gloss on the representation of Heracles here underpins the view of violent acts as performances of the heroic self. Theatricality is linked to the repetitiveness of killing as well as to the accomplishment of a role that is normally assigned to the heroic subject.[18] In both Hughes' and Armitage's plays Heracles' murders ensue from the theatrical/cinematic revival of his heroic deeds. Hughes' Heracles projects the killing of his family when he re-enacts his labours. Before committing the murders, Armitage's Heracles experiences a state of mental disorder which 'whips up a version of his life'.[19] At the end of Armitage's play, Heracles hopes to be given shelter 'as circuses house freaks'.[20] Since the heroic performances of Heracles culminate in the murder of his family, Heracles leaves the theatre of action to dwell in the degenerate form of a freak-show, where he will only be stared at. The burlesque re-enactment of the labours in Hughes' version also consigns the hero to the world of low-brow spectacle.[21]

Armitage merges the metatheatrical element with the elimination of theological reference, rendering Theseus' line about Heracles' murders, 'This is Hera's work',[22] as 'Tragedy, friend, is what you look upon.'[23] The term 'tragedy' here is not merely used in its everyday sense to describe the aftermath of Heracles' deed. The interplay between the name of the dramatic genre and the catastrophe dramatised in the play is so effective that Armitage might well be inviting the audience to see his own rewriting of Euripides' text as a tragedy.

The way in which *Mister Heracles* and *Alcestis* construe violence is decidedly post-Nietzschean. Violence is disconnected from any Dionysiac creative drive or from any claim of immanence in human nature. In Armitage's version all references to Dionysus in the Greek text are translated as 'violence',[24] which is revealed as a particularly astute rendering when the prototype and the rewriting are read in juxtaposition. By showing violence as a core constituent of narratives of masculinity and heroism, the plays actually deconstruct the hero in the most efficacious way.[25] Going even further in this direction, Kennelly's *The Trojan Women*, which provides the next focus of this paper, offers an alternative idea of heroism to

212

that criticised by Hughes and Armitage through its representation of the female characters.

Among the many responses to Barthes' theoretical displacement of the Author, Seán Burke suggests that instead of renunciation, a more salutary strategy would be to reposition him/her as the conduit of socio-political procedures.[26] The late twentieth-century versions of Greek tragedy under examination point towards a solution to the theoretical impasses that poststructuralist analysis entails. The amalgamation of translation and adaptation found in these versions resists the notion of the single author as the originator of the text and shows that language indeed governs the process of writing. However, language here is not the abstract process described by Barthes, but a commonality that the author shares with the community,[27] in order to channel specific cultural, ideological and political codes.

Kennelly's version of Euripides' play, written in 1993, is the third part of a Greek 'trilogy', following his *Antigone* in 1987 and *Medea* in 1988. Irish poets have been particularly amenable to the translational tendency which mixes translation and adaptation to address issues of Ireland's post-colonial identity.[28] Such a use of the classical text could be viewed as a questioning not only of authorship but of authority in a broader sense. For Kennelly, the topographical context is wedded to the feminist questions tackled in his versions of Greek tragedy. In his version of *The Trojan Women* the author is displaced both as male and individual: Kennelly's version amplifies Euripides' text and gives prominence to the female perspective; furthermore, his interventions in the prototype situate the female experience within an Irish context. Close translation of the prototype is constantly infused with the social experience of the playwright's community. The female socio-political perspective advocated by Kennelly and the hybrid nature of the text combine to undermine the patriarchal principle,[29] in both its social configurations as well as in its embodiment in the authorial figure. Kennelly's writes in the introductory note to the play:

> I heard women in the village where I grew up say of another woman, 'She's a Trojan', meaning she had tremendous powers of endurance and survival ... and seemed eternally capable of renewing herself.[30]

His theatrical language consequently mediates the women's experiences and values. Warfare is depicted as a male activity involving slavery and maltreatment for women. The vocabulary employed by Kennelly to emphasise the sexual exploitation of the Trojan captives is much more charged than Euripides' language. It is repeatedly said that Hecuba is destined not only to slavery but to become a concubine of Odysseus,[31] in contrast to her Euripidean antecedent.

Kennelly's interpolations also problematise myth and literature as embodiments of male authority. The present ordeal of the women is opposed to the fabricated male truths: 'I am not fooled by songs or plays / or tales and legends / because I have stood there, in the presence of men ....'[32] In vivid contrast, women embody the silenced truth of their land. As a woman of the chorus says: 'Women, we are become this city, / we are become its untold loss / its forgotten truths, commemorated lies, its unspoken and unwritten history.'[33]

Feminist criticism has laid bare the gender relations entrenched in the metaphors of translation.[34] As epitomised in Gilles Ménage's epithet 'les "belles infidèles" ', brought to the attention of literary and translation studies by Roger Zuber in 1968,[35] the feminine conceptualisation of (mis)translation and the male dictate for fidelity are inextricable; translation must be faithful to the original text like an obedient woman to her spouse. It could be argued that Kennelly's *The Trojan Women* offers a positive re-evaluation of the feminine metaphorics of translation. Opposed to the 'belles infidèles', Kennelly's Trojan women prove translation to be essentially feminine, not because it betrays the source text, but because it bears the hallmarks of the feminine values of renewal and survival.

Kennelly's attempt to channel the unheard voices of the women of Ireland through the Euripidean text features prominently in the performance of his *Trojan Women*. His translation in performance literally embodies and gives voice to the Trojan women of his country; on the other hand, the communal element intrinsic in Kennelly's use of the language entails the communication of his text to an audience which is not limited to the playwright's local community. My next paradigm showcases even more explicitly how a translation which consistently inscribes the communal element onto the prototype can secure a wider reception of the classical text.

The cultural exchange inherent in every act of translation seems to condition the peculiar translational practice in Soyinka's *The Bacchae of Euripides* (1973). The interweaving of translation and adaptation forms the basis of his various encounters. Soyinka reads the *Bacchae* via the Yoruba, Greek and Christian myths. The prominent question of authorship is readdressed as a question of cultural ownership of texts. Soyinka's version shows that the text is not produced in a vacuum through the single agency of language, as Barthes maintains, but in a process of reception through the agency of cultural currents as well as past texts.

It is not only the idea of the sacred original, but the original in its most pragmatic sense that is rendered problematic in the case of Soyinka's *Bacchae*. For Soyinka the 'original' is constituted not by a unique text, but by a corpus of past translations. His version is allegedly based on the translations of Murray, Arrowsmith and Cavander, although the author must have had some limited access to the ancient text. As already mentioned, Brecht's version of *Antigone* is based on Hölderlin's translation; similarly, many adaptations of Greek tragedy by Müller use the earlier established translations of Hölderlin and Peter Witzmann. In Soyinka's case, the challenge to the notion of the original text involves the postcolonial negotiation of the textual culture. Femi Osofisan, a Nigerian writer and translator of classical literature himself, discusses the issue of the access to classical culture in the post-colonial era: 'when we talk of classical Greek theatre … in Nigeria, we are talking of such theater as given to us through the efforts of English-speaking translation and also, as well, through written texts'.[36]

Soyinka does not modernise Euripides' tragedy in order to communicate it to the target audience by means of eliminating the mythological references or alluding to specific events. On the contrary, the mythological basis of the prototype is kept intact, while elements of the Yoruba mythical tradition are layered upon it. Rather than a manifestation of *difference*, the displacement of the classical text becomes an indication of cultural *affinity*. In Soyinka's version the fusion of the ritual elements emphasises the common aspects shared by the Dionysian, Ogun and Christian visions.[37] The grounding of Soyinka's version in cultural affinities recalls Walter Benjamin's claim in his early essay 'On Language as Such and on the Language of Man' (1916),[38] that the kinship of languages is the prerequisite for and the *raison d'être* of every translational praxis.

Soyinka offers a politicised reading of the ritual; both the Dionysiac and Ogun rites substantiate social equality. His translation emphasises the god's potency to abolish the boundaries of age and class, which is endemic in the prototype.[39] 'He [Dionysus] has broken the barrier of age, the barrier of sex or slave and master. It is the will of Dionysos that no one be excluded from his worship.'[40] The boundaries between cultures are challenged in a similar way. The most explicit statement of cultural reassessment is given in the following passages, which provide an example of the amplification of the original lines:

> Pentheus: We have more sense than barbarians
>   Greece has a culture
> Dionysus: Just how much have you travelled Pentheus?
>   I have seen even among your so-called
>   Barbarian slaves natives of lands whose cultures beggar yours.[41]

In the preface to his *Bacchae* Soyinka views the Dionysiac *sparagmos* as an expression of the human impulse to partake in the natural process of catastrophe and revitalisation:

> I see the *Bacchae*, finally, as a prodigious barbaric banquet, an insightful manifestation of the universal need of man to match himself against Nature. The more the hinted-at-cannibalism corresponds to the periodic needs of humans to swill, gorge and copulate on a scale as huge as Nature's on her monstrous cycle of regeneration.[42]

The cannibalism theme can be further related to the speculation on

215

post-colonial translation proffered by Haraldo de Campos, who sees it as an act of cannibalism and vampirisation in which the translator devours the western original in order to nourish his/her own culture.[43] Here the old Romantic principle of foreignisation is recast, but there is a notable shift in emphasis from the linguistic to the cultural aspects of translation. The advocates of verbatim translation, Friedrich Schleiermacher and Wilhelm von Humboldt, assert that the literal translation which preserves the foreignness of the prototype enriches the receiving language.[44] The cannibalism metaphor implies that textual transformation invigorates the target culture. Susan Bassnett argues that the image of cannibalistic translation relates to 'post-modernist post-colonial translation theory ...; for what all have in common is a rejection of the power hierarchy which privileged the author and relegated the translator to a secondary role'.[45]

Soyinka's version absorbs rather than devours the prototype text(s), as indeed it absorbs the predominant Western ideas about tragedy; and it absorbs it in order to produce a text which introduces new elements into the translator's own culture. Soyinka's version is not a demonstration of difference, but an erasure of difference on the grounds of cultural kinships. Soyinka changes the Euripidean ending and closes his play with the scene of communion. Just as the tragic *sparagmos* is offset by the festive resolution at the end of Soyinka's play, the translational strategy adopted also surpasses the violence implied in the cannibalism metaphor. Recently, Michael Walton has adopted the term transubstantiation in his discussion of the translation of classical literature.[46] Communion involves a process of transubstantiation (wine into blood, bread into flesh), which culminates in a symbolic act of unity. This is especially apt here where Soyinka transubstantiates Euripides' *Bacchae* into a text to be commun(icat)ed to different cultures, thereby establishing through the multiple cultural referents a wider sense of Turner's *communitas* in the performance proper.

Notes

1. The chapter presented here is part of a broader inquiry on the rewriting of Greek tragedy in the last three decades. The conference on the performance reception of the classical texts gave me the chance to rethink aspects of this work in the light of parallel developments in the field of performance studies. Special thanks are due to Edith Hall for inviting me to take part in this debate. Helene Foley's response to my paper was of great help. Fiona Macintosh's feedback contributed significant insights into this paper as well as to my study of the recent reception of Greek tragedy.

2. See Jauß 1982.

3. Fischer-Lichte 2005: 111.

4. On the other hand, certain conventions, linked to practical conditions of the ancient theatre, such as the announcement of entrance and exits, is eliminated.

5. Hardwick 2000: 12.

6. Barthes 1977: 142-8, 155-69.

7. The selection of Hölderlin's also signifies a reinterpretation of tradition. What

seems to be of particular importance is that Hölderlin's text is an already inscribed one, despite and because of its closeness to the Greek original. Steiner (1975) repeatedly refers to Hölderlin's paradigmatic translations of Greek tragedy.

8. In the introductory scene, Antigone and Ismene are presented in Germany after the blitz, the role of Teiresias is changed so that it no longer bears any theological reference, and Creon's role as an authoritarian ruler is reflected in the common mode of address directed toward him, 'Führer'. The play closes with the announcement of the death of Creon's second son (Megareus), which is only mentioned briefly in Sophocles' *Antigone*, but more fully developed in Euripides' *Phoenissae*.

9. Kraus 1985: 301.

10. Hughes' play was published posthumously in 1999.

11. See Carlson's (1984) discussion on Blau's response to Turner, in particular.

12. Riley (2008) compares MacLeish's and Armitage's reworkings of Euripides' *Heracles*. Riley argues that the interpretation of Heracles insanity as intrinsic in heroic nature, as Willamowitz-Moellendorff argues, already marks a departure from Euripides, who presents Heracles noble, and it is mainly based on Seneca.

13. The striking similarities between the plays make the hypothesis of an immediate influence very plausible.

14. Riley 2008: 314.

15. Jones 1996.

16. Many version of Greek tragedy, such as Frank McGuiness' *Electra* (1997) and *Hecuba* (2004) also eliminate mythological and theological references, but this alteration does not bear further implications.

17. The absence of gods is expressed eloquently in the translation 'enough to make even a desert weep', as opposed to 'even a god' in Armitage 2000: 43.

18. *Herakles 5* by Heiner Müller (1966) bears striking similarities. Before cleaning the Augean stables, Heracles re-enacts some of his past labours in the mode of a performance. The hero wears a mask, while the Thebans watch and applause enthusiastically in the place of an audience. In Müller's play, the heroism of Heracles is also imposed by the community.

19. Armitage 2000: 35.

20. Armitage 2000: 51.

21. There is an additional level of metatheatricality here with the burlesque representation of Heracles, as the afterlife of *Alcestis* on the British stage includes many burlesque adaptations. See Macintosh (2001).

22. *Heracles Furens* 1189.

23. Armitage 2000: 46.

24. In Hughes 1999: 7, Death provides a Nietzschean presentation of Apollo: 'You and your bright ideas, for one / You fill the minds of human beings / With lunatic illusions / A general anaesthesia / A fuzzy euphoria ...'.

25. In Armitage 2000: 31, Heracles confesses 'I like fighting / It seems to keep me alive.'

26. Burke 1992.

27. This is very evident in the cases of versions of Greek tragedy which make use of specific idioms, such as *Medea* by Liz Lochhead (2000) who uses the clash between Scottish and standard English.

28. See McDonald and Walton (2002) for a list of these plays.

29. Kennelly 1991: 8, discusses the mixed reception of his *Medea*; while the play met the approval of many women spectators, Kennelly has been labelled as a misogynist by others.

30. Kennelly 1993: 5.
31. Kennelly 1993: 31, 73, 77.
32. Kennelly 1993: 75.
33. Kennelly 1993: 34.
34. Bassnett 1993 and Chamberlain 1992.
35. Zuber 1968.
36. Osofisan quoted in Olaniyan 1995: 328. Also Lefevere 1992: 109-10 – 'for readers who cannot check the translation against the original, the translation *is* the original' (*emphasis original*).
37. See Mary-Kay Gamel's chapter in this volume on the elements of Christian ritual in Lee Breuer's famous adaptation of *Oedipus at Colonus, Gospel at Colonus*.
38. Benjamin 1999.
39. *Bacchae* 208-9, 421-2.
40. Soyinka 1973: 26.
41. Soyinka 1973: 43.
42. Soyinka 1973: x-xi.
43. See Bassnett 1993: 138-61 and Vieira 1999.
44. Schleiermacher 1992 and Humboldt 1992.
45. Bassnett 1993: 115.
46. See Walton 2005.

Acting Perspectives: The Phenomenology of Performance as a Route to Reception

Jane Montgomery Griffiths

I am looking at a photograph of a woman hitting another woman. Or rather, not hitting her; not yet. She is about to, though; preparing the blow, positioning her left arm at full extension to make the most of the moment, to make the effort of the blow worthwhile. Her eyes are closed in concentration and effort; her mouth is open and contorted with strain. Is it the strain of preparing for the hit, or the force of the words she might be speaking that puts such tension in her jaw? Hard to say, because her words have gone: whatever she might, or might not, have been saying at this moment is lost in the silence of the image. No words, just the photograph to help me surmise the action. Her appearance is incongruous: a wedding dress and veil, right and tight and white; but strange. Its conservatism is confounded by the stains on the dress hem and by the actions of the body which is wearing it. With her right hand, she is holding onto the other woman. Onto her neck? Her hair? Difficult to know for sure, but there is violence in the hold. And the force of this hold has had a curious effect on the woman being held, because she has lost her face. Swung round by the violence of the pull, her head is a blur. Pushed down by force and blurred by speed: the photograph has captured the energy of this moment by abnegating the image of the recipient of the force. Perhaps in doing so, the photograph has also captured the essential of this moment, trapping forever the dual functions of the force: a face made unrecognisable by the violence of another; a body bowed, always about to receive, never quite receiving, the final blow. The photograph puts the recipient out of focus: a victim, an object. Her face and hair are there but smudged; her dress is fore-grounded (recognisable as a dirty shift in contrast to the other's stained trousseau) but is still not the focus. The only part of the victim to be as clear as the perpetrator is her foot: bare, scratched, swollen, bending slightly to accommodate the other's pressure.

What am I seeing when I look at this picture? A moment trapped in time? Real bodies and real sensation captured and pressed and transplanted to an image? A shadow of a dream or a memory of a feeling? In just a second or so, the bent-over woman will be hit, will feel the sensation – a pain, a tingling, a somatic, sensory reaction to add to the burn at the nape of her neck. The woman who hits will feel the dull thud of the other's flesh on her own gloved hand. But in this picture, these women do not, cannot feel: their sensory reactions can only be implied by the combined efforts of the picture's frozen energy and my own imaginative inference. They cannot feel, but they can make me feel. These bodies, which once were all sensation – which, in the moments before and after the photograph, experienced the violence of that hair-pull and sting of that slap – these bodies still emit a violence, even in their static, two-dimensional form. They force their story on me. They force me to tell their story; to name them; to name my affiliation to them.

This is not simple. Their story is complex; an intricate nap, with several strands that trail off, despite my attempts at neatening them. The energy of this always-impending, frozen moment of imminent (not to say, immanent) violence carries over into the moment of my looking at the picture. It forces me to articulate the picture (flailing limbs and all); it forces me to name the picture to tell the story, and in naming it, to name myself. Not just a picture, but a picture of a play. Not just a play, but the play 'Electra'. Not just two women, but an aggressor and a victim, a mother and a daughter, a Clytemnestra and an Electra, an actress and an actress; namely Beatrice Comins and myself, in the production of Sophocles' Electra by Compass Theatre Company, which toured the UK from January to July in 1999 (see Fig. 8). So I am looking at a photograph of a woman who is about to hit me, after she has hit me, many years after, while all the time knowing that she never actually hit me (even though I felt the blow); all the time knowing that she only ever hit Electra, six nights a week and twice on Saturdays, for six months nine years ago, frozen in time in a photo on a laptop, scanned from a publicity shot taken days before the production had even opened.

In many ways, trying to decipher this picture and work out the layers of meaning and identification is precisely what we attempt to do in performance reception. We look at the frozen images of a once living form; we decode the hieroglyphs from pictorial representations and inscriptions – inscribed words, inscribed pictures – in the hunt for the physical reality, the historical actuality, the contextual factuality. We try to read back from the material prop, the image of set, the description of a costume the *experience* of its use. We try to glean the truth from its representation. We behave, in short, like the most faithful of textual critics searching for the *philogia perennis* (*pace* Pfeiffer): *recensio* and *emendatio*, to piece together the fragments of the play.

This approach, however, does not altogether sit comfortably with the subject that is being studied. Just as in editorial theory, where there is always the nagging suspicion that there is not actually an original to which to return, so in performance reception, there is always a problem about the ontological status of the performance event we try to recover.[1] Theatre is the most tricky of art forms to pin down. By nature ephemeral, in essence collaborative, it is always haunted by multiple ghosts. As Marvin Carlson argues,

Fig. 8. Sophocles' *Electra*, Compass Theatre Company, UK tour 1999. Jane Montgomery Griffiths as Electra and Beatrice Comins as Clytemnestra.

> Everything in the theatre, the bodies, the materials utilized, the language, the space itself, is now and has always been haunted, and that haunting has been an essential part of the theatre's meaning to and reception by its audiences in all times and all places.[2]

Performance reception is the study of ghosts; and in many ways, our attempts to capture that ghostly essence are doomed to be as reductive as all those efforts of Mr Hudson and Mr Reeves, the darlings of Victorian spiritualism, who tried so hard, through the wonders of photography, to make material the immaterial; to capture for posterity the 'invisible emanations' of the long since departed, by freezing them in time on a treated glass plate.[3]

One of the questions that performance reception must ask is 'How do we pin down a ghost?' I would suggest not, necessarily, through historiography. That is not to denigrate in any way the work of theatre historians/ theorists who have found a vocabulary for their branch of reception studies in the language of cultural materialism. The importance of the work of Hall, Macintosh et al. in highlighting the need to recognise the socio-historical and cultural Zeitgeist of a play's transmission, reincarnation and reception cannot be over-emphasised. It should also be noted that Hall's excellent essay, 'Towards a Theory of Performance Reception' provides an admirable model for discussion of many of the methodological and theoretical problems inherent in the study of performance. But that is something different from what I am talking about here. The New Historicist approach to performance reception aims to examine the classical influence by capturing a bygone context, but not, necessarily, a bygone presence. It does not ask us to feel an absence; and although reports of audience responses to a production can go far to make us appreciate the political importance of a given play in a given society (and from that, the nature of the society itself), they do not necessarily ask us to find an analogous response in ourselves. Ironically, the discipline that grew from reader response theory, often, inadvertently, forgets to ask the new reader to interrogate their own response. What do we feel when we read of these performances that took place ages and worlds away? *How* do we feel? Why should it matter?

Reading the current corpus of classical performance reception, I do, however, interrogate my response. The very name of the sub-discipline makes me interrogate it: 'Classical'; 'performance'; 'reception'. Three words that carry with them such a weight of baggage: the authoritative solidity and resonances of respectability contained in the word 'Classical'; the polyvalence of approach (and the lack of respectability) contained in the word 'performance'; and the theoretical open-endedness, with all its protean possibilities, contained in the word 'reception'. The connotative force of these words makes me readdress my identity in relation to them – erstwhile actor, current classicist, accidental academic – causing me just as much confusion as when I look at that picture of myself (who was not I), beaten by a woman who was, once upon a time, at one-in-the-same-time, my mother (who was no mother) and my colleague (who was just playing a part when she hit me each night). My confusion has to do with shifting identities, morphing subjectivities, and disappearing presences. It has, in particular, to do with what every actor and audience member both knows and feels is the essence of performance: the absence and presence of the body. '[T]heatre', writes Simon Shepherd, 'is, and has always been, a place which exhibits what a human body is, what it does, what it is capable of.'[4] In this respect, performance reception is not just the study of how plays have been adapted, appropriated and made manifest in different cultural contexts, but is also the study of how bodies have operated in, on, and around the performance event. These bodily operations perform on various levels: the mimetic platform of the stage, on which the actor's body works as both signifier and sign, simultaneously representing and becoming the character; the receptive arena of the audience, where the spectator's body reacts on multiple planes to the experience before her, redoubling that energy to be received again by the performer; and the uncontainable receptacle of memory – somatic, intellectual, emotional – on which and in which the performance event replays its effect. For Blau, this at the crux of theatre:

> It is exactly what goes out of sight that we most desperately want to see. That's why we find ourselves, at the uttermost consummation of perform-ance, in the uncanny position of *spectators*. It is uncanny because, in some inexplicable way (though Freud comes uncannily close to explaining it), *we are seeing what we saw before*.[5]

The strange belatedness of this predicament is just where we find our-selves as we try to conjure up the image of the ephemeral theatrical event. We feel haunted by the details of that past performance, we can almost conjure up the picture, but we cannot find the means and vocabulary to reify the ghost, revivify the experience and explicate the strangeness of the effort. Like the brain-itching frustration of straining to remember that early morning dream, each attempt to capture the essence of that 'utter-most consummation of performance' leaves us floundering for words and trapped in the discomfort of the familiar yet the uncanny. Susan Melrose puts this well:

> ... *when it works*, theatre work gives place to the means to something *felt* and virtually **un-speakable**. To something momentary and – for all its force – weak. To a gasp and a quickening of the pulse. A body chaos of shortlived but effective kind. Something painful in its pleasing.[6]

In performance reception, we should not only be trying to analyse the receiving culture of a particular play in a particular time; we should also

223

be trying to pick up the vibrations of that 'gasp and … quickening of the pulse' as a means not of trying to imagine the hypothetical response of an imagined past audience, but, rather, of addressing our own interaction with the disciplinary discourse, with the play itself, and with the mutable medium of theatre.

To do so, of course, requires an approach quite alien to the disciplinary rigour and analytical objectivity that is the foundational underpinning of most Classical scholarship. It is a rare Classicist who will write about her or his own emotional connection to a play.[7] It is a rare Classicist who will, for that matter, actually write about a play *as* a play. When proposing a chapter for a forthcoming book on Greek drama, I was recently asked to cut out all the sections on performance. Caring for Classicist credibility, I did just as I was told: I concentrated on the philology, cut out the perform- ance angle, and ended up with an article that was the closest I shall probably ever come to writing a 'proper' bit of Classics. The message was clear: Classics does not 'do' performance; at least, not in a way anyone who has worked in a drama department or been an actor would recognise. We study plays as texts; we study theatre as historians; we might develop a performative or metatheatrical reading of a play from its intradialogic clues; but that is where the disciplinary border is reached. To step over that border is to enter no-man's land; and perhaps that is where classical performance reception finds itself now: one foot in Classics, the other reaching over into performance studies, and not quite supple enough to make the straddle comfortably. The problem of the sub-discipline's iden- tity is not only about its need to be flexible, however. It is more about the difficulties of its discovering where it belongs. However some occasional 'narrowness' in Classical Studies might seem a little unpalatable, there is no guarantee that the green pastures of performance studies will be any easier to digest. There is an (albeit benign) ideological and methodological fissure found again and again as scholars of theatre and performance try to define a vocabulary for its study. One has only to note the subtle differentiation between organisational structures across universities to see this in practice: Drama departments vie with Theatre Studies depart- ments which all tend to face it out with Performance Studies centres; each section with different competing priorities, different theoretical position- ings, different methodological leanings, and even different operational vocabularies. Theatre historians engage in a discourse quite discreet from that of their colleagues in performance theory: and into this milieu, who knows where the 'theatre maker' or 'performance practitioner' can, or even should, fit?

The variety and eclecticism of these different approaches to the study of the theatrical event do, however, provide a significant pointer to a possible direction for classical performance reception. The key lies in their parallel, yet occasionally wildly heterogeneous, approaches to the same end: complementariness through diversity and multiplicity. Performance

224

is so unwieldy. It is difficult to write about; it is difficult to define. It does not give itself easily to the Cartesian surety of analytic objectivity. In other words, it needs multiplicity: it needs multiple aims, multiple theories and multiple voices to give anything like a half-way decent representation, let alone analysis, of this once live event that has been and gone, yet lingers still in material and affective traces. This is the pursuit of the ghostliness of theatre; and this pursuit ultimately creates the possibility for a methodology of classical performance reception based on an inclusive phenomenological model that embraces the uncanniness of 'ghosting':

> The missing person is recurrently there insisting that his story be told, both playing and giving up the ghost. In our work, we have tried to make this uncentering dilemma into the methodology at the heart of the story, what I have described as ghosting.[8]

In Blau, we have a practitioner/theorist speaking; one whose theoretical stance and conceptual understanding of the performance event has been completely moulded by his own practice. Yet interestingly, as one reads his work, it is plain that this is a reciprocal interaction: practice has also developed out of theory. The magpie-like interdisciplinarity that makes him both frustrating and so inspiring to read is, in itself, a form of performance reception, where his prose 'performs' the synthesis of his practice-based theorising and his theory-based practice, staging the synergy of his influences and interpretations. It is an interesting combination, and a style that finds parallels in the writing of the most interesting performance theorists – a shared thread of interdisciplinarity that stretches across former theoretical demarcations. On some level, of course, this is not a matter of methodology, but of prose style. Peggy Phelan, Bert O. States and Elin Diamond can make us feel the uncanny excitement of the long gone theatrical event through the beauty or confrontational force of their prose: performative language in more ways than one. They attempt on some level to make the reader feel the academic narrative in an affective sense, in a way that usually exists more in prose poetry than essays on performance. But there is also a methodological issue at stake here to do with how one tries to link theory and practice in academic analysis. Definitions of performance constantly slip and slide, and if there are no bounds to performance, everything is open and worthy of consideration. If there is no adequate methodology to explore performance in an academic text, all methodologies, all theoretical stances, can be of use. Post-modern relativism it might well be, but in its willingness to move between disciplines, to be open to possibility and to embrace non-dualistic modes of discourse, an eclectic disciplinary approach tries to – and sometimes succeeds in – reflecting the polyvalent nature of performance.

Such a way of looking at performance analysis and performance reception is something that would benefit classical performance reception. Each time we look at the transmission of a Greek tragedy, we have to question the transhistoricity or cultural specificity of emotions and behaviour, endlessly – and often unsuccessfully – juggling the synchronic and diachronic as we tentatively tease out the specific from the universal.[9] Perhaps one reason it is difficult to find the words to express this tricky act of plate stacking is that we have yet to find the right vocabulary. Perhaps we need a vocabulary that recognises that when we try to describe performance, we are engaging in a rhizomatic or planar activity: branches leading from branches, or plateaux upon plateaux, in a Deleuzian approach that can lead us to jettison preconceptions about the academic pre-eminence of the binary, and to embrace the multiple. This is something easier said than done, of course. As Eve Kosofsky Sedgwick explains, it is not so easy to side-step the dualistic in practice as it is to suggest it in theory:

> A lot of voices tell us to think nondualistically, and even what to think in that fashion. Fewer are able to transmit how to go about it, the cognitive and even affective habits and practices involved, which are less than amenable to being couched in prescriptive forms … it's far easier to deprecate the confounding, tendentious effects of binary modes of thinking – and to expose their often stultifying perseveration – than it is to articulate or model other structures of thought. Even to invoke *non*dualism … is to tumble right into a dualistic trap.[10]

Kosofsky Sedgwick both recognises the difficulties and circumvents them, not only through dense argument that manages to meld phenomenology with Austinian speech act theory and Foucauldian queer theory, but by the use of the curiously resonant preposition, 'beside':

> … the most salient preposition … is probably *beside*. Invoking a Deleuzian interest in planar relations, the irreducibly spatial positionality of beside also seems to offer some useful resistance to the ease with which beneath and beyond turn from spatial descriptors into implicit narratives of, respectively, origin and telos. *Beside* is an interesting preposition also because there's nothing very dualistic about it. *Beside* comprises a wide range of desiring, identifying, representing, repelling, paralleling, differentiating, rivalling, leaning, twisting, mimicking, withdrawing, attracting, aggressing, warping, and other relations.[11]

For me, *besideness* is exactly descriptive of our engagement with an ancient text. The multiplicity contained in its tumbling connotations perfectly captures the twisting negotiations we must make as we grapple with the morphing identities of Greek and Roman drama. *Beside* is the preposition of lateral connection that allows both for distanced perspective and for intense energetic engagement. It is the preposition governing every fresh attempt by every translator and adaptor, composer and designer, by every director and actor. It is the preposition of the gasping vibration. There is an exercise that actors sometimes do in rehearsal as a means of finding energetic connection. Two actors stand face to face and hold their palms out towards each other. Slowly, the actors bring their hands together, but stop before touching, stop at the moment they feel the 'pranic' energy, the pulsating force-field of magnetic resistance that vibrates between their palms. Sometimes, the distance at which this force-field is felt is only a centimetre or so; sometimes it can be as big as two feet. Who knows why some actors have such strong magnetism, such immanent energy, and others do not; why some connect, and some do not? The connection comes not through intellect, necessarily, but through sensation: Melrose's 'quickening pulse' and 'body chaos'; an affective association that feels while it does not touch, and experiences although it cannot, as yet, articulate why in a jumble of synaesthetic aliveness. The exercise is a demonstration of the power of *besideness*. It is also a parallel to how the new creative team, and the scholars who would study them, try to find the point of energetic connection with the ancient tradition and the ancient text.

When the actor meets her character for the first time, there is a *besideness* to the encounter. The meeting occurs not merely through the authorising frame of the translator's and publisher's printed text, but through a complex paratext (*besideness*, again) through which the actor eventually comes to see, feel and be the character. To some extent, this 'paratext' corresponds to Genette's definitions: it is a 'fringe ... [which] constitutes, between the text and what lies outside it, a zone not just of transition but of *transaction*'.[12] Whereas Genette's paratext is a composite of the material and abstract weave that includes the peritext (of preface, title and *dramatis personae*) and the epitext (of externally manufactured readerly knowledge), the actor's paratext is a personal threshold; one that emits the unique energies of the actor, and receives the vibrations of the text and the part. This process is anything but neutral, linear, and objective for the actor: the actor will enter this meeting with numerous motivations and intentions, numerous assumptions and prejudices, and an infinite number of influences that will ultimately shape the interpretation. There is the cultural historicity of the part, and, in the case of Greek drama, the connotations of a part's name – Oedipus, Medea, Electra – can be infinitely more pervasive than the denotative force of it as a character from the play. The name can inspire or confound, as an exemplum of the grandeur or excess of Greek tragedy. It can terrify or excite as the 'female Hamlet': one of the canonically great tragic heroines along with Lady Macbeth and Hedda Gabler.[13] It can carry with it the weight of other performances and representations, from different productions and adaptations. The name, encrusted with 'sedimentation', is at the beginning of the actor's accretive process. She cannot come to the text without looking beside, and skirting around the potential that lies within the name. In her approach to the name, the actor's characterisational process necessarily, and intuitively, is both a continuation of the theatre's endless ghostings, and also an on-going example of living reception.

Added to the ghostly traces of past performances, there is also the somatic force of the actor's embodiment: the 'phenomenological frontality', as States would say, through which the actor presents his/her new self – complete with new textual weave – to the audience. In so doing, the actor both objectifies herself and reconfigures herself in a new subjectivity that is not hers, but that will encrust and seep into her:

> ... in the theater we see an object in its 'embodied form' as having a double aspect, one of which is significative, the other ... self-given. Phenomenology occurs in the 'seam' between these two faces of the object.[14]

States' point is important, since it highlights the uncanniness of the actor's position. Operating as she does simultaneously through an internal and external frame, she elides the boundaries of her self and her character. Her character lives within her, but is not she; her character maps itself onto her, and so is she. The boundaries of character and actor are semi-permeable, and through their availability to the gaze of the audience, create an ever growing and, indeed, potentially infinite paratext to the play and the character. The audience interprets this through a complicated process of 'besideness', juggling their pre-existing transtextual knowledge of the inscribed text and the practitioner before them with their immediate decoding of the persona presenting itself to them on stage. As Alice Rayner says, in her description of the phenomenology of the actor taking as Ophelia:

> The performer stands directly in the face and presence of the audience, with a combination of the conscious choices and the baggage of both bodily presence and unconscious determinants, all of which are manifest in externals. How that presence signifies to an audience is historically bound to conceptions of both real persons and conventions of theatricality. The actress herself is already a signified body as well as a performer who chooses to signify.[15]

Hence, through this phenomenological 'besideness' which is at the heart of the actor's relationship with the audience, the actor's body becomes both the recipient of the character, and the conduit through which it will be received by others. The actor's body becomes, in other words, the core of performance reception.

Given that, one would imagine that the experience of actors would figure a little more prominently than it actually does in classical performance reception studies. It is a curious anomaly that this fledgling sub-discipline, which spends so much of its time analysing the cultural phenomena of past theatrical production, spends so little of its time actually investigating the phenomenological processes of the current performance event.[16] It is as though performance is the means to the end of reception: it creates the conditions for the object of study, but is not, in itself, worthy of much analysis. Its constituent parts can be: costume, *mise-en-scène*, the epi- and para-textual baggage of programmes and posters and fliers are all deemed suitable subjects for analysis. But the actual phenomenon of performance and the experience of the performer slip under the radar: something too nebulous to be categorised, too ephemeral to be archived; something which perhaps exists only in practice and not in theory.

The vocabulary of 'besideness' can perhaps help us find a way into investigating and categorising the actor's experience and thereby into addressing the extraordinary insights that the performer's sensory and somatic connection to a part can throw on our understanding of the source text. For me, this is still very much work in progress. Currently, I am trying to explore this area by attempting to synthesise the responses of a number of actors to a specific part: parallel voices, touched by the same yet parallel character. Over the last few years, I have been interviewing performers who have played Sophocles' Electra. Most of them came to the part without prior knowledge of the play, or its performance history. All of them, however, use remarkably similar language when describing the part; talk, in identical terms, about the need for similar physicalities; describe the invasion of the part into their bodies – in all cases, to the detriment of their health; and also all say that they found in the part a spiritual connection that was beyond anything any of the interview participants had experienced before: a 'beauty' in the character, a 'terrible loveliness' in who Electra is, a spirituality that was 'the nearest I have come to god'.[17]

This is interesting because some of these statements confound so thoroughly the academic discourse on the play. It is interesting, too, because the actor's memory of the part plays so uncannily with absence, presence, liveness and the past. The actor, as someone who, while performing, exists in an anarchy of amorphous temporality and spatiality, is uniquely privileged as one who can perhaps marry the problems of transhistoricity versus historicity. Her connection to the part belies all normal definitions of physical containment and the ephemerality of liveness. The actor continues to be the means and ends of reception long after the performance has concluded and the theatre has made way for a shopping mall. Each performance invades the mind and body of the actor; each performance forces a blending of the personal and private of the performer's subjectivity with the communal and public of the play's and part's historicity. There is violence in this invasion: it is a sensory assault on, and in, the actor's body; the sheer viscerality of which necessitates a reframing of the traditional means of analysing production data. Despite the fact that a production has been and gone, traces of the force of this experience linger in the affective

229

aftermath of performance. I would argue that these traces need to be analysed with as much seriousness as is accorded by the theatre historian to the material evidence of a production's history. Behind the photograph of an actor hitting another actor, there is an emanation of energy; behind the picture of an actor wearing a costume, there is a trace of a body that feels the constriction or nakedness of cloth on skin; behind a specific translation, there is the echo of a voice that came into being in the speaking of those words. Somewhere along the line as we engage in the rigorous academic discipline of Classics, it becomes easy to forget that theatre is about bodies, and sensation, and feeling – about affect; because it is hard to articulate affect, and even harder to convey in words its power in the ephemeral theatre event, we stumble as we try to create a methodology of performance reception, and we feel uncertain as to whether we should even try. We don't tend to ask actors and audiences how they felt, and if we do, we often don't know what to do with the information once we have it. I don't know either, but I do think it is something worth investigating, because I believe reception studies allows a dialogic, heteroglossial *besideways* engagement between the text and the practitioner, between the performance and the audience, that can tell us something both about the receiving culture, and about the text that is being received. However difficult it is to capture a ghost, the attempt is worth the effort.

Notes

1. For an application of theories of editorship and textual criticism to performance, see Worthern. Ubersfeld, from a semiotic approach, is representative of the synergies between editorial and performance theory.
2. Carlson 2003: 15.
3. Sussman 2007: 339.
4. Shepherd 2006: 1.
5. Blau 1987: 173.
6. Melrose 1994: 62-3 (her emphasis).
7. For the uses of personal voice theory and the Classics, see Hallet and Van Nortwick 1997; and Arethusa 34.2 (2001).
8. Blau 1982: 282-3.
9. See Hardwick 2003 and Hall 2004a for further discussion of the link between historicism and transhistoricism in performance reception.
10. Kosofsky Sedgwick 2003: 1.
11. Kosofsky Sedgwick 2003: 6 (her emphasis).
12. Genette 1991: 261.
13. For instance Walter 1999: 222 holds up Electra as at the 'pinnacle' of the 'sparsely spaced pyramids' of great female roles; Hazel 2002 talks of the 'Hamletization' of Electra.
14. States 1992: 375. For phenomenology of the actor and the medial role of the body on stage, see also Garner 1994: 1-17, 26-8, 43-49); see also Melrose 1994, who combines semiotics and phenomenology in her theory of 'somatographia'.
15. Rayner 1996: 31-2.

16. I am talking here in relative terms: there are very honourable exceptions to this omission, most notably the work of Lorna Hardwick and her colleagues at the Open University's database, whose attempts to document the experience of practitioners have uncovered some real insights.

17. Expressions taken from interviews with Penny Layden, Zoe Wanamaker and Fiona Shaw.

Physical Performance and the Languages of Translation

Stephe Harrop

1. Performance and physicality

Performance is a physical experience. The words spoken in a theatre are mediated through, and interpreted by, an actor's body, and received by physically-present spectators experiencing a specific set of corporeal conditions. As Erika Fischer-Lichte reminds us, 'a performance takes place in and through the bodily co-presence of actors and spectators'.[1] As a spectator, my engagement with Greek tragedy is strongly coloured by the bodily experience of the theatre-event. For example, the National Theatre of Scotland's 2007 *Bacchae* is primarily registered in my memory as a burning sensation of the eyes.[2] By contrast, recalling *In Blood: The Bacchae* conjures the smell of theatrical smoke, the waft of displaced air hitting my face, and a dizzy sense of the room spinning.[3] Each remembered experience brings with it a set of characteristic physical associations, which are central to my understanding of the performance.

It has been suggested by some dance theorists that 'viewer's bodies, even in their seated stillness' can actually 'feel what the dancing body is feeling – the tensions or expansiveness, the floating or driving momentums that compose the dancer's motion'.[4] I suspect that the intensity of this posited identification between dancer and spectator is at least partially the result of the degree to which dancers and their audiences (often themselves the recipients of dance training) share a detailed kinaesthetic knowledge of specific movement vocabularies, which permits a high degree of corporeal empathy between performer and observer. Still, even the untrained observer receives and remembers and interprets the theatre-event partly through its impact upon their physically present body.

As a performer, my relationship with the languages of ancient tragedy in translation is even more profoundly corporeal. Different texts feel different, breathe differently, taste different in the mouth. Each variant version, each different cluster of morphemes, breath-patterns, vowels, consonants, and pauses has a different impact upon the body.[5] And the performer's response to these somatically experienced differences has consequences not only for the physical enactment

232

of the drama, but also for the physically-present spectator's reception of a text-in-performance.

Our lack of reliable information concerning the physical and choreographic aspects of ancient tragic performance permits modern writers to construct their own imaginative re-creations of the ancient text/body relationship in a wide variety of modes.[6] The range of ways in which texts translated or adapted from ancient tragedy are capable of suggesting performative physicalities is accordingly broad. However, we often respond to these new theatre works as if they were linguistic artefacts, as if theatre translation were merely the replacement of one counter with another in a word game played out at the level of the printed text, and relayed to an audience without the crucial corporeal intervention of breath, bone, tissue and muscle. This chapter is concerned with what physically happens in that moment when the written text of a drama is filtered and resonated and shared though the medium of an actor's body. It is also concerned with the opportunities presented by the multiple re-versioning of Greek drama in the contemporary theatre to explore the multiple ways in which the formal qualities of dramatic text, especially poetic texts, can influence the physical life of a performance.

2. Language in the body

Speech is an intensely physical act. As well as the obvious motions of the lips and tongue, the frictions of breath being shaped against the larynx, teeth and palate, many other areas of the body are involved:

> The most active part of the body as we vocalize is the breath system: the rib cage, diaphragm and the deeper support muscles of the abdomen going down as far as the groin. Literally half of your body and a number of organs housed in your torso are utilized to manufacture the breath necessary to produce human sound.[7]

Speech is the result of a complex set of physical actions and reflexes. Some specialists argue that 'it is impossible even to *think* of a word without moving':

> Language-based thought (and most thought is contained in language) is accompanied by the beginnings of the motor actions required to articulate the words aloud. The area of the brain most closely concerned with speech production, Broca's area, is essentially a movement area – it triggers activity in the muscles that allows the lips, tongue and throat to produce sounds. When people read, even quietly, alone, to and for themselves, this area produces tiny contractions of those muscles, even if we long ago learned to stop our lips moving.[8]

Even silent reading (and readers were not silent in antiquity[9]) may contain the roots of physical motion. All articulated speech is certainly motion. However, poet Robert Pinsky is a relatively lonely voice among his literary colleagues in asserting that 'poetry is a vocal, which is to say, a bodily, art':

> The medium of poetry is a human body: the column of air inside the chest, shaped into signifying sounds in the larynx and the mouth. In this sense, poetry is just as physical or bodily an art as dancing.[10]

In this chapter I contend that the textual choices of the translator, a writer's individual responses to a set of lexical and stylistic variables presented by the translation process, significantly affect the bodies as well as the minds and voices of performers. The performer putting their bodily all into saying 'Ten years since' is actually physically different from the same person embarking upon a speech that begins 'Ten years ago', and different again from that same person wrapping themselves around a chorus beginning 'The tenth year this'. In each case, the body changes in response to the varying demands of the language being enunciated. Further, I would suggest that any engagement with dramatic text remains incomplete so long as it fails to recognise and respond to the physical qualities of embodied language.

3. The actor and the text

Voice practitioners primarily concerned with the performance of Shakespeare give us a good place to start. The methods of Cicely Berry, and those who have been inspired by and developed her work, encourage performers to engage personally and with physical as well as intellectual commitment to the aural qualities of spoken language, especially the challenging and complex language of formal dramatic speech. This approach stresses the importance of a detailed awareness of the contours of a poet's language and argument as defined by metrical phrasing and punctuation.[11] Berry emphasises the performative importance of understanding and possessing a character's thought and speech patterns as encoded in dramatic verse 'physically through the breath'.[12]

Likewise, Patsy Rodenberg insists upon the insight that 'proper voice work is very physical' and 'involves the use of the entire body'.[13] One of Rodenberg's rehearsal exercises gives some idea of the range of physical movements and movement qualities which can be prompted by the process of becoming bodily receptive to the influence of poetic speech:

> Walk while speaking the text, allow the different rhythms, phrasing units, changes of thought and emotional mood swings to shift the direction, speed and quality of your walking. In this exercise you will discover many corners, bends and U-turns in the journey of a text. Don't be frightened of permitting the text to throw you forward, slow you down, make great sweeping walks or runs across the room or even stop you cold or mow you down. You are making

the intellectual, emotional and *physical* journey of the words actual and real. Imagine that if someone was observing you from above they would see a journey traced out below them, a picture drawn in time and space. When you return to speaking the text standing still, allow your body and voice to be filled with the physical journey you have just experienced.[14]

The great joy of this sort of approach to appreciating the somatic qualities of a text is its accessibility. Almost anyone can pick up a text, and start reading aloud and pacing round the room. In fact, if no one's watching, then I strongly recommend that you have a go right now, with these three different *Agamemnon* choruses for starters:[15]

> Ten years ago
> The sons of Atreus,
> Menelaus and Agamemnon,
> Both divine kings,
> Assembled a thousand ships
> Crammed with the youth of Hellas
> And sailed across the sea to punish Priam.

> Ten years since clanchief Menelaus
> and his bloodkin Agamemnon
> (the twin-yoked rule from clan-chief Atreus –
> double thronestones, double chief-staves)
> pursued the war-suit against Priam,
> launched the thousand-ship armada
> off from Argos to smash Troy.

> The tenth year this, since Priamos' great match,
> King Menelaos, Agamemnon King,
> – The strenuous yoke-pair of the Atreidai's honour,
> Two-throned, two-sceptered, whereof Zeus was donor –
> Did from this land the aid, the armament dispatch,
> The thousand-sailored force of Argives clamouring
> 'Ares' from out the indignant breast …

The first of these extracts (from Ted Hughes' 1999 *Agamemnon*) travels in a straight line, with weighty, deliberate steps rising and falling in time with the verse's long vowels, sometimes stretching out the short lines into a sombrely intoned slow-march. The second provokes a more urgent and complex forward propulsion, with steps of different sizes and direction, and my weight sometimes taken on the ball (rather than the heel) of the foot. This walk is an incipient dance, with some pretty fancy footwork needed to keep pace with the 'short vowels' and 'sensuous consonantal quality' of Tony Harrison's *Agamemnon* for masks (1980).[16] The third comes from a 'transcript' of Aeschylus generally considered to be utterly unplayable,[17] and the twists of the verse might seem to corroborate this judgement, but in walking this bit of Robert Browning's *Agamemnon*

(1877) the ensuing tongue-and-foot tangle, with its directional complexity, can actually make it easier to get to grips with the semantic logic of the different fragments of the choppy text. The conflict the verse describes is going on in my mouth, which recruits the rest of my body into the struggle to turn tragic violence into meaningful poetic utterance.

Of course, these are my personal responses, and everyone's personal response will be different. But even something as simple as walking whilst speaking a text can reveal crucial characteristics of phrasing, breath patterning, stress and emphasis, verbal register, pace and style, all of which impart different qualities to a speaker's physical movement. The body discovers difficulties and possibilities in a spoken text that the silently reading eye is blind to. This sort of exercise can be intensely personally liberating, as well as revealing of the workings and resonances of a dramatic text.

What both Berry and Rodenberg offer are ways in which individuals (not just professional actors) can become more sensitively attuned to the qualities of dramatic language, and especially the qualities of theatrical verse. However, the central concern of this work is with 'communication through the word'.[18] It is based upon the attempt to develop a conscious awareness of the physical presence of language within our own bodies, in order that our intellectual selves can make more purposeful and skilful decisions about the speech-acts that we perform. Despite the immense range of physical possibilities implicit in this sort of voice work, the vocal techniques associated with classical western acting are built around the idea that speech is the primary physical process. Vigorous physical activity, in this tradition, is regarded as a menace to diction and clarity, with potential physical expressivity being more or less ruthlessly subjugated to semantic comprehensibility and aural beauty. Peter Hall speaks for a sizeable section of the theatrical establishment when he authoritatively pronounces that 'eloquent movement destroys eloquent words'.[19]

4. Psychosomatic co-operation

By contrast, Jerzy Grotowski (pioneer of the cruel and holy theatres of the 1960s and 70s), proposed a method of exploring heightened, traditional verses which demanded the deliberate subjugation of the conscious, self-critical mind to the deep, somatic, irrational impulses of embodied language. This work was inspired by the visionary manifestos of Antonin Artaud who, in a 1933 *Letter on Language,* demanded:

> Let there be the least return to the active, plastic, respiratory sources of language, let words be joined again to the physical motions that gave them birth, and let the discursive, logical aspect of speech disappear beneath its affective, physical side, i.e., let words be heard in their sonority rather than be exclusively taken for what they mean grammatically, let them be per-

ceived as movements, and let these movements themselves turn into other simple, direct movements as occurs in all the circumstances of life but not sufficiently with actors on the stage, and behold! the language of literature is reconstituted, revivified.[20]

Grotowski was fascinated by the way the reactions of the body to intensely experienced vocal stimuli can illuminate aspects of a role that evade intellectual analysis. In his work in collaboration with Thomas Richards, Grotowski explored the potential of poetic language to act upon and provoke the elusive psycho-physical 'impulses' which lie at the root of bodily action, and which he considered to be the 'morphemes', or 'basic beats' of performance.[21] This work drew upon 'the traditional song' which was used as a 'mantra' for the actor, a vocal tool which might release them from a fixation upon the *meaning* of words, instead allowing them to focus on experiencing the *vibratory qualities* of language:

> When we begin to catch the vibratory qualities, this finds its rooting in the impulses and the actions. And then, all of a sudden, the song begins to sing *us*.

The resulting 'song-body' – a body in which the qualities of the song are concretely, visibly manifested – depends upon the recognition that 'the impulses which run in the body are exactly that which carries the song'.[22] As Richards described the process:

> When a doer begins to sing a song of tradition, and begins to initiate something of the inner process, the song and the melody will start to descend in the body. The melody is precise. The person, who is singing begins to let the song descend into the organism, and the sonic vibration begins to change. The syllable and the melody of these songs begins to touch and activate something I perceive to be like energy seats in the organism.[23]

Within this singularly intense mode of working, the sonic qualities of the embodied song have the power to alter the psycho-physical impulses of the sensitised and attentive performer. This is quintessentially 'holy theatre', a 'Theatre of the Invisible-Made-Visible', with the usually intangible vibratory qualities of embodied sound forming the basis for physical performance.[24] The processes Grotowski and Richards describe offer a way of conceptualising the links between the words performers put into their mouths, the psycho-somatic impulses resulting from this ingestion, and the impulse-activated physical actions that can be the external product of this procedure.

Grotowski's experiments and insights, which inspired a generation of avant-garde theatre-makers, potentially point the way to a fully-embodied relationship between the sensitive, disciplined performer and the dramatic language they articulate. Poet and dramatist Ted Hughes, who became familiar with the ideas of Grotowski through director Peter Brook,[25] had his own belief in the fundamental corporeality of poetic language reinforced by the experience: 'Poetry is not made out of thoughts or casual fancies. It is made out of experiences which change our bodies, and spirits, whether momentarily or for good.'[26]

In a detailed study of the poems of Coleridge and Hopkins,[27] Hughes elaborated upon his idea that poetic language can 'compel the reader to co-operate physically':

> Each line is like a dancer who, if you are going to read the line at all, forces you to be a partner and dance ... You can pronounce the line as silently as you like, but that launching of the inner self into full kinaesthetic participation is, so to speak, compulsory. Otherwise you can't read the line. You have to back off, stay a wallflower, and call it 'unsayable'. As everybody knows, between the sitting or standing person and that same person dancing there gapes an immense biological gulf ... In fact, what is required is that the familiar person becomes, in a flash, an entirely different animal with entirely different body chemistry, brain rhythms and physiological awareness.

This 'psychosomatic co-operation with the vitality of the statement' is a powerful and persuasive imagining of the potential of heightened language, whether poetic or dramatic, to transform the body through which its resonances and meanings are transmitted.[28] The all-encompassing physical and spiritual demands of Grotowski's avowedly cruel theatre might be well beyond the aspirations of most readers and players of ancient drama. Still, the idea that the performer capable of abandoning conventional psycho-physical restraint, of deciding – in Hughes' terms – not to be a wallflower, might thereby free themselves to become increasingly responsive to the impulses contained within dramatic language is both suggestive and seductive.

5. The corporeality of the word

Peter Hall outlines the following prescription for an adequate appreciation of the words of a theatre text: 'We must add to these words an understanding of how they operate when spoken aloud, and what their form, shape and rhythm contribute to the emotional meaning of the character who is speaking them. We must also be aware of what the dramatist was asking of the actor – indeed almost what kind of acting is indicated by the text.'[29] I go further than Hall, and consider not only *what kind of acting* but also *what kind of physical presence and/or movement* might be indicated to, or demanded of, the performer by the verbal score of a dramatic text. The spoken word, absorbed into the receptive body, can be a powerful shaper of physical presence and motion.

There are many difficulties attached to exploring this complex and analysis-resistant area of performance. Different actors, with different physiologies, different trainings in enunciation and breath control and different intellectual readings of a text's meanings will all respond differently to the somatic promptings of a script. Directors, choreographers and designers also exert significant controls upon the appearance and motion of the performer's body, their decisions and demands often serving concepts and ideas not necessarily related, or sympathetic to the somatic promptings of embodied language. This is a mode of exploration which resists formal theorisation, which depends upon intuitive, subjective and highly personal experience. But even if the challenge of unravelling the elusively symbiotic relationship between spoken text and the performer's body is ultimately unachievable, still the process of attempting to engage with and understand the physical life of a text within a body can only enrich our experience and understanding of ancient drama, indeed any drama, in performance.

This question is particularly relevant to the study of the reception of ancient drama, as our grasp of what might constitute an appropriate physical response to the ancient dramatic text is partial, vague and therefore open to a wide range of interpretations in different times and places, different cultures, and in the variously plausible speculations of different scholars and theatre-makers. Multiple re-visionings and re-versionings each contain within their texts a set of assumptions about, aspirations for and parameters defining their possible onstage embodiment. The attempt to get at and make use of the implicit information about physical presence and/or movement embedded within dramatic text is a complex, often intuitive and inevitably subjective one. But only by risking our own bodily engagement with a text can we begin to excavate and appreciate these latent provocations and promptings concerning the potential physical life of ancient drama in subsequent theatrical performance.[30]

Notes

1. See Fischer-Lichte in this volume, p. 29.
2. Text by David Greig, directed by John Tiffany. Lyric, Hammersmith (London), September 2007.
3. Text by Frances Viner, directed by Noah Birkstead-Breen. Arcola Theatre (London), January 2009. My experience of this show was perhaps more physically memorable than most. See review at: http://www.londontheatreblog.co.uk/in-blood-the-bacchae/ (accessed 14 March 2009).
4. Leigh Foster 2008: 49.
5. Thus 'vocality always brings forth corporeality': see Fischer-Lichte in this volume, p. 34.
6. There is far more (albeit circumstantial) evidence for the dancers of ancient myth in the 'pantomime' of the Roman Empire. See Webb 2008.
7. Rodenberg 1997: 6.
8. Carter 2006: 140.
9. See Goldhill 1999a.
10. Pinsky 1998: 8.

11. However quixotic this veneration for the minutiae of inevitably imperfect and corrupted period source-text(s) might seem.

12. Berry 2000: 26.

13. Rodenberg 1997: 8.

14. Rodenberg 1993: 144.

15. Always bearing in mind that such choral lyrics would probably have been sung, or at least intoned to aulos accompaniment, in ancient performance. See Hall 1999 and 2002b.

16. Harrison 2002: 22.

17. Though I would contend otherwise: an argument made briefly in Harrop and Wiles 2008, and at length in Harrop 2007.

18. Harrop and Wiles 2008: 54.

19. Hall 2000. 30.

20. Artaud 1958: 119.

21. Richards 1995: 95.

22. Richards 1995: 127-8.

23. Schechner 2001: 437.

24. Brook 1968: 47.

25. Brook's celebrated version of Seneca's *Oedipus* (Old Vic, London, 1968), and the *Orghast* project (CIRT, 1970-1) resulted from this collaboration.

26. Hughes 1967: 32.

27. It ought to be noted that the latter was deeply influenced by the lyric poetry of Aeschylus.

28. Hughes 1994: 334-5.

29. Hall 2000: 14.

30. Further analysis of the issued raised here can be found in Harrop and Wiles 2008, and at greater length in Harrop 2007. I am grateful to David Wiles for his support and criticism, and to Edith Hall for commenting on an earlier version of this chapter.

'Spatial Poetics' and Greek Drama: Scenography as Reception

Paul Monaghan

In one of his groundbreaking 1930s essays on theatre, 'Production and Metaphysics', Antonin Artaud urged his readers to consider what he called 'spatial poetics', the spatial equivalent of a language-based poetry:

> I maintain the stage is a tangible, physical place that needs to be filled and it ought to be allowed to speak its own concrete language ... [This 'spatial poetry'] is composed of everything filling the stage, everything that can be shown and materially expressed on stage, intended first to appeal to the senses, instead of being addressed primarily to the mind, like spoken language.[1]

'Spatial poetry', in other words, exists and has its effect on the spectator's senses and consciousness quite independently of words. The more accepted terms today for Artaud's 'spatial poetry', which he also refers to as 'the physical temptation of the stage', are 'performance text',[2] the 'weave of actions'[3] or simply 'mise-en-scène'. Artaud goes on in the same passage to specifically mention 'architecture, lighting and décor', or what we now call 'design' or 'scenography'.

It is my aim in this essay to offer the Reception Studies scholar and student a means and a language with which to conceptualise, describe and analyse scenography as reception. As Marvin Carlson asserts, theatre is 'a ground for the encounter of the spectator and the performer';[4] the way that 'ground' or 'space' is constituted, physically as well as psychically, then, is of enormous consequence for the experience and interpretation of the performance. This approach to 'reception' involves understanding the visual, spatial and kinaesthetic dynamics of scenography, the work of objects and light in theatre, the importance of architectural forms, and the way that these forms in space express our relationship to, and understanding of the world, as well as our attempts to shape it and orient ourselves in it.

Analysis of scenography is significantly under-represented in Reception Studies (and to some extent even in theatre and performance theory). One of the reasons for this shortfall may be that scenography is one of the most difficult areas of theatre to analyse and articulate in writing, and as

Svoboda asserts, 'true scenography is what happens when the curtain opens and can't be judged in any other way'.[5] Moreover 'spatial poetry' is precisely what is absent and often difficult to imagine from the page and thus can easily be underrated or overlooked by those whose contact with drama (including Greek drama) is primarily through reading.

Space is a fundamental of human society, and any shaping of space is already a culturally situated expression before anything occurs inside it. As the foremost theorist of space in the twentieth century, Henri Lefebvre, asserts,

> Vis-à-vis lived experience, space is neither a mere 'frame', after the fashion of framing a painting, nor a form or container of a virtually neutral kind ... Space is social morphology: it is to lived experience what form itself is to the living organism, and just as intimately bound up with function and structure.[6]

Lefebvre is not alone in this view. Heidegger suggested that architecture was a revelation of the human metaphysical situation between earth and sky.[7] Kant had earlier asserted that architecture is 'the art of *exhibiting concepts* of things that are possible only through art'.[8] Similarly Pallasmaa notes that buildings and towns 'are devices, which structure and articulate our existential experience'. Such an architectural metaphor is 'a highly abstracted and condensed ensemble that fuses the multitude of human experiences into a single image'.[9] Taking a slightly different angle, Bachelard suggested in 1958 that all constructions of space are an attempt to give shape, intimacy and meaning to an otherwise vast and forbidding universe.[10] Or as urban theorist, Kevin Lynch, stated in his pivotal 1960 work *The Image of the City*, 'We are continuously engaged in an attempt to organise our surroundings, to structure and identify them.'[11]

Lynch reminds us that one of the largest constructions of social morphology is the city, within which architectural ensembles of all kinds, including theatre spaces, organise and shape our experience.[12] Joseph Svoboda, former Professor of Architecture and one of the most influential scenographers of the twentieth century, was convinced that 'the best preparation for a scenographer is the study of architecture'.[13] The scenographic composition of a performance space involves architectural principles: the articulation of space through the construction or use of existing boundaries, the placement of objects and bodies, and the dialectic of revealing and concealing through the use of light. The 'canons' of architecture with which an architect constructs his/her expression, says Henricksson, are 'time, space, person, and building',[14] and it is easy to see how strongly these canons relate to the 'canons' of theatre: time, space, performance (including the actor, but also scenographic, kinaesthetic and other elements) and audience. All of these factors are embedded in the term 'scenography', which Svoboda defined as 'The interplay of space, time, movement and light on stage.'[15]

In the same way that all architecture is culturally situated, all sceno-graphic compositions for performance (Artaud's 'spatial poetics') are intimately related to their contemporary culture in one way or another. They are what Foucault called a 'heterotopia',[16] a kind of mirror in which each age can recognise its own world, whether in a more concrete or abstract form. 'The stages of every society are different', writes Aronson, 'and yet each of those societies saw its theatre as a reflection of its world.' Just as we must be able to recognise that 'a collection of marks on a page is written language', he writes, so too must we recognise that a particular arrangement of space is a stage and that somehow, when looking at that arrangement of space, we are seeing our world. In order for this to occur, the stage must be 'readable', that is, 'we must be able to comprehend the stage both visually and spatially'.[17] Architecture and scenography, then, embody and express each society's understanding of space, a conclusion reached also by Wiles, who states that 'The context for a history of performance space is a history of *space*.'[18] Such a history involves philo-sophical, theological, socio-political, cultural, artistic and other factors that are the very stuff of Reception Studies.

When we are examining scenography as reception, as cultural negotia-tion and exchange, we need to be able to identify those elements of a production's scenography that are significant 'statements'. Artaud as-serted that spatial poetry 'can only ever be fully effective if it is *tangible*, that is to say, if it objectively produces something owing to its *active presence* on stage'.[19] Simply being there is not enough – to be *tangible*, to have an *active presence,* a production's 'architecture, lighting and décor' needs to 'make [thought] develop, guiding it, destroying it or decisively changing it'. Spatial poetry has an *active presence* in as much as it 'exerts itself directly on the stage without passing through words'.[20] An element of scenography is 'active' when it has been structured into the specific space-time-action matrix of a production in such a way that without it the production concept would fall apart, or change in such a way as no longer to be the same production. Whether a costume is red or pink, or one kind of chair is substituted for another, however important these choices may be semiotically, may not cause the performance to change radically; nor might those choices 'make [thought] develop'. But the existence of a huge staircase dominating the presentational space (such as in Reinhardt's 1905-12 *Oedipus*, Terence Gray's 1931 *Antigone* or Svoboda's 1963 *Oedi-pus*) is a major statement, and leaving it out would radically alter the experience and interpretation of a production. The same can be said of the use of a rapid sequence of contemporary tourist slides at regular intervals in a contemporary production of a Greek tragedy.[21]

Scenography includes the effect on the experience of a theatrical event of a theatre's location in the city, as well as the context of that building (its immediate environment), its approach, façade, entrance, internal organi-sation and so on.[22] These are aspects that, whether we are aware of them

Paul Monaghan

or not, have already influenced our experience of a performance before it begins. But the four most immediately important areas of scenographic analysis in general are first, scenographic composition, or spatial poetics, including both the internal architectonic articulation of the space by objects, walls, light and so on, and its physical framing; secondly, the relationship between that which is physically present in the performance space and that which it represents (either a fictional or 'real' space); thirdly, the physical and psychic distance between the performance space and the spectator;[23] and fourthly, the way that this ensemble of factors shifts and transforms through the time period of the performance. In what follows, I work with these areas of analysis in order to identify the 'actively present' features of four broad scenographic 'styles' ('realist/naturalistic', 'modernist', 'postmodern' and 'postdramatic'), and identify the typical feature that sets up interpretive frameworks in that style's 'spatial poetics'.

To create 'realist/naturalistic'[24] scenography is to attempt to present a stage world that 'corresponds' (visually, spatially, aurally and behaviourally) to the world of daily private and social experience.[25] However, since 'realist art' is by definition not 'natural' or 'real' but artificially constructed, the realist artist attempts to present and 'frame' the dramatic world as if there were no presenter, no author, no artifice. As Demastes puts it, realism presents itself as 'objective', as 'a faithful rendering of existence without biased impositions on the part of its creators'.[26] Realist scenography therefore mirrors the world of the auditorium in an *iconic* way, as if spectators are looking through the front door of a *real* private dwelling at predominantly domestic, internal, private space inhabited by people just like themselves. In order to achieve this 'objective' view, the realist stage is necessarily held at an aesthetic distance from the viewer, more or less sealed off from the world of the auditorium in order to preserve the 'illusion of reality' that it seeks to create. For this reason, the proscenium arch theatre, with its two distinct chambers facing each other (one for the performance and one for the audience), and hence an ability to control the visual field, remains the preferred site of realist/naturalistic performance.[27]

The *sine qua non* of realist scenography is the chair, for as States asserts, 'what the chair made possible … was conversation',[28] and realist theatre is almost unimaginable without characters sitting around talking. Greek tragic personae were mostly mythic beings in an amplified world, and thus rarely sat down (or ate, or did the shopping). But realist characters are a part of the same world as the daily lives of the spectators who also live in houses and sit on chairs. Moreover, the space we see onstage (a living room, or bedroom) is continuous and contiguous with an imagined (and often partially visible) offstage space (the rest of the house, perhaps the garden, seen through an open door),[29] and stage lighting needs to be as realistically motivated (the morning sun through the window, a real candle or electrical fixture at night)[30] as Stanislavski's actors.

What is most valuable to Reception Studies is that realist/naturalistic

244

scenography is underpinned by cultural and philosophical assumptions. The idea that art, and specifically theatre, could and should 'mirror' the real social world gained strength in the nineteenth century both as a corollary to scientific and intellectual developments (Marx, Darwin, Freud) and as a reaction against the overly mannered 'well-made plays', melodramas and morality of the Victorian era. The dominant use of the proscenium arch theatre for realism/naturalism also carries with it philosophical baggage. Wiles locates the basis of the proscenium theatre in Plato's cave and Cartesian dualism, arguing that the separation of audience (mind) and actor (body) in the proscenium arch theatre was the logical theatrical analogue of Descartes' dualism, in which mind and body are seen as separate substances. 'Cartesian space', Wiles argues, is 'ocular ... It does not submit to any embodied immersion in space'.[31] And when Wagner first turned off the lights in the auditorium, says Wiles, 'casting the spectators into darkness, and tying them with invisible bonds that prevented them from looking to left or right', then the logic of Plato's cave was carried to its conclusion.[32] And as States also notes, the use of chairs carries with it identifiable philosophical assumptions:

> to *sit* is to *be*, to exist suddenly and plentifully in the material world ('I sit, therefore I am *here*'); and in this sense classical characters are bodiless: they exist in a vague intersection between elsewheres established by poetry.[33]

Like many other productions, especially of Euripides' plays, the scenography for Wesley Enoch's *Black Medea* (Sydney and Melbourne, 2005) used a realistic table, chairs and wooden floor (albeit inside a cave-like setting with a semi-transparent upstage drape evoking traditional Indigenous dot paintings), and the production overall located the Medea story inside 'real' contemporary Indigenous Australian issues (domestic violence, loss of land). There was certainly no metaphysical other in this production.

Aronson points out that 'modern' stage design – and by 'modern' here he means what others refer to as 'modernist',[34] that is the anti-realist/ naturalistic strand in theatre from the late nineteenth-century Symbolists onwards – was 'characterised by the presence of a strong metaphorical or presentational image or related series of images' creating a 'meta-narrative that attempts to encompass the world within a unified image'.[35] There was (and is) in this style a sense of singular, 'organic' and 'monolithic' unity about these images, characterised by 'simplicity, suggestion, abstraction, and grandeur within the context of a three-dimensional sculptural setting that would unify the performer and the stage space' within an overall aesthetic of 'pleasure and harmony'.[36] Modernist presentational space tends not to be 'illusionistic', as in realist/naturalistic scenography, but instead focuses on the creation of a 'fundamental concept or metaphor of the production' using, more often than not, 'platforms, ramps, steps, screens, walls and curtains'.[37] These tendencies of modern(ist) scenography are aptly described by Jean-François Lyotard's definition of modernism as 'a meta-discourse ... making an explicit appeal to some grand narrative'.[38]

Steps and staircases, Pallasmaa argues, are a resonant 'architectural metaphor' expressing cultural values,[39] and their use in modernist scenography is revealing.[40] Cooper reports that, in the mythology of many cultures, stairs connote the 'passage from one plane to another or from one mode of being to another' and represent 'communication between heaven and earth with a two-way traffic of the ascent of man and the descent of the divinity'.[41] The modernist 'grand narrative', particularly prevalent in early Modernist art, is the notion that, with appropriate (and usually philosophically guided) behaviour and actions here in this world, humanity could either ascend out of the degraded human world towards divinity or some higher plane of being, or that divinity or the world spirit could descend into human lives (or both). Indeed, modernism featured true believers attempting to spiritualise the world through their art. Thus the staircase featured frequently in *fin de siecle* Symbolist paintings as a metaphor for the gradual spiritualisation of the material world, but it was the Swiss scenographer and director Adolphe Appia who brought the multi-level stage floor and staircase most forcefully into theatrical practice in his work with Emile Jacques-Dalcroze at Hellerau, Germany, from around 1908, and especially after their new studio was built there in 1912. The staircase then became a standard trope of Expressionist drama and theatre, with German director Leopold Jessner using them so often that they became known as the *Jessnertreppen* ('Jessner's Steps').[42] Symbolist and Expressionist theatre was underpinned by a desire to transcend or spiritually transform the material world, but while Symbolist theatre retained nineteenth- century pictorial staging in proscenium arch theatres, Expressionist performance, with its steps, platforms and staircases, tended to seek a more embodied experience in spaces where the separation between stage and auditorium had been minimised or abolished.

Many modernist productions of Greek drama similarly featured the staircase and/or multi-level floor, such as Max Reinhardt's *Oedipus* (1905-1912), Appia's designs for *Prometheus* (1910), Terence Gray's *Oresteia* (1926), *Prometheus* (1929) and *Antigone* (1931), the production of Sophocles' *Women of Trachis* choreographed by members of the Jaques-Dalcroze's school in Syracuse (1933), and many more. By focusing on the 'actively present' staircase in the scenography of these productions, then, one can identify their culturally situated metaphor of aspiration to a higher plane of being. It could be argued, however, that by the mid to late 1920s (in Terence Gray's productions, for example), the fervour of the metaphor had waned, and the staircase remained as a theatrical device somewhat divorced from its zealous metaphorical beginnings.

The over-arching supposition of *post*modernism, however, is the demise of the belief in a single, monolithic truth and its accompanying 'grand-narrative'. Postmodernism is consequently signalled by the primacy of what Jean Baudrillard called 'simulacra', essentially a multiplicity of copies without any originating essence, or Plato's *phenomena* without their *noumenon*. Postmodern scenography revels in multiplicity, in a playfulness of images and an 'intentionally radical disruption of pleasing aesthetic synergy', a strategic 'juxtaposition of seemingly incongruous elements within the unifying structure of the stage frame', with the intention to 'create a referential network within the mind of the viewer that extends beyond the immediately apparent world of the play'.[43] Note the assumed validity of multiple perspectives in the word 'network'. Thus postmodern scenography often makes overt or covert reference to other works (both contemporary from the past), and incongruously places contemporary and past referents inside the one frame.

Because of its preoccupation with the image, postmodern scenography is in many ways very 'nineteenth century', in the sense that production tends to be conceived with a strong focus on specifically *pictorial* composition. The proscenium arch remains the preferred site of postmodern as much as realist performance, and the proscenium frame that encloses the stage picture not only disconnects the world of the stage from any supposed unitary truth, but also from 'the world of the auditorium'.[44] Images seem to exist for their own pleasure and experiential force, especially in the case of the so-called 'theatre of images' of Robert Wilson, Richard Forman, Lee Breuer and the like.[45] The pictorial focus of the proscenium arch theatre (or *Theatre à l'Italien* as it was then called) has been its strength since it developed in the seventeenth century out of the 'visual' preoccupations of the Italian Renaissance.[46] Not surprisingly, then, contemporary digital projections have featured strongly in postmodern scenography.[47]

The postmodern tendency to mix chronologies is naturally evident in productions of Greek tragedy. American designer Ming Cho Lee's 1964 design for *Electra*, for example, which Aronson notes was a landmark production for postmodern scenography, included three large upstage panels that evoked the ruins of ancient stone temples, but the panels were suspended off the ground, suggesting abstract art, and the stage floor consisted of a roughly stepped platform recalling modernist designs.[48] Australian director Barry Kosky has produced numerous such 'postmodern' tragedies in Australia, Berlin and Vienna, including his 2005 *Medea* in Vienna and his 2008 *Women of Troy* in Melbourne and Sydney. These productions feature purposefully incongruous scenographic elements drawn from various styles including vaudeville.

The final style of scenography I discuss here is 'postdramatic', which needs some explanation. In *The Postdramatic Theatre* (2006), Lehmann argues that the form we call 'drama' is historically determined, with Aristotle and Hegel playing key roles in its formulation,[49] and therefore not inherent to the theatre as a medium. Ever since Aristotle's *Poetics*, he writes, where it was proposed that tragedy is an imitation or representation (*mimesis*) of an action (*praxis*), the 'trinity of drama, imitation and action' has been almost indivisible. The 'postdramatic' theatre begins when the 'trinity of drama, imitation and action' has lost its hold.[50] After Aristotle, the concept and form of 'drama', argues Lehmann, derive in large part from Hegel. History is made, according to Hegel, from a process of dialectical conflict and resolution in new syntheses, and drama expresses this process.[51] Drama relies on the linear story in which individual 'characters' inhabit a closed, fictive universe (expressed scenographically as well as in other ways), and in which conflict moves through various stages towards resolution of some kind.[52] Dialogue is the primary expression of drama because 'in dialogue the characters can express themselves and so drive the action forward ... action is produced by a character as an act of will'.[53] The 'post' of 'postdramatic' does not indicate a total rejection of drama; rather it 'denotes a theatre that feels bound to operate beyond drama, at a time "after" the authority of the dramatic paradigm in theatre'.[54]

Although 'drama' is expressed scenographically in various ways according to the style in question (as shown above), there tends to be a distinct separation between the world of the drama and the world of the auditorium, even where the open stage theatre is used. By contrast, the scenographic expression of the postdramatic involves the dissolution of this separation, and there is thus a strong sense that the designed space of the performance is continuous and contiguous with the world of those witnessing it; both spaces are seen to be 'real', as opposed to the performance space being symbolic and metaphoric of the real world. Consequently, we are no longer sure what is 'staged' and what is 'real', and it is precisely on this borderline that the postdramatic theatre thrives.[55] The radical difference between this sense of continuity/contiguity and that of 'realist' scenography is that in the latter case the (private) space seen through the front door, as it were, *stands in for* (represents) the 'real' world, whereas here the two are not easily distinguished. Postdramatic scenography does not set out to create a separate world; rather it uses the tools of scenography to set up a dialogue, not between characters within the dramatic world, but with the 'visitors' to the postdramatic space.[56] Thus the 'mirror' function of drama, which relies on aesthetic distance, has been disrupted;[57] the 'postdramatic' stage no longer *represents* the societies from which it derives.

Yet Aronson's assertion regarding the recognisability of the stage remains true for the postdramatic theatre. Although not a 'mimesis' of the world in the sense that is inherent to 'drama', nevertheless the new form does derive (and how could it not?) from the world as it is experienced. As Karen Jürs-Munby writes in the Introduction to Lehmann's work, the postdramatic is:

> a theatre that does not make the world 'manageable' for us – fundamentally because the world we live in, globalized and multiply mediatized as it is, *is* less 'surveyable' and manageable than ever.[58]

There is something about the apparent unruliness and potentially cata-strophic violence of the contemporary world that seems not to fit into the old dramatic form. This is exactly what we recognise in the scenography when we 'visit' a postdramatic performance.

A typical example is *medEia* (1998-2007) by the Dutch group Dood Paard.[59] In this production, the three actors speak directly to the audience for most of the show, in the persona of the chorus. They do not *enact* the story or become the personae of the narrative; at times they are narrators, at other times they speak to the audience (or each other) with the words of one character or another, much as an ancient bard might have done with the poems of Homer. There is no pretence at any time that the performance space is anything other than the actual space in which they stand. At the beginning of each segment, two of the performers raise a patchy white backdrop by means of ropes and pulleys, and the performers stand in front of it. At the end of each segment, the backdrop is torn down again, a new one is raised further down stage, the lights are dimmed, and a long series of slides shown in rapid succession. After the slide show, the performers take their places in front of the new backdrop, and resume the narrative. Thus there is no dramatic artifice, yet the performance is powerfully theatrical and effective in communicating the experience of the Medea story.

In this essay I have only scratched the surface of a complex area. I have focussed on only four styles amongst many, and much more work needs to be done on how scenography can be analysed as reception in relation to ancient Greek drama, and on analysing how the composition of a stage space 'performs' the cultural negotiation that is central to Reception Studies. A far more detailed examination of the relationship between 'the secret geometry of the work',[60] or as Goldhill puts it, 'the logic of space written into' the play being staged,[61] and a production's scenographic style and detail would also be most welcome. Most importantly, more thought needs to be given to the practising scenographer's perspective on ancient drama.

Notes

1. Artaud 1974: 27-8.
2. Elam 2002: 29-86.
3. Barba 1985.
4. Carlson 1989: 6.
5. Svoboda, in Burian 1971: 15.
6. Lefebvre 1991: 93-4.
7. Heidegger 1971: 143-159.
8. Kant in Winters 2007: 1-2 (my emphasis).
9. Pallasmaa 2000: 7-8.
10. Bachelard 1958: 3-37 and *passim*.
11. Lynch 2007: 38.

12. See also Tilghman and Sparshott in Mitias 1994.

13. Svoboda 1992: 12.

14. In Parment 2000: 20.

15. In Howard 2002: xiv.

16. A *heterotopia* is a counter-site 'in which the real sites, all the other real sites that can be found within the culture, are simultaneously represented, contested and inverted' (Foucault 1986: 24).

17. Aronson 2005: 104.

18. Wiles 2003: 4.

19. Artaud 1974: 28.

20. Artaud 1974: 28-30.

21. Dood Paard's 1998-2007 *medEia* – see Monaghan 2009.

22. Carlson 1989 and McAuley 2000.

23. States comments that 'the history of theatre can be viewed as a history of flirtation with the psychical distance between stage and audience' (States 1985: 96).

24. There are ultimately important differences between 'realist' and 'naturalistic' theatre (with or without the latter term's connection to scientific 'naturalism'), but the two terms are so often used either interchangeably or with exactly the opposite meaning to their use somewhere else, that for this discussion I will use the shorthand 'realist/naturalistic'. For a fuller discussion see Furst and Skrine 1971; Grant 1970.

25. Grant 1970: 9ff.

26. Demastes 1996: x.

27. Although open stage theatres have increasingly been used for this purpose since at least the 1970s, there is always – except in an end-on configuration that mimics the proscenium arch – a diminution of 'the illusion of reality', because spectators in an open stage are confronted to a greater or lesser degree by the presence of other spectators.

28. States 1985: 45.

29. Rokem 1986: 11.

30. Palmer 1985: 122.

31. Wiles 2003: 7.

32. Wiles 2003: 229.

33. States 1985: 45.

34. The use of the terms 'modern' and 'modernist' in performance and other theory is quite confused and confusing (see Habermas 1998: 2-3 and Diamond 2003: 5-6). Aronson refers to designs here as 'modern' that many would refer to as 'modernist' (anti-realist) in their tendency towards abstraction and metaphor.

35. Aronson 2005: 13-14.

36. Aronson 2005: 15.

37. Aronson 2005: 17.

38. Lyotard cited in Aronson 2005: 14.

39. Pallasmaa 2000: 9.

40. See Monaghan 2008.

41. Cooper 1978: 94.

42. Patterson 1981: 93.

43. Aronson 2005: 18.

44. Aronson 2005: 26.

45. See Marranca 1997.

46. Wiles 2003: 216.

47. See Oddey and White 2006.
48. Hainaux 1973: 28, fig. 31.
49. Lehmann 2006: 39-45.
50. Lehmann 2006: 37.
51. Lehmann 2006: 39; see Kruger 2003: 81.
52. Lehmann 2006: 31.
53. Shepherd and Wallis 2004: 167-8.
54. Lehmann 2006: 27.
55. Lehmann 2006: 99-104.
56. Lehmann 2006: 12, 150.
57. Lehmann 2006: 150.
58. Lehmann 2006: 11.
59. See Monaghan 2009.
60. A phrase used by Yannis Kokkos in regard to his own 1995 production of Racine's *Le Thébaïde* – Smith 2001: 60.
61. Goldhill 2007: 29, 38.

Translating Greek Drama for Performance

Blake Morrison

I speak a little warily, as someone with small Latin and no Greek.[1] Thereby hangs a rather tragic tale, because I liked Latin and was reasonably good at it, until a timetable clash at grammar school forced me to drop it in the fifth form, year 11. Had I done it for O-level, who knows, I might have gone on to study it at A-level, along with Ancient Greek, and my whole career might have been different – then I could stand here speaking from a position of authority, instead of, as I fear it is, one of at best amateurish enthusiasm and at worst sheer effrontery.

Let me begin with something where I feel on firm ground – an experience not of adapting but of being adapted. A memoir I wrote about my father has recently been turned into a film. I feel fortunate in what the screenwriter, producer, director and actors have done with my book.[2] But being alive and able to raise my voice, as Goldoni, Kleist, Sophocles and Aristophanes haven't been able to with me, I did query some of the changes being proposed to the original, one of them in particular. In the memoir I describe how, after my father died at home, my mother wanted his body and face to remain uncovered until the undertaker came to remove him the next day. It was unconventional behaviour, perhaps, but I completely understood her reasons for it – 'why would anyone,' I wrote, 'except in the movies, draw [the bedsheets] over his head and shut out before time what will soon be unseeable forever'. When I was sent the penultimate draft of the screenplay, however, I discovered that the screenwriter had my mother and me doing exactly what we hadn't done either in life or in the book, that's to say draw the sheet over my father's head. This was an untruth too far. And – almost as bad – a movie cliché. I made my objection. The screenwriter made the change. And the film, I think, is the better for honouring what was in the original.

I find that image – the sheet being discreetly drawn over the corpse – suggestive in a couple of ways. First, as a reminder that the customs surrounding dead bodies are still important to us today, just as they were in the age of Sophocles, whose Antigone, Ismene and Creon argue over the rights and wrongs of covering the corpse of Polyneices. Second, the image strikes me as a metaphor for the whole question of adaptation. I think we all disapprove of the way that some translators – not necessarily Victorian ones, either – have handled classical authors, Aristophanes in particular, shying away from the naked truth of his language for fear the British public, over two thousand years later, will find it too troubling, too obscene. Perhaps they have a point: a Tory councillor in Bury St Edmunds tried to prevent my version of *Lysistrata* being performed there this autumn, feeling that such filth wasn't the right way to commemorate the theatre's re-opening after extensive refurbishment. Still, the procedures of the abridgers and prettifiers remind me of how after my mother died in a nursing home a yellow rose was placed between her hands, a prettifying symbol of which she, as a doctor, wouldn't have approved. When an ancient Greek play is being adapted, we want to feel the raw power, the cold truth, the uncomfortable reality. Because of course respecting the primary text means respecting its lack of respect – the departure from the norms of its time that made it a classic in the first place. Those giant phalluses in *Lysistrata* must remain in any modern production; and Oedipus must appear in all his eyeless bloody horror – the shocks registering now as they did then, without being exaggerated on the one hand or tamed on the other.

Still, a naked translation of a classical play – in the sense of a word-for-word literal transcription – can never work on the stage. Literalism is a lifeless corpse – what one wants from a play in a dead language is to see not just the life it once had but the life it still has in another language. So my concern in adapting classics for the stage has been to produce texts which are speakable rather than – as some versions I have come across can be – unspeakable; texts that actors can stand and deliver without sounding as if their mouths are full of mothballs; texts that have drive, energy, resonance and the inflexions of contemporary speech and/or authentic dialect; texts that are playscripts not scholarly translations. Of course to produce such scripts I first have to immerse myself in already existing English translations – preferably annotated scholarly translations – in order to understand what it is I'm adapting. But there comes a point when you have to set aside your inhibitions about line-by-line fidelity and let rip.

My task has been made simpler in that the five classics I've so far adapted – three of them ancient Greek, one eighteenth-century Italian and one nineteenth-century German – have all been for a single theatre company, Northern Broadsides, whose founder, director and lead actor, Barrie Rutter, is a man with a clear mission. That mission is to take plays on tour around the country, sometimes to unusual venues, including disused mills, warehouses and cattle markets: the 200-seat theatre at the company's home base in Halifax is a dank vaulted basement that used to be a turning space for the railway engines that fetched and carried to Dean Clough, once the largest carpet factory in Europe. Northern Broadsides reach audiences which theatre doesn't always reach but there's no dumbing down: Rutter's only interest is in producing Shakespeare and European (preferably ancient Greek) classics, almost always written in verse form. It is a populist mission but also a purist one. The commitment is to live theatre: no video screens or pre-recorded music, only the actors' own faces, gestures, voices and instrumental skills. Props are minimal: the blind Tiresias gets a white stick but that's about it.

Writing for Northern Broadsides I'm writing for the stage rather than writing for the page. The difference is important and it was brought home to me by the only two bits of adapting I've done which weren't for Northern Broadsides. With the first, I translated five poems by the German Friedrich Rückert on the death of children (two of his own children having died from scarlet fever) which Gustav Mahler set to music for his *Kindertotenlieder* (1905); the commission was for a musical play about Mahler created by the Canadian director Robert Lepage.[3] Without using rhyme, I tried to represent the meaning of the euphony in the German original, in those sounds *gegangen* and *gelangen* and *verlangen*, or *schon* and *hoh'n*, the repetition being kind of mantra of denial from the bereaved father, who wants to believe his children aren't dead but just out walking. For the stage version, I wanted room for a sense of hopeless repetitiveness to accrue, but when I later included the translation in my *Selected Poems* (1999) I reworked it, paring it right down, because the reader, unlike someone in an audience, has time to sit and linger over the words – so the final version has only thirteen lines, just as Rückert's did. I also hoped the reader might linger over the phrase 'pipe down' and make a subliminal or conscious connection with the Pied Piper, who led children away onto (and under) a hill:

> I often think: they're out walking, that's all.
> Any minute they'll be back.
> It's a lovely day. Relax.
> Listen hard and you'll hear their cries.
>
> Pipe down. They're out walking.
> And off they've wandered
> Further than usual, up the hill,
> We'll soon catch up with them.
> They're run ahead, that's all.
> When the sun's out on the hill,
> We can catch up with them.
> Listen hard and you'll hear their cries.
>
> It's a lovely day, up on the hill.

Writing for the stage is different from writing for the page: the effect has to be immediate, in the moment, and can't be dwelt on or revisited. I found this again when I was commissioned to transform Jules Verne's novella *Dr Ox's Experiment* (1872) into a libretto for an opera of the same name by the composer, Gavin Bryars.[4] With a libretto, however singable

254

the words, only a tiny percentage of what you write will be caught by the audience. The great advantage of the theatre, or at any rate Northern Broadsides theatre, is that you know every word will be heard.

But what is it that an audience does hear? Carlo Goldoni, whose *Servant of Two Masters* (1745) I reworked in 2006 as *The Man with Two Gaffers*, says in his *Memoirs* that for a translation to work the thoughts, imagery, erudition, phrasing and style 'must be adapted to the taste of the nation into whose language the translation is made'.[5] Ibsen said more or less the same thing when he wrote in a letter of 1872 that 'a poem ought to be translated in the way the poet himself would have composed it, had he belonged to the nation for which he is being translated'. On that basis, when I resituated Goldoni's play in nineteenth-century Yorkshire, I changed names as well as places: instead of a Venetian merchant called Pantalone, we have a Dales farmer called Towler; instead of fricandeau, hotpot; instead of the Rialto, the Leeds-Liverpool canal. But above all it was the language that had to change, which gave me an excuse to draw on a two-volume dictionary of dialect words in use in Craven in the early nineteenth century. Since Goldoni's Venetian plays were written in dialect, and he so cherished the city's street-talk that he had plans to compile a Venetian dialect-dictionary, I felt that was apt. And there was the hope that, though my English-language audiences would have to do some translating too, they'd relish, as I had, the discovery of evocative dialect words. 'Bummelkites' for blackberries. 'Cobby' for lively. 'Gut-scraper' for fiddler. 'Lig-a-bed' for lazy. And so on.

I'd previously used dialect – taken from a different dialect dictionary – in my first collaboration with Northern Broadsides, a version of Heinrich von Kleist's comedy *Der Zerbrochene Krug*, normally translated as *The Broken Jug*, which, it so happened, I knew from studying German A-level at grammar school. (See, there were compensations in dropping Latin.) Kleist wrote the play early in the nineteenth century (it was first performed in 1808) but set it in Utrecht in 1770; it centres on a local judge called Adam, who's both hearty and manipulative, Falstaffian and Machiavellian, and the guilty party in a case over which he's presiding, which involves the breaking of a jug. My first draft version of the play stuck closely to the original – too closely for Barrie Rutter, who had read a long dialect poem I'd written called 'The Ballad of the Yorkshire Ripper'. Use that kind of idiom, Rutter urged me; 'It's the music of the monosyllable we want to hear.' So that's the music I tried to write, switching the play from early eighteenth-century Utrecht to early nineteenth-century Skipton (the town where I'd studied Kleist at grammar school), and allowing the characters to speak in the regional vernacular. Neither this adaptation nor the Goldoni was a nostalgic venture to revive lost folk-speech, but a recognition that dialect words are at best simply more alive and expressive than their smoothed-off estuary-English equivalents. Is there a better word for a hedgehog than a 'prickyback' or for diarrhoea than 'scutters', or for a cup of tea (that traditional accompaniment of conversation) as 'chatter-watter'?

Anyone coming to adapt Kleist's play will want to shift the time and setting and idiom to provide an alternative, more readily recognizable historical context; a 1994 version by the novelist John Banville moved the play to Ireland during the famine and made the visiting magistrate an Englishman. Changing the plot or structure of a play is a different matter. During rehearsals of *The Cracked Pot*, Barrie Rutter, in the role of Judge Adam, worried that for a play centring on a crime and a court case there was no tension of a 'whodunit' kind – perhaps, he felt, I ought to rewrite the play to make his guilt less obvious. I was sceptical and we agreed to wait to see how the previews went. The moment the play had its first performance, we understood why Kleist wrote it as he did: the audience are never in doubt that Adam is guilty, but they enjoy watching him cover his tracks and feel complicit with his cunning, and that's where the pleasure of the play lies. Whereas in *Oedipus Rex*, the audience know what the hero doesn't (which adds to the sense of doom and tragedy), in Kleist audience and hero both know (which adds to the sense of comedy).

The classics always adapt; that's why they're classics. But the adaptor who doesn't respect the spirit of the original is irresponsible and self-defeating. Often it's the local detail that carries the emotional kick and authenticity of a work, so ironing out the idiosyncrasies of an original for the sake of some global goo or Esperanto or readily attainable 'relevance' is counter-productive. If something seems obscure and archaic, don't just cut it – work at it and see if you can find some equivalent. On the other hand, you do want the freedom to make adjustments and even additions:

> He is translation's thief that addeth more
> As much as he that taketh from the store
> Of the first author.[6]

So Marvell wrote, but I confess to having added a speech for one of the characters in *The Cracked Pot*: everyone else in the small cast had his or her set-piece or aria and it seemed odd for this character not get one too. You should also be ready to exploit not just the particular talents of your cast (which in the case of the current production of my version of *Lysistrata* includes their musical talents) but also the opportunities which a production will throw up. A week before *The Cracked Pot* Barrie Rutter had his hair shaved off, in preparation for the part of Judge Adam, who must sit in court bare-headed having lost his wig. It wasn't the most successful of shaves: the barber had left nicks and scratches on the glazed white dome of Rutter's head. But since in the play Adam has taken a battering the night before, we made a virtue of it, and I added a couplet, for when a horrified Adam looks at himself in the mirror:

Crudding tuptails! I'm like a sheep that's just been fleeced: my skin's
Riddled with cuts where t'farmer's shears have dug in.

The couplet isn't in Kleist, but it adds to the sense of place: Skipton is the
gateway to the sheep-farming Dales.

Rehearsals are a testing period for any adaptation. However many
drafts you've done, it's only when you stand people up that the words fall
flat, because inert or forced or saccharine or (the great sin with Rutter)
'middle-class'. So I often find I'm rewriting up to the dress rehearsal – and
beyond. That's the one advantage a living playwright has over a dead one,
at least to a director. To the actors, forced to learn new lines at a late stage,
it can seem a serious *dis*advantage.

After *The Cracked Pot*, it was natural to turn to *Oedipus*. Though one
is a comedy and the other a tragedy, both have club-footed heroes who are
guilty of the crime they are investigating. And themes of blindness,
judgment and sexual transgression are common to both. Having no Greek,
I did feel daunted when the idea was first proposed. But I was encouraged
by reading the standard 1982 'Penguin' translation by Robert Fagles
which, however accurate, had – it seemed to me – severe limits as a
speakable or actable piece of theatre.

Working on the play in the spring of 2001 I had the excitement of
discovering the way in which a classic, whatever its era, belongs to every
other era. (People talk of 'contemporary classics' but the phrase is tauto-
logous: classics are contemporary by definition.) The opening lines of the
play describe a plague afflicting Thebes, and that spring Britain was
struggling with a plague of its own, the foot-and-mouth epidemic. Sophocles speaks of dying cattle and blighted fields, and I knew that when the
play toured in rural areas (one of the venues was Skipton cattle market),
there'd be huge resonance in those lines.

> The place is falling apart, waste and rubble
> everywhere you look. Nothing works
> and no one visits. Barren harvests,
> cows with their ribs showing like roof-slats,
> vast pyres of mouldering sheep – that's the meadows.
> Here in town we've got it as bad or worse.
> Fever trickles in beads down lime-white cheeks.
> Babies whine for their mums and mums keen o'e'r
> their babies. The plague's left its mark on every door.[7]

In the spring of 2001, the plague meant foot and mouth. But by the time
the play opened, two days after 9/11, the image of a ruined Thebes –
reeking with smoke, ringing with cries, a panicked people massing in the
squares – took on an additional set of meanings none of us could have
anticipated. Jocasta, praying at a stone altar, resembled the bewildered
relatives at Ground Zero. Oedipus' promise to find the perpetrator and

bring him to justice had the immediacy of a George Bush press briefing on CNN. And Tiresias' tirade against the hubristic Oedipus – when he tells him that his conspiracy-theories are foolish, and that the real culprit is himself – reminded me of the pundits who were saying that the US 'had had it coming'.

In my view, audiences should be allowed to make such connections for themselves, rather than being clubbed over the head with them. At any rate, with *Oedipus* I avoided specifying a time and place for the action; the characters kept their names but there was no mention of Thebes, let alone New York. My use of dialect was more sparing this time, too, since the universality of the play seemed resistant to anything too narrowly regional. There's a northern flavour at times, nevertheless. And in a sense that was the challenge I was trying to meet with this play, to see whether a northern idiom, usually associated with comedy and with low-life characters and 'bit parts', could achieve poetry in the mouth of a tragic hero. So the two great set-pieces in the play had nothing to do with any pressingly immediate historical parallel but with two great 'timeless' narratives, first Oedipus' account of how he unwittingly killed his father and, second, the servant's account of Jocasta's suicide and Oedipus' blinding of himself.

> ... I took to the road,
> sleeping rough, not caring where I ended up,
> so long as I avoided my parents
> and kept the gods from winning their bet.
> One day on my wanderings I happened on the spot
> where you say Laius met his death. A beck
> running by, a drystone wall, a hawthorne tree
> shaved slantwise by the wind: there I am,
> sun beaming down, scrats of cloud in the sky,
> minding my own, pondering which road to take,
> when along comes a coach party – a driver,
> two men on horseback, a messenger boy
> running ahead, and a man inside the carriage,
> just as you said. There's plenty of room to pass,
> but the driver and the bigwig inside
> scream at me to clear out the bloody way.
> If only they'd ask nicely I'd not mind,
> but when the driver tries to force me off the road
> I see red and fetch him one full in the face.
> and then the old fellow inside the carriage
> leans out and raddles me with a spiked club
> or something, and keeps thumping me over the head
> till I lose patience and learn him a lesson,
> my blows are flisky little tigs, that's all,
> but before I know it he's reeling under 'em,
> he's rolling through the door of the carriage,
> he's laid out on his back eyeing the heavens
> and the body I'm battering is a corpse.[8]

258

To me, Oedipus' story of how he came to kill Laius gains power from having a particular setting: seeing is believing, and it's as he revisualises the scene that the full appalling truth dawns on him. So though the language is spare, I've risked adding detail here – and risked turning a spot which Fagles refers to only as a 'triple crossroad' into a specific place I could almost take you to on the Yorkshire moors or 'tops'. There's a similar risk when, coming in on an argument between Creon and Oedipus, Jocasta exasperatedly bursts out 'What a family! Aren't you ashamed to make such a din',[9] which might be a line from a soap but is there to remind us that Sophocles' play is indeed, just as soaps are, a story about families.

Classics can reach us at any time, but we reach out to them most eagerly at times of crisis, as if to put our own troubles in a broader perspective. I found that to be the case, again, in 2003, with *Antigone*, which I was working on while the invasion of Iraq was unfolding on television. *Antigone* picks up the story of Oedipus a few years on, with the Thebans no longer huddled in panic but celebrating the quick conclusion of a war: the enemy has been sent packing and a new regime is in place. But winning the peace is less straightforward than appears. In his euphoria, Creon, as leader, overestimates people's willingness to pull together. There are still conflicting loyalties and pockets of resistance. And his brutal enforcement of a vindictive law – that enemy corpses be left to rot – becomes the trigger for further death and violence.

Antigone has had many different treatments down the years. But what struck me in 2003 was that it's a play about bodies. After the Somme, the Nazi Holocaust, Cambodia and Rwanda, we have, understandably, become fixated by images of the war dead – and preoccupied with the dignities and indignities of their disposal. Article 17 of the Geneva Conventions in respect of the war dead states that they should be 'honourably interred', according to their religion, and that any possessions found on them be placed in 'sealed packets', so that they can be identified. We know such standards haven't been met in Iraq or in many other wars. The ethos of Creon – that the enemy, deserving no better, be left to jackals and vultures (including the jackals and vultures of the media) – is hard to dislodge.

Good plays have their moment; with great plays, that moment never ends. One enduring aspect of *Antigone* is its concern with gender. To Ismene, being a woman is incapacitating ('women aren't built / to do battle. Men's wills are like iron. / To live with them, women have to give'[10]). To Antigone, femaleness is a mark of moral superiority – only women know how to look after bodies and do right by family, she believes. To Creon, masculinity means playing the hard man and making an example of Antigone; he accuses his son Haemon of effeminacy for taking her side and snarls at Antigone's feminine logic:

> I'll not take lessons from a girls' school.
> No woman's going to lord it over my rule.[11]

Blake Morrison

There are similar lines in *Lysistrata* – evidence, if we needed it, that the war of the sexes is a timeless phenomenon. But the problem with translations is that, by speaking in the idiom of their day, they quickly date – and therefore date the original, too, rather than allowing it its timeless moment. Here, for instance, from four of the best-known twentieth-century translators of Sophocles, is the opening of the famous choric ode to man:

> Wonders are many; yet than Man
> None more wonderful is there known. (Trevelyan, 1924)

> Wonders are many, but none there be,
> So strange, so fell, as the Child of Man. (Murray, 1941)

> Wonders are many, yet of all
> Things is Man the most wonderful. (Kitto, 1962)

> Numberless wonders terrible wonders walk the world
> but none the match for man. (Fagles, 1982)

As I understand it, the original Greek in the lines above rests on an ambiguity – the word *deinon*, meaning both 'wonderful' and 'terrible' – which can't easily be expressed in English. But why do the first three sound pre-Wordsworth, never mind pre-Eliot and pre-Pound? The problem is their piety towards Sophocles' grandiloquence, which makes them invert normal word-order (and in Trevelyan's case quite a bit more besides) in the vain hope that it will add poetic lustre. Fagles, while avoiding such quaintness, is not much better – can wonders be said to 'walk'? – and a few lines on he too falls into inversion: 'the blithe, lightheaded race of birds he snares'. Blithe? Lightheaded? Race? You can already hear the clatter of tipped-up seats as the audience streams towards the exit.

The better versions of *Antigone* in recent years have come from poets, including Brendan Kennelly (1996) and Tom Paulin. Paulin's *The Riot Act* ranges from Northern Irish dialect (*eejit, scrake, stinty, sleaked, clemmed*) to the windy politico-babble of Creon, whose opening address sounds uncannily Blairite, even though Paulin's version dates back to 1985: 'Thank you all for coming, and any questions just now? We have one minute. (Flashes stonewall smile).'[12] There's no press conference in the original, of course, but Paulin isn't taking liberties with Sophocles, he's liberating him. Good translations and productions do this. Fidelity doesn't preclude a little invention, or a little cheek. In my version, the archaic 'Wonders are many' becomes the vernacular 'Wonders never cease'[13] – a wearily sarcastic phrase in modern idiom, but here I hope reanimated and purged of cynicism.

Having done earlier drafts of *Antigone* against the backdrop of the invasion of Iraq, I did the last ones during the Hutton Enquiry, the starting-point for which wasn't a war so much as a single, exposed dead

260

body, that of Dr David Kelly.[14] And the issue of weapons of mass destruction was still there when I embarked on my adaptation of *Lysistrata* two or three years ago. The play was first staged just a year after the disastrous Sicilian expedition in 411 BCE, in which thousands of young Athenian lives were lost – a military catastrophe and civic trauma on the scale of Vietnam or Iraq. The play contains two plot-hinges – first a sex strike (women refusing to sleep with men until they stop fighting), and second an occupation (women taking over an exclusively male domain – the Acropolis in the original – in order to starve the military of funds and equipment). Neither of these strands is difficult for a modern audience to engage with: in recent years, women have used sex strikes as a means of political persuasion in several countries, including Columbia, Turkey and Poland. And there was a famous anti-war occupation by women at Greenham Common in the early 1980s – one which formed the basis for Tony Harrison's version of *Lysistrata*, *The Common Chorus* (1992).[15]

Despite the Aristophanic play's sense of familiarity, it's a tricky one to adapt, something underlined by the fact that Harrison's play, though commissioned, was never staged. How, for instance, do you avoid the taint of misogyny in the presentation of the women? And how do get round the seeming illogic of the strike itself – the premise that a man cannot find sexual relief if his wife refuses him was clearly ridiculous in ancient Athens, where large numbers of rent boys and prostitutes were available, and it's no less ridiculous in the era of dogging and Internet porn. And if the men are away fighting, how will the sex strike affect them anyway?

The play's strain on credulity is something I learned about the hard way. I was originally commissioned to adapt it for television – but television being an overwhelmingly realist medium, the would-be producers wanted to use realist conventions (for example, they wanted each member of the largely anonymous male and female choruses to have a 'back story'), and when I didn't come up with the goods they dropped the project. And yet I thought I'd given the play a believable contemporary context by setting it in a northern mill-town where racial tension is rife: instead of the women of Athens and Sparta joining forces to stop their men fighting, in my version they're white and Muslim; and instead of them occupying the Acropolis, they occupy the factory at which most of the men earn their livelihood, thereby hitting them, as one of the women puts it, 'in their wallets as well as their bollocks'. I even, I thought, prevented such a setting seeming too local and small-scale in comparison to the original. Just as Aristophanes' women make startling discoveries about the world of politics when they enter the Acropolis, so the women in my version *Lisa's Sex Strike* discover that the components being manufactured at the occupied factory are being supplied to the arms trade, and are thus part of the global war between whites and Asians, Christians and Muslims, First World and Third.

All of this is pretty apposite and contemporary, especially when you consider that in the original there's also an exchange about Lysistrata wearing a veil, which one of the male authority figures derides, in the manner of Jack Straw, prompting her to remove it and stick it on his head instead.[16] There was never any danger of the play not being topical. While working on it I assembled a mass of cuttings and news items about sex strikes, gang wars, veils, hoodies, Islamophobia, the British arms trade and even knitting as an expression of political activism. But what I'd neglected was the farcical and absurdist spirit of the original, so much so that I was in danger of turning a comedy into a tragedy. It was Conrad Nelson, the director of the stage version for Northern Broadsides, who brought that home to me, over the course of numerous rewrites. My prosily realist first drafts were gradually abandoned in favour of half-rhyming couplets; then the half-rhymes slowly became fuller. (The odd thing about rhyming couplets is that once they're established the audience almost stop noticing them, or start to miss them when they aren't there.) The sections of dance and music were also extended, which meant new songs had to be composed and lyrics written. Conrad's versatility as a composer, and our wish for the play to be both eclectic and multi-ethnic, resulted in an extraordinary mixture of musical traditions: a George Formby ukelele number satirising British 'bobbies' (policemen), a Bollywood ballad, an accelerating *Zorba the Greek*-type solo for the goddess of peace, a First World War marching song and, most spectacularly perhaps, a rap number in which a preening chorus of male workers celebrate their masculinity by stripping, to the amusement of the watching female chorus and to their own eventual humiliation.[17] In Jack Lindsay's 1925 version of *Lysistrata*, the men kick off their *Full Monty* routine[18] with the lines:

> Come, let vengeance fall,
> You that below the waist are still alive,
> Off with your tunics at my call – Naked, all.
> For a man must surely savour of a man. (Lindsay, 1925)

In our version, the male chorus is given more room to flex its muscles, but the message is the same: men rule the world!

> MEN Yo, we're the archetypal primate, Mr Macho Man
> The father figure for Goliath and c-Caliban,
> The proud descendant of the ape and the orang-utan
> Next to us the women pale cos we're the race called men
> Men are God's first creature
> His leading feature,
> Pure hunks of meat, dear,
> Nothing in the world tastes sweeter,
> Men began with Adam
> Who taught his madam
> To serve her lad
> We're the rulers of the world

You can't thump us we're all pumped up with testosterone
Don't be a prat or you'll be battered with this knucklebone
Our booming voices carry miles without a megaphone
We're made of stone, we're in the zone, we are the race called men ...
Men, we sup our lager
Just like our fathers
Cos we feel harder
When the booze is in our larder
Men, including poofs, dear,
Carry in their nuts here
Something to fear
We're the rulers of the world.
Cos we're the undisputed owners of huge abs and pecs
Sumo wrestlers run for cover when our stomachs flex
In any bout we'll knock you out cos we're the stronger sex
Beneath our vests we've massive chests, we are God's musclemen
Men, we win each tussle
Don't make no fuss, girl
Come feel this muscle,
It's the size of a double decker bus, girl
Men, we box like Rocky
Our cocks are cocky,
No one dare mock
We're the rulers of the world
WOMEN Oh, we've listened to your rapping but it's just a rant.
Now we wonder what you look like in your underpants.
If we whip round, will you strip down for a raunchy dance?
Please don't be shy, just show us why you are the race called men.
Men, don't act like Jessies
Come and impress us
Let's see those chests puff,
We want to see you with your vests off,
Men, if you're not losers
Show us your bruises
Come light our fuse
You're rulers of the world.

Perhaps the number that best illustrates the role which music can play in a production is a blues song which comes early on in what I think of as Act 2 of the play. This is the point at which, to her exasperation, Lysistrata's sex strike is collapsing, as the women, in their desperation for orgasm, seemingly attainable only through penetrative sex with their husbands, try to sneak off home. It's a scene that can seem both unfunny – all those Benny Hill *doubles entendres* – and misogynistic, and though we used some of the original gags (for example, with the first woman who says she has to go home because there are mothballs in her wool, we kept the joke, because she'd been established as a woman who loves to knit) some we quietly dropped. In the original Lysistrata's clinching argument is that if the women can only hold out a little longer, they've been promised victory by the oracle; in our version, she reads out entries from a horoscope in a woman's magazine, *Heat*, on which the women have earlier sworn their oath. Our key departure, though, was to bring back Lampito – Lysistrata's Spartan ally, her key collaborator in organising the sex strike, who, so Lysistrata assumes, is still on her side. This assumption is quickly demolished as Lampito – Loretta, an Afro-Caribbean in our version – sides with the defecting women by singing of her sexual frustration. Here goes:

> Got the celibacy blues, girl, pining for my loving man.
> Miss the touch of him so bad, yeh, his sweet wet tongue and gentle hand.
> Without my man to bring me comfort, I cain't reach the promised land.
> Baby kisses on my belly, on my buttock and my thigh,
> His hairy chest against my nipple, my legs wrapped round him as we lie.
> Don't need no dope or whisky, one whiff of my man gets me high.
> Yes, when a woman's feeling lonely, there ain't but one known solid cure.
> Only a man can bring jouissance, only a man can bring amour.
> No dildo dong done ever come, man, nor do it make this girl come too.
> Just wanna lie back on the pillow with my hands behind my head
> Let my man make all the running till I'm clutching at the bed
> When I go down and kiss him back, hon, I'll give him love he won't forget.
> Got the celibacy blues, girl, pining for my loving man.
> Miss the touch of him so bad, yeh, his sweet mouth and gentle hand.
> I've tried so hard to keep my promise but I hate this loving ban.

One of the incidental pleasures of this production lay in exploiting the talents of the cast both to function as members of a chorus – speaking with one voice – and to emerge as individuals. So there's Loretta, who sings the blues. And there's a male factory worker who suffers from a condition akin to Tourette's syndrome, who in his struggles to get words out invariably stutters or stumbles into an f-word that's not the f-word he's looking for but does have its own kind of zany inventiveness – 'that fecund woman', 'just pistachio out of it', 'him and me are fitting twins', 'we're fruiting all in the same fishy fix'. (The language of Aristophanes' original play is incredibly obscene, so Greek scholars assure me, but obscenity is so integral to the English spoken by men and women in Britain today that it's no longer shocking or surprising to hear it onstage – and we wanted the demotic speech of our characters to be more inventive than the usual four-letter expletives.) Or there's Amit, tormented by his giant erection, who hankers nostalgically for a minuscule, detumescent penis – in a nice inversion of the usual male anxiety, he'd like nothing better than to be smaller. It's a play that allows you to have fun with stereotypes – of ethnicity and old age as well as gender – and if you miss that opportunity you're being untrue to the spirit of the original, much more so than if you tamper here and there with the play's structure.

I mention tampering with structure because with this play, more than any other I've adapted, we did tamper – just as we brought back Lampito, or Loretta, so we also brought back the key male authority figure (a magistrate in the original, a factory owner in my version) who in Aristophanes disappears in the play's first half. 'The original is unfaithful to the translation,' Borges once said about a translation he particularly admired,[19] and we had the same heretical thought about *Lysistrata* – that the play lets itself down towards the end, but that with a change or two it could be made truer to Aristophanic spirit than Aristophanes himself was. So the factory owner returns to threaten the peace, thereby preventing the play from petering out and making the ultimate triumph of peace – in the play's song-and-dance-routine finale – all the sweeter.

I seem to be saying that it's possible to be true to the spirit of an original while making radical changes. And in the end, that's what I feel. The translator is sometimes spoken of as a sort of delivery boy – 'the mailman of human thought and sentiment' in George Steiner's phrase. But surely this allows too little to the translator, and even more so to the adaptor, who, unlike the mailman, has to know what's inside the package as well as delivering it to the right address. What's more, adaptors can never be anonymous; they'll always leave their thumbprints on the envelope. Rather than being mailmen, adaptors are mediators. On the one hand they're conscious of the original authors they're adapting, who peer over their shoulder as they work; on the other hand, they're aware of the audience to which the adaption is being aimed, who need to feel a sense of recognition or relevance or ownership if they are going to respond.

Put like that, adaptation sounds much like the process of writing itself, where the task is to make potentially obscure or private experiences knowable to others, so that an audience feel 'Yes, here's something I recognise and can relate to'. The adaptor works with a pre-existing text, of course. But poets or novelists have a pre-existing text, too, the Utopian model in their head of what the work should be. It's not a question of the author being free to imagine whereas the adaptor is shackled by duty to an original. Both will feel a notion of service, and a strange mixture of constraint and liberation, fidelity and freedom, euphoria and hard labour. When I wrote that memoir of my father, I had the task of making my family – with its idiosyncratic customs – intelligible to a wider audience, and in a way, bizarrely, when adapting classical plays I feel to be doing the same. At the root of both endeavours is the struggle to make the alien familiar – but not so familiar that the audience won't be provoked, entertained and disturbed.

Notes

1. This essay is a transcript of a talk given in Oxford, at the Archive of Performances of Greek & Roman Drama, on 26 November 2007.

2. The film, *And When Did You Last See Your Father?* (directed by Anand Tucker, 2007) was based on Morrison 1993.

3. Robert Lepage's *Kindertotenlieder* opened at the Lyric, Hammersmith on 14 May 1998.

4. The opera was first performed by the English National Opera on 15 June 1998.

5. Goldoni 1828: 143.

6. 'To his Worth Friend Doctor Witty upon his Translation of the "Popular Errors"', 1651, lines 13-15.

7. Morrison 2003: 7.

8. Morrison 2003: 34-5.

9. Morrison 2003: 28.

10. Morrison 2003: 69.

11. Morrison 2003: 85.

12. Paulin 1985: 17.

13. Morrison 2003: 77.

14. Dr David Kelly was a civil servant who worked for the UK Ministry of Defence. He was found dead in July 2003 in mysterious circumstances, shortly after appearing before a parliamentary committee investigating a scandal related to the government's information about alleged weapons of mass destruction in Iraq. Lord Hutton was in charge of the enquiry into his death.

15. *The Common Chorus* is included in Harrison 2002.

16. In October 2006, the Labour politician Jack Straw angered some British Muslims by suggesting in a newspaper article that the custom of wearing the veil made community relationships more difficult.

17. There is a recording of the musical numbers in *Lisa's Sex Strike* available for consultation at the Archive of Performances of Greek & Roman Drama in Oxford.

18. The movie *The Full Monty* (1997), directed by Peter Cattaneo, narrated how six unemployed former steel workers begin an alternative career as male strippers.

19. Borges 1973: 140.

Bibliography

Adorno, T.W. (1973), *Philosophy of Modern Music* (tr. A.G. Mitchell and W.V. Blomster, London: Sheed and Ward).

———— (1992), *Quasi Una Fantasia: Essays on Modern Music* (tr. R. Livingstone, London: Verso).

Altena, H. (2005), 'The Theater of Innumerable Faces', in J. Gregory (ed.) *A Companion to Greek Tragedy* (Oxford: Blackwell), 472-89.

Alverson, H. (1994), *Semantics and Experience: Universal Metaphors of Time in English, Mandarin, Hindi, and Sesotho* (Baltimore: Johns Hopkins University Press).

Andreach, R.J. (1996), 'Charles L. Mee's *Orestes*: A Euripidean Tragedy as Contemporary Transvaluation', *Classical and Modern Literature* 16.3, 191-202.

Andrews, M. (2007), 'The Importance of Ephemera', in S. Eliot and J. Rose (eds) *A Companion to the History of the Book* (Oxford: Blackwell), 434-50.

Ang, I. (2001), 'On the Politics of Empirical Audience Research', in M.G. Durham and D. Kellner (eds) *Media and Cultural Studies: Keyworks* (Oxford: Blackwell), 177-97.

Appiah, K.A. (1993), 'Thick Translation', *Callaloo* 16.4, 808-19.

———— (2006), *Cosmopolitanism: Ethics in a World of Strangers* (New York: Norton).

Armitage, S. (2000), *Mister Heracles: After Euripides* (London: Faber).

———— (2006), *Homer's Odyssey* (London: Faber).

Arnott, P. (1987), 'North America', in J.M. Walton (ed.) *Living Greek Theatre: A Handbook of Classical Performance and Modern Production* (Santa Barbara: Greenwood Press), 355-82.

Aronson, A. (2005), *Looking into the Abyss: Essays on Scenography* (Ann Arbor: University of Michigan Press).

Arrowsmith, W. (tr.) (1959), *Euripides I-IV* (Chicago: University of Chicago Press).

Artaud, A. (1958), *The Theatre and its Double* (tr. M.C. Richards, New York: Grove Press).

———— (1974) *The Theatre and its Double* (tr. V. Corti, London: Calder).

Assman, A. (2002), 'Beyond the Archive', in B. Neville and J. Villeneuve (eds) *Waste-Site Stories: The Recycling of Memory* (New York: State University of New York), 71-84.

Aston, E. and G. Savona (1991), *Theatre as Sign-System: A Semiotics of Text and Performance* (London: Routledge).

Astrié, C. (2002), 'C. # 01', in C. Astrié, J. Kelleher and N. Ridout (eds) *Idioma Clima Crono. Quaderni dell' itinerario* (Cesena), 8-10.

———— (2006) *Programme of the Brussels Kunsten Festival des Arts*. www.kunsten-festivaldesarts.be (last accessed 28 March 2009).

Auslander, P. (1999), *Liveness: Performance in a Mediatized Culture* (London: Routledge).

Austin, T.R. et al. (1996), 'Defining Interdisciplinarity', *PMLA* 111.2, 271-82.

Bibliography

Bachelard, G. (1958), *The Poetics of Space* (Boston: Beacon).

Baker, M. (1992), *In Other Words* (London: Routledge).

Bakhtin, M. (1986), 'Response to a Question from the Novy Mir Editorial Staff', in C. Emerson and M. Holquist (eds) *Speech Genres and Other Late Essays* (Austin: University of Texas Press), 1-9.

Bal, M. (1999), *Quoting Caravaggio: Contemporary Art, Preposterous History* (Chicago: University of Chicago Press).

Barba, E. (1985), 'The Nature of Dramaturgy: Describing Actions at Work', *New Theatre Quarterly* 1, 75-78.

Barcelona, A. (ed.) (2000), *Metaphor and Metonymy at the Crossroads: A Cognitive Perspective* (Berlin: Mouton de Gruyter).

Barish, J.A. (1981), *The Antitheatrical Prejudice* (Berkeley: University of California Press).

Barnes, H. (1964), 'Greek Tragicomedy', *Classical Journal* 60, 125-31.

Barnstone, W. (1993), *The Poetics of Translation: History, Theory, Practice* (London: Yale University Press).

Baron-Cohen, S. (1995), *Mindblindness: An Essay on Autism and Theory of Mind* (New York: MIT Press).

Barish, J. (1994), 'Is there "Authenticity" in Theatrical Performance?', *Modern Language Review* 89.4, 817-31.

Barrault, J.-L. (1961), *The Theatre of Jean-Louis Barrault* (tr. J. Chiari, New York: Hill and Wang).

Barthes, R. (1972), 'Putting on the Greeks', in *New Critical Essays* (Avanston: Northwestern University Press), 59-66.

—— (1974), *S/Z* (tr. R. Miller, (Oxford: Blackwell).

—— (1977), *Image Music Text* (tr. S. Heath, London: Fontana).

—— (2002) *Écrits sur le théâtre* (Paris: Editions du Seuil).

Bassnett, S. (1993), *Comparative Literature: A Critical Introduction* (Oxford: Blackwell).

—— (2002), *Translation Studies* (London: Routledge).

Bassnett, S. and A. Lefevere (1998), *Constructing Cultures: Essays on Literary Translation* (Clevedon: Multilingual Matters).

Bates, W.N. (1930), *Euripides: A Student of Human Nature* (Philadelphia: University of Pennsylvania Press).

Batstone, W.W. (2006), 'Provocation: The Point of Reception Theory', in C. Martindale and R.F. Thomas (eds) *Classics and the Uses of Reception* (Oxford: Blackwell), 14-20.

Battezzatto, L. (1999-2000), 'Dorian Dress in Greek Tragedy', *Illinois Classical Studies* 24-25, 343-62.

Baxandall, M. (1985), *Patterns of Intention: On the Historical Explanation of Pictures* (New Haven: Yale University Press).

Becker, O. (1937), *Das Bild des Weges und verwandte Vorstellungen im frühgriechischen Denken* (Hildescheim: Weidmann).

Bell, C. (1914), *Art* (London: Chatto & Windus).

Bending, L. (2000), *The Representation of Bodily Pain in Late Nineteenth-Century English Culture* (Oxford: Clarendon Press).

Benjamin, W. (1992), *Illuminations* (tr. H. Zohn, London: Fontana).

—— (1999), *Selected Writings Volume I: 1913-1926* (Cambridge: Harvard University Press).

Bennett, S. (1997), *Theatre Audiences: A Theory of Production and Reception* (London: Routledge).

Bibliography

Benstein, C.L. (2007) 'Beyond the Archive: Cultural Memory in Dance and Theater', *Journal of Research Practice* 3.2. http://jrp.icaap.org/index.php/jrp/article/viewFile/110/141 (accessed 20 March 2009).

Bentley, E (1975), *The Life of the Drama* (New York: Atheneum).

Bergson, H. (1956), 'Laughter', in W. Sypher (ed.) *Comedy* (London: Doubleday, 1956), 61-192.

Bermel, A. (2001), *Artaud's Theatre of Cruelty* (London: Methuen).

Berry, C. (2000), *The Actor and the Text* (London: Virgin).

Birett, H. (ed.) (1980), *Verzeichnis in Deutschland gelaufener Filme. Entscheidungen der Filmzensur 1911-1920 Berlin, Hamburg, München, Stuttgart* (München: Saur).

Blau, H. (1982), *Take Up the Bodies: Theater at the Vanishing Point* (Champaign: University of Illinois Press).

―――― (1987), *The Eye of Prey: Subversions of the Postmodern* (Bloomington: Indiana University Press).

―――― (1990), *The Audience* (Baltimore: Johns Hopkins University Press).

Bleeker, M., L. Van den Dries, A. Van Hoof and K. Vanhoutte (2002), 'Romeo Castellucci. Interview', in M. Bleeker, S. De Belder, K. Debo, L. Van den Dries and K. Vanhoutte (eds) *Bodycheck: Relocating the Body in Contemporary Performing Art* (Amsterdam: Rodopi), 217-31.

Bloch, M. (2006), *L'anthropologie cognitive à l'épreuve du terrain: l'exemple de la théorie de l'esprit* (Paris: Collège de France Fayard).

Bogue, R. (1989), *Deleuze and Guattari* (London: Routledge).

―――― (2003), *Deleuze on Cinema* (London: Routledge).

Bolla, P. de (2001), *Art Matters* (Cambridge: Harvard University Press).

Bonta, M. and J. Protevi (2004), *Deleuze and Geophilosophy: A Guide and Glossary* (Edinburgh: Edinburgh University Press).

Borges, J.L. (1973), *Other Inquisitions* (London: Souvenir Press).

Bradley, H. (1999), 'The Seductions of the Archive: Voices Lost and Found', *History of the Human Sciences* 12.2, 107-22.

Braidotti, R. (1994), *Nomadic Subjects: Embodiment and Sexual Difference in Contemporary Feminist Theory* (New York: Columbia University Press).

―――― (2006) *Transpositions: On Nomadic Ethics* (Cambridge: Polity Press).

Braund, S. and G.W. Most (eds) (2003), *Ancient Anger: Perspectives from Homer to Galen, Yale Classical Studies 32* (Cambridge: Cambridge University Press).

Breuer, L. (1989), *Gospel at Colonus* (New York: Theatre Communications Group).

Brilliant, R. (1991), *Portraiture: Essays in Art and Culture* (Chicago: Reaktion Books).

Brook, P. (1968), *The Empty Space* (London: Penguin).

Brown, P. (2004), 'Greek Tragedy in the Opera House and the Concert Hall of the Late Twentieth Century', in E. Hall, F. Macintosh and A. Wrigley (eds) *Dionysus Since 69: Greek Tragedy at the Dawn of the Third Millennium* (Oxford: Oxford University Press), 285-310.

Budelmann, F. (2006), 'Körper und Geist in tragischen Schmerz-Szenen', in B. Seidensticker and M. Vöhler (eds) *Gewalt und Ästhetik: Zur Gewalt und ihrer Darstellung in der griechischen Klassik* (Berlin: De Gruyter), 123-48.

―――― (2007), 'The Reception of Sophocles' Representation of Physical Pain', *American Journal of Philology* 128, 443-67.

Budelmann, F. and P.E. Easterling (2010), 'Reading Minds in Greek Tragedy', in *Greece and Rome* 57.

Bulman, J. (1996a), 'On Being Unfaithful to Shakespeare: Miller, Marowitz, and Wesker', *Journal of Theatre and Drama* 2, 59-73.

────── (1996b), *Shakespeare, Theory and Performance* (London: Routledge).

Burian, J. (1971), *The Scenography of Josef Svoboda* (Middletown: Wesleyan University Press).

Burke, S. (1992), *The Death and Return of the Author: Criticism and Subjectivity in Barthes, Foucault and Derrida* (Edinburgh: Edinburgh University Press).

Burkert, W. (1983), *Homo Necans: The Anthropology of Ancient Greek Sacrificial Ritual and Myth* (tr. P. Brieg, Berkeley: University of California Press).

Butler, J. (1990), *Gender Trouble: Feminism and the Subversion of Identity* (London: Routledge).

────── (1993), *Bodies that Matter: On the Discursive Limits of 'Sex'* (London: Routledge).

Cacoyannis, M. (tr.) (1982), *Euripides. The Bacchae* (New York: Plume).

Calder, W.M. (2005), 'Aeschylus, Prometheus: A DDR Interpretation', in *Theatrokratia: Collected Papers on the Politics and Staging of Greco-Roman Tragedy* (Hildesheim: Olms), 41-51.

Call, J. and M. Tomasello (2008), 'Does the Chimpanzee Have a Theory of Mind? 30 Years Later', *Trends in Cognitive Science* 12, 187-92.

Campbell, J. (1968), *The Masks of God: Creative Mythology* (London: Secker & Warburg).

Campbell, P.A. (2008), 'Medea as Material: Heiner Müller, Myth, and Text', *Modern Drama* 51.1 (Spring), 84-103.

Carlson, M. (1984), *Theories of the Theatre: A Historical and Critical Survey from the Greeks to the Present* (Ithaca: Cornell University Press).

────── (1989), *Places of Performance: The Semiotics of Theatre Architecture* (Ithaca: Cornell University Press).

────── (1994a), 'The Haunted Stage: Recycling and Reception in the Theatre', *Theatre Survey* 35, 5-18.

────── (1994b), 'Invisible Presences – Performance Intertextuality', *Theatre Research International* 19.2, 111-17.

────── (2003), *The Haunted Stage: The Theatre as Memory Machine* (Ann Arbor: University of Michigan Press).

Carlson, M. (2002), 'Performative Pain: Building Culture on the Bodies of Actors and Artists', unpublished PhD dissertation (City University of New York).

Carroll, J. (2004), *Literary Darwinism: Evolution, Human Nature, and Literature* (London: Routledge).

Carruthers, P. and P.K. Smith (eds) (1996), *Theories of Theories of Mind* (Cambridge: Cambridge University Press).

Carruthers, P., S. Laurence and S. Stich (eds) (2005-7), *The Innate Mind* (Oxford: Oxford University Press).

Carter, D.M. (2007) *The Politics of Greek Tragedy* (Exeter: Bristol Phoenix Press).

Carter, R. (2006), 'The Limits of Imagination', in R.H. Wells and J. McFadden (eds) *Human Nature: Fact and Fiction* (London: Continuum), 128-46.

Carter, S. (1993), *Pecong* (New York: Broadway Play Publishing).

Case, S.E. (2007), 'The Masked Activist: Greek Strategies for the Streets', *Theatre Research International* 32.2, 119-29.

Cassens Stoian, L. (2002), 'Learning Performance by ~~Doing~~ Archiving Performance', *Performance Research* 7.4, 128-34.

Castellucci, R. (2002), 'Letter about the Goat that Once Gave its Name to Tragedy', in C. Astrié, J. Kelleher and N. Ridout (eds) *Idioma Clima Crono. Quaderni dell' itinerario* (Cesena), 3.

Castellucci, R., C. Guidi and C. Castellucci (2001), *Epopea della polvere: Il teatro*

Bibliography

della Socìetas Raffaello Sanzio 1992-1999. Amleto, Masoch, Orestea, Giulio Cesare, Genesi (Milan: Ubulibri).

Chadwick, O. (1970), *The Victorian Church: An Ecclesiastical History of England* (Oxford: Oxford University Press).

Chaikin, J. (1972), *The Presence of the Actor* (New York: Theater Communications Group).

Chamberlain, L. (1992), 'Gender and the Metaphorics of Translation', in L. Venuti (ed.) *Rethinking Translation: Discourse, Subjectivity, Ideology* (London: Routledge), 57-72.

Cixous, H. (1976), 'The Laugh of the Medusa' (tr. K. Cohen and P. Cohen), *Signs* 1.4, 875-93.

Cole, T.R. (1997), *The Journey of Life: A Cultural History of Aging in America* (Cambridge: Cambridge University Press).

Colebrook, C. (2006), *Deleuze: A Guide for the Perplexed* (London: Continuum).

Conboy, K., N. Medina and S. Stanbury (eds) (1997), *Writing on the Body: Female Embodiment and Feminist Theory* (New York: Columbia University Press).

Connor, S. (1997), *Postmodernist Culture: An Introduction to Theories of the Contemporary* (Oxford: Blackwell).

Contat, M. and M. Rybalka (eds) (1976), *Sartre on Theater* (tr. F. Jellinek, London: Quartet Books).

Cooper, J.C. (1978) *An Illustrated Encyclopaedia of Traditional Symbols* (London: Thames and Hudson).

Craik, T.W. (ed.) (1995), *Shakespeare: Henry V* (London: Routledge).

Crane, M.T. (2001), *Shakespeare's Brain: Reading with Cognitive Theory* (Princeton: Princeton University Press).

—— (2002), 'What Was Performance?', *Criticism* 43, 169-87.

Crisp, P. (2003), 'Conceptual Metaphor and its Expressions', in J. Gavins and G. Steen (eds) *Cognitive Poetics in Practice* (London: Routledge), 99-113.

Croft, W. and D.A. Cruse (2004), *Cognitive Linguistics* (Cambridge: Cambridge University Press).

Crombez, T. (2005), 'The Stain and Deficiency of Tragedy. An Interpretation of Romeo Castellucci's Tragedia Endogonidia', *Janus* 19, 93-100.

—— (2008), *Het anti-theater van Antonin Artaud: Een onderzoek naar de veralgemeende artistieke transgressie toegepast op het werk van Romeo Castellucci en de Socìetas Raffaello Sanzio* (Ghent: Academia Press).

Cropper, W.H. (1970), *The Quantum Physicists and an Introduction to their Physics* (New York: Oxford University Press).

Cross, J. (1998), *The Stravinsky Legacy* (Cambridge: Cambridge University Press).

Csapo, E. and W.J. Slater (1995), *The Context of Ancient Drama* (Ann Arbor: University of Michigan Press).

Curtius, E.R. (1953), *European Literature and the Latin Middle Ages* (tr. W.R. Trask, London: Routledge & Kegan Paul).

Damasio, A. (1994), *Descartes' Error: Emotion, Reason, and the Human Brain* (New York: Avon Books).

Davis, R. (2002), Review of Aeschylus' *Oresteia* by David Johnston, *Communications from the International Brecht Society* 36, 86-90.

Decreus, F. (2005), 'The Long Expected Discovery of Physicality', in S. Raeymaekers (ed.) *Body Language* (Bruges: Brugge Cultuurcentrum), 48-55.

—— (2008), 'The Nomadic Theatre of the *Socìetas Raffaello Sanzio*. A Case of Postdramatic Reworking of (the Classical) Tragedy', in L. Hardwick and C. Stray (eds) *A Companion to Classical Receptions* (Oxford: Blackwell), 274-86.

Bibliography

———— (forthcoming, 2009), 'The Reptilian Brain and the Representation of the Female in Theodoros Terzopoulos' Bacchai', in *Acta of the XIIIth International Meeting on Ancient Drama* (Delphi: Delphi Cultural Centre).

Deleuze, G. (1962), *Nietzsche et la philosophie* (Paris: Presses Universitaires de France).

———— (1995), *Negotations 1972-1990* (New York: Columbia University Press).

———— (1980), *A Thousand Plateaus – Capitalism and Schizophrenia 2* (Minneapolis: University of Minnesota Press).

Deleuze, G. and F. Guattari (1972), *Anti-Oedipus – Capitalism and Schizophrenia* (Minneapolis: University of Minnesota Press).

Dellheim, C. (1982), *The Face of the Past: The Preservation of the Medieval Inheritance in Victorian England* (Cambridge: Cambridge University Press).

Demastes, W.W. (1996), *Realism and The American Dramatic Tradition* (Tuscaloosa: University of Alabama Press).

———— (1998), *Theatre of Chaos: Beyond Absurdism, into Orderly Disorder* (Cambridge: Cambridge University Press).

Denton, M. (ed.) (2006), *Playing With Canons: Explosive New Works from Great Literature by America's Indie Playwrights* (New York: The New York Theatre Experience, Inc.).

De Preester, H. (2007), 'To Perform the Layered Body: A Short Exploration of the Body in Performance', *Janus Head* IX.2, 349-83.

Derrida, J. (1996), *Archive Fever: A Freudian Impression* (Chicago: University of Chicago Press).

Detienne, M. (1981), *L'Invention de la Mythologie* (Paris: Gallimard).

Diamond, E. (2003), 'Modern Drama / Modernity's Drama', in R. Knowles, J. Tompkins and W.B. Worthen (eds) *Modern Drama: Defining the Field* (Toronto: University of Toronto Press), 3-14.

Dilthey, W. (1913-1958), *Gesammelte Schriften*, vols 1-12 (Stuttgart: Vandenhoeck & Ruprecht).

Dodds, E.R. (ed.) (1960), *Euripides Bacchae* (Oxford: Clarendon).

Dove, R. (1994), *The Darker Face of the Earth* (Brownsville: Story Line Press).

Dover Wilson, J. (1947), *Shakespeare: Henry V* (Cambridge: Cambridge University Press),

Dunbar, R. (2000), 'On the Origins of the Human Mind', in P. Carruthers and A. Chamberlain (eds) *Evolution and the Human Mind: Modularity, Language and Meta-Cognition* (Cambridge: Cambridge University Press), 238-53.

Dürrenmatt, F. (1982), 'Problems of the Theater', in V. Sander (ed.) *Plays and Essays* (New York: Continuum).

Dutton, D. (2003), 'Authenticity in Art', in J. Levinson (ed.) *The Oxford Handbook of Aesthetics* (Oxford: Oxford University Press), 258-74.

Eagleton, T. (1991) *The Ideology of the Aesthetic* (Oxford: Blackwell).

———— (2000), *The Idea of Culture* (Oxford: Blackwell).

———— (2003), *Sweet Violence: The Idea of the Tragic* (Oxford: Blackwell).

Easterling, P.E. (1990), 'Constructing Character in Greek Tragedy', in C.B.R. Pelling (ed.) *Characterization and Individuality in Greek Literature* (Oxford: Clarendon Press), 83-99.

———— (1996), 'From Repertoire to Canon', in P.E. Easterling (ed.) *The Cambridge Companion to Greek Tragedy* (Cambridge: Cambridge University Press), 211-27.

———— (ed.) (1997a), *The Cambridge Companion to Greek Tragedy* (Cambridge: Cambridge University Press).

―――― (1997b), 'Gilbert Murray's Reading of Euripides', *Colby Quarterly* 33.2, 113-27.

―――― (2005), 'Ancient Plays for Modern Minds', *Inaugural UCL Housman Lecture*.

―――― (forthcoming, 2010), 'Sophoclean Journeys', in T. Mathews and J. Parker (eds) *Tragedy, Trauma, Translation: The Classic and the Modern* (Oxford: Oxford University Press).

Edelman, G. (1992), *Bright Air, Brilliant Fire: On the Matter of the Mind* (Jackson: Basic Books).

Edwardes, J. (2007), Interview with Katie Mitchell in *Time Out* (12 November 2007), http://www.timeout.com/london/theatre/features/3819.html#articleAfterMpu (accessed 16 December 2007).

Elam, K. (2002), *The Semiotics of Theatre and Drama* (London: Routledge).

Elder, J. (2000), 'Culture as Decay: Arnold, Eliot, Snyder', in L. Coupe (ed.) *The Green Studies Reader: From Romanticism to Ecocriticism* (London: Routledge), 227-34.

Eliot, T.S. (1944), *What is a Classic?* (London: Faber).

―――― (1951), *Selected Essays* (London: Faber).

Erikson, E.H. (1975), *Studies of Play* (New York: Arno Press).

Evans, H.A. (ed.) (1903), *Shakespeare: Henry V* (London: Methuen).

Ewans, M. (1982), *Wagner and Aeschylus: the Ring and the Oresteia* (London: Faber).

―――― (2007), *Opera from the Greek: Studies in the Poetics of Appropriation* (Aldershot: Ashgate).

Farber, Y (2008), *Molora* (London: Oberon Books).

Fauconnier, G. and M. Turner (2002), *The Way We Think: Conceptual Blending and the Mind's Hidden Complexities* (Jackson: Basic Books).

Felski, R. (ed.) (2008), *Rethinking Tragedy* (Baltimore: Johns Hopkins University Press).

Fernandez, J.W. (ed.) (1991), *Beyond Metaphor: The Theory of Tropes in Anthropology* (Stanford: Stanford University Press).

Finkelstein, D. and A. McCleery (eds) (2006), *The Book History Reader* (London: Routledge).

Fischer-Lichte, E. (1988), *Semiotik des Theaters* (Tübingen: Francke).

―――― (1992), *The Semiotics of Theatre* (tr. J. Gaines and D.L. Jones, Bloomington: Indiana University Press).

―――― (1998), *Theater seit den sechziger Jahre* (Tübingen: Francke).

―――― (2004), 'Thinking about the Origins of Theatre in the 1970s', in E. Hall, F. Macintosh and A. Wrigley (eds) *Dionysus Since 69: Greek Tragedy at the Dawn of the Third Millennium* (Oxford: Oxford University Press), 329-60.

―――― (2005), *Theatre, Sacrifice, Ritual: Exploring Forms of Political Theatre* (London: Routledge).

―――― (2006), 'Frank Castorfs Spiele mit dem Theater: Wie das Neue in die Welt kommt', *Forum Modernes Theater* 21.1, 5-24.

―――― (2008), *The Transformative Power of Performance: A New Aesthetics* (London: Routledge).

―――― (2009a), 'Politicizing Antigone', in S.E. Wilmer and A. Zukauskaite (eds) *Interrogating Antigone: From Philosophy to Performance* (Oxford: Oxford University Press).

―――― (2009b). 'Theater als Resonanz-Raum', in K. Lichau, V. Tkaczyk and R. Wolf (eds) *Resonanz. Potentiale einer akustischen Figur* (Munich: Fink).

Bibliography

Fischer-Lichte, E. and A. Fleig (eds) (2000), *Körper-Inszenierungen* (Tübingen: Attempto).

Fischer-Lichte, E., C. Horn and M. Warstat (eds) (2001), *Verkörperung* (Tübingen: Francke).

Fish, S. (1980), *Is There a Text in This Class? The Authority of Interpretive Communities* (Cambridge: Harvard University Press).

Flashar, H. (1991), *Inszenierung der Antike. Das griechische Drama auf der Bühne der Neuzeit 1585-1990* (Munich: Beck).

Fleishman, M. (1990), 'Workshop Theater as Oppositional Form', *South African Theatre Journal*, 4.1, 88-118.

Foley, H.P. (1980), 'The Masque of Dionysus', *TAPA* 110, 107-30.

—— (1985), *Ritual Irony: Poetry and Sacrifice in Euripides* (Ithaca: Cornell University Press).

—— (2004), 'Bad Women: Gender Politics in Late Twentieth-Century Performance and Revision of Greek Tragedy', in E. Hall, F. Macintosh and A. Wrigley (eds) *Dionysus Since 69: Greek Tragedy at the Dawn of the Third Millennium* (Oxford: Oxford University Press), 77-112.

—— (2008), 'Generic Boundaries in Late Fifth-Century Athens', in M. Revermann and P. Wilson (eds) *Performance, Iconography, Reception: Studies in Honour of Oliver Taplin* (Oxford: Oxford University Press), 15-36.

Foley, W.A. (1997), *Anthropological Linguistics: An Introduction* (Chichester: Wiley-Blackwell).

Fonseca, L.H. da and T. Kliche (eds) (2006), *Verführerische Leichen – verbotener Verfall: 'Körperwelten' als gesellschaftliches Schlüsselereignis* (Lengerich: Pabst-Verlag).

Foster, S.L. (2008), 'Movement's Contagion: The Kinaesthetic Impact of Performance', in T.C. David (ed.) *The Cambridge Companion to Performance Studies* (Cambridge: Cambridge University Press), 46-59.

Foster, V.A. (2004), *The Name and Nature of Tragicomedy* (Aldershot: Ashgate).

Foucault, M. (1976), *The Archaeology of Knowledge* (New York: Harper & Row).

—— (1976-1984) *Histoire de la sexualité, I-III* (Paris: Gallimard).

—— (1986), 'Of Other Spaces', *Diacritics* 16.1, 22-7.

Frankland, G. (2000), *Freud's Literary Culture* (Cambridge: Cambridge University Press).

Freeman, D.C. (1993), ' "According to My Bond": King Lear and Re-Cognition', *Language and Literature* 2, 1-18.

Freeman, M.H. (2000), 'Poetry and the Scope of Metaphor: Toward a Cognitive Theory of Literature', in A. Barcelona (ed.) *Metaphor and Metonymy at the Crossroads: A Cognitive Perspecitve* (Berlin: Mouton de Gruyter), 253-81.

Freshwater, H. (2002), 'Anti-Theatrical Prejudice and the Persistence of Performance', *Performance Research* 7.4, 50-8.

—— (2003), 'The Allure of the Archive', *Poetics Today* 24.4, 729-58.

Fuchs, E. (1996), *The Death of Character: Perspectives on Theater after Modernism* (Bloomington: Indiana University Press).

Furst, L. and P. Skrine (1971), *Naturalism* (London: Methuen).

Galinsky, K. (1975), *Ovid's* Metamorphoses: *An Introduction to the Basic Aspects* (Oxford: Blackwell).

Gallagher, S. (2001), 'The Practice of Mind: Theory, Simulation or Primary Interaction?' *Journal of Consciousness Studies* 8.5-7, 83-108.

Gallese, V. and G. Lakoff (2005), 'The Brain's Concepts: The Role of the Sensory-Motor System in Conceptual Knowledge', *Cognitive Neuropsychology* 22, 455-79.

Bibliography

Gamel, M.-K. (2002), 'From *Thesmophoriazousai* to *The Julie Thesmo Show*: Adaptation, Performance, Reception', *American Journal of Philology* 123. 3, 465-99.

Gardiner, C.P. (1987), *The Sophoclean Chorus: A Study in Character and Function* (Iowa City: University of Iowa Press).

Garner, S.B. (1994), *Bodied Spaces: Phenomenology and Performance in Contemporary Drama* (Ithaca: Cornell University Press).

Gassner, J. (1956), *Form and Idea in Modern Theatre* (New York: Dryden Press).

Gavins, J. and G. Steen (eds) (2003), *Cognitive Poetics in Practice* (London: Routledge).

Gellrich, M. (1988), *Tragedy and Theory: The Problem of Conflict since Aristotle* (Princeton: Princeton University Press).

Genast, E. (1862/66), *Aus dem Leben eines Schauspielers* (Leipzig).

Genelli, C. (1818), *Das Theater zu Athen* (Germany).

Genet, J. (1962), *Our Lady of the Flowers* (tr. B. Frechtman, New York: Grove Press).

Genette, G. (1991), 'Introduction to the Paratext', in *New Literary History* 22.2, 261-72.

—— (1997), *Palimpsests: Literature in the Second Degree* (tr. C. Newman and C. Dobinsky, Lincoln: University of Nebraska Press).

Giannisi, P. (2006), *Récits des voies: chant et cheminement en Grèce archaïque* (France: J. Millon).

Gibbs, R.W. (1994), *The Poetics of Mind: Figurative Thought, Language, and Understanding* (Cambridge: Cambridge University Press).

—— (2006), *Embodiment and Cognitive Science* (Cambridge: Cambridge University Press).

Gibbs, R.W. and G.J. Steen (eds) (1999), *Metaphor in Cognitive Linguistics: Selected Papers from the Fifth International Cognitive Linguistics Conference, Amsterdam, July 1997* (Herndon: John Benjamins).

Gilbert, J. (2000), 'Falling in Love With Euripides (*Andromeda*)', *Illinois Classical Studies* 24-5, 75-92.

Gill, C. (1996), *Personality in Greek Epic, Tragedy, and Philosophy* (Oxford: Oxford University Press).

Gillespie, S. and P. Hardie (eds) (2007), *The Cambridge Companion to Lucretius* (Cambridge: Cambridge University Press).

Gilloch, G. (2002), *Walter Benjamin: Critical Constellations* (Cambridge: Polity Press).

Ginzburg, C. et al. (1995), 'Inter/disciplinarity: A Range of Critical Perspectives', *The Art Bulletin* 77.4, 534-52.

Goff, B. (2000), 'Try to Make it Real Compared to What? Euripides' *Electra* and the Play of Genres', *Illinois Classical Studies* 24-5, 93-106.

—— (ed.) (2005), *Classics and Colonialism* (London: Duckworth).

Goff, B. and M. Simpson (2007), *Crossroads in the Black Aegean: Oedipus, Antigone, and Dramas of the African Diaspora* (Oxford: Oxford University Press).

Golder, H. (1996) 'Geek Tragedy? – Or, Why I'd Rather Go to the Movies', *Arion* 4.1, 174-209.

Goldhill, S. (1986), *Reading Greek Tragedy* (Cambridge: Cambridge University Press).

—— (1991), *The Poet's Voice: Essays on Poetics and Greek Literature* (Cambridge: Cambridge University Press).

—— (1994), Review of Marvin Carlson's *Theories of the Theatre* in *Bryn Mawr Classical Review*, 05.01.

——— (1999a), 'Body/Politics: Is There a History of Reading?', in J. Peradotto, T.M. Falkner, N. Felson and D. Konstan (eds) *Contextualizing Classics: Ideology, Performance, Dialogue* (Boulder: Rowman & Littlefield), 89-122.

——— (1999b), 'Programme Notes', in S. Goldhill and R. Osborne (eds) *Performance Culture and Athenian Democracy* (Cambridge: Cambridge University Press).

——— (2002), *Who Needs Greek?: Contests in the Cultural History of Hellenism* (Cambridge: Cambridge University Press).

——— (2007), *How to Stage Greek Tragedy Today* (Chicago: Chicago University Press).

——— (2008), 'Generalizing about Tragedy', in R. Felski (ed.) *Rethinking Tragedy* (Baltimore: Johns Hopkins University Press), 45-65.

Goldman, M. (1975), *The Actor's Freedom: Toward a Theory of Drama* (New York: Viking Press).

——— (2000), *On Drama: Boundaries of Genre, Borders of Self* (Ann Arbor: University of Michigan Press).

Goldoni, C. (1828) *Memoirs of Goldoni, Written by Himself* (tr. J. Black, London: Henry Colburn).

Gombrich, E. (1965), *Meditations on a Hobby Horse and Other Essays on the Theory of Art* (London: Phaidon).

Goodman, T. (2006), 'Performing a "New" Nation: The Role of the TRC in South Africa', in J.C. Alexander, B. Giesen and J.L. Mast (eds) *Social Performance: Symbolic Action, Cultural Pragmatics and Ritual* (Cambridge: Cambridge University Press), 169-92.

Gottschall, J. and D.S. Wilson (eds) (2005), *The Literary Animal: Evolution and the Nature of Narrative* (Evanston: Northwestern University Press).

Graham, J. (1985), *Difference in Translation* (Ithaca: Cornell University Press).

Grant, D. (1970), *Realism* (London: Methuen).

Green, A.S. (1994) *The Revisionist Stage: American Directors Reinvent the Classics* (Cambridge: Cambridge University Press).

Gregory, J. (2000), 'Comic Elements in Euripides', *Illinois Classical Studies* 24-5, 59-74.

——— (ed.) (2005), *A Companion to Greek Tragedy* (Oxford: Blackwell).

Greig, D. (2007), *Euripides, The Bacchae. A Version by David Greig* (London: Faber).

Gridley, S. (2006), *Post-Oedipus* (New York: Playscripts, Inc.).

Griffith, R.D. (1988), 'Disrobing in the Oresteia', *Classical Quarterly* 38.1, 552-4.

Griffiths, J.M. (2007), 'The Experiential Turn: Shifting Methodologies in the Study of Greek Drama', *New Voices in Classical Reception Studies* 2 (Spring), http://www2.open.ac.uk/ClassicalStudies/GreekPlays/newvoices/issue2/issue2 index.htm (accessed 19 July 2008).

Grimm, G. (1977), *Rezeptionsgeschichte: Grundlegung einer Theorie* (Munich).

Guidi, C. (2002), '1st Grammatical Project with 20 Amino Acids', in C. Astrié, J. Kelleher and N. Ridout (eds) *Idioma Clima Crono. Quaderni dell' itinerario* (Cesena) 3-4.

Gurr, A. (ed.) (2005), *Shakespeare: King Henry V* (Cambridge: Cambridge University Press).

Habermas, J. (1998), 'Modernity – An Incomplete Project', in H. Foster (ed.) *The Anti-Aesthetic – Essays on Postmodern Culture* (New York: The New Press), 1-15.

Hacking, I. (1999), *The Social Construction of What?* (Cambridge: Harvard University Press).

Bibliography

Hainaux, R. (1973), *Stage Design Throughout the World since 1960* (Brussels: Editions Meddens).

Hainge, G. (2005), 'No(i)stalgia: On the Impossibility of Recognising Noise in the Present', *Culture, Theory and Critique* 46.1, 1-10.

Hall, E. (1997), 'The Sociology of Athenian Tragedy', in P. Easterling (ed.) *The Cambridge Companion to Greek Tragedy* (Cambridge: Cambridge University Press), 93-126.

—— (1999), 'Actor's Song in Tragedy', in S. Goldhill and R. Osborne (eds) *Performance Culture and Athenian Democracy* (Cambridge: Cambridge University Press), 96-124.

—— (2002a), 'The Ancient Actor's Presence since the Renaissance', in P. Easterling and E. Hall (eds) *Greek and Roman Actors: Aspects of an Ancient Profession* (Cambridge: Cambridge University Press), 409-34.

—— (2002b), 'The Singing Actors of Antiquity', in P. Easterling and E. Hall (eds) *Greek and Roman Actors: Aspects of an Ancient Profession* (Cambridge: Cambridge University Press), 1-38.

—— (2004a), 'Towards a Theory of Performance Reception', *Arion* 12.1, 51-89.

—— (2004b), 'Why Greek Tragedy in the Late Twentieth Century', in E. Hall, F. Macintosh and A. Wrigley (eds) *Dionysus Since 69: Greek Tragedy at the Dawn of the Third Millennium* (Oxford: Oxford University Press), 1-46.

—— (2005a), 'Aeschylus' Clytemnestra versus her Senecan Tradition', in E. Hall, F. Macintosh, P. Michelakis and O. Taplin (eds) *Agamemnon in Performance, 458 BC to AD 2004* (Oxford: Oxford University Press), 37-52.

—— (2005b) 'Iphigenia and her Mother at Aulis: A Study in the Revival of a Euripidean Classic', in S. Wilmer and J. Dillon (eds) *Rebel Women: Staging Ancient Greek Drama Today* (London: Methuen), 3-41.

—— (2006), *The Theatrical Cast of Athens: Interactions between Ancient Greek Drama and Society* (Oxford: Oxford University Press).

—— (2007), 'Aeschylus' *Persians* via the Ottoman Empire to Saddam Hussein', in E. Bridges, E. Hall and P.J. Rhodes (eds) *Cultural Responses to the Persian Wars* (Oxford: Oxford University Press), 167-200.

—— (2008a), 'Putting the Class into Classical Reception', in L. Hardwick and C. Stray (eds) *A Companion to Classical Receptions* (Oxford: Blackwell), 386-98.

—— (2008b), *The Return of Ulysses: A Cultural History of Homer's Odyssey* (London: I.B. Tauris & Co.).

—— (forthcoming, 2010), *Greek Tragedy: Suffering Under the Sun* (Oxford).

Hall, E. and F. Macintosh (2005), *Greek Tragedy and the British Theatre 1660-1914* (Oxford: Oxford University Press).

Hall, E., F. Macintosh and A. Wrigley (eds) (2004), *Dionysus Since 69: Greek Tragedy at the Dawn of the Third Millennium* (Oxford: Oxford University Press).

Hall, E. and R. Wyles (eds) (2008), *New Directions in Ancient Pantomime* (Oxford: Oxford University Press).

Hall, P. (2000), *Exposed by the Mask: Form and Language in Drama* (London: Oberon).

Hallet, J.P. and T. Van Nortwick (eds) (1997), *Compromising Traditions* (London: Routledge).

Hardwick, L. (2000), *Translating Words, Translating Cultures* (London: Duckworth).

—— (2003), *Reception Studies, Greece & Rome: New Surveys in the Classics 33* (Oxford: Oxford University Press).

Bibliography

———— (2004), 'Greek Drama and Anti-Colonialism: Decolonizing Classics', in E. Hall, F. Macintosh and A. Wrigley (eds) *Dionysus Since 69: Greek Tragedy at the Dawn of the Third Millennium* (Oxford: Oxford University Press), 219-42.

———— (2005) 'Refiguring Classical Texts: Aspects of the Post-Colonial Condition', in B. Goff (ed.) *Classics and Colonialism* (London: Duckworth), 107-17.

———— (2006), 'Remodelling Receptions: Greek Drama as Diaspora in Performance', in C. Martindale and R.F. Thomas (eds) *Classics and the Uses of Reception* (Oxford: Blackwell), 204-15.

———— (2007), 'Shades of Multi-Lingualism and Multi-Vocalism', in L. Hardwick and C. Gillespie (eds) *Classics in Post-Colonial Worlds* (Oxford: Oxford University Press), 305-28.

———— (2008), 'Translated Classics around the Millennium: Vibrant Hybrids or Shattered Icons?', in A. Lianeri and V. Zajko (eds) *Translation and the Classic* (Oxford: Oxford University Press), 341-66.

———— (2009a), 'Is the "Frail Silken Line" worth more than "A Fart in a Bearskin"? or How Translation Practice Matters in Poetry and Drama', in S.J. Harrison (ed.) *Living Classics* (Oxford: Oxford University Press), 39-61.

———— (2009b), 'Can (Modern) Poets do Classical Drama? The Case of Ted Hughes', in R. Rees (ed.) *Ted Hughes and the Classics* (Oxford: Oxford University Press).

———— (forthcoming, 2010a), 'Fuzzy Connections', in J. Parker and T. Mathews (eds) *Translation, Trauma and Tradition*.

———— (forthcoming, 2010b), 'The Problem of the Spectators, Ancient and Modern', in A. Bakogianni (ed.) *Modern Receptions of Greek and Roman Drama*.

———— (forthcoming, 2010c), 'Antigone's Journey: From Athens to Edinburgh, via Paris and Tblisi' in H. Foley and E. Mee (eds) *Mobilizing Antigone on the Contemporary World Stage* (Oxford : Oxford University Press).

Hardwick, L. and C. Gillespie (eds) (2007), *Classics in Post-Colonial Worlds* (Oxford: Oxford University Press).

Hardwick, L. and C. Stray (eds) (2007), *A Companion to Classical Receptions* (Oxford: Blackwell).

Harris, W.V. (2001), *Restraining Rage: The Ideology of Anger Control in Classical Antiquity* (Cambridge: Harvard University Press).

Harrison, T. (2002), *Tony Harrison: Plays 4* (London: Faber).

Harrop, S (2007), *The Body in Translation: The Relationship between Text and Movement in Modern Poetic Versions of Greek Tragedy*, unpublished PhD thesis (University of London).

Harrop, S. and D. Wiles (2008), 'Poetic Language and Corporeality in Translations of Greek Tragedy', *New Theatre Quarterly* 24.1, 51-64.

Hart, F.E. (2006), 'Performance, Phenomenology, and the Cognitive Turn', in B. McConachie and F.E. Hart (eds) *Performance and Cognition: Theatre Studies and the Cognitive Turn* (London: Routledge), 29-51.

Hartley, A.J. (2001), 'Sots and Snots: The Specter of Authenticity in Performance Scripts', *Theatre Topics* 11.2 , 173-86.

Hazel, R. (2002), ' "Tis not alone my inky cloak, good mother ...": the Hamletization of *Electra*', *Didaskalia* 5.3, http://www.didaskalia.net/issues/vol5no3/hazel.html (accessed 29 March 2009).

Heidegger, M. (1971) *Poetry, Language, Thought* (tr. A. Hofstadter, New York: Harper and Collins).

Hell, J. (2006), 'Remnants of Totalitarianism: Hannah Arendt, Heiner Müller, Slavoj Žižek, and the Re-Invention of Politics', *Telos* 136, 76-103.

278

Bibliography

Herington, C.J. (1963), 'The Influence of Old Comedy on Aeschylus' Later Trilogies', *TAPA* 94, 113-25.

Hertmans, S. (2000), *Mind the Gap* (Amsterdam: Meulenhoff).

—— (2007), *Het zwijgen van de tragedie* (Amsterdam: De Bezige Bij).

Heskel, J. (1994), 'Cicero as Evidence for Attitudes to Dress in the Late Republic', in J.L. Sebasta and L. Bonfante (eds) *The World of Roman Costume* (Madison: University of Wisconsin Press), 133-45.

Heuser, A (ed.) (1987), *Selected Literary Criticism of Louis MacNeice* (Oxford: Oxford University Press).

Hexter, R. (2006), 'Literary History as a Provocation to Reception Studies', in C. Martindale and R.F. Thomas (eds) *Classics and the Uses of Reception* (Oxford: Blackwell), 23-31.

Hirst, D.L. (1984), *Tragicomedy* (London: Methuen).

Hodgdon, B. (1996), 'Looking for Mr. Shakespeare after "The Revolution": Robert Lepage's Intercultural *Dream* Machine', in J.C. Bullman (ed.) *Shakespeare, Theory and Performance* (London: Routledge), 68-91.

—— (2003), 'Photography, Theater, Mnemonics. Or, Thirteen Ways of Looking at a Still', in W.B. Worthen and P. Holland (eds) *Theorizing Practice: Redefining Theatre History* (London: Routledge), 88-119.

Hodgdon, B. and W.B. Worthen (2005), *A Companion to Shakespeare and Performance* (Oxford: Blackwell).

Hogan, P.C. (2003), *Cognitive Science, Literature and the Arts: A Guide for Humanists* (London: Routledge).

Holland, E.W. (1999), *Deleuze and Guattari's Anti-Oedipus* (London: Routledge).

Hollander, A. (1993), *Seeing Through Clothes* (Berkeley: University of California Press).

Holmes, J. (2004), *Merely Players?: Actors' Accounts of Performing Shakespeare* (London: Routledge).

Holub, R.C. (1984), *Reception Theory: A Critical Introduction* (London: Routledge).

—— (1995), 'Reception Theory: School of Constance', in R. Selden (ed.) *Cambridge History of Literary Criticism* (Cambridge: Cambridge University Press).

Hope, C. (1980), *Titian* (London: Jupiter).

Hornby, R. (1986), *Drama, Metadrama, and Perception* (Lewisburg: Bucknell University Press).

Hourmouziades, N. (1965), *Production and Imagination in Euripides: Form and Function of the Scenic Space* (Athens).

Howard, P. (2002), *What is Scenography?* (London: Routledge).

Hughes, T. (1994), *Winter Pollen: Occasional Prose* (London: Faber).

—— (1999), *Euripides' Alcestis: In a New Version by Ted Hughes* (London: Faber).

Humboldt, W. von (1992), 'From Introduction to his Translation of *Agamemnon*', in R. Schulte and J. Biguenet (eds) *Theories of Translation: An Anthology of Essays from Dryden to Derrida* (Chicago: University of Chicago Press), 55-9.

Humphrey, S.C. (2004), 'Classics and Colonialism: Towards an Erotics of the Discipline', in *The Strangeness of Gods* (Oxford: Oxford University Press), 8-50.

Humphreys, A.R. (1968), *Shakespeare: Henry V* (London: Penguin).

Hutcheon, L. (2006), *A Theory of Adaptation* (New York: Routledge).

Ibsen, H. (1972), *The Oxford Ibsen*, ed. J.W. McFarlane (Oxford: Oxford University Press).

Innes, C. (1993), *Avant Garde Theatre 1892-1992* (London: Routledge).

Irigaray, L. (1985), 'The Stage Setup', in *Speculum of the Other Woman* (tr. G. Gill, Ithaca: Cornell University Press).

Bibliography

Iser, W. (1972), 'The Reading Process: A Phenomenological Approach', in *The Implied Reader: Patterns of Communication in Prose Fiction from Bunyan to Beckett* (Baltimore: Johns Hopkins University Press).

―――― (1978), *The Act of Reading: Theory of Aesthetic Response* (London: Routledge).

―――― (1984), *Der Akt des Lesens* (Munich: Fink).

―――― (1987), *Walter Pater: The Aesthetic Moment* (Cambridge: Cambridge: University Press).

―――― (1988), *Shakespeares Historien. Genesis und Geltung* (Constance: Universitätsverlag Konstanz).

Jameson, E. (1990), *Signatures of the Visible* (London: Routledge).

Jamesson, F. (1981), *The Political Unconscious* (Ithaca: Cornell University Press).

Jauss, H.R. (1970), *Literaturgeschichte als Provokation* (Frankfurt: Suhrkamp).

―――― (1977), *Ästhetische Erfahrung und literarische Hermeneutik* (Munich: Fink).

―――― (1982), *Toward an Aesthetic of Reception* (Brighton: Harvester).

Johnson, M. (1987), *The Body in the Mind* (Chicago: University of Chicago Press).

Johnson, R. (2002), 'Many Languages, A Common Passion', in *Los Angeles Times*, June 2002.

Jones, A.R. (1981), 'Writing the Body: Toward an Understanding of "L'Ecriture Feminine" ', *Feminist Studies* 7.2, 247-63.

Jones, R. (1996), 'Author(s) and Authority: Brian Friel's *Living Quarters*' http://www2.open.ac.uk/ClassicalStudies/GreekPlays/conf96/jones.htm (accessed 12 September 2007).

Jordanova, L. (2000), *Defining Features: Scientific and Medical Portraits 1660-2000* (University of Chicago Press).

Kallendorf, W. (ed.) (2007), *A Companion to the Classical Tradition* (Oxford: Blackwell).

Kant, I. (1952), *The Critique of Judgement*, tr. J.C. Meredith (Oxford: Clarendon Press).

Kapilow, R. (2008), *All You Have to Do is Listen: Music from the Inside Out* (Hoboken: Wiley).

Kennelly, B. (1991), *Euripides' Medea: A New Version* (Newcastle upon Tyne: Bloodaxe).

―――― (1993), *Euripides' The Trojan Women: A New Version* (Newcastle upon Tyne: Bloodaxe).

―――― (1996), *Sophocles' Antigone: A New Version* (Newcastle upon Tyne: Bloodaxe).

Kierkegaard, S. (1987), *Either / Or Part I* (tr. H.V. Hong and E.H. Hong, Princeton: Princeton University Press).

Kimmel, M. (2004), 'Metaphor Variation in Cultural Context: Perspectives from Anthropology', *European Journal of English Studies* 8, 275-94.

Kitto, H.D.F. (1956), *Form and Meaning in Drama* (London: Methuen).

Kivy, P. (1995), *Authenticities: Philosophical Reflections on Musical Performance* (Ithaca: Cornell University Press).

Klein, J. (1996), *Crossing Boundaries: Knowledge, Disciplinarities, and Interdisciplinarities* (Virginia: University Press of Virginia).

―――― (1990), *Interdisciplinarity: History, Theory, and Practice* (Detroit: Wayne State University Press).

Knowles, M. and R. Moon (2006), *Introducing Metaphor* (New York: Routledge).

Knowles, R.P. (2004), *Reading the Material Theatre* (Cambridge: Cambridge University Press).

Bibliography

Knox, B.M.W. (1970), 'Euripidean Comedy', in A. Cheuse and R. Koffler (eds) *The Rarer Action* (New Jersey: Rutgers University Press), 68-96.

Konijn, E. (2000), *Acting Emotions: Shaping Emotions on Stage* (Amsterdam: Amsterdam University Press).

Konstan, D. (2006), *The Emotions of the Ancient Greeks: Studies in Aristotle and Classical Literature* (Toronto: University of Toronto Press).

Kosofsky Sedgwick, E. (2003), *Touching Feeling: Affect, Pedagogy, Performativity* (Durham: Duke University Press).

Kövecses, Z. (2002), *Metaphor: A Practical Introduction* (Oxford: Oxford University Press).

—— (2005), *Metaphor in Culture: Universality and Variation* (Cambridge: Cambridge University Press).

Kramer, L. (2007), 'Wittgenstein's Chopin: Interdisicplinarity and "the Music Itself" ', in G. Beer, M. Bowie and B. Perrey (eds) *In(ter)discipline: New Languages for Criticism* (London: Legenda), 41-51.

Kraus, M. (1985), 'Heiner Müller und die griechische Tragödie: Dargestellt am Beispiel des *Philoktet*', *Poetica: Zeitschrift für Sprach- und Literaturwissenschaft* 17.3-4, 299-339.

Kristeva, J. (1997), 'Modern Theater Does Not Take (A) Place', in *SubStance* 19.19, 131-34.

—— (2002), *The Portable Kristeva* (New York: Columbia University Press).

Kruger, L. (2003), 'Making Sense of Sensation: Enlightenment, Embodiment and the End(s) of Modern Drama', in R. Knowles, J. Tompkins and W.B. Worthen (eds) *Modern Drama: Defining the Field* (Toronto: University of Toronto Press), 80-101.

Lada-Richards, I. (2002), 'The Subjectivity of Greek Performance', in P.E. Easterling and E. Hall (eds) *Greek and Roman Actors: Aspects of an Ancient Profession* (Cambridge: Cambridge University Press), 395-418.

—— (2005), 'Greek Tragedy and Western Perceptions of Actors and Acting', in J. Gregory (ed.) *A Companion to Greek Tragedy* (Oxford: Blackwell), 459-71.

Lakoff, G. (1987), *Women, Fire, and Dangerous Things: What Categories Reveal About the Mind* (Chicago: University of Chicago Press).

Lakoff, G. and M. Johnson (1980), *Metaphors We Live By* (Chicago: University of Chicago Press).

Lakoff, G. and M. Johnson (1999), *Philosophy in the Flesh: The Embodied Mind and Its Challenge to Western Thought* (Jackson: Basic Books).

Lambropoulos, V. (2006), *The Tragic Idea* (London: Duckworth).

Langer, S.K. (1953), *Feeling and Form: A Theory of Art Developed from Philosophy in a New Key* (London: Routledge & Kegan Paul).

Lawson, C. and R. Stowell (1999), *The Historical Performance of Music: An Introduction* (Cambridge: Cambridge University Press).

Lefebvre, H. (1991), *The Production of Space* (Cambridge: Blackwell).

Lefevere, A. (1992), *Translation, Rewriting and the Manipulation of Literary Fame* (London: Routledge).

Le Goff, J. and N. Truong (2003), *Une histoire du corps au Moyen Age* (Sumter: Lévi).

Lehmann, H.T. (2006), *Postdramatic Theatre* (tr. K. Jürs-Munby, New York: Routledge).

Leppard, R. (1988), *Authenticity in Music* (London: Faber).

Levinson, S.C. (2003), *Space in Language and Cognition: Explorations in Cognitive Diversity* (Cambridge: Cambridge University Press).

Bibliography

Lévi-Strauss, C. (1966), *The Savage Mind* (London: Weidenfeld and Nicolson).
—— (1969), *The Raw and the Cooked* (New York: Harper and Row).
Ley, G. (2007), *The Theatricality of Greek Tragedy: Playing Space and Chorus* (Chicago: University of Chicago Press).
Lianeri, A. and V. Zajko (eds) (2008), *Translation and the Classic: Identity as Change in the History of Culture* (Oxford: Oxford University Press).
Llewellyn-Jones, L. (2001), 'The Use of Set and Costume Design in Modern Productions of Ancient Greek Drama', http://www2.open.ac.uk/ClassicalStudies/GreekPlays/essays/essayindex.htm (accessed 20 March 2009).
Lloyd, G.E R. (2007), *Cognitive Variations: Reflections on the Unity and Diversity of the Human Mind* (Oxford: Oxford University Press).
Lorraine, T. (1999), *Irigaray and Deleuze: Experiments in Visceral Philosophy* (Ithaca: Cornell University Press).
Lowe, N.J. (2000), *The Classical Plot and the Invention of Western Narrative* (Cambridge: Cambridge University Press).
Lynch, K. (2007), 'The Image of the City', in R.T. Gates and F. Stout (eds) *The City Reader* (New York: Routledge).
Lyne, R. (2006), '*Volpone* and the Classics', in G.A. Sullivan Jr., P. Cheney and A. Hadfield (eds) *Early Modern English Drama: A Critical Companion* (Oxford: Oxford University Press), 177-88.
Lyons, J. (1977), *Semantics* (Cambridge: Cambridge University Press).
Lyotard, J.F. (1977), 'The Unconscious as Mise-en-Scène', in M. Benamou and C. Caramello (eds) *Performance in Postmodern Culture* (Madison: Coda), 87-98.
MacDonald, M.F. (ed.) (2003), *Whistler's Mother: An American Icon* (Farnham: Ashgate).
Macfarlane, R. (2007), *Original Copy: Plagiarism and Originality in Nineteenth Century Literature* (Oxford: Oxford University Press).
Macintosh, F. (2000), 'Introduction: The Performer in Performance', in E. Hall, F. Macintosh and O. Taplin (eds) *Medea in Performance, 1500-2000* (Oxford: Legenda), 1-31.
—— (2001), '*Alcestis* on the British Stage', *Cahiers du Gita* 14, 281-308.
—— (2004), 'Oedipus in the East End: from Freud to Berkoff', in E. Hall, F. Macintosh and A. Wrigley (eds) *Dionysus Since 69: Greek Tragedy at the Dawn of the Third Millennium* (Oxford: Oxford University Press), 311-27.
—— (2007), 'From the Court to the National: The Theatrical Legacy of Gilbert Murray's *Bacchae*', in C. Stray (ed.) *Gilbert Murray Reassessed: Hellenism, Theatre and International Politics* (Oxford: Oxford University Press), 133-44.
—— (2008), 'An Oedipus for Our Times? Yeats' Version of Sophocles' *Oedipus Tyrannos*', in M. Revermann and P. Wilson (eds) *Performance, Iconography, Reception: Studies in Honour of Oliver Taplin* (Oxford: Oxford University Press), 524-47.
MacNeice, L. (1935), Review of Aeschylus, *The Seven Against Thebes*, tr. Gilbert Murray, *Spectator*, 10 May 1935.
Mandler, P. (1997), *The Fall and Rise of the Stately Home* (London: Yale University Press).
Marowitz, C. (1978), *The Marowitz Shakespeare* (London: Marion Boyars).
Marranca, B. (1996), *Ecologies of Theater: Essays at the Century Turning* (Baltimore: Johns Hopkins University Press).
—— (1997), *The Theatre of Images* (New York: Drama Book Specialists).
Marranca, B. and G. Dasgupta (eds) (1999), *Conversations on Art and Performance* (Baltimore: Johns Hopkins University Press).

Marsh, D. (2007), 'Italy', in C.W. Kallendorf (ed.) *A Companion to the Classical Tradition* (Oxford: Blackwell), 208-21.

Martindale, C. (1993), *Redeeming the Text: Latin Poetry and the Hermeneutics of Reception* (Cambridge: Cambridge University Press).

———— (2005), *Latin Poetry and the Judgement of Taste* (Oxford: Oxford University Press).

———— (2006), 'Introduction: Thinking Through Reception', in C. Martindale and R.F. Thomas (eds) *Classics and the Uses of Reception* (Oxford: Blackwell), 1-13.

———— (2007), 'Reception', in C.W. Kallendorf (ed.) *A Companion to the Classical Tradition* (Oxford: Blackwell), 297-311.

Martindale, C. and R.F. Thomas (eds) (2006), *Classics and the Uses of Reception* (Oxford: Blackwell).

Marx, K. (2004), *Capital: Critique of Political Economy*, vol. 1 (London: Penguin Classics).

Mason, H. (1977), 'Wyatt's Birds of Fortune', *Cambridge Quarterly* 7, 281-96.

Mastronarde, D.J. (2000), 'Euripidean Tragedy and Genre: The Terminology and its Problems', *Illinois Classical Studies* 24-5, 23-40.

———— (2002), *Euripides: Medea* (Cambridge: Cambridge University Press).

Matejka, L. and I.R. Titunik (eds) (1976), *Semiotics of Art – Prague School Contributions* (London: MIT).

McAuley, G. (2000), *Space in Performance* (Ann Arbor: University of Michigan Press).

McClure, M. (1985), *The Beard and Vktms* (New York: Grove Press).

McConachie, B. (2001), 'Doing Things with Image Schemas: The Cognitive Turn in Theatre Studies and the Problem of Experience for Historians', *Theatre Journal* 53, 569-94.

———— (2002), 'Using Cognitive Science to Understand Spatiality and Community in the Theater', *Contemporary Theatre Review* 12.3, 97-114.

———— (2006), 'Cognitive Studies and Epistemic Competence in Cultural History: Moving Beyond Freud and Lacan', in B. McConachie and F.E. Hart (eds) *Performance and Cognition: Theatre Studies and the Cognitive Turn* (London: Routledge), 52-75.

———— (2008), *Engaging Audiences: A Cognitive Approach to Spectating in the Theatre* (London: Routledge).

McConachie, B. and F.E. Hart (eds) (2006), *Performance and Cognition: Theatre Studies and the Cognitive Turn* (London: Routledge).

McDonald, M. (1993), 'Orestes' *Mania*: Euripides', Mee's and Bogart's Apocalyptic Vision', *Illinois Classical Studies* 18, 73-81.

———— (2001), *Sing Sorrow: Classics, History, and Heroines in Opera* (London: Greenwood Press).

———— (2003), *The Living Art of Greek Tragedy* (Bloomington: Indiana University Press).

McDonald, M. and J.M. Walton (eds) (2002), *Amid Our Troubles: Irish Versions of Greek Tragedy* (London: Methuen).

McLeish, K. and F. Raphael (1994), *Medea* (London: Nick Hern Books).

Mee, C.L. (1998), *History Plays* (Baltimore: Johns Hopkins University Press).

Melrose, S. (1994), *A Semiotics of the Dramatic Text* (London: Macmillan).

Melzack, R. (2001), 'Pain', in G. Underwood (ed.) *The Oxford Guide to the Mind: Understanding Everyday Mysteries of the Human Mind* (Oxford: Oxford University Press), 86-8.

Melzack, R. and P.D. Wall (1991), *The Challenge of Pain* (London: Penguin).

Merrill, L. (1992), *A Pot of Paint: Aesthetics on Trial in Whistler v. Ruskin* (Washington: Smithsonian Press).

Mervant-Roux, R.-R. (1998), *L'assise du theatre: pour une etude du spectateur* (Paris: CNRS).

Michelakis, P. (2006), 'Reception, Performance and the Sacrifice of Iphigenia', in C. Martindale and R.F. Thomas (eds) *Classics and the Uses of Reception* (Oxford: Blackwell), 216-26.

―――― (2008a), 'Performance Reception: Canonization and Periodization', in L. Hardwick and C Stray (eds) *A Companion to Classical Receptions* (Oxford: Blackwell), 219-28.

―――― (2008b) '*The Legend of Oedipus*: Silent Cinema, Theatre, Photography', in I. Berti and M.G. Morcillo (eds) *The Ancient Greek World in Cinema* (Stuttgart: Franz Steiner Verlag), 75-88.

―――― (forthcoming, 2009), 'Dancing with Prometheus: Performance and Spectacle in the 1920s', in F. Macintosh (ed.) *Greek Drama and Modern Dance* (Oxford: Oxford University Press).

Miller, J. (1986), *Subsequent Performances* (New York: Viking).

Mitias, M. (ed.) (1994), *Philosophy and Architecture* (Amsterdam: Rodopi).

Monaghan, P. (2008), 'Bodies and Stairs: Modernist Theatrical Space and Consciousness', in T. Mehigan (ed.) *Frameworks, Artworks, Place: The Space of Perception in the Modern World* (Amsterdam: Rodopi).

―――― (2009), ' "I can not act / Cause I'm no actor" – Dood Paard's Postdramatic *medEia*', *Didaskalia* 7.2.

Moran, J. (2002), *Interdisciplinarity* (London: Routledge).

Morris, D.B. (1991), *The Culture of Pain* (Berkeley: University of California Press).

Morrison, B. (1993), *And When Did You Last See your Father?* (London: Granta).

―――― (1999), *Selected Poems* (London: Granta).

―――― (2003), *Oedipus and Antigone by Sophocles* (Halifax: Northern Broadsides).

Morwood, J. (ed.) (2007), *Euripides: Suppliant Women* (Oxford: Oxbow).

Most, G. (2000), 'Generating Genres: The Idea of the Tragic', in M. Depew and D. Obbink (eds) *Matrices of Genre: Authors, Canons, and Society* (Cambridge: Harvard University Press), 15-36.

Muecke, F. (1982), ' "I Know You – By your Rags": Costume and Disguise in Fifth-Century Drama', *Antichthon* 16, 17-34.

Müller, H. (1984), 'Wasted Shore Medeamaterial Landscape with Argonauts', in C. Weber (ed.) *Hamletmachine and Other Texts for the Stage* (New York: Performing Arts Journal Publications), 126-35.

Murnaghan, S. (2007), Review of C. Martindale and R.F. Thomas, *Classics and the Uses of Reception*, *Bryn Mawr Classical Review*, 02.19.

Murray, P. and P. Wilson (eds) (2004), *Music and the Muses: The Culture of Mousikê in the Classical Athenian City* (Oxford: Oxford University Press).

Murray, T. (ed.) (1997), *Mimesis, Masochism, and Mime: The Politics of Theatricality in Contemporary French Thought* (Ann Arbor: University of Michigan Press).

Nellhaus, T. (2006), 'Performance Strategies, Image Schemas, and Communication Frameworks', in B. McConachie and F.E. Hart (eds) *Performance and Cognition: Theatre Studies and the Cognitive Turn* (London: Routledge); 76-94.

Nestle, W. (1930), *Die Struktur des Eingangs in der attischen Tragödie* (Stuttgart).

Nightingale, A.W. (2001), 'On Wandering and Wondering: Θεωρία in Greek Philosophy and Culture', *Arion* 9.2, 23-58.

―――― (2004), *Spectacles of Truth in Classical Greek Philosophy: Theoria in its Cultural Context* (Cambridge: Cambridge University Press).

Bibliography

Novati, G.C. (2006), *Tragedia Endogonidia: The Embodiment of the Tragedy: The Power of Essences* (Dublin: Samuel Beckett Centre).

Oddey, A. and C.A. White (2006), *The Potentials of Spaces: The Theory and Practice of Scenography and Performance* (Bristol: Intellect Books).

Olaniyan, T. (1995), *Scars of Conquest Masks of Resistance: The Invention of Cultural Identities in African, African-American and Caribbean Drama* (Oxford: Oxford University Press).

O'Mahony, J. (2000), 'The Mighty Munchkin', *Guardian Saturday Review*, 20 May, 6-7.

Orgel, S. (1987), *The Authentic Shakespeare* (Tasmania: University of Tasmania).

Orr, J. (1991), *Tragicomedy and Contemporary Culture: Play and Performance from Beckett to Shepard* (London: Macmillan).

Ortony, A. (ed.) (1993), *Metaphor and Thought* (Cambridge: Cambridge University Press).

Padel, R. (1992), *In and Out of the Mind: Greek Images of the Tragic Self* (Princeton: Princeton University Press).

Pallasmaa J. (2000), 'Stairways of the Mind', *International Forum of Psychoanalysis* 9, 7-18.

Palmer, R.H. (1985), *The Lighting Art: The Aesthetics of Stage Lighting Design* (Englewood Cliffs: Prentice-Hall).

Parment, U.B. (2000), 'What is Architecture About? Interview with Jan Henriksson, Professor of Architecture', *International Forum of Psychoanalysis* 9,19-27.

Pater, W. (1913), *Appreciations: With An Essay on Style* (London: Macmillan).
—— (1980), *The Renaissance: Studies in Art and Poetry, The 1893 Text* (Berkeley: University of California Press).

Patten, R.L. (2006), 'When is a Book Not a Book?', in D. Finkelstein and Alistair McCleery (eds) *The Book History Reader* (London: Routledge).

Patterson, M. (1981), *The Revolution in German Theatre 1900-1933* (Boston: Routledge and Kegan Paul).

Pattison, G. (1992), *Kierkegaard: The Aesthetic and the Religious* (London: Macmillan).

Paulin, T. (1985), *The Riot Act: A Version of Sophocles' Antigone* (London: Faber).

Paulus, D. (2006), 'It's all About the Audience', *Contemporary Theatre Review* 16, 334-47.

Pavis, P. (1980), *Dictionnaire du théâtre: termes et concepts de l'analyse théâtrale* (Paris: Editions Sociales).

Pearson, M. and M. Shanks (2001), *Theatre/Archaeology* (London: Routledge).

Peters, J.S. (2000), *Theatre of the Book 1480-1880: Print, Text, and Performance in Europe* (Oxford: Oxford University Press).

Pfeiffer, R. (1968), *History of Classical Scholarship* (Oxford: Clarendon Press).

Phillips, A. (2007), 'Does the Book Have a Future?', in S. Eliot and J. Rose (eds) *A Companion to the History of the Book* (Oxford: Blackwell), 547-59.

Pickard-Cambridge, A. (1988), *The Dramatic Festivals of Athens* (rev. J. Gould and D.M. Lewis, Oxford: Oxford University Press).

Pinsky, R. (1998) *The Sounds of Poetry: A Brief Guide* (New York: Farrar, Straus and Giroux).

Pisters, P. (2003), *The Matrix of Visual Culture: Working with Deleuze in Film Theory* (Chicago: Stanford University Press).

Plantinga, T. (1980), *Historical Understanding in the Thought of Wilhelm Dilthey* (Toronto: University of Toronto Press).

Plessner, H. (1970), *Laughing and Crying: A Study of the Limits of Human Behaviour* (tr. J.S. Churchill and M. Greene, Evanston: Northwestern University Press).

Pointon, M. (1993), *Hanging the Head: Portraiture and Social Formation in Eighteenth Century England* (London: Yale University Press).

Pomian, K. (1990), 'Museum und kulturelles Erbe', in G. Korff and M. Roth (eds) *Das historische Museum: Labor – Schaubühne – Identitätsfabrik* (Frankfurt: Suhrkamp Verlag), 41-64.

Poole, A. (2005), *Tragedy: A Very Short Introduction* (Oxford: Oxford University Press).

Premack, D. and G. Woodruff (1978), 'Does the Chimpanzee Have a "Theory of Mind" ', *Behavioral and Brain Science* 4, 515-26.

Prettejohn, E. (2007), *Art for Art's Sake: Aestheticism in Victorian Painting* (London: Yale University Press).

Quinn, M.R. (1990), 'Celebrity and the Semiotics of Acting', *New Theatre Quarterly* 22, 154-61.

Rabkin, G. (1984), 'Interview with Lee Breuer', *Performing Arts Journal* 22, 48-51.

Rampell, C. (2008), *'The Persians* Revisited', in *Smithsonian Magazine*, http://www.smithsonianmag.com/arts-culture/persians.html (accessed 1 April 2009).

Ranciere, J. (2007), 'The Emancipated Spectator', *ArtForum* March, 271-7.

Rani, M.X. (2008), 'An Overview of Traditional Dance in South African Townships: Lost Meaning – New Traditions –The Effects of Modernity', in S. Friedman and N. Lock (eds) *Confluences 5: Proceedings of the Fifth South African Dance Conference* (Cape Town: University of Cape Town), 123-32, http://web.uct.ac.za/depts/ballet/confluen/confluences5.pdf (accessed 20 September 2008).

Rayner, A. (1994), *To Do, To Act, To Perform* (Ann Arbor: University of Michigan Press).

—— (2006), *Ghosts: Death's Double and the Phenomena of Theater* (Minneapolis: University of Minnesota Press).

Reason, M. (2003), 'Archive or Memory? The Detritus of Live Performance', *New Theatre Quarterly* 19.1, 82-89.

—— (2006), *Documentation, Disappearance, and the Representation of Live Performance* (New York: Palgrave Macmillan).

Rehm, R. (2003), *Radical Theatre: Greek Tragedy and the Modern World* (London: Duckworth).

Revermann, M. (2006), *Comic Business: Theatricality, Dramatic Technique, and Performance Contexts of Aristophanic Comedy* (Oxford: Oxford University Press).

Richards, T. (1995), *At Work with Grotowski on Physical Actions* (London: Routledge).

Richardson, A. and F.F. Steen (2002), 'Literature and the Cognitive Revolution: An Introduction', *Poetics Today* 23, 1-8.

Richardson, E. (2008), *The Failure of History: Nineteenth-Century Britain's Pursuit of the Ancient World*, unpublished PhD thesis (University of Cambridge).

Ridley, M. (2003), *Nature Via Nurture* (London: Fourth Estate).

Riley, K. (2004), 'Heracles as Dr Strangelove and GI Joe: Male Heroism Deconstructed', in E. Hall, F. Macintosh and A. Wrigley (eds) *Dionysus Since 69: Greek Tragedy at the Dawn of the Third Millennium* (Oxford: Oxford University Press), 113-41.

—— (2008), *Reasoning Madness: The Reception and Performance of Euripides' Herakles* (Oxford: Oxford University Press).

Bibliography

Ringer, N. (1998), *Electra and the Empty Urn: Metatheater and Role Playing in Sophocles* (Chapel Hill: University of North Carolina Press).

Ritvo, H. (2007), 'Manchester v. Thirlmere and the Construction of the Victorian Environment', *Victorian Studies* 49.3, 457-82.

Rodenberg, P. (1993), *The Need for Words: Voice and the Text* (London: Methuen).

—— (1997), *The Actor Speaks: Voice and the Performer* (London: Methuen).

Rokem, F. (1986), *Theatrical Space in Ibsen, Chekhov, and Strindberg: Public Forms of Privacy* (Ann Arbor: UMI Research Press).

Rokotnitz, N. (2006), ' "It Is Required / You Do Awake Your Faith": Learning to Trust the Body through Performing *The Winter's Tale*', in B. McConachie and F.E. Hart (eds) *Performance and Cognition: Theatre Studies and the Cognitive Turn* (London: Routledge), 122-46.

Rose, J. (2001), *The Intellectual Life of the British Working Classes* (London: Yale University Press).

Rose, L. (2001), *The Survival of Images: Art Historians, Psychoanalysts, and the Ancients* (Cambridge: Hackett).

Rose, P.W. (1992), *Sons of the Gods, Children of Earth: Ideology and Literary Form in Ancient Greece* (Ithaca: Cornell University Press).

Rose, S. (2005), *The 21st-Century Brain: Explaining, Mending and Manipulating the Mind* (New York: Vintage Books).

Rüter, C. (ed.) (1991), *Die Perser / Aischylos* (tr. P. Witzmann, rev. H. Müller, Berlin: Hentrich).

Ryan, K. (1989), *Shakespeare* (London: Harvester).

Said, E. (1983), *The World, the Text and the Critic* (Cambridge: Harvard University Press).

Sampatakakis, G. (2004), *Bakkhai-Model: The Re-Usage of Euripides' Bakkhai in Text and Performance*, unpublished PhD thesis (University of London).

Sanders, J. (2006), *Adaptation and Appropriation* (New York: Routledge).

Sartre, J.-P. (1964), *Words* (tr. I. Clephane, London: Hamish Hamilton).

—— (1970), 'L'art cinématographique', in M. Contat and M. Rybalka (eds) *Les Écrits de Sartre* (Paris: Gallimard), 456-52.

—— (1976) *Sartre on Theater* (tr. F. Jellinek, New York: Random House).

Sauter, W. (2000), *The Theatrical Event: Dynamics of Performance and Perception* (Iowa: University of Iowa Press).

Scarry, E. (1985), *The Body in Pain: The Making and Unmaking of the World* (Oxford: Oxford University Press).

Schechner, R. (ed.) (1970), *Dionysus in 69* (New York: Farrar, Straus and Giroux).

—— (1982) *The End of Humanism* (Cambridge: Performing Arts Journal Press).

Schechner, R. and L. Wolfson (eds) (2001), *The Grotowski Sourcebook* (London: Routledge).

Schiller, F (1993), 'Letters on the Aesthetic Education of Man', in *Essays* (tr. W. Hinderer and D.O. Dahlstrom, New York: Continuum).

Schironi, F. (2007), 'A Poet without "Gravity": Aristophanes on the Italian Stage', in E. Hall and A. Wrigley (eds) *Aristophanes in Performance: Peace, Birds and Frogs, 421 BC-AD 2007* (Oxford: Legenda).

Schlegel, A.W. (1846), *A Course of Lectures on Dramatic Art and Poetry* (tr. J. Black, London: Bohn).

Schleiermacher, F. (1992), 'On the Different Methods of Translating', in R. Schulte and J. Biguenet (eds) *Theories of Translation: An Anthology of Essays from Dryden to Derrida* (Chicago: University of Chicago Press), 36-54.

Schneider, R. (2001), 'Performance Remains', *Performance Research* 6.2, 100-8.

287

Schoenmakers, H. (ed.) (1992), *Performance Theory: Reception and Audience Research* (Netherlands: Tijdschrift Voor Theaterwetenschap).

Schumacher, C. (ed.) (1989), *Artaud on Theatre* (London: Methuen).

Scott, W.C. (1984), *Musical Design in Aeschylean Theater* (Newtown: Hanover Press).

Scuderi, A. (2000), 'Updating Antiquity', in J. Farrell and A. Scuderi (eds) *Dario Fo: Stage, Text and Tradition* (Carbondale: Southern Illinois University Press), 39-64.

Seaford, R. (ed.) (1996), *Euripides: Bacchae* (Warminster: Aris & Phillips).

Secord, J. (2000), *Victorian Sensation: The Extraordinary Publication, Reception, and Secret Authorship of Vestiges of The Natural History of Creation* (Chicago: University of Chicago Press).

Segal, C. (1981), *Tragedy and Civilization: An Interpretation of Sophocles* (Cambridge: Harvard University Press).

———— (1982), *Dionysiac Poetics and Euripides' Bacchae* (Princeton: Princeton University Press).

Segal, E. (1995), ' "The Comic Catastrophe": An Essay on Euripidean Comedy', in A. Griffiths (ed.) *Stage Directions: Essays in Ancient Drama in Honour of E.W. Handley* (London: BICS Supplement 66), 46-55.

Seidensticker, B. (1978), 'Comic Elements in Euripides' *Bacchae*', *American Journal of Philology* 99, 303-20.

———— (1982), 'Palintonos Harmonia. Studien zu komischen Elementen in der griechischen Tragödie', *Hypomnemata* 72.

Seigel, J. (2005), *The Idea of the Self: Thought and Experience in Western Europe since the Seventeenth Century* (Cambridge: Cambridge University Press).

Shepherd, S. (2006), *Theatre, Body and Pleasure* (London: Routledge).

Shepherd, S. and M. Wallis (2004), *Drama/Theatre/Performance* (London: Routledge).

Sickinger, J.P. (1999), *Public Records and Archives in Classical Athens* (Chapel Hill: University of North Carolina Press).

Silk, M.S. (1988), 'The Autonomy of Greek Comedy', *Comparative Criticism: An Annual Journal* 10, 3-37.

———— (ed.) (1996), *Tragedy and the Tragic: Greek Theatre and Beyond* (Oxford: Oxford University Press).

Slingerland, E. (2008), *What Science Offers the Humanities: Integrating Body and Culture* (Cambridge: Cambridge University Press).

Smethurst, M. (1989), *The Artistry of Aeschylus and Zeami: A Comparative Study of Greek Tragedy and Nō* (Princeton: Princeton University Press).

Smith, B.H. (2005), *Scandalous Knowledge: Science, Truth and the Human* (Durham: Duke University Press).

Smith, B.R. (1988), *Ancient Scripts and Modern Experience on the English Stage 1500-1700* (Princeton: Princeton University Press).

Smith, K.M. (2001), 'Designing Readers: Redressing the Texts of Classic Drama', *Design Issues* 17.3 , 56-66.

Snell, B., R. Kannicht and S.L. Radt (eds) (2004), *Tragicorum Graecorum Fragmenta* (Göttingen: Vandenhoeck & Ruprecht).

Snipe, T.D. (1996), 'African Dance: Bridges to Humanity', in K. Welsh-Asante (ed.) *African Dance: An Artistic, Historical and Philosophical Inquiry* (Trenton: Africa World Press), 63-77.

Sofer, A. (2003), *The Stage Life of Props* (Ann Arbor: University of Michigan Press).

Sommerstein. A., S. Halliwell, J. Henderson and B. Zimmermann (eds) (1993),

Bibliography

Tragedy, Comedy and the Polis: Papers from the Greek Drama Conference. Nottingham, 18-20 July 1990 (Bari: Levante Editori-Bari).

Sontag, S. (1994), *Against Interpretation* (London: Vintage).

Soyinka, W. (1973), *The Bacchae of Euripides: A Communion Rite* (London: Norton).

Sperber, D. (2000), *Metarepresentations: A Multidisciplinary Perspective* (Oxford: Oxford University Press).

Spolsky, E. (2001), *Satisfying Scepticism: Embodied Knowledge in the Early Modern World* (Aldershot: Ashgate).

States, B.O. (1985), *Great Reckonings in Little Rooms: On the Phenomenology of Theater* (Berkeley: University of California Press).

–––––– (1992), 'The Phenomenological Attitude', in J.G. Reinelt and J.R. Roach (eds) *Critical Theory and Performance* (Ann Arbor: University of Michigan Press).

Steidle, W. (1968), *Studien zum antiken Drama: unter besonderer Berücksichtigung des Bühnenspiels* (Munich).

Steiner, G. (1975), *After Babel: Aspects of Language and Translation* (Oxford: Oxford University Press).

–––––– (1984), *Antigones: The Antigone Myth in Western Literature, Art and Thought* (Oxford: Oxford University Press).

–––––– (1996a), *The Death of Tragedy* (London: Yale University Press).

–––––– (1996b), 'Tragedy, Pure and Simple', in M.S. Silk (ed.) *Tragedy and the Tragic: Greek Theatre and Beyond* (Oxford: Clarendon), 534-46.

–––––– (2000), *Grammars of Creation* (London: Yale University Press).

–––––– (2008), ' "Tragedy" Reconsidered', in R. Felski (ed.) *Rethinking Tragedy* (Baltimore: Johns Hopkins University Press), 29-44.

Steinmeyer, E. (2007), 'Post-Apartheid Electra: In the City of Paradise', in L. Hardwick and C. Gillespie (eds) *Classics in Post-Colonial Worlds* (Oxford: Oxford University Press), 102-18.

Stern, J. (2001), 'Knowledge by Metaphor', *Midwest Studies in Philosophy* 25.1, 213-14.

Stocking, G.W. (1987), *Victorian Anthropology* (New York: Free Press).

Stockwell, P. (2002), *Cognitive Poetics: An Introduction* (London: Routledge).

Strathern, M. (2004), *Commons and Borderlands: Working Papers on Interdisciplinarity and the Flow of Knowledge* (Wantage: Kingston).

–––––– (2007), 'Interdisciplinarity: Some Models from the Human Sciences', *Interdisciplinary Science Reviews* 32.2, 123-34.

Strauven, W. (ed.) (2006), *The Cinema of Attractions Reloaded* (Amsterdam: Amsterdam University Press).

Styan, J.L. (1977), *The Shakespeare Revolution: Criticism and Performance in the Twentieth Century* (Cambridge: Cambridge University Press).

Sugiera, M. (2002), 'Theatricality and Cognitive Science: The Audience's Perception and Reception', *SubStance* 31, 225-35.

Sussman, H. (2007), 'The Perfect Medium: Photography and The Occult', in *Victorian Literature and Culture* 35, 338-43.

Svich, C. (2003), *Trans-global Readings: Crossing Theatrical Boundaries* (Manchester: Manchester University Press).

–––––– (ed.) (2005), *Divine Fire: Eight Contemporary Plays Inspired by the Greeks* (New York: Back Stage).

Svoboda, J. (1992), 'The Secret of Theatrical Space', in *Theatre Design and Technology* (vol. 1), xxviii.5, 12.

Bibliography

Sutcliffe, T. (1996), *Believing in Opera* (Princeton: Princeton University Press).

Swenson, A. (2007), *Conceptualising 'Heritage' in 19th and early 20th Century France, Germany and England* , unpublished PhD thesis (University of Cambridge).

Szondi, P. (1965), 'The Play of Time: Wilder', in M. Hays (ed.) *Theory of the Modern Drama* (Cambridge: Polity Press).

Taplin, O. (1977), *The Stagecraft of Aeschylus* (Oxford: Oxford University Press).

———— (1978), *Greek Tragedy in Action* (Oxford: Oxford University Press).

———— (1986), 'Fifth-Century Tragedy and Comedy: A Synkrisis', *Journal of Hellenic Studies* 106, 163-74.

———— (1989), *Greek Fire* (London: Random House).

———— (1992), *Homeric Soundings: The Shaping of the Iliad* (Oxford: Oxford University Press).

———— (1996), 'Comedy and the Tragic', in M.S. Silk (ed.) *Tragedy and the Tragic: Greek Theatre and Beyond* (Oxford: Oxford University Press), 188-202.

———— (2001), 'The Experience of an Academic in the Rehearsal Room', *Didaskalia* 5.1, http://didaskalia.net/issues/vol5no1/taplin.html (accessed 20 March 2009).

Taplin, O. and P. Wilson (1993), 'The "Aetiology" of Tragedy in the Oresteia', *PCPS* 39, 169 -80.

Taruskin, R. (1988), 'The Pastness of the Present and the Presentness of the Past', in N. Kenyon (ed.) *Authenticity and Early Music: A Symposium* (Oxford: Oxford University Press), 137-219.

Taylor, G. (ed.) (1982), *Shakespeare: Henry V* (Oxford: Oxford University Press).

———— (1991), *Reinventing Shakespeare: A Cultural History from the Restoration to the Present* (London: Vintage).

Teraoka, A.A. (1996), *East, West, and Others: The Third World in Postwar German Literature* (Lincoln: University of Nebraska Press).

Thom, P. (1993), *For an Audience: a Philosophy of the Performing Arts* (Philadelphia: Temple University Press).

Thomas, R. (1992), *Literacy and Orality in Ancient Greece* (Cambridge: Cambridge University Press).

Thompson, A. and J.O. Thompson (eds) (1987), *Shakespeare: Meaning and Metaphor* (Brighton: Harvester).

———— (2005), 'Meaning, "Seeing", Printing', in D.A. Brooks (ed.) *Printing and Parenting in Early Modern England* (Aldershot: Ashgate), 59-88.

Tilley, C. (1999), *Metaphor and Material Culture* (Oxford: Blackwell).

Toelken, F. (1842), 'Über die Eingänge zu dem Proszenium und der Orchestra des alten griechischen Theaters', in A. Boeckh, E. Toelken and R. Foerster, *Antigone des Sophokles und ihre Darstellung auf dem Königl. Schloßtheater im neuen Palais bei Sanssouci* (Berlin: Schröder).

Trilling, L. (1971), *Sincerity and Authenticity* (Cambridge, MA: Harvard University Press).

Tsur, R. (2003), *On the Shore of Nothingness: Space, Rhythm, and Semantic Structure in Religious Poetry and its Mystic-Secular Counterpart: A Study in Cognitive Poetics* (Charlottesville: Imprint Academic).

Turner, M. (1987), *Death Is the Mother of Beauty: Mind, Metaphor, Criticism* (University of Chicago: Chicago Press).

———— (1991), *Reading Minds: The Study of English in the Age of Cognitive Science* (Princeton: Princeton University Press).

———— (1996), *The Literary Mind* (Oxford: Oxford University Press).

Turner, V. (1969), *The Ritual Process – Structure and Anti-Structure* (London: Routledge).

—— (1972), 'Variations on a Theme of Liminality', in S.F. Moore and B.C. Myerhoff (eds) *Secular Ritual* (Asser: Van Gorcum).

Ubersfeld, A. (1999), *Reading Theatre* (tr. F. Collins, Toronto: University of Toronto Press).

Ungar, S. (1983), *Roland Barthes: The Professor of Desire* (Lincoln: University of Nebraska Press).

Van den Dries, L. (2002a), 'The Sublime Body', in M. Bleeker, S. De Belder, K. Debo, L. Van den Dries and K. Vanhoutte, *Bodycheck: Relocating the Body in Contemporary Performing Art* (Amsterdam: Rodopi), 71- 96.

—— (2002b) 'De grenzen van de semiotiek', in L. Van den Dries, S. De Belder and K. Tachelet (eds) *Verspeelde werkelijkheid. Verkenningen van theatraliteit* (Leuven: Van Halewyck) 21-38.

Van Houtte, K. (2002), 'Het lichaam als inzet: de theoretische weddenschap van het theater', in L. Van den Dries, S. De Belder and K. Tachelet, *Verspeelde werkelijkheid. Verkenningen van theatraliteit* (Leuven: Van Halewyck), 39-54.

Van Wyenberg, A. (2008), 'Rewrite this Ancient End! Staging Transition in Post-Apartheid South Africa', *New Voices in Classical Reception*, 31-46, http://www2.open.ac.uk/ClassicalStudies/GreekPlays/newvoices/issue3/issue3 index.htm (accessed 24 March 2009).

Van Zyl Smit, B. (2010), 'Orestes and the Truth and Reconciliation Commission', *Classical Receptions Journal* 2.

Vance, N. (1985), *The Sinews of the Spirit: The Ideal of Christian Manliness in Victorian Literature and Religious Thought* (Cambridge: Cambridge University Press).

Vellacott, M. (1977), 'Has Good Prevailed? A Further Study of the *Oresteia*', *Harvard Studies in Classical Philology* 81, 113-22.

Veltrusk, J. (1977), *Drama as Literature* (Lisse: Peter de Riddler).

Vernant, J.P. (1998),'The Tragic Subject: Historicity and Transhistoricity' in J.P. Vernant and P. Vidal-Naquet, *Myth and Tragedy in Ancient Greece* (Brooklyn: Zone Books), 237-48.

Vico, G. (1948), *The New Science* (tr. T.G. Bergin and M. Fisch, Ithaca: Cornell University Press).

Vidal-Naquet, P. (1988),'Oedipus in Vicenza and Paris', in J.P. Vernant and P. Vidal-Naquet, *Myth and Tragedy in Ancient Greece* (Brooklyn: Zone Books), 361-80.

Vieira, E.R.P. (1999), 'Haroldo de Campos' Poetics of Transcreation', in S. Bassnett and H. Trivedi (eds) *Post-Colonial Translation: Theory and Practice* (London: Routledge), 95-113.

Walcott, D. (1998), 'The Antilles: Fragments of Epic Memory', in *What the Twilight Says* (London: Faber), 65-84.

Wall, P.D. (1999), *Pain: The Science of Suffering* (Troy: Phoenix).

Walter, H. (1999), *Other People's Shoes* (London: Viking Penguin).

Walton, J.M. (2005), 'Translation or Transubstantiation', in F. Macintosh, P. Michelakis and E. Hall (eds) *Agamemnon in Performance, 458 BC to AD 2004* (Oxford: Oxford University Press), 189-206.

—— (2006), *Found in Translation: Greek Drama in English* (Cambridge: Cambridge University Press).

Walton, K. (2004), 'Make-Believe and its Role in Pictorial Representation and the Acquisition of Knowledge', *Philosophic Exchange* 23, 81-95.

Warning, R. (ed.) (1979), *Rezeptionsästhetik. Theorie und Praxis* (Munich).

Webb, R. (2008), 'Inside the Mask: Pantomime from the Performer's Perspective',

Bibliography

in E. Hall and R. Wyles (eds) *New Directions in Ancient Pantomime* (Oxford: Oxford University Press), 44-60.

Webster, T.B.L. (1970), *The Greek Chorus* (London: Methuen).

Weimann, R. (1984), *Structure and Society in Literary History* (Baltimore: Johns Hopkins University Press).

Weiss, G. and R. Wodak (eds) (2003), *Critical Discourse Analysis: Theory and Interdisciplinarity* (Basingstoke: Palgrave Macmillan).

Weissbort, D. and A. Eysteinsson (eds) (2006), *Translation Theory and Practice: A Historical Reader* (Oxford: Oxford University Press).

Welton, D. (1999), *The Body: Classic and Contemporary Readings* (Oxford: Blackwell).

Wetmore, K.J. (2002), *The Athenian Sun in an African Sky* (London: McFarland).

––––– (2003), *Black Dionysus: Greek Tragedy and African American Theatre* (London: McFarland).

Wheeler, M. (2006), *The Old Enemies: Catholic and Protestant in Nineteenth-Century English Culture* (Cambridge: Cambridge University Press).

Whistler, J.M. (1967), *The Gentle Art of Making Enemies* (New York: Dover).

Whiten, A. (2000), 'Chimpanzee Cognition and the Question of Mental Re-Representation', in Dan Sperber (ed.) *Meta-Representations: A Multidisciplinary Perspective* (Oxford: Oxford University Press) 139-67.

Whittall, A. (2003), *Exploring Twentieth-Century Music: Tradition and Innovation* (Cambridge: Cambridge University Press).

Wilamowitz-Moellendorff, U. von (1930), *My Recollections, 1848-1914* (tr. G.C. Richards, London: Chatto & Windus).

Wilde, O. (1989), 'The Decay of Lying', in I. Murray (ed.) *Oscar Wilde* (Oxford: Oxford University Press).

Wiles, D. (2000), *Greek Theatre Performance: An Introduction* (Cambridge: Cambridge University Press).

––––– (2003), *A Short History of Western Performance Space* (New York: Cambridge University Press).

––––– (2007), *Mask and Performance in Greek Tragedy: From Ancient Festival to Modern Experimentation* (Cambridge: Cambridge University Press).

Wilke, S. (1999), 'The Role of Art in a Dialectic of Modernism and Postmodernism: The Theatre of Heiner Müller', *Paragraph* 14.3, 276-89.

Williams, R. (1966), *Modern Tragedy* (Stanford: Stanford University Press).

––––– (1994), 'Afterword' to J. Dollimore and A. Sinfield (eds) *Political Shakespeare: Essays in Cultural Materialism* (Manchester: Manchester University Press), 281-9.

Wilson, D.H. (1993), *Staging Politics: The Lasting Impact of Shakespeare's Historical Plays* (New York: New York University Press).

Wilson, N.L. and R.W. Gibbs (2007), 'Real and Imagined Body Movement Primes Metaphor Comprehension', *Cognitive Science* 31, 721-31.

Wiltshire, B. (1982), *Role Playing and Identity: The Limits of Theater as Metaphor* (Bloomington: Indiana University Press).

Winkler, J. and F. Zeitlin (eds) (1990), *Nothing to do with Dionysos? Athenian Drama in its Social Context* (Princeton: Princeton University Press).

Winters, E. (2007), *Aesthetics and Architecture* (New York: Continuum).

Wise, J. (2008), 'Tragedy as "an Augury of a Happy Life" ', *Arethusa* 41.3, 381-410.

Wittreich, J.A. Jr. (ed.) (1970), *The Romantics on Milton: Formal Essays and Critical Asides* (Cleveland: Press of Cape Western Reserve University).

Worthen, W.B. (1997), *Shakespeare and the Authority of Performance* (Cambridge: Cambridge University Press).

Bibliography

———— (2003), *Shakespeare and the Force of Modern Performance* (Cambridge: Cambridge University Press).

Wright, M. (2005), *Euripides' Escape-Tragedies: A Study of Helen, Andromeda and Iphigenia Among the Taurians* (Oxford: Oxford University Press).

Wyles, R. (2007), *The Stage Life of Costume in Euripides' Telephus, Heracles and Andromeda,* unpublished PhD thesis (University of London).

Yu, N. (1998), *The Contemporary Theory of Metaphor: A Perspective from Chinese* (Herndon: John Benjamins).

Zacharia, K. (1995), 'The Marriage of Tragedy and Comedy in Euripides' *Ion*', in S. Jäkel and A. Timonen (eds) *Laughter Down the Centuries* (Turku: Turun Yliopisto), 45-62.

Zeitlin, F. (2004), '*Dionysus in 69*', in E. Hall, F. Macintosh and A. Wrigley (eds) *Dionysus Since 69: Greek Tragedy at the Dawn of the Third Millennium* (Oxford: Oxford University Press), 49-75.

Zuber, R. (1968), *Les 'Belles infidèles' et la formation du goût classique* (Paris: Colin).

Zunshine, L. (2004), 'Richardson's *Clarissa* and a Theory of Mind', in A. Richardson and E. Spolsky (eds) *The Work of Fiction: Cognition, Culture, and Complexity* (Aldershot: Ashgate), 127-46.

———— (2006), *Why We Read Fiction: Theory of Mind and the Novel* (Ohio State University Press).

Index

295

Index

Index

Index

television, 11, 261
Terzopoulos, Theodoros (director), 86, 124, 133, 183
 Ajax (2005), 39
text, textual, textuality
 compared with performance, 6, 34, 181-9
 fragments, 35
 meaning of, 3, 34-7, 72-3
Thalheimer, Michael (director, 1965-)
 Oresteia (2006), 4
theatre, theatres, theatrical
 architecture, 36, 198n.27, 241-9, 253
 history, historiography, methodology in, 31, 43-55, 95-107, 108, 222-5, 230
 participation, 153
Theatre of the Absurd, 140, 146, 148
Theatre of the Republic, Paris, 26
theatre studies (academic discipline), 2, 26, 43-4, 49, 109, 111, 183, 208, 224
Thucydides, 54, 175
Tieck, Ludwig (poet and director, 1773-1853)
 Antigone (1841), *see* Mendelssohn
Tiffany, John (theatre director, 1971-),
 Bacchae (2007), 141-4 with fig.5, 146, 194-9, 232
time, 21, 24-5, 115, 128, 242-3
Titian (Tiziano Vecelli) (artist, 1488(?)-1576), 62-4, 80
tragedy, the tragic, 6, 16, 123-36, 137-41, 150, 212, 247-8
tragicomedy, 6, 137, 140, 148, 150
translation, translations
 as transubstantiation, 216
 categories of, 12
 comparison of different, 193-205, 210-16, 234-6, 261, 262-3
 dialect in, 255-60
 for performance, 6, 34, 42n.11, 53, 98, 156, 172, 192-205, 232-3, 235, 239, 252-64
 history of, 14-15, 230
 impossibility of faithful, 112, 211, 253, 265
 languages of, 6, 14-15, 235-6, 238-9, 254-65
 literary, 6

methodology in writing, 253-7, 260-1, 264-5
 rhyme in, 254, 262
 romantic, 216
 speakability of, 232-6, 253, 257
 stylistic features in, 144, 235-6, 254-64
 theories, theorists of, 209-11, 216
Trier, Lars von (director and screenwriter, 1956-), 86
Turner, Victor (anthropologist, 1920-1983), 38, 45, 211, 216

utopia, utopian, 25, 265

Verfremdungseffekt, 44, 117, 159
Vernant, Jean-Pierre (anthropologist, 1914-2007), 14
Vico, Giovanni Bttista (philosopher, 1668-1744), 3, 4, 21, 26, 85, 93n.1
Vidal-Naquet, Pierre (classical historian, 1930-2006), 7, 13
violence, 25, 62, 99-102, 105, 129, 131-2, 145, 146, 150, 198, 199, 211-16, 219-23, 229-30, 236
Virgil, 60-2, 65, 75, 79, 131, 183
visual arts, 3, 1, 10, 11, 31, 75
voice, vocality, 7, 11, 34, 36, 155, 230, 232-9, 254

Wagner, Richard (composer, 1813-1883), 57, 68, 75, 77, 78, 245
Wajda, Andrej (director, 1926-)
 Antygona (1984), 26
Walcott, Derek (poet and playwright, 1930-), 194
Walton, Michael (theatre scholar), 216
Wanamaker, Zoe (actress, 1949-), 229n.17
Warner, Deborah (theatre director, 1959-)
 Medea (2000-2002), 144-6
Wase, Christopher (translator, 1625(?)-1670)
 Electra (1649), 14-15
Weimann, Robert (drama theorist and historian), 14, 26
Weimar Theatre, 41n.3
Whistler, James McNeil (artist, 1834-1903), 56-7